In Darwin's Wake
REVISITING BEAGLE'S SOUTH AMERICAN ANCHORAGES

In Darwin's Wake

REVISITING *BEAGLE*'S SOUTH AMERICAN ANCHORAGES

JOHN CAMPBELL

For Lana, who happens to be my best friend as well as my wife.

Acknowledgements

I would like to thank the crew, Nick, Chris and Tony the Doc., for their mostly cheerful compatibility, and especially Jeff, who against all odds, managed to keep all the machinery running. I, and all the crew, owe a big thanks to Lana, who had the most difficult job on board, keeping us all fed, which she did admirably.

Also I would like to thank Dennis O'Sullivan, whose timely encouragement stopped the writing project foundering, and to Denny Desoutter, who has helped greatly with all my various writing endeavours.

Last but not least, I would like to thank *The Owner*. After all, he paid for the voyage

This edition first published in 1997 by
Sheridan House Inc.
145 Palisade Street
Dobbs Ferry, NY 10522
First published in Great Britain by Waterline Books,
an imprint of Airlife Publishing Ltd

Library of Congress Cataloging-in Publication Data
Campbell, John, 1946–
In Darwin's Wake: revisiting Beagle's South American anchorages/
John Campbell.
p. cm.
ISBN 1-57409-025-9
1. South America – Description and travel. 2. Darwin, Charles,
1809–1882 – Journeys – South America. 3. Beagle expedition
(1831–1836). 4. Campbell, John, 1946– – Journeys – South America.
I. Title.
F2225.C36 1997
918.04'39–dc21
96-49604
CIP

Printed in Great Britain

ISBN 1-57409-025-9

Contents

Chapter 1

Because It Is There

I looked out of the hatch. The horizon to the east was beginning to lighten. Dawn would soon be here. Just 9 miles away was the unmistakable shape of Cape Horn, silhouetted against the pre-dawn sky.

It had been a long night. I suppose I had dozed, but every little puff of wind, each whisper of breeze in the rigging, even the noise of the crew changing watch on the even hour had brought me wide awake. I was as nervous as a cat, being anchored for the night within sight of Cape Horn.

The barometer was still high, but as I reached over and gave it a tentative tap on the glass, the pointer edged down towards its more usual position. This spell of good weather would not last much longer. We should not be sitting here waiting to get thrashed, we should be heading up into more sheltered waters before the next gale arrived. In fact, if I had had my way we would not even have stopped for the night. We would have dashed north as soon as we had rounded the Cape, and spent the night in the comparative shelter of Puerto Williams.

But we had not done that. We had stayed the night at Hermite Island for the simple reason that the owner of the boat was snoring away in the after cabin. It is hard to argue with the man who writes the cheques! He had wanted to round the Horn from east to west, which we had done the previous afternoon. Now, after spending the night at Hermite Island, he felt that by sailing back, he could claim a rounding from west to east. Who was I to argue? I was only the captain, he was the owner.

I felt that by lingering there we were thumbing our collective nose at Cape Horn. The longer we stayed, the more likely it became that Cape Horn would flex its metaphorical muscles, and perhaps blow us to eternity.

I went out into the cockpit. Nick, who was on watch, grinned at me with a cheery 'G'day mate'. There was no hiding his Australian origins.

He seemed oblivious to the enormity of the whole thing. He was sheltering from the cool pre-dawn breeze, lurking under the spray dodger, his red woolly hat clamped firmly in place by the earphones of his Walkman, from which he was seldom parted. He was beating a tattoo on his knees in accompaniment to the music I could faintly hear coming from his earphones.

I prised one earphone out far enough for him to hear me. 'Why don't you go and roust the others out. I'd like to head out as soon as it's light.' Let the Boss have his second rounding of Cape Horn, and then we could get north, into sheltered waters sooner rather than later.

As the sky began to get lighter, the clouds took on a more ominous look. The weather was definitely changing, and in that part of the world, it can do that all too quickly.

Too nervous to bother about breakfast, I sat in the cockpit, waiting for the others to get woken up, dressed and fed. Then we could recover our anchors and move out. I could hardly take my eyes off Cape Horn. It was hard to believe that we were really there, anchored barely 9 miles from the most famous, most treacherous headland in the sailors' world.

Lana and I had been working on the boat, *Thalassi*, for almost a year. We had joined it in Spain, and now we had achieved a long-held ambition of mine – we had sailed to Patagonia.

Jeff came into the cockpit for his pre-breakfast cigarette. He was almost a chain-smoker, but was good about not smoking below. He sniffed the breeze, peered at the gathering clouds, and rather unnecessarily said, 'It's going to come on to blow.' Then he huddled down under the spray dodger to light up.

Despite his sometimes pessimistic outlook on life, I thought again how lucky we had been to find him. Jeff was our engineer, and not only had he managed to keep all the mechanical bits and pieces running relatively smoothly, but he had also turned out to be a good shipmate.

The only job more demanding than Jeff's was Lana's. She had to keep the crew fed, and especially in the case of Nick and Chris, the two young deckhands, this was a daunting task. They say that growing gannet chicks eat their own bodyweight in food each day; Nick and Chris seemed to come close to that at times.

The five of us had sailed *Thalassi* down from Spain. We had recently signed on Tony, a young Irish doctor, whom we had found in the Falklands. He had spent the winter in the Antarctic, and joined us to replace Chris, who was scheduled to fly back to reality, from Punta Arenas, in a few days.

Then there was the owner. He has requested anonymity – from

whom, one can only guess. So for the purpose of this narrative, he shall appear as 'the Boss'. Suffice it to say, he is a Spanish hotel owner, made rich by the package tourists who flock to Mallorca. He would join us from time to time, in various places, occasionally with guests. The rest of the time he would be busy at home, taking care of his many business interests, while we moved the boat to the next area that he wanted to visit. Meanwhile there he was, tucked up in his bunk, still snoring.

The Boss's plan was to circumnavigate South America. Lana and I soon realised that we would more or less be following the route that Darwin had taken on the survey ship *Beagle*, 150 years earlier. For us, cruising is more interesting if we have a project or a theme, so we decided to try and share as many anchorages as we could with the ghost of the *Beagle*. Wigwam Cove, in the shadow of Cape Horn, was just one of them. We were following in Darwin's wake.

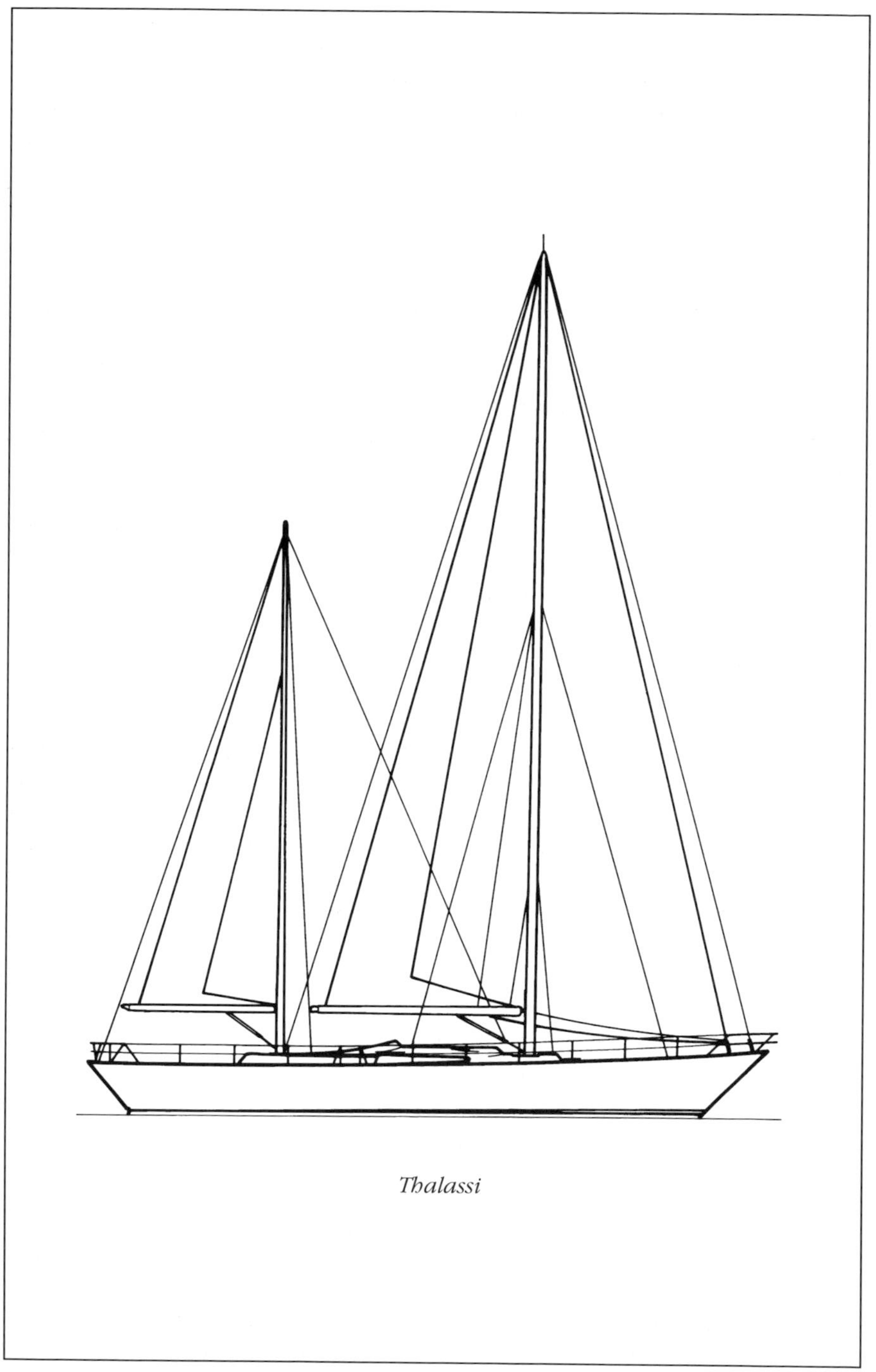

Thalassi

Chapter 2

Preparations

After *Thalassi* had been built in Spain, she had done a double Atlantic crossing, partly as a shakedown and partly so that she could be shown in a couple of American boatshows to advertise the builders. The trip gave her a good shakedown alright, and the crew had arrived back at the builders with a long list of problems. They gave the list to the yard and then promptly left the boat, to go sailing elsewhere.

When Lana and I took over the running of *Thalassi*, we found her in the little Spanish harbour of Calpe. Her 83ft length seemed enormous in the tiny, congested harbour, and her 100ft mainmast towered above every other boat there.

We took over the work list from the previous skipper, and before we had been there a month, we had added almost as many items of our own.

In addition to the work list, we inherited two crew. It is extremely difficult to find five or six people who can live and work together, in close quarters, twenty-four hours a day, seven days a week. Many people see only the glamorous side of the job, and overlook the difficult, strenuous and tedious aspects. The choice of crew can make the difference between a successful, happy voyage, and one that is a chore, when everybody is thankful that it is over.

We were faced now with two crew – Nick, a deckhand, and Tim, the engineer – who had been on board for several months, and had become established in their own routines. They were both late-night people, and it was their habit to disco the night away, and get back to the boat at 4 or 5 a.m. Trying to get them to turn to at 7.30, when the yard started work, was impossible. Yet a lot of the work that needed to be done was in the engine room, and Tim should certainly have been supervising that.

As the days passed, Lana and I realised that Tim thought he could run the boat, and felt he should have been given the skipper's job. Tensions rose. I was determined to do things my way, which basically is to get the work done first, then we can all play.

I tried explaining my views to Nick and Tim, but it had little or no

effect. I appealed to the Boss to let me hire my own crew, but he felt that Tim was vital to the whole operation. Finally Lana and I became so frustrated that we went to him with an ultimatum: it was to be Tim or us. We were not going to start a voyage with tensions so high and morale so low. If *Thalassi* could not become a happy ship, then we would rather not sail on her.

Finally the Boss relented. We could fire Tim and hire our own crew. We told Nick he was on a month's probation, and he had to prove himself an asset in that time, or follow in Tim's footsteps.

Nick seemed almost relieved that he no longer had to try to keep up with Tim's drinking and partying, and he enjoyed having a full night's sleep; an average of two or three hours a night had just about worn him out. He began to put in a full day's work, and was cheerful about it.

The day we fired Tim, there was a knock on the hull. It was a young Englishman called Chris. He told us that Tim had said he could come as crew, and he had flown out from England on the strength of that promise. My every instinct told me that we should not take on a legacy from Tim, but poor Chris looked so woebegone when I told him the situation that I took pity on him. He too was hired on a month's probation, and turned out to be quite a good crew.

At last we could concentrate on getting items crossed off the job list. The sooner the list was finished, the sooner we could leave.

To be fair to the builders, many of the items were minor, but we were heading for remote areas where repairs would be difficult, so it was in our interest to ensure that the boat was in the best possible condition. Sometimes it was hard to convince the yard that a particular job was important. All too often, we had to go through a time-consuming process of repeated and complicated explanations through the various bureaucratic layers of the boatyard management. For the most part these were concluded in fractured Spanish. At least, I thought it was Spanish I was learning from the workers, but it turned out that it was Catalan, which is not even as close to Spanish as Dutch is to German.

Nick was becoming as anxious to sail as we were, and began to show a spark of initiative by taking things into his own hands. The yard, in its infinite wisdom, perhaps to save $50 on the $2 million project, had decided to drain the two forward showers using a single pump. One shower served Nick and Chris, while the other was for Lana and myself. Not a major problem, one might suppose. However, whenever Nick or Chris pumped out their shower, such an evil smell came out of ours, that Lana and I had to evacuate our cabin.

We explained the problem to José, our beleaguered project

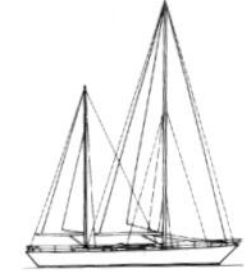

manager, and requested that they install a second pump, so that each shower could be pumped independently of the other. Instead of just taking our word for it and asking somebody to fit the extra pump, José had to satisfy himself that there was indeed a problem with the system, which it turned out he had designed. He went down on his hands and knees and sniffed our shower drain while the other was pumped out. He must have had some kind of nasal problem, because he swore that he could not smell anything untoward.

Nick was feeling as frustrated as I was, and finally solved the problem as only an Australian could. 'Try one more time, mate,' he said, running water into the other shower. José got back on his knees and Nick crept up close behind him. Drowning the noise with a discrete cough, Nick, who seemed able to do these things to order, made a smell that registered even with José's insensitive nose. The second pump was fitted the next day, but the explanations had already wasted half a day.

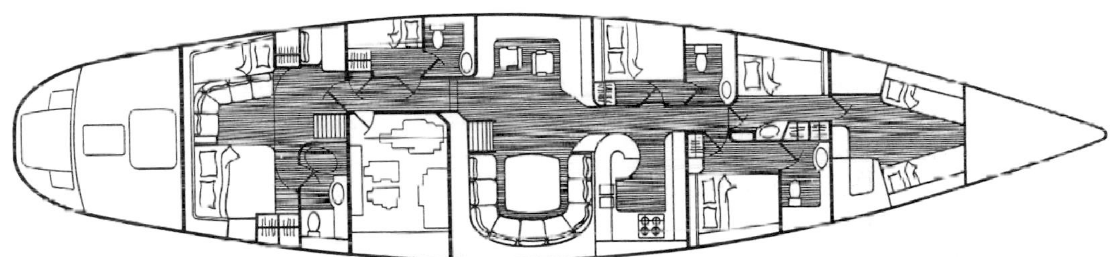

Thalassi – *accommodation plan.*

A much more serious problem occurred with the mast. It just did not seem strong enough. The previous skipper had said they had had trouble with it bending too much. We kept taking the boat out sailing, and tuning and retuning the rig, but to no avail. In the slightest breeze the mast would bend alarmingly. 'Put more tension on,' said the racing pundits. We cranked up on the hydraulic mast jack until there was 60 tons of compression on the mast at rest and went out for a sail; the mast bent worse than ever.

'Too much compression.' said the cruising men, scratching their collective beards. We slackened everything off, but if anything the mast bent more than before. Finally we did what we should have done at the start: we got somebody down from the mast-maker in Holland. Their chief rigger, Hans, arrived, brimming with confidence, expecting to be finished in an hour or two.

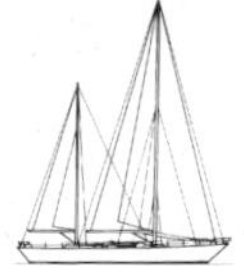

He spent four days with us, tweaking the rigging and testing. He fitted two additional stays about two-thirds of the way up the mast and said that was the best he could do. It did not look very much better than before he came. Off the record, he suggested that what was needed was a stronger mast. We all agreed, but we were unable to convince the owner. The mast was to prove a constant source of worry for the next 30,000 miles.

Between these various trials and tribulations, we sailed over to the island of Mallorca for a bit of a shakedown, and to let the Boss show the boat off to his friends. Although we had not missed Tim's presence in the engine room, I knew that we had to find ourselves an engineer as soon as possible. There was a lot of machinery to take care of, and I did not want to have to look after it all myself. There was the main diesel engine of course, and two generators. Then we had a machine for making fresh water from sea water, the refrigeration compressors, the air-conditioning system and the hydraulics. The hydraulic system in itself was very complicated. The sails were hoisted, furled, reefed and trimmed by hydraulic power. The centreboard was raised and lowered by hydraulics. The bow thruster, (a propeller mounted in the bows to help manoeuvre the boat) was also hydraulically operated. All this mechanical help let one or two people sail the boat efficiently, provided it all worked. We needed a good engineer to keep it all in order.

Palma, Mallorca, is a good place to look for crew. There are always people changing boats or looking for something better. We put the word out and were soon inundated with literally dozens of people claiming to be 'qualified marine engineers', whatever that might mean.

What Lana and I were most anxious to avoid was some prima donna who thought he was indispensable. The crew were finally starting to work together so I wanted to find somebody who could fit in and not upset the system. Hopefully they would also be good at maintaining and mending things.

We waded through the list of 'qualified marine engineers' and interviewed at least a dozen candidates without finding anybody Lana and I felt comfortable with. At all costs we wanted to avoid signing on another Tim. We were beginning to feel a bit despondent when we heard about Jeff.

He had not applied for the job, but a friend told us about him and said he was good at fixing things. I tracked him down at the bar which was his contact address and second home. About the first thing he said was, 'I'm not exactly a qualified marine engineer, but I can fix things'. Maybe he was what we were looking for.

He came down to the boat, and Lana and I had a long talk with him. He had an engineering background, and had done a lot of sailing, skippering a boat only a little smaller than *Thalassi* for a number of years. We hired him that afternoon, and never regretted it.

Now that the crew was complete, we decided to declare the boat to be as ready as she was going to get. September, and the beginning of the Austral summer, was upon us. It was time to get down to Patagonia. The Boss was now becoming as anxious as we were for the boat to leave. If we did not go soon, we would have to wait until the following season; we did not want to be poking around Cape Horn in the winter. So we said *adios* to Spain and headed west, towards Gibraltar. The voyage had begun.

Beagle's refit did not go any quicker than ours. In fact they were even further behind schedule than we were. It was to be December before they got away, and nobody wants to sail down channel that late in the year if they can help it.

Late or not, the fact that she was going at all was almost entirely due to her captain, a gentleman by the name of Robert Fitzroy.

Some five years previously, in 1826, the Admiralty had sent *Beagle* to South America under the command of Captain Pringle Stokes. They were sent to survey the coast from Rio de Janiero to Cape Horn, then up the Chilean coast to Chiloe. While they were in the deep south, in the Straits of Magellan, Captain Stokes was overcome with 'a fit of melancholy', and committed suicide. The mate sailed the ship back up to their base in Montevideo. The powers that be chose Lieutenant Fitzroy, who was serving on HMS *Ganges*, to take over. They promoted him, and gave him command of the *Beagle*. He was just twenty-three years old, more or less the same age as 'our' Nick and Chris! Hard to imagine.

Had it not been for the demise of Captain Stokes, Fitzroy might never have got command of the ship, and as we shall see, Darwin would probably not have had the chance to make his voyage, and so to propound his theory of evolution.

As soon as Fitzroy took command of the ship, he proved himself to be enthusiastic about the job, as well as very capable. He quickly realised that although the survey work was undoubtedly important, they were missing a huge opportunity to take other scientific observations, just because they had nobody on board who was capable of doing so. He made a vow that if he ever got the chance to command a similar voyage, he would ask the Admiralty to add geological and zoological studies to the ship's task, and to put a scientist on board.

Until such time as he could sail with a scientist on board, Fitzroy was doing his best to record his own, layman's observations. In an attempt to understand the local Fuegans better, he decided to try and educate one. To this end, he bought a teenage boy from his parents, for the princely sum of one pearl button, with the idea of taking him back to England.

While Fitzroy was mulling over his scientific thoughts, the *Beagle* was anchored back down in the Straits of Magellan, off Tierra del Fuego, close to where his predecessor had caught the 'melancholies'. Another series of incidents occurred that was going to affect future events and ensure that Darwin would make his voyage.

Theft by the natives was a continuous problem, and when a whaleboat was stolen from the ship, Fitzroy ordered the crew to capture three Fuegans as hostages, against the return of the boat. So, temporarily at least, they now had four Fuegians aboard. Suddenly a gale blew up. Their anchorage quickly became untenable, and Fitzroy had no choice but to slip his anchor and run before the rising wind.

The plan had been to return at least the three hostages, but the gale drove them out of the Straits, far out to sea. Perhaps it was nearly time to head for home anyway, because Fitzroy decided not to try and beat back into the Straits, but to head for England, taking the four Indians with him. He thought he might try and educate all four of them, in the hope that if he could teach them some English, he might be able to learn a little of their ways. He promised them that he would return them on the next voyage, which he felt certain would be ordered by the Admiralty.

Sadly, one of the Fuegans died from smallpox within days of reaching England, but the others survived, were treated well, and even had tea with the King and Queen. The only fly in the ointment was that Britain was suffering a recession, and cutbacks had been ordered in the Admiralty. All future surveys of South America were cancelled, or at least postponed for the forseeable future.

Now Captain Fitzroy was a gentleman, and in those days a gentleman's word was his bond. He had said he would take the Fuegans back, and take them back he would. He had some money put by, and started to fit out a small ship at his own expense, with the sole purpose of sailing the Indians back home.

Then he had a stroke of luck. A distant uncle, who was in the Admiralty, heard what his nephew was trying to do, and started to pull some strings. Decisions were reversed, and once more Captain

Fitzroy was given command of the *Beagle*, ostensibly to continue the survey of Patagonia, but in fact to let him take the Fuegans home at the taxpayers' expense.

Fitzroy's enthusiasm was not to be underestimated. He took the appointment seriously, and pretty soon *Beagle*'s voyage was becoming a full-blown expedition. True to the promise he had made to himself in the Straits of Magellan, he approached the Hydrographer to authorise the signing on of a civilian scientist.

The Hydrographer was Captain Beaufort, who shortly afterwards became an admiral. We remember him today by his Beaufort Scale, which is still used to describe wind strengths. He listened to Fitzroy's arguments, and eventually agreed; *Beagle* would take a scientist on the voyage.

The fates that brought Charles Darwin to the ship are even stranger than those which put Captain Fitzroy in command. Darwin was only twenty-two years old, and far from qualified technically for such an onerous post as scientific observer to an Admiralty expedition. His grandfather, Erasmus Darwin, would have been more suited, had he still been alive. He had been a well-respected doctor, and had published a number of medical treatises, although his favourite writings were, believe it or not, botanical poems! He not only became wealthy, but also well connected. One of his friends was James Watt, of steam engine fame, but the friend who was to influence the aspect of history in which we are interested was Josiah Wedgwood, the pottery man. The ensuing generations of Darwins and Wedgwoods were to remain fast friends and become connected through marriage.

Erasmus had three children. Charles (our Charles's uncle), Erasmus junior and Robert. Charles was chosen to follow in his father's footsteps and take over the still lucrative medical practice. Unfortunately he died before he even qualified, of blood poisoning contracted when he cut himself while doing a dissection.

Erasmus now turned his attention to Robert, the youngest, and decided that he should become the doctor, even though the sight of blood upset him. Meanwhile Erasmus junior became depressed, perhaps because his father's attention was being lavished on his younger brother, and drowned himself. So Robert became a slightly reluctant doctor, and sole heir to the family fortune and the medical practice.

Robert, whose financial well-being was already assured, married Susannah Wedgwood, who stood to inherit a substantial fortune from her father, Josiah. So young Charles was born to wealthy parents, on 12 February 1809. He had four sisters and a brother.

From a very early age Charles became a collector of things,

especially small animals. The habit was encouraged by his mother, who had known and admired his grandfather. Unfortunately she died when Charles was only eight, and he grew up rather in awe, and perhaps somewhat in fear, of his father. The latter tended to be a little distant with the children, but did sometimes take young Charles on his medical rounds with him, and would often take the trouble to identify animals that they spotted along the way.

Robert assumed that Charles would become the third generation to run the practice, but Charles was not so sure. His aversion to blood was even stronger than his father's. Despite this, he was sent to study medicine at Edinburgh University, but it soon became obvious that he was not applying himself. The realisation that his father would leave him well off and without the need to earn a living, was probably no help to his motivation.

This is where fate once again changed the course of history. Robert finally realised that his son was not going to be the one to continue the family tradition, and decided that the only other respectable occupation for him would be the Church. Charles was sent off to Cambridge University to read theology.

Through friends he made there, he became interested in entomology, or bug hunting as he preferred to call it. Despite the bugs and other distractions, he got his divinity degree, and only needed two years of residence to be ordained. Fortunately for history, he had attracted the attention of two professors, one his maths tutor and the other a teacher of mineralogy. They were friends of Captain Beaufort, who had asked them to suggest a scientist for the *Beagle*. They must have recognised some spark of genius in Darwin because, despite the lack of any technical qualifications, they recommended him for the job.

At first Darwin's father was against his going on the expedition. It took his uncle, Josiah Wedgwood, to help him persuade his father to agree, but eventually Robert gave his somewhat reluctant consent for him to apply for the position.

Darwin travelled to London to be interviewed by Captain Fitzroy, and took an immediate liking to him. But Fitzroy, who studied physiognomy, decided that he did not like the shape of the prominent nose, which for generations had been a Darwin trademark. He and the naturalist would be living in close quarters, and as we had found, Fitzroy knew it would be impossible to live in harmony on a small ship with somebody who did not fit in. His study of physiognomy told him plainly that somebody with such a big nose would be a misfit. He started making excuses, and might have put Darwin off the venture if it had not been for the young man's mounting enthusiasm.

Finally Fitzroy relented. He decided to ignore the nose and hire him for the voyage.

Once the Admiralty had decided that the voyage was to go ahead, they spared little expense to refit the ship. She had a complete new deck laid, and while they were at it Fitzroy had them raise the after deck some 12in. This gave more room below, and increased the freeboard aft to make her drier in a following sea. The bottom of the ship was sheathed with 2in fir planks, which were then covered with copper sheets bedded in felt. This added 15 tons to her displacement, but reduced leaks to a minimum, and the copper sheathing would keep her bottom relatively free from seaweed and barnacles.

Fitzroy knew that much of the survey work would be done from small boats. He asked for seven new ones to be built, and when the Admiralty balked at the cost, he had two of them built at his own expense. Getting them built was not the only problem; it required some ingenuity to stow them all on board the *Beagle*.

The smallest, the Captain's jolly-boat, was carried astern in davits. It became known as the dinghy, and it is thought that this term was

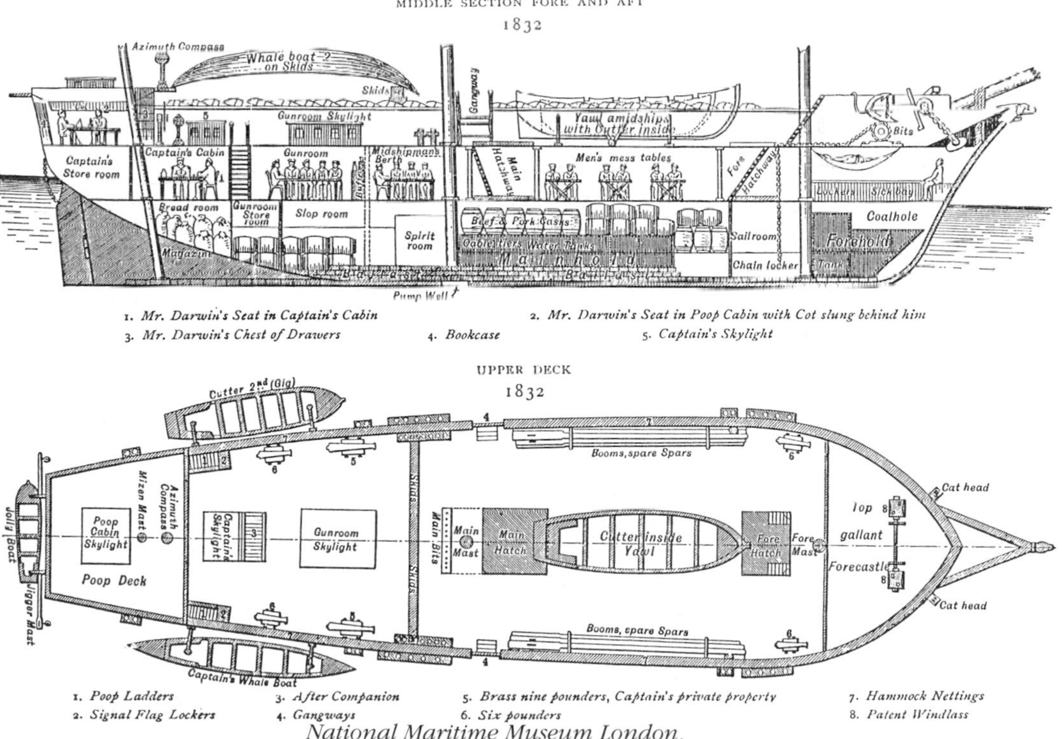

National Maritime Museum London.

in fact coined aboard the *Beagle*. The biggest boat was the yawl. It was 28ft long, and it stowed on deck between the fore and mainmasts. Stowed inside that was the cutter which, at 25ft, was only a little smaller. Both of these boats were built by the new method of double diagonal planking. The foreman of the Plymouth dockyard, where they were built, was given £300 in recognition of his invention of this building method.

Captain Fitzroy's own two 25ft whale-boats were stowed in skids over the quarterdeck, with a third, similar whale-boat hung in iron davits on the starboard quarter. The last boat was a smaller, lighter cutter, which became known as the gig. It was hung in davits on the port quarter.

Beagle's refit began in July, and it was early September when Darwin saw her for the first time. She was in the Royal Naval Dockyard in Devonport, and he was appalled at what he saw. There were no masts stepped, and she looked more like an old hulk destined for the scrapyard than a Royal Navy ship getting ready for a voyage round the world. Not only did the apparent chaos concern him, but the ship was much smaller than he expected. Indeed at 98ft overall she was only about 15ft longer than *Thalassi*, yet she was going to sail with seventy-four crew. I think she would have seemed small to me too, if we had had a crew of that size.

The crew consisted of thirty-four seamen who, together with six apprentices, would take care of the physical aspects of sailing the ship. Captain Fitzroy and his twenty-four officers would do the organising, and undertake the survey work. Then there were nine supernumeraries, of which Darwin was one. He took along his own servant, as did the Captain. In addition to medical men and a chaplain, they took a ship's artist, whose job it was to record the places they visited. Then there were the three Fuegans whom they were taking home.

Finally there was George Stebbing who was to tend the chronometers. One of the tasks given to the ship was to fix the longitude of the various places they visited accurately. When taking a sun sight with a sextant, it is easy enough to fix one's latitude very accurately, without having to know the time. To measure the longitude, however, one must know the time very accurately. Any small error in time can result in large inaccuracies in the longitude. *Beagle* was to carry twenty-two chronometers, whose rates could be compared. Any obviously inaccurate readings would be discounted. The chronometers were suspended in gimbals in wooden boxes, which in turn were cushioned in 3in of sawdust. Part of Fitzroy's cabin was cleared for the chronometers, which were placed on the centre-line of the

ship, and as low down as possible, to reduce the motion to a minimum. Stebbing, who was the son of the watchmaker who had made several of the chronometers, wound them daily at 9 a.m. Once again, Fitzroy took the task very seriously. He was not satisfied with the seventeen chronometers that the Admiralty supplied, so he bought five more with his own money.

Even the best of the chronometers ran at different speeds as the temperature changed, so whenever the ship was in a port whose position was accurately known, the officers took a series of sights. Any discrepancy between their calculated position and the known one had to be due to an error in time, and it was then a simple matter to correct the chronometers for the error. By repeating the exercise over a six-day period, they could see at what rate the chronometers were gaining or losing time at that particular temperature. That correction would be applied each day for the next leg of the voyage.

When they arrived at a port whose position was not known, they repeated the same procedure of daily sights for six days. By comparing the daily differences, they could again calculate the daily error and re-rate the chronometers. By the end of the voyage, after five years, eleven of the chronometers were still running reasonably accurately.

Beagle displaced 240 tons, which is about three times the displacement of *Thalassi*, so *Beagle* obviously had quite a lot more volume than we did. She did not have the benefit of all the hydraulic winches which we had on *Thalassi* (provided Jeff could keep them all running), so she needed the muscle provided by the extra crew. A patent anchor winch was fitted during the refit, and although it was still manually operated, it was much more efficient than the capstan it replaced.

Beagle's sails, all twenty-one of them, were hoisted and trimmed by the 'Armstrong method' – lots of people pulling on ropes. The crew had to go aloft to reef or stow the heavy flax square sails, whereas we could do everything from the deck, mostly with a push of a button.

It was bad enough for us trying to provision *Thalassi*, but for them, trying to stow provisions for seventy-four people for a five-year voyage must have been a nightmare. They did not have the benefit of either refrigeration or canned food as we know it. They did, however, ship some of the newly available preserved food from Kilner and Moorson, a company which was pioneering the preservation of food in sealed glass jars, and which supplied the ship with preserved vegetables, soup and a small amount of meat.

Fresh vegetables such as potatoes, cabbages and onions will keep

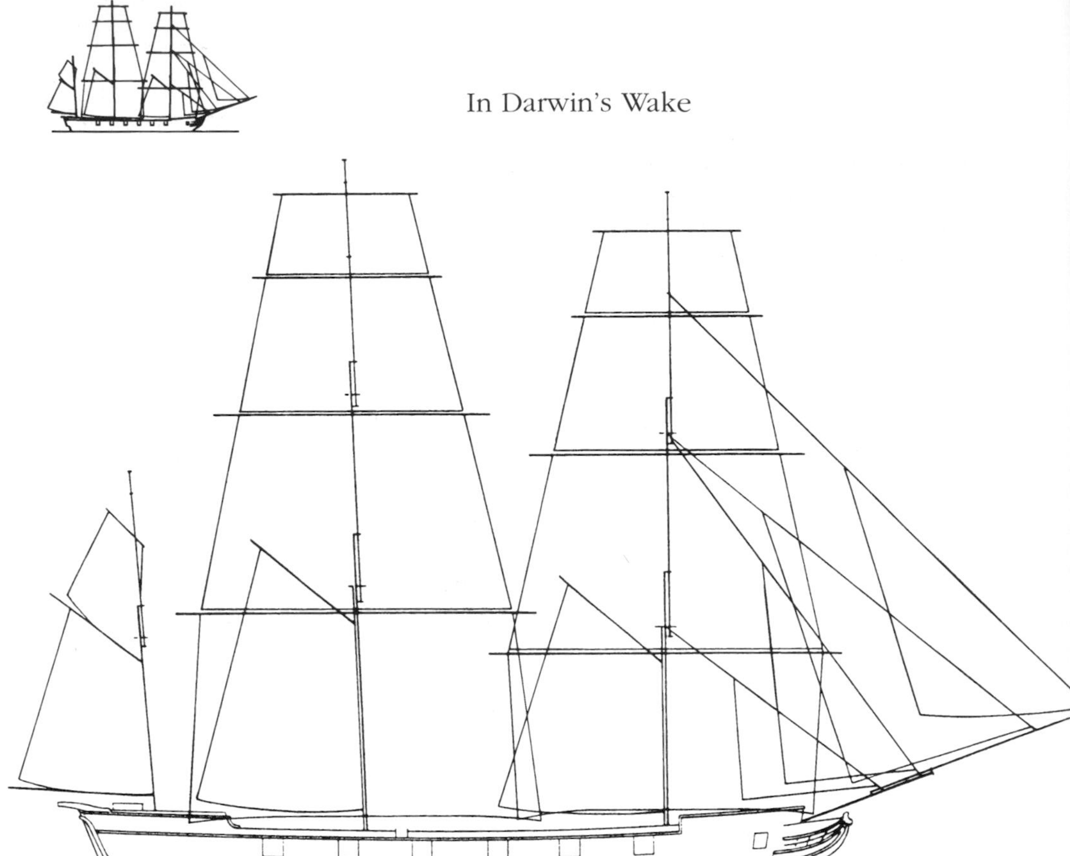

This sailplan of the Beagle *as she was fitted for surveying is based partly on the tables and drawing found in John Edye's* Naval Calculations *of 1832 and partly on contemporary sketches of the* Beagle.

for a month or two. They would therefore be replaced whenever possible, but when they were gone the carbohydrate content of the diet would consist of ship's biscuits. Towards the end of the voyage, these biscuits would have been adding to the protein in their diet – the biscuits always became infested with weevils.

The effects of scurvey were well known at this time, and as antiscorbutics they took along dried apples, pickles and lemon juice. They carried other dried fruit such as raisins and sultanas, but at least for the crew forward of the mast, these would be limited to the weekly 'duff', a kind of suet pudding usually served as a Sunday treat.

Meat was not much easier to store. Salt pork, and to a lesser extent salt beef, stowed in barrels of brine, were the mainstay. The sailors often disparagingly referred to it as 'Salt horse', and they were perhaps nearer the mark more often than they realised. The chandlers who supplied the ship knew that their products would often not be eaten for a year or more, and that it could be as much as three or

four years before a ship would be back. They could be sure, therefore, that the chance of ever receiving a complaint was small.

On such a diet, our crew would have lasted about a day. With Lana's careful planning, and *Thalassi*'s large coolers and freezers, we ate a 'normal' diet for the whole trip.

As big a problem as food storage was for the *Beagle*, the supply of fresh water was even more important. The ship's tanks held 15 tons of water, and although the crew would never miss a chance to top them up whenever good water was available, fresh water was on permanent ration. Indeed, water was usually the deciding factor in how long a vessel could stay at sea, or in a remote location. Even now, on the older charts for many of the remoter areas of the world which have not yet been superseded by modern insipid metric charts, we can still see notes saying, 'Good water here', 'Watering place', 'Sweet spring water' and similar helpful comments. Finding a supply of fresh water was often literally a matter of life and death.

On *Beagle*, the afterguard, as the officers were termed, had jugs of water brought to their cabins regularly throughout the day, but the crew would draw it by the mugful from the 'Scuttlebut', a barrel on deck. This was filled each day, so consumption could be closely monitored. Sailors would often linger at the scuttlebut and swap news with other crew members. Even now, we refer to nautical gossip as scuttlebut.

Little if any fresh water would be wasted on washing. Clothes, dishes and bodies would all be washed in sea water, unless a timely rain squall served. This was not too much of a problem in the tropics, but in Patagonia, with a sea temperature close to freezing, it was a different matter altogether.

On *Thalassi*, we carried about 3 tons of water, and what with daily showers, the washing machine and the dishwasher, the five of us used as much water each day as the seventy-four men on the *Beagle* did. Despite this profligate use, we never had to carry buckets of water from nearby streams to top up the tanks, as *Beagle*'s crew did. All we had to do was hope that Jeff could keep the water maker running. This machine turns sea water into drinking water at the rate of about 50 gallons an hour, so we could top up the tanks more or less at will. Provided we had fuel enough for the generator to run the water maker, we effectively had an infinite supply of water.

When all the stores and water were finally aboard the *Beagle*, and Captain Fitzroy deemed the ship ready to go to sea, the supernumeraries joined the ship. Darwin moved his gear aboard on 21 November. They were already more than a month late, yet still more delays held

them up for another three weeks before they finally hoisted the anchor and stood out to sea.

It was by now winter, and they sailed straight into a strong south-westerly gale. Darwin took to his hammock, sicker than he thought it possible to be. *Beagle*, like all square-riggers, could not sail very close to the wind. The best she could manage was about 65 or 70 degrees. *Thalassi* can do some 30 degrees better than that, and because of her efficient keel, she does not make as much leeway (slipping sideways) as the *Beagle* did. The gale blowing up the English Channel effectively stopped the *Beagle* in her tracks.

After a fruitless thirty-six hours, they gave up and ran back into the shelter of Plymouth harbour to wait for the gale to abate.

It finally blew itself out ten days later. A day or two ashore had quickly renewed young Darwin's adventurous spirit, and he was excited when they set sail once more, on 21 December. Unfortunately the excitement was short-lived. An awkward gust caught them aback, and they ran hard aground off Drake's Island, still within the confines of the harbour. By the time she was refloated, the wind was back in the south-west, so Captain Fitzroy elected to spend Christmas at anchor.

The morning of 27 December dawned dull but calm. Indeed, there was no wind at all. While that would have suited us quite nicely, *Thalassi*'s Mercedes diesel being able to push her along at 10 knots if needed, *Beagle* had no engine and could only wait for the wind.

While waiting, Darwin, the Captain and some of the officers lunched ashore on mutton chops and champagne. With a meal like that inside him, it was no wonder that Darwin was again sick when they set off, even though they had a fair wind from the east. The favourable breeze sent them bowling down channel.

Darwin's outlook was not improved the next day when Captain Fitzroy ordered the flogging of the worst of the Christmas drunkards. It was a salutary reminder that they were on a naval vessel and naval discipline would rule.

Despite the inauspicious start, Darwin was excited. They were off to the Canary Islands, and around the world – much more interesting than learning to be a vicar.

Chapter 3

The Voyage Begins

Beagle's passage across Biscay was not an easy one. The weather was cold, the skies grey. The wind had dropped a little, but was still quite strong. The ship was very heavily laden, and she rolled and rolled on the big swell left over from the winter gales. It is very tiring just trying to live under these conditions. In a big swell the boat can be rolling 30 or 40 degrees one way then the other, the whole cycle being repeated several times a minute. It is hard to sleep, and difficult to prepare or even eat food. Nothing can be put down without wedging it firmly in place.

Darwin was sick. He mostly stayed in his hammock, but occasionally lay on the sofa in Fitzroy's cabin. If Fitzroy was having second thoughts about the suitability of his naturalist, he did not show it. He was sympathetic, and saw to it that Darwin was always looked after.

Darwin ate little. He found he could not face the shipboard meals at all, and for almost the whole of the first week, all he ate was a few raisins. Not even the sighting of the island of Madeira could entice him from his bunk.

Even though Darwin could not be bothered to get up to see it, the passing of Madeira marked a turning point in the voyage. The bad weather ended, the clouds parted, and the grey skies and seas turned blue. It was *Beagle*'s eighth day out from England. Darwin finally ventured out on deck, and found life was not so bad after all. He managed a bite or two of food, and made the first entry in his journal.

Just twenty-four hours later they sighted Tenerife, the biggest of the Canary Islands. As a child, Darwin had read an account of a visit to Tenerife written by the German explorer Baron Alexander von Humboldt (after whom the current in the Pacific is named). Something in the account caught his imagination, and it became his strong ambition to visit the island. Indeed, it was perhaps the promise of that particular landfall that had made him determined to go on the voyage in the first place. *Beagle* sailed south, between Tenerife and Gran Canaria. As the sun rose, and the clouds cleared, Darwin saw the snow-tipped peak of Tenerife's volcano. He was about to live one of his earliest dreams, or so he thought.

Unfortunately, it was not to be. As they anchored off the town of Santa Cruz, they were met by the British Consul. They always say that bad news travels fastest. The Consul told them that reports had been received of an outbreak of cholera in England. The island's officials had therefore decided that all ships arriving from England were to be quarantined for twelve days. Nobody would be allowed ashore during this period, so that they could be sure that none of the crew had cholera.

Despite Darwin's pleas, Fitzroy refused to wait for the twelve days. They were already behind schedule and he was determined to press on south. They were allowed to buy fresh fruit and vegetables, but by nightfall *Beagle* was once more underway, headed south.

As if to tantalise Darwin further, the wind went light, and they were becalmed in sight of the island for the whole of the next day. Darwin could hardly bear to take his eyes off the volcanic peak, until darkness finally blotted it out.

The wind gradually returned that night, and by the following morning, Tenerife was no more than a memory.

By starting from southern Spain, we avoided the cold, ugly thrash down channel that *Beagle* had had to endure. Our first passage was a nice gentle reach westwards to Gibraltar, which let us all find our sea legs in the easiest possible way.

In Gibraltar, our main task was to collect a big box of spare parts which had been sent down from England for us. The easy part was unpacking the extra anchors, rope and various odds and ends. The hard part was finding places to stow them all.

Lana co-opted Nick and Chris to bring back what appeared to be about half the stock of the Safeway supermarket. *Thalassi* was beginning to bulge at the seams.

Jeff showed the same interest in *Thalassi*'s fuel tanks that Captain Fitzroy had shown in the *Beagle*'s water tanks. Neither of them ever missed an opportunity to fill up. *Thalassi* carries 3 tons of diesel fuel, which of course supplies the main engine, but also runs the generators. The electricity from the generators not only makes the fresh water, but also charges the batteries for lighting and keeps the freezers frozen. Without an ample supply of diesel fuel, life would quickly become almost as basic as aboard the *Beagle*, and nobody wanted that. We were all becoming thoroughly spoilt by *Thalassi*'s luxuries!

Once Jeff had topped up the fuel tanks, and Lana had organised the stowing of the last of the provisions, we were ready to head westwards once more.

For a sailing vessel trying to leave the Mediterranean, the Straits of Gibraltar can be a difficult passage. Because of the evaporation from the surface of the enclosed sea, there is almost always a current flowing into the Mediterranean. Moreover, the prevailing wind is from the west. Indeed, the only time it ever seems to blow from the east is when one is trying to sail into the Med!

Fortunately, the west wind was fairly light, so we were able to motorsail against it quite easily. Picking a gap in the endless stream of ships, we dashed across to the African side. We passed a few miles north of Tangier, and before dusk we were clear of the narrow section and the almost constant procession of ships. We were able to set our course towards the Canaries, 600 miles to the south-west. At last we felt that the voyage had begun. The Atlantic Ocean lay ahead.

The Boss was not with us, at least not in the flesh. Sometimes, however, it seemed as if he was there in spirit. Lurking next to the chart table, in a shiny brown plastic case, was a telex machine. Aboard the *Beagle*, they might literally go for years without news from home or fresh orders. On *Thalassi*, we were never out of range of the long arm of the Boss. Via the telex, he could reach us any time he wanted, which was not always an advantage.

Via the ham radio, we were able to speak to our neighbour in Ireland, and to George, who was the Boss's Agent in Britain. Sometimes the miracles of modern communication work to our advantage, but on other occasions it would have been nice to sail in blissful ignorance.

As we cleared the straits, the telex started chattering away. There was a change of plans already. Instead of Tenerife, we were to make Lanzarote our Canary Island landfall. Although Tenerife was the *Beagle*'s first destination, and our usual stopping place in the Canaries, we were happy enough to divert and visit Lanzarote instead. Tenerife has suffered greatly at the hands of the developers, and is perhaps the most commercialised of the islands. Besides, none of us had been to Lanzarote before.

Although he would not be meeting us there, the Boss told us to go to a little bay at the south end of the island called Playa Blanca. He was planning to build a hotel or two there, and he wanted us to show off his boat to his partner, who also happened to be Mayor of the nearby town.

The harbour was tiny; I was sure there would not be room for *Thalassi*'s 83ft, and was all set to anchor out in the bay, when Lana

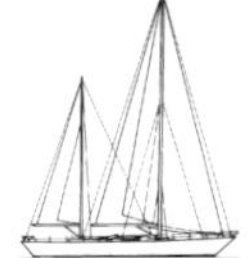

spotted somebody on the quay waving for us to come in. We crept in, and turned round to facilitate our eventual escape. There was not much room to manoeuvre, but *Thalassi*'s bow thruster, known familiarly as the thrutcher, made the turn possible. The thrutcher is close to the bows of the boat, and consists of a propeller on the end of a retractable leg. When the leg is lowered, the propeller is used to push the bows from side to side. It certainly makes life easier when trying to manoeuvre the boat in tight spaces.

There was a group of yachties watching us, with uniformly open mouths, as we wriggled into a space about a foot longer than the boat. Not one of them came to catch our lines; they just stood and watched – not a very friendly reception.

Thalassi *laying alongside in the harbour at Playa Blanca, in Lanzarote.*

All was made clear the next day. We discovered that the Harbourmaster, on the instruction of the Mayor, who had got word from the Boss, had moved six yachts to make space for us. They had all thought they were settled in that particular corner of the harbour for the winter and none of them was happy at having to move for our short visit.

Feeling a bit like the Royal Yacht, we duly entertained the Harbourmaster, the Mayor and the editor of the local newspaper.

Once we had done our duty, we felt that we had better make the expedition that Darwin might have made had he been there. Lana and I drove up into the interior of the island in a rented car. Even knowing little or nothing about geology, we could see that Lanzarotte is volcanic. The whole island looks pretty much like a great big heap of cinders.

As we drove up into the centre, to the National Park, the cliché of a 'lunar landscape' kept springing to mind. There was mile after mile of black sand and heaps of jagged cinder-like lava, with absolutely nothing growing, for as far as the eye could see.

In the main part of the park, there is a restaurant, built beside a series of hot volcanic vents. One such vent comes to the surface strategically close to the kitchen door. A heavy steel grille has been built over the vent, and an endless supply of steaks and chicken are barbecued on it, courtesy of the hidden volcano.

After the visit to the restaurant, we decided to take a camel ride up the side of one of the volcanos. Perhaps because Lanzarote is so close to Africa, camels have become the accepted beasts of burden on the island. Camels walk differently from horses, and indeed from most other animals. Rather than moving diagonally opposite legs at the same time, they move both legs on one side, then both on the other. We had heard them called 'ships of the desert' before, and I had thought the name just referred to the fact that they could cross ocean-sized tracts of desert. Lana and I rode double on one camel, and as soon as it lurched to its feet, we realised that the name had probably been given for other reasons. The curious lurching gait gave a motion similar to a less than sea-kindly vessel in a rolling swell. By the time we reached the top of the volcano, we were both a little green around the gills, and feeling decidedly camel-sick.

Perhaps of more interest to Darwin would have been the vineyards a little further north. Grapes are grown, under seemingly impossible conditions, for a locally produced wine. No ordinary grapevine could survive for long on the dry, windswept slopes of the mountains, but over the years the islanders have developed a special plant, and a unique technique for growing the grapes.

The grape vines which are grafted onto cactus roots to enable them to grow in the very dry climate. In this instance, man has modified Darwin's Law of Evolution, to allow a plant to survive where it could not do naturally. The stone walls shelter the plants from the incessant wind.

For each plant, a hollow is dug into the volcanic ash, and any stones or lava are heaped up in a horseshoe shape on the windward side. This gives the growing plant a little shelter from the almost perpetual wind. In the centre of each hollow, they then plant a cactus, which is allowed to grow until it is well established. Once it is well rooted, they cut it off just above ground level, and graft on the grapevine. The vine is not supported in any way, but allowed to grow on the ground, up the sides of the hollow. Rain is rare on Lanzarote, but this hybrid plant is able to absorb enough moisture from the dew not only to survive, but to flourish and produce grapes.

It was of course later in his voyage that Darwin first developed his theories of natural selection, whereby plants and animals change to adapt to certain conditions, but here was a case where man was helping nature develop a unique plant for a specific environment.

By chance we stumbled across another curious crop that the people of Lanzarote cultivate. We saw several small fields of cacti growing, and assumed that they were there to provide root stock for further generations of vines. We were wrong. It turned out that they were prickly pear cacti being grown because they were the favourite food of the cochineal beatle.

Somewhere in the dim recesses of my mind, I knew that the food colouring cochineal came from squashed beetles, but I had never stopped to wonder where those beetles came from. Now we knew. Cochineal beetles are an important export from Lanzarote, even in this day of artificial colourings and 'E' numbers'.

As usual, before we left, Lana visited the local market to load up with fresh fruit and vegetables, and Jeff had managed to persuade the driver of a little fuel truck to come down to the dock to top up the fuel tanks. We had entertained the Boss's friends, done a little exploring, and now we were ready to follow the *Beagle* south. The Cape Verde Islands lay ahead.

Chapter 4

To the Cape Verdes

As we left the Canaries behind us, the wind was fair and the weather became warmer by the day. Chris began to work seriously on his suntan, and despite his shipmates casting doubts on his masculinity, he tried to bleach his hair in the sun, using the juice of lemons filched from Lana's galley.

The days passed easily enough for all of us except Nick, who was getting low on cigarettes. He and Jeff were the only smokers. Jeff was a fifty-a-day man, and in Gibraltar he had filled every spare inch of his cabin with cartons of duty-free cigarettes. He reckoned he had enough to last him as far as Brazil, and was quite rightly reluctant to give any to Nick, just because Nick had not bothered to stock up. At first Nick was philosophical about it, saying that he wanted to give up smoking anyway. But as the days passed, he became more and more fidgety and less the happy-go-lucky, easy-going Nick that we knew.

As we approached the Cape Verde Islands, the visibility steadily became worse. Eventually it was down to a couple of miles. It was not foggy or misty; the air was very dry. What was reducing the visibility was dust in the air, and indeed a fine red dust was beginning to settle all over the boat.

The poor visibility was no real problem for us, as the satellite navigator was ticking away, updating our position regularly, and the radar did not even know that there was a haze; it could still see everything around us for 30 miles or more. But there was not much for us to see from on deck.

We closed the north eastern-most island, Sal, in the late afternoon, and sailed gently down the west coast as the sun set. A developer's potential paradise, the island looks to be composed of a series of sand dunes fringed with virgin white sand beaches.

There was just the occasional house and one small village, but we did not see any particularly inviting anchorages, so I decided to sail on through the night and go to Brava, which I knew has a well protected bay on its south side.

We sailed gently through the night, passing to the north of Santiago, to make a picture-book landfall at dawn, off the island of Fogo. This island is an almost perfectly conical volcano, rising straight out of the sea. At dawn, the whole island was visible, but as soon as the sun began to rise, clouds formed at the peak. As the sun got higher, the clouds worked their way steadily down the mountain. By breakfast time they had enshrouded at least half the island.

The last of the breeze vanished with the dawn, so we motored the remaining few miles towards Brava, the south western-most island in the group. Lana spotted a small boat, perhaps half a mile off the shore. Through the binoculars we could see that the three crew members were all waving furiously. Thinking that they might have broken down and be in danger of drifting out to sea, we motored over to them. It transpired that they were fishermen with a large catch of lobsters, and they were hoping for a bit of early-morning business.

Communication presented a bit of a problem. While it was obvious that they were trying to sell lobsters to us, we had difficulty explaining that we did not even know what their local currency was, nor did we have any of it. We showed them the bundle of pesetas that we had left over from the Canaries. They realised it was money, but had never seen anything like it before. They seemed happy enough to give us two buckets of lobsters in exchange for a bundle of the mysterious notes, and were all set to pass up a third bucketful before the cook called a halt. I hope they were not disappointed when they managed to change the pesetas.

As we motored round the corner into Blacksmith's Bay, we were met by a flotilla of six more fishing boats. They did not try to sell us anything, they were just curious. It must be rare enough for a yacht to come into their bay. Even after the anchor was down, the boats continued to circle around us, just looking, for the most part smiling, and occasionally waving.

Perched up on the cliff, high above the bay, was a small village of about half a dozen houses. Perhaps this was how Darwin saw Praia. Certainly few changes can have occurred here, in this little bay, in the last 150 years. There was still no electricity nor running water, and little contact with the rest of the island, let alone the outside world.

The Boss had already informed us of his anticipated arrival date in Brazil, still some 1400 miles away. Since we were supposed to be there for his arrival, we did not have much time to spare. We would only be able to spend the day in Brava, and then we would have to leave that night to stay on schedule.

By anchoring in such a secluded bay, I must confess, we had hoped to avoid any contact with officialdom. Normally we play

strictly by the rules, but on this occasion, with our stop being only for eight or nine hours, I had decided, mainly to save time, to take a chance and not clear with the authorities in the main town of Faja, on the north side of the island.

We were just getting ready to put our dinghy over the side when we saw one of the small boats heading our way rather purposefully. An older man was sitting in the stern sheets, and two youths were rowing him directly towards us. Sure enough, they came alongside.

My heart sank when I realised that he was telling us that he represented officialdom. I could do nothing but invite him aboard. They seemed to understand our Spanish without difficulty, but there was little in their Portuguese reply that was intelligible to us. However, we did understand that he wanted to make a note of the ship's particulars, although it turned out that he had neither pen nor paper.

Lana presented him with a notebook and ballpoint pen, and told him that he could keep them both. He was so pleased with them that he forgot to write anything down. We gave him and each of his muscular rowers a can of Coke to drink. None of them knew how to open the cans. Perhaps it was the first time they had seen drinks in cans, although they all recognised the Coca Cola symbol, so knew what was in the can.

Formalities completed, cans of drink safely opened, there were smiles all round. We felt it was safe enough to go ashore. Jeff offered to stay aboard to keep an eye on the boat; he wanted to check over everything in the engine room ready for the crossing to Brazil. It was much easier for him to work in the engine room while we were anchored in the shelter of the bay, rather than rolling about in mid-Atlantic. Lana said she would stay as well. The lobsters were taking it in turns to climb out of the buckets, so she decided to quieten them down by cooking them.

So it was the three of us, Nick, Chris and I, who set off ashore. We decided to walk up to the village overlooking the bay, with Nick hoping to find a village shop that stocked his brand of cigarettes.

As soon as we got ashore, it seemed as if every child for miles around came to follow us up the track. There were dozens of them – far more, we thought, than the few houses in the village could possibly accommodate. So, feeling more like the Pied Piper than Charles Darwin, I led the procession up the steep path to the village.

When we finally panted our way to the top of the path, we found several people who had obviously been watching our trek up the hill. They were sitting on a bench in the shade of the single tree which was growing in front of the cluster of houses. 'Where d'you reckon the supermarket is then?' asked Nick. It did not look too promising

Looking down from the village, at Thalassi *anchored in Blacksmith's Bay.*

for much in the way of shopping. The houses were little more than shacks, and none of them looked like a shop.

Nods and smiles were exchanged with the row of watchers. Between the three of us, we discussed whether we should attack the next section of path, which vanished up the mountain. It looked even steeper than the one we had just struggled up. Nick, never one for unnecessary exercise, was for once eager to try, in case we might be able to find a cigarette shop. Chris and I were less enthusiastic. We were still debating what to do when a young man stood up, walked over and introduced himself. To our ears, his name was totally unpronounceable, and it sounded different each time we got him to repeat it. The closest we could get was 'Himself', so Himself he became for the duration of our visit.

By dint of some fractured Spanish, a lot of sign language and a few drawings in the dust, we understood that Himself was offering to take us to the valley where the villagers grew their food.

He led us along a narrow rocky track over the escarpment to the east. We crested a ridge, and suddenly the valley was there in front of us; a splash of brilliant green among the dusty, barren red hills that made up most of the island. As we walked down the side of the valley, Himself showed us a large stone cistern, brimming full of water. This, he explained, was where they got their drinking water, and then, as if to prove how good the water was, he peeled off his shirt and jumped in. He beckoned us to join him, and I must admit it looked tempting, but we wondered how the village elders might feel if they found three very sweaty yachties frolicking in their drinking water. We declined as graciously as we could.

We were very curious, however, about the source of the water. It was obvious from the parched countryside that it rarely if ever rained, and yet in this little valley, they had water apparently to spare.

Once we could get Himself out of the water tank, he gave us the answer, or at least a part of it. He took us past the rocky outcrop against which the big stone tank nestled, and showed us the beginning, or I suppose more technically the end, of a long, intricate series of stone aqueducts.

We could see the network of supporting stone walls zigzagging its way up the mountain, at least a couple of miles from the valley. Offshoots went down into the valley itself, while one branch ensured that the cistern remained full. There was not a lot of water coming down the stone channel, but there was at least a steady trickle. The clouds which were gathered round the tops of the mountains suggested that there would always be water up there, even if it never rained down where we were.

We wanted to know who had undertaken this immense engineering project. Clearly it would have been beyond the scope of the few villagers who lived there. We asked Himself who had built the aqueducts. His reply was puzzling, and a little disturbing. Nobody had built them, he said, and he was adamant on this point. Nobody had built them, they had always been there. It was an enigma for somebody with a better grasp of the Portuguese language to solve.

He showed us an ancient grindstone, where the villagers crushed sugar cane. The cane juice was used to brew the local hooch. When he asked us if we would like something to drink, I feared that he was about to produce some of the home brew. The boys said yes, they

---

(Opposite) Nick walking along one of the mystery aquaducts on Brava. Our guide, 'Himself', insisted that nobody had built them, they had always been there.

were thirsty, and I had visions of them becoming blind or going mad through drinking the local grog.

I was much relieved when our man nipped up the nearest palm tree and cut a young coconut for each of us. Once he was safely back on terra firma, Himself cut the top off each nut, and we gratefully drank the surprisingly cool milk. It was sweet and refreshing and, more to the point, would not make the boys go blind!

The expedition was deemed complete, and Himself led us back down through the village. He vanished momentarily inside a house, to reappear clutching three eggs. He gave one to each of us. We asked if they were cooked, but he said they were not, they had just been laid. Each of us solemnly carrying an egg, we walked back down to the beach.

We took our guide out to the boat, together with two of his young friends. How could we repay them? All we could think of was a can of Coke each, and a packet of biscuits. Then Chris had a bright idea, and produced a couple of old T-shirts. It was little enough to repay their generosity when they had so little, and we appeared to have so much.

As the sun began to set, we could see a group of people gathering beneath the tree. Motoring out of the bay, I blew the horn in salute to our audience.

We made sail as darkness fell with tropical rapidity. As we looked back towards the bay, there was not a single glimmer of light to be seen. There was not even a moon to silhouette the island, and the perpetual dusty haze hid the stars. It was as black as the inside of a cow. Only the radar told us that the island, and no doubt the people of Blacksmith's Bay, were still there. As each of us took a piece of the three-egg omelette that Lana had made, we drank a toast to them.

Aboard the *Beagle*, things were continuing to look up. They too had a fair wind and warmer weather. Darwin began to take more of an interest in his studies as his sea legs developed. He made a bag to tow behind the ship, in order to collect plankton. When he examined his catch under the microscope, he saw a bewildering array of tiny plants and animals of every conceivable shape and form. In his journal he expressed 'an unhappy wonder at so much beauty for, it seems, so little purpose'.

Like us, Darwin read a lot on passage. I am afraid that at sea our

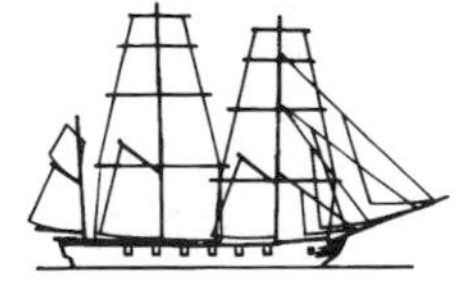

reading is mainly limited to 'airport' novels. Most of the time we find it difficult to concentrate on anything more erudite when sailing. We did have our moments though. There was a full set of Encyclopaedia Britannica on board, and that was used almost every day to settle an argument, or to start another. Chris was especially good at checking facts and figures, and it got to the point when one could hardly make any statement at all without every nuance being verified by Chris.

Darwin spent a lot of time reading a recently published tome on geology. Much of what it said went against the current religious dogma relating to the age of the earth. The author of the book was convinced that the world was much older than the Bible would allow.

As they approached the islands, the visibility was about as bad as we were experiencing. However, they were without any of the modern electronics that made navigation so easy for us. Fitzroy had only his sextant and a compass to work with, so their exact position was often a little uncertain.

The persistent haze made star sights impossible and sun sights difficult. To take a sextant sight of the sun, or indeed any heavenly body, as the stars and planets are quaintly called, one has to be able to see the horizon. One trick when taking sights in reduced visibility is to get low down, as close to the water as possible. This has the effect of bringing one's horizon closer, hopefully within the limits of the visibility. Captain Fitzroy took sights whenever he was able, and breathed a small sigh of relief when the first land eventually appeared through the haze.

Darwin noticed the same red dust landing on the decks as we had, but instead of cursing it for making more clean-up work, he carefully swept up samples and examined them under his microscope.

We had assumed that it was dust blowing out from the Sahara Desert. After all, the easterly trade winds were always blowing over the desert and out to sea, and deserts must be dusty old places.

We were almost correct, but not quite. Darwin described the dust as being composed of 'Infusoria, with siliceous shields'. Our dictionary says that 'Infusoria' are 'a group of protozoans frequently developed in infusions of decaying matter and stagnant water'. So what we had dismissed as dust was actually lots of little one-celled animals which had come from stagnant water. Stagnant water in the desert?

By the time he had sifted through his various samples of dust, Darwin had identified sixty-seven types of protozoa, including flagellates, amoebas and ciliates. We had guessed that the wind had carried them over the 300 miles from the mainland, so it was not too surprising that he found that all but two were fresh rather than seawater species.

The big surprise came later, when he got back to England and identified some that he was having trouble with. He found that two species were not to be found in Africa at all. They were unique to South America. Had some of the red dust which landed on the *Beagle*, and even now was being crunched underfoot on *Thalassi's* deck, originated in South America? If so, the trade winds had carried the little animals almost three-quarters of the way round the world before dropping them on us.

In 1832, the Cape Verde Islands were a Portuguese colony, inhabited by a few hardy settlers from West Africa and from Portugal itself. In the 1970s, when colonialism was becoming a dirty word, the islands achieved a quasi-independence. When Portuguese Guinea broke away from Portugal to become Guinea Bissau, the islands were lumped in with them, to be ruled by the same political party.

That state of affairs did not last long. By the time we arrived, they had been a completely independent country for five years, largely supported, it seems, by the many Cape Verdians who have emigrated to the north-eastern USA.

Beagle sailed into the port of Praia, on the island of Santiago, which is now the country's capital. The total population of the Cape Verde Islands is about 350,000, and almost half of that number live on the island of Santiago. Praia, which Darwin describes as a small village, now has in excess of 60,000 inhabitants.

He describes Puerto Praia as having a desolate aspect, saying that volcanic activity and the searing sun had rendered much of the soil unfit for cultivation. However, he was still interested to get ashore, to start his field work, and put his new-found geological knowledge to the test. After so long at sea, it was exciting to be walking through a strange land, and to stroll through his first grove of coconut trees was an added thrill.

He remarked that compared with the English countryside, the landscape looked sterile. Indeed, there was almost nothing green to be seen growing on the lava plains, yet there were goats and a few cattle that seemed able to survive. When he asked some of the settlers about this, he was told that, on average, it rained there but once or twice a year. But when it does rain, the vegetation springs up quickly, much of it literally growing up overnight. It soon dies down again in the hot sun, but it forms a natural hay for the animals to eat, and survive on until the next time it rains.

Darwin was able to make a couple of expeditions with Rowlett, the purser, and Byrne, the assistant surgeon, who both shared his interest in exploration. One day they rode over to Ribera Grande, a village to the east. There they found the remains of a large stone fort, and a big cathedral. They had been built when the adjacent bay was the main anchorage for the ships visiting the island. Now, for some reason, the bay had become silted and too shallow for ships to enter. The town had been more or less abandoned, and everybody moved lock stock and barrel to Praia, where the anchorage was still deep.

Another day they crossed the central plain to a little village called St Domingo. On the plain itself, Darwin was intrigued by the stunted acacia trees growing there. Every one was leaning to the south-west, sculpted by the incessant wind. The village, they found, was in a small valley, which was fed by a little stream. The whole valley was a veritable oasis. Fruits, vegetables and plants of all descriptions were growing in profusion there, in stark contrast to the rest of the island.

There was so much for him to see, and he wanted to see it all. Everything was very different from what he was used to in England, and every new sight stimulated new thoughts.

While at Praia, he did a little marine biology, scouring the rock pools at low tide. He found some sea slugs and watched octopuses change colour as he teased them, but it was geology that really drew his attention.

He decided to try and draw a map of the geological structure of the whole island. One day, while working on his map, he took a rest at the foot of a low lava cliff. He was marvelling at the sun, the bright coral reef and the tropical plants, when he had a sudden vision of where his life's work might lead. He began by thinking that instead of just recording everything for the Admiralty, perhaps he should try and write a book comparing the geological aspects of the various lands he was about to visit. Then it occurred to him that he should include his other studies. He was already finding that his books on tropical flora and fauna were woefully inadequate. Maybe he could add to and improve on them. So really it was here, sitting on the water's edge in the Cape Verdes, that the seeds were sown for *The Origin of Species*, which was to make him famous.

Chapter 5

St Peter and St Paul Rocks

Beagle left the Cape Verdes, and set off across the Atlantic towards the north-east corner of Brazil. Their course took them close to the St Peter and St Paul Rocks, so naturally Darwin was anxious to stop and visit them.

The rocks – they can hardly be called islands – are just over 50 miles north of the Equator and 540 miles off the coast of Brazil, to whom they nominally belong. They stick up only about 50ft above the sea, and there is deep water close up to them. It was not going to be an easy landfall for Captain Fitzroy to make.

Almost as soon as they left the Cape Verdes, Darwin became seasick once again. A couple of days out, they met a north-bound packet-ship called the *Lyra*. Captain Fitzroy ordered the *Beagle* hove to so that he could stop and talk to the other captain. The *Lyra* stopped and *Beagle*'s gig was launched to take Captain Fitzroy over for a visit.

The *Lyra* was bound for England, and offered to take mail for them. Despite feeling wretched with seasickness, Darwin wrote a hasty letter to his father. He was surprisingly enthusiastic, and said that he was 'Unreservedly glad that he had not missed the opportunity of the century'. He intimated, even at this early stage, that he might be able to do some original work in some branch of natural history.

Underway once more, Darwin began to settle into the shipboard routine, and despite the lethargy caused by the seasickness, he kept busy sorting his collections and writing his notes. He began to enjoy the imposed regularity of the ship's routine, and he got on well with the officers. They nicknamed him the Flycatcher, and despite the fact that he was younger than all of them, just twenty three-years old, they often referred to him as the Dear Old Philosopher.

As they neared the rocks, Captain Fitzroy grew more and more nervous. He took sights of the stars at dawn and dusk, and at least three sights of the sun by day. His star sights at dawn on their eighth day out, put him a scant 15 miles off the rocks. They sailed cautiously onwards, and as soon as the sun rose, the mast-head lookout spotted the rocks to the south, gleaming white in the early light.

Landfall at St Peter and St Paul Rocks. Our electronic navigation aids made our landfall easy. Captain Fitzroy must have been very nervous of approaching these tiny rocks, in the middle of the ocean, with only his celestial navigation to guide him.

They hove to near to the rocks, and put a boat over the side. It is far too deep to anchor, even very close to the rocks, so the ship stood off, and one of the whale-boats took Darwin and a few of the officers ashore. They landed in the little bay between the two islands, which is rather hopefully marked on the Admiralty chart as an anchorage.

Darwin scrambled ashore and set to work. Part of his interest in the rocks was their actual structure. With his new-found geological knowledge, he discovered that they were composed of two types of rock, chert and feldspar. He realised that this was unusual, since all the other offshore, remote islands in the world, with the exception of the Seychelles in the Indian Ocean, are composed of either coral or volcanic matter. With his chipping hammer he knocked off a few pieces of rock to add to his collection.

He was also fascinated by the white coating that covered much of the rock. He found that it was very hard – hard enough in fact to scratch glass. The coating was about ⅒in thick, and consisted of many thin layers. He decided that it was probably formed by the action of rain and salt spray on the accumulated bird droppings. What intrigued him was the similarity of this coating to the mother of pearl

which lines living shells. It was almost as if the rock itself was alive and secreting the covering.

Darwin found that there are only two types of bird living on the rocks. The bigger is the booby, a type of gannet. Much smaller is the little noddy tern. Both birds are very prolific. The booby does not bother to build a nest, it just lays its eggs on the bare rock. The little terns, however, build quite intricate nests. They use the only materials available to them – seaweed and their own droppings.

In his journal, Darwin enumerates the spiders and other insects that he found there, including a woodlouse that lives beneath the guano. When we landed there, however, we were not about to pick through the bird droppings to see whether the lice were still there.

The only other fauna are the many bright red crabs and flora is non existent. Other than seaweed in the tidal zone, there are no living plants on the rocks, not even a lichen.

While Darwin was ashore, listing the species for scientific posterity, many of the crew were off in the boats also looking for fauna, but of the edible variety. All around the rocks they found the fishing to be good, although they sometimes had difficulty landing hooked fish before they were stolen by sharks. Nevertheless, enough was caught for all the crew to enjoy a meal of fresh fish. This made a welcome change from the normal diet of salted and dried food. The leftovers were hung in the rigging, to be dried for later use.

Late in the afternoon Darwin was summoned from his labours. Captain Fitzroy was anxious to get clear of the rocks before the dark. The boats were hoisted on board, sails loosened and a course set for the Equator, which they crossed early the next morning.

There is a strong tradition amongst most seafarers that people crossing the Equator for the first time (called pollywogs) are initiated by King Neptune (a seasoned sailor in disguise). After a suitable ceremony, usually involving some kind of penance, they are promoted to the rank of shellback. Surprisingly, Darwin makes no mention in his journal of being initiated, and in his account Captain Fiztroy rather disdainfully dismisses the ceremony as 'one to divert the childish minds of the men'. But *Thalassi*'s crew was not going to get off as lightly as Darwin – they were going to suffer thoroughly at the hands of the childishly-minded skipper.

(Opposite) The birds nesting on the rocks have little in the way of raw materials to construct their nests – just a few bits of seaweed and their own droppings.

Our course from the Cape Verdes towards Brazil was nearer south than west. I do not think any of us had realised quite how far east the continent of South America lies. Indeed, it was only when Chris dug out the atlas that we could see that almost the whole of South America is further east than most of the east coast of North America. Since we were aiming for the easternmost bulge of the continent, we had very little westing to make.

It felt a little odd to be crossing the Atlantic by sailing south, but at least this course gave us fairly comfortable sailing on a broad reach across the trade winds, rather than a roly-poly downwind run. The Cape Verdes were quickly left far astern.

Unfortunately we soon ran out of the trade winds, into the area of fluky winds known as the doldrums. We had plenty of fuel, however, and the engine kept us right on schedule, averaging about 170 miles a day.

The fishing was good – we caught two large dorado and a wahoo. Lana cooked them all, and after the fourth consecutive meal of fish, the crew unanimously agreed to stop fishing.

Each of us found different ways to help pass the time. Lana did some sketching. Jeff got his sextant out and took at least three sights a day for practice. Chris worked hard on his suntan and hair bleaching, while Nick grew grumpier by the day now that his cigarettes were but a distant memory.

Our landfall on St Peter and St Paul Rocks were easy enough – in fact it was a little anti-climactic. Jeff's sights and the satellite navigator both told us that we were getting close, and they appeared as two little green blips on the radar when they were still over 30 miles away – no anxiously peering lookout at the mast-head for us.

If finding them was almost too easy, getting ashore certainly was not. Although the wind had been light for several days, there was quite a big swell running. The rocks were not big enough to give us much shelter, and *Thalassi* was rolling heavily.

Thalassi has two boats on deck: 16ft hard-bottomed inflatable with a 40-horsepower outboard, and a smaller, but almost as heavy, fibreglass pulling boat. We tried to put the inflatable over. In calm water it is easy enough, lifting it over the rail with the mizzen staysail halyard on a hydraulic winch. But with *Thalassi* rolling it was a different matter. As soon as we lifted the dinghy clear of its chocks, despite everybody hanging on to it, it started crashing from side to side. Somebody was going to get hurt.

Hastily we dropped it back onto the deck and lashed it down again. What to do next? The pulling boat was almost as heavy, and it would probably not be much easier to handle. Should we abandon the

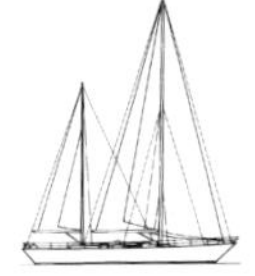

project, and sail on for Brazil?

Jeff was all for pressing on. Nick was by now desperate for cigarettes and was eager to get to the mainland. Lana did not want the skipper to leave the boat in mid-Atlantic. Only Chris shared my enthusiasm to try and land on the rocks.

We decided to swim in. Jeff was well able to handle *Thalassi.* He would take her in near to the rocks, drop us off for the swim in, then stand by at a safe distance. When he saw us getting ready to come back, he would bring *Thalassi* back in close, to save us having to swim too far. Lana thought we were mad, and retreated to the galley.

Chris and I both put on diving fins to help with the swim, and as Jeff brought *Thalassi* to a stop, about 75yd from the rocks, we jumped off the stern. Despite being so close to the rocks, the depth sounder said the water was over 500ft deep. It was a dark inky blue. Although neither of us would admit it to the other, I think we were both a bit worried about swimming in such deep water. It is entirely irrational, since once one is out of one's depth, it is academic whether it is by 1ft or several hundred. Despite knowing this, and trying hard to rationalise it, I swam as fast as I could to get to the rocks, and Chris was going even faster than me.

About halfway there, a large and excessively curious booby tried to land on Chris's head. The bird had probably never seen a human head swimming off its rock before, and had decided to investigate. Between giggles I told Chris that I thought it was attracted to the lemon juice he was still using to bleach his hair 'beach-bum blond'.

At first Chris was amused, but after the second or third aborted landing, he began to get annoyed. Finally I think the big bird frightened him, because his stroke rate almost doubled, and he beat me to the rock with some 20yd to spare.

Having reached the nearest rock – we were not sure whether it was St Peter or St Paul – we found that landing was not going to be easy. Although we were on the lee side, the swell was breaking on the rocks, and the water was rising and dropping 4 or 5ft every few seconds, with each wave. After a quick discussion we decided the thing to do was to take our fins off, so that once we did gain terra firma, we could scramble up the rocks unimpeded. We threw the fins ashore, above the wave line. Now we were committed to landing, if only to recover the fins.

Chris went first, and timed it to perfection. He grabbed hold of a rock as a wave lifted him high, and as the water fell away, scrambled nimbly ashore. I did not manage it quite so gracefully. As I crawled up the rocks I made a Darwinian observation. He had noted that the pearly white concretion on the rocks was hard enough to scratch

glass. I discovered that it was also well able to cut knees. As a corollary to this observation, I later found that these cuts took over two months to heal. Whatever the white stuff is, not only is it hard, but it is also powerful.

Notwithstanding the slight loss of blood, I followed Chris up to the summit of the rock. The birds were going crazy. There were hundreds, maybe thousands, of them swooping low over us, all wanting to take a look at these strange creatures that had emerged from the sea.

We found the bird-dropping nests, but did not dig into them to see if the woodlice were still living there. There were also crabs by the million. Everywhere we looked there were these bright red creatures scuttling to and fro across the rocks. Indeed, close to the water's edge, it was hard to walk without treading on them, there were so many.

From our perch on the top of the northernmost rock, we could look down into the so-called anchorage. It was a veritable cauldron from the swell that day. We realised that even if we had been able to launch the inflatable, we would have been hard pressed to get ashore without swimming the last bit. It must have been exceptionally calm for Darwin's visit if they were able to step dry-shod from the whaleboat.

Looking across at the other rock, we could see the tangled, rusted remains of what looked like a light tower. In bad weather, waves must have washed right over the rocks, taking everything, including the bird-dropping nests and most of the light tower with them. The birds, with an infinite supply of building materials, had rebuilt their nests, but it did not look as if anybody had been near the tower for several years.

Feeling well satisfied that we had accomplished our mission, we waved at the distant Jeff to bring *Thalassi* closer and made our way down the rocks ready for the swim back to the boat.

It was only once we were back on board, and reread Darwin's account, in which he mentioned the numerous sharks, that we thought that perhaps we had been a little rash, especially as both my knees were leaving a steady stream of blood behind us on the swim back to the boat.

I was determined that our crew of pollywogs would be properly initiated at the Equator, and I spent most of my night watch making up a King Neptune costume, which actually turned out rather more like Father Time.

Having broken the watch schedule while we messed about at St Peter and St Paul Rocks, I decided to move the Equator 93 miles south, so that we could cross it at 'happy hour', just before supper,

The Author ashore on St Paul Rock. The birds were very interested in us – they don't get many visitors.

rather than at 5.30 a.m.

Nick was on watch for the geographical crossing just before dawn. He took a series of photographs of the satellite navigator counting the latitude down to zero, and finally clicking over to south. Although he still had no cigarettes, he was a little more cheerful to be back in 'his' hemisphere.

For the ceremonial crossing later that day, I had to be a little circumspect, since I was the only shellback and so was outnumbered four to one.

Once King Neptune appeared, clad in his Father Time disguise, the first thing he did was to co-opt a queen. Since Lana was the only candidate, and following the maxim of never upsetting the cook, she got the mildest of initiations. She was made to promise not to cook any more of the King's fishy subjects, and 'tattooed' with 'save the fish' slogans in marker pen. After taking the solemn oath, she became a shellback, and Neptune's Queen. That evened the numbers a little.

We decided to set about Jeff first. King Neptune accused him of being a perpetually oily engineer who left cigarette ash everywhere. Both accusations were patently false, as Jeff was always clean and tidy in his work, but mere facts were not going to stop the King. After being made to promise to do better, he was anointed with an evil mixture of olive oil and cigarette ash. A good squirt of aerosol shaving soap completed the job; Jeff was now a shellback and could help us with the boys, who were both looking a little apprehensive by this time.

Nick was next. I had been trying to persuade him to let Lana cut his long and straggly hair before our landfall in Brazil. I wanted to arrive with a smart-looking crew, not a bunch of hippies. He had steadfastly refused, so King Neptune took matters, and a large pair of scissors, into his own hands. Nick got the shortest haircut he had ever had. By the time the Queen had tidied up the King's enthusiastic work, he no longer looked like a hippy, more like a bottle brush.

That left Chris as the last pollywog. He was actually shaking, perhaps more in anticipation than fear. The King told him that putting lemon juice on his hair was not a very macho, salty thing to do, and if he was to be shellback, then he must use the King's mixture. For a moment or two Chris looked relieved that he was not to get the same haircut as Nick, but when he saw that the mixture which the King was holding had burned through the bottom of the plastic cup containing it, fear returned. The mixture contained quick-setting epoxy, which the King used to make two large spikes out of Chris's hair.

Poor Chris took it in good part, even when the epoxy started burning his scalp. He had to virtually shave the crown of his head, almost like a monk's tonsure, to get rid of the epoxy. His suffering was compounded over the next few days when his newly acquired bald spot became badly sunburned, but at least he, like all the rest of the crew, was now officially a shellback.

Chapter 6

Fernando de Noronha and Natal

Our first destination in Brazil was to be Natal, where we were to meet the Boss and friends. From the telex we learned that he was bringing two Spanish film-makers with him, and we would back-track a little to take them to the island of Fernando de Noronha, to make a documentary film.

Beagle did not have any owners to collect, so from St Peter and St Paul Rocks, they sailed straight for Fernando de Noronha. Although they were not faced with deadlines as rigid as ours, Fitzroy was still concerned about being behind schedule, so once again they lingered for only one short day. The moment the anchor was down, Darwin went ashore. He was determined to make the most of the short visit.

The most prominent feature of the island is the gigantic spike of rock which overlooks the north-western corner of the island. It rises straight up for some 1000ft, and actually overhangs its base on one side. It was this rock that drew Darwin's attention first. He put on his geologist's hat, so to speak, and attacked the rock with his chipping hammer. He found that the pinnacle was composed of a rock called phonolite, which is volcanic in origin.

Once he had finished his studies of the rock, there was time for only a short walk in the woods. At least he got a taste of the tropical rain forest which lay in store for him on the mainland.

All too soon it was time for him to return on board. He was not too disappointed to leave after such a short visit, because he was becoming more and more excited about what lay ahead.

The curious spire of rock, overlooking the anchorage at Fernando do Noronha. Darwin, of course, went over to chip a piece off it, to analyse what it was made of.

Fernando de Noronha and Natal

Our course to Natal took us close by Fernando, but as time was pressing, and we were due to come back with the Boss, we did not stop, but sailed onwards towards Natal.

We made our landfall off Cabo São Roque, the north-eastern tip of Brazil. Natal lies about 50 miles south of the cape, a couple of miles up the Potengi River. Looking at the chart, we could see that shallow water extends out to sea for several miles, with a distant bar across the entrance to the river. Although the channel into the river is clearly shown on the chart, and there appeared to be plenty of water for us to get over the bar, I was still a bit nervous. The south-east trade winds were blowing hard onshore, and the shallow water was likely to be breaking. I knew we would have to get it right first time; it would be difficult or impossible to turn the boat round if we missed the channel or ran aground.

Through the night we had slowed the boat down, so I could time our arrival on the bar just before high tide. This would give us a few extra feet of water, and if we could carry the very last of the flood tide into the river, the seas on the bar would be calmest – or rather least rough.

As we closed the shore we raised the centreboard. With the board up *Thalassi* draws almost 9ft of water, which can cause problems enough, but with it down, she needs all of 16ft. The board was almost up when we heard a loud 'clunk', and the boat lurched. I almost had cardiac arrest. Just for an instant, I thought we had run aground, but the depth sounder showed 30ft. We could not be aground.

'Did we hit a log or something?' asked Jeff.

Nick ran to the stern and looked back. 'Nothing came out this end,' he reported.

'What the hell was it then?' I wondered.

Jeff and I had the same thought at the same time. It must be the centreboard hoist. 'We need somebody to go and take a look,' I suggested hopefully. Without any discussion, all eyes turned on Nick, who was the youngest and was usually 'volunteered' for any nasty jobs.

He hardly grumbled at all as we strapped him into a facemask and tied a rope around his waist. He hesitated for a moment on the boarding ladder, when Chris started making unhelpful comments about shark bait, but he was far enough down for a gentle shove from Jeff to ensure that he did not change his mind.

He had not been in the water more than thirty seconds before he confirmed our worst fears. 'The bloody board's all the way down.' Some part of the mechanism joining the hydraulic ram to the board had broken. The ram was all the way up and the board was all the

way down.

There was not much we could do rolling about in the open sea, so while Chris and Jeff retrieved Nick, I recalculated the depth of water over the bar. It looked as though there would be just about enough for us to get over with the board down. Even if we touched, the board would probably swing back safely as long as we were going forwards. The only danger would be if the board hit the seabed as a wave dropped us straight down, or if we were swept sideways by the current onto a shoal. Then the board would certainly be damaged, and perhaps the hull as well.

We crept in over the bar in our deep-draught mode. At times there were just inches to spare, but we did not touch at all. Finally we were able to anchor in the middle of the river, off the little yacht club, just as the ebb tide started. I calculated that there would be just enough water for us at low tide.

We were still getting organised for a celebratory end-of-passage drink when a very agitated Harbour-master appeared in his launch. He took great exception to our being anchored in the middle of the channel, which, he explained, is used by big commercial ships. He wanted us to move closer to the yacht club, and refused to believe that we drew some 5m of water. At low tide, we would be close enough to touching bottom where we were, never mind moving in any nearer to the shore. I had hoped to postpone raising the board until the next day, but it was obviously not going to be. We would have to do it now, or risk the wrath of the harbour authorities.

The river was a muddy chocolate brown, not the best water for diving in, but there was no other way. The board weighed almost 2 tons, so we would have to find some way to secure a rope under its tip and winch it up with the hydraulic sheet winches.

A year or two previously, in a very similar-looking river in Panama, I had seen numerous big crocodiles (I suppose technically they were caymans, but they all look the same to me, or at least their big teeth do). I was very nervous about diving in what was obviously going to be near zero visibility. It is all too easy to imagine big jaws full of crocodile teeth appearing out of the muddy water to remove a leg or an arm in a single munch. I decided that a quick expedition ashore to the yacht club would be prudent, to ask them about crocodiles in the river.

The woman in the club office was young, attractive and spoke good English. Our three bachelor crew members immediately, and to a man, fell in lust with her. There were no crocodiles in the river, she assured us. Then, as we turned to leave, she added that there were hardly any piranha either.

We had all read accounts of how schools of these voracious fish are supposed to be able to strip a cow to its bare bones in a matter of moments, and we had no wish to test the veracity of these tales, in the flesh, as it were. There was a discussion about who was to go in the water. Chris had never scuba dived, so he was off the hook. 'I've done a bit,' conceded Jeff, 'but I never did get certified.' If I had known Jeff better than, I would have realised that for him to admit to having done a bit meant he was a very accomplished diver – as he turned out to be. Lana, who is a qualified dive-master, sloped off to the galley, muttering, 'If you want feeding tonight, you can count me out.' Nick, who had already regaled us all with tales of diving in Australia, could not come up with an excuse. So it came down to him and me to brave the piranhas, and attach the rope to the board.

It was not easy. The ebb current was by now quite strong. The visibility was close to zero, and in my imagination, swarms of hungry piranhas circled us, licking their fishy little lips. It took us about an hour to position, move and refasten ropes, but finally the board was near enough up, held in place by a rope passing under the hull from side to side. We weighed anchor and moved *Thalassi* out of the channel into her designated anchorage off the yacht club. The postponed arrival celebrations could begin.

The next job was to prove even more time-consuming. We had to clear Customs and Immigration, or as they came to be known on *Thalassi*, 'Costumes and Intimidation'. It was to take three days to get all the paperwork in order. On the way across the Atlantic, I had managed to speak on the radio to several hams in Brazil. Having made contact with one, I was introduced to several more, and finally spoke to one in Natal. He was a German called Peter, who had lived there for several years. He met us at the yacht club, and explained how to change money on the black market at almost double the official rate, and how, and in what order, to deal with officialdom. He gave us a street map with all the various offices marked.

The first part of the procedure was a visit to the hospital for clearance by the Ministry of Health. Lana came with me. We took a taxi, and despite having the map with all the streets named, we got hopelessly lost. The taxi driver had very thick glasses, and it transpired that even with them on, he was still so short-sighted that he could not see the map – and perhaps not very much of the other traffic either. As soon as we realised that, we paid him off and searched for another taxi.

The second driver had better eyesight, at least sufficient to read the map, but we did not fare much better. He stopped twice to ask the way, and eventually, more by a process of elimination than anything else, we found the hospital. We arrived at 5.25 p.m., to be told that they closed at 5.30 and we should come back the next day! At least we now had a fix on where the hospital lay.

On our return the following morning, they said a doctor had to go down to the boat to check for rats and breeding mosquitoes. We piled into a hospital jeep and drove down to the yacht club for the inspection. It turned out to be a very cursory one, and once it was finished the doctor announced that we all had to get yellow fever injections. To do this, we had to go back up to the hospital! There was no charge for the shots, but they did economise by using the same needle on all five of us. It pays to know your shipmates well!

Fortunately that was the only time we had to deal with the Ministry of Health. Now all that was left was to have papers stamped by the Port Captain, the Federal Police and the Customs. The papers had to be obtained and stamped in a specific order, and naturally the offices were far apart and kept different hours. Peter warned us that this procedure was going to have to be repeated at every port we visited. Without exception, the officials were friendly and helpful, but it was annoying to say the least.

What was even more confusing than dealing with officialdom was the currency. Just a few months before our arrival, as part of the grand economic plan for Brazil, the government had knocked three zeros off the value of the notes. Some new notes had been printed, but many of the old ones were still in circulation. Lana almost came to blows with one taxi driver when she insisted on trying to pay him one thousandth of what he wanted, as that was what was showing on the meter. We would go shopping with a fistful of notes with a lot of zeros and feel quite well off. When we came to work out the actual value in 'real' money, however, it was worth almost nothing.

Between tracking down the officials and placating taxi drivers, we did get to see quite a bit of the town. Natal is a very old place, founded by the Portuguese in 1597. Indeed, many of the ramshackle buildings looked as though they dated back almost that far. It is the main port and capital of the northern state of Rio Grande.

Much to everyone's relief, Nick found a tobacconist, renewed his habit and quickly became his old cheerful self again. Lana located the market, and arrived back laden with fresh fruit and vegetables. Meanwhile Jeff had tracked down a good hardware shop and got most of the various bits and pieces he needed for the engine room. The stern gland, which stops water coming into the boat along the propeller shaft, was leaking, and Jeff was doing his best to stop it. While all this was going on, Chris had almost taken up residence in the yacht club, where he was trying to learn Portuguese (he said),

from the lovely secretary.

Natal is a busy fishing port, and every morning and evening we could watch the fleet sailing in and out. Almost all the boats were engineless, and relied completely on sail power. There were two distinct types. One was like a raft, with almost no freeboard, while the other was larger, and more like a conventional boat. Although the two designs were so different, they shared the same rig. Without exception the boats had a curious mast, with the top third bent back through about 45 degrees. This does make for a very efficiently shaped sail, and perhaps it had evolved over the years because of the prevailing onshore winds. Every trip out across the bar would entail a heavy beat to windward, and the more efficiently this could be done, the quicker and easier it would be for the crew to reach their fishing grounds.

Nick and Chris befriended a young Brazilian man who worked as a translator for one of the oil companies. With his help Jeff managed to find somebody who would deliver diesel oil to the dock, and got permission for us to go alongside to receive it.

All too soon, it seemed, the Boss and his two friends arrived. His friends were brothers, but very different from each other. One was small, serious and eternally pessimistic, while the other was tall, always joking and a born optimist. Their names were, respectively, Paco and Pedro, but before the first day was over, they became known as Paco and Wacko.

On our way back out to the offshore islands, we were surprised to see the little boats from Natal 30 miles or more from shore. They were well out of sight of land, bobbing along, apparently quite happily, in the big swell and brisk trade wind – rather them than me.

Our first stop was to be a little atoll called Atol das Rocas, about 150 miles from the mainland. The Boss wanted to stand a watch during the night, and insisted that Paco and Wacko do likewise. It was a mistake to leave them unsupervised. When I came up on deck at the end of the Boss's watch, he proudly announced that he had been able to steer a lot closer to the wind than the compass course I had given him. Meanwhile one of the trio had been fiddling with the satellite navigator, and had got it so confused that it had stopped working.

So there we were, barrelling along through a dark night, sailing towards an unlit coral reef, and we did not have a clue where we were. Being virtually awash, the reef would not even show up on the radar. The only prudent thing to do was to heave to while we tried to get the satellite navigator running again, or took dawn star sights if we could not make it work by then.

The film crew started to complain that we were wasting time – they

wanted a full day on the atoll for filming. The Boss did not seem to be able to grasp that I did not know where we were, nor what course to steer for our destination, and retired to his cabin in a bit of a huff.

Despite the navigational problems, we found our way to Atol das Rocas by mid morning. Paco and Wacko had been seasick since leaving Natal, and they were dismayed to find that the little atoll gave almost no lee. We were rolling at anchor worse than we had been while sailing. They were more than anxious to get ashore. Nick and Chris wanted to help them and were also eager to see what lay ashore. I stayed on board, ostensibly to help Jeff with a few engine-room problems, while Lana was to cope with the domestic chores. In fact the three of us were just glad to have a break from the film team.

The shore party set off in the inflatable dinghy, with film equipment, dive gear and a lot of optimism. Nick returned about half an hour later with a deflated dinghy and an account of how everybody and everything was dumped in the surf. They had underestimated the size of the waves, gone straight into the beach, and been tipped over by the first wave. The dinghy had been punctured by the sharp coral.

We had another smaller inflatable dinghy stowed in the lazarette, so we hoisted the big one on deck for repairs and sent Nick back ashore in the little one.

When the film crew returned, they were still damp and a little chastened. It had been too rough to dive, and apart from an overwhelming number of birds, there had been little of interest to film ashore. Almost as a final insult, between the five of them they managed to puncture the second inflatable on *Thalassi*'s exhaust pipe while unloading the film gear. It joined the big one on deck to be repaired. It was not an auspicious start to the film expedition.

On the overnight sail to Fernando de Noronha, I decided that we would keep a better eye on the Boss and his friends. This time I would do the watch with Paco and Wacko, while Jeff could keep a surreptitious eye on the Boss. Everybody was forbidden to touch the satellite navigator.

During the watch, I quizzed the brothers about their proposed film. Paco explained that the island of Fernando was little visited, and in his words 'pristine'. Living among the coral along its shores, he told me, is a particular worm, which is unique to this island. Their intention was to do a background of this 'pristine' island, then study and film the worm. The fact that they had only five days to do it, and that they were not quite sure what the worm looked like, did not seem to bother them at all.

We spotted Fernando's rock pinnacle soon after dawn, and by lunch time we were anchored in its shadow, in Bahia Antonio towards the northern end of the island. The trade winds were blowing hard, and there was some swell working its way into the anchorage. Through the binoculars, we could see a good-sized surf breaking on the beach.

Paco was visibly disappointed to find eleven other yachts anchored in the bay, which he had expected to find deserted – and 'pristine'.

On their first foray ashore, with the Boss in command of the repaired dinghy, they again misjudged the size of the waves, and were dumped in the surf one more. When they finally got ashore to find a rather scruffy little town, Paco reached hitherto unplumbed depths of gloom. 'This is like a little New York,' he said – surely the biggest exaggeration of the voyage so far. Wacko took his unexpected swim in good part, and officially named the landing area 'Killer Beach'.

Despite the problems of negotiating Killer Beach, we enjoyed our visits ashore. We found the island interesting, and learned a little of its colourful history. It was given to its Portuguese discoverer, after whom it is named, in 1504. History does not relate what Fernando did with his island, but it was soon seen to be of strategic importance. As a result it was attacked several times by various nations in the seventeenth and eighteenth centuries. It remained under Portuguese control until as recently as 1942, when it became a territory of Brazil.

Shortly after Darwin's visit, it became a penal colony – Portugal's equivalent of Devil's Island. During this period much of the forest that Darwin walked through was cut down. Some was used for fuel, but much was destroyed to stop the prisoners building boats in which they could escape to the mainland.

In the late 1950s and early 1960s, the Americans built a tracking station on the island to monitor the early space shots from Cape Canaveral. The buildings of the defunct tracking station have now become a very low-key hotel. From a peak of several thousand in its heyday, the island's population is down to a little over 900, and is steadily declining. There is little work to be had, and like so many other island communities, the young are leaving for the bright lights of the mainland.

The Boss and his men went to do some research for their film, and quickly met another setback. The only dive operation on the island was fully booked for the next two weeks by, insult of insults, another film crew. They would not be able to dive with our men at all, and if they knew anything about Paco's coral worm, they were not saying.

Wacko, the cameraman of the duo, seemed content to move the operation ashore and film birds instead of worms. The three of them piled into a rented jeep, and with the Boss in command, vanished off to the other end of the island in a cloud of dust.

Guns guarding the main anchorage at Fernando. We found British Admiralty arrows still visible on the guns. How did British guns end up here?

Their departure gave the rest of us a little time to explore the town. We found a very large abandoned church, and then a big stone fort overlooking our anchorage. In the fort we found some rusty old cannon, which still bore the imprint of the British Admiralty. It would be interesting to track down where they came from: the island has never been British, so the cannon must have been captured elsewhere, in some battle, and brought there. Alas, there was no time on that visit to find out more – maybe one day we can go back, when everybody is not in such a hurry.

The Boss told us that he wanted his men to film us sailing *Thalassi* into a small bay which they had found further down the coast. The three of them would be on the cliff top, Wacko filming, while the Boss controlled the operation by radio. We dutifully hoisted anchor and sails, and found the bay we were supposed to sail into. Perhaps it looked bigger from the top of the high cliffs, but from where we were, it hardly looked big enough for *Thalassi* to turn around in.

The Boss was very emphatic with his instructions over the radio. We were to sail into the bay, and we were not to begin to turn until he gave us the appropriate order. As we got into the bay, Jeff must have seen that I was getting a bit nervous. 'Should I fire up the main engine, just in case?' He asked. I nodded.

We got closer and closer to the rocks. The Boss's voice on the radio kept saying, 'Don't turn yet. Don't turn yet.'

Jeff commented, 'If we don't turn soon they'll be able to film the sucker running up the rocks.' Finally I put the engine into astern to

Looking across the anchorage and 'Killer Beach' at Fernando.

slow us down. We crept closer and closer to the shore. Seemingly inches from the rocks, the Boss was finally satisfied. 'Turn now,' came the order.

'About bloody time,' responded Nick as he got ready to release the jib sheet for tacking. There really was not room to turn, so with the engine hard astern we backed out, with sails still set and drawing.

Chris gave a chuckle, and said 'That'll look like they've got the film running backwards.

Back in the anchorage off Killer Beach, we were able to talk to the crews of a few of the other yachts there. They all told us that we had to visit Dolphin Bay, at the south end of the island. For some reason a large group of dolphin have chosen to live in this bay, and provided one does not wear scuba tanks, they are happy for people to swim with them. But everybody warned us that the dolphin are frightened of divers with tanks.

The film crew wanted to continue their work ashore the next day, so after depositing them again at Killer Beach, Lana and I took the dinghy down the coast to Dolphin Bay. As we got close, dolphins came to inspect us, jumping in the bow-wave of the dinghy. The motor did not frighten them at all – the faster we went, the more they seemed to enjoy it.

We anchored the dinghy at the head of the bay, put on masks and fins, and jumped in the water. Immediately we were surrounded by fifty or more dolphins. They appeared to be as intrigued by us as we were by them. What surprised us most was the noise. We could clearly hear the squeaks and grunts as the dolphins talked to each other and examined us with their sonar.

As we swam along, they swam with us. If we dived, they dived. We saw several mother and child pairs, and as they swam close to us we could see the child occasionally reaching out to touch its mother, as if for reassurance. Sometimes if the baby lagged behind a little so that the mother could no longer see it, she would reach out a fin to feel if it was still there. We felt a bit like animals in a zoo, as parents showed their children these funny creatures that had dropped into their world from above. They did not want us to get near enough to touch them, but they would frequently swim up close in front of us and gaze into our masks. It was a strange feeling to make such intimate eye contact with a wild animal.

When we were physically and emotionally exhausted, we climbed back into the dinghy and headed back to *Thalassi.* Jeff, Nick and Chris were eager to have a visit, and came back as excited by the experience as we had been.

Over dinner that night, the five of us were going on so much about the dolphins that the Boss became a bit irritated that we had done it first. He intimated that it had always been their plan to film the dolphins, and that they would do so the next day.

We weighed anchor right after breakfast, and sailed to the south end of the island. The Boss was taking Paco and Wacko in the dinghy so that they could film us along the way. The dolphins came out to play in *Thalassi's* bow wave and escorted us the last little bit into their bay.

We anchored in the middle of the bay, and the trio started to get their gear together. When the Boss told Nick to get three sets of scuba gear ready, I repeated the warnings we had heard about the dolphins being frightened of tanks. The Boss dismissed it as irrelevant, and said, 'We need to be wearing tanks if we are to make a professional film.'

We could only do as we were told, and helped them load all their gear into the dinghy. But all five of us stayed on board *Thalassi*. We watched them anchor the dinghy near where we had anchored it the previous afternoon. The Boss put his tank on and was the first to jump into the water. I doubt whether he had drawn a single breath from his tank before the dolphins came together in a tight group and, leaping from wave to wave, left the bay *en masse* and headed straight out to sea.

The Boss and his men were oblivious to what had happened, and spent half an hour searching in vain for the dolphins. They eventually came back to the boat and tried to blame us for coming to the wrong spot, arriving too late, or maybe even exaggerating the whole thing.

We spent the rest of the day there, waiting, but in vain. No more dolphins appeared. Two boats from the hotel came past, also searching for the dolphins to show to their guests, but they too were destined to be disappointed.

After retreating to Killer Beach for the night, we tried again the next morning. This time we managed to persuade them at least to have one dive first without tanks. They finally agreed and off they went, with the camera but without tanks. Once more the expedition degenerated into a farce. Wacko was first in this time, and since he was without a tank, he was immediately surrounded by dolphins. True to form he became overly excited and yelled at the Boss to pass him the camera quickly. In the rush and excitement, he dropped the camera, and it soon sank from sight into 50ft of water. It was a chastened trio that returned on board; that was their only underwater camera.

Out came the scuba gear once more. They were determined to

look for the camera, and to hell with the dolphins. It was a fairly small area to search, and there was a good chance of finding it. Nick and I agreed to dive with them, to help them look, while Chris followed us in the dinghy. We made up several floats on long ropes that we could anchor, in order to mark out the area and search it methodically.

But there appears to be something in the Spanish nature that precludes doing anything in a methodical way. No sooner had we reached the seabed, than the three of them swam off hither and yonder, leaving Nick and me with an armful of floats, gazing at each other. Of course we found no camera.

We finally retreated to *Thalassi* for lunch. The Boss decided that the camera was a lost cause, but Nick was keen to have another go. During siesta time, he, Jeff and I donned scuba gear, and once more Chris manned the dinghy. We established a base line with the floats, and began a systematic search pattern with the three of us in line abreast, just in sight of each other. On the second pass, Nick spotted the camera, and we were back on board before siesta was over.

Of course with all the scuba activity the dolphins were far away, and since we had to leave the next day for our men to catch their flight out from Recife on the mainland, that was the end of the filming exploits.

Just like Darwin, we did not feel we had done justice to the island, but also like him, we were excited about the prospect of seeing more of the mainland of Brazil.

Chapter 7

Recife and Salvador

On their way south from Fernando de Noronha, *Beagle* bypassed Recife, or Pernambuco as it was called then, and went straight to Salvador. They did, however, stop there on their way back to England, towards the end of their voyage. However, to avoid confusion I intend to describe their ports of call geographically, rather than strictly chronologically.

When the *Beagle* reached Recife, Fitzroy decided to anchor outside the reef which shelters the town. It was his intention to stop for only six days, to check and rate the chronometers. He soon realised, however, that even for a short stay, it was going to be too uncomfortable. The ship was rolling heavily in the swell. They hoisted the anchor once again, and sailed in through the gap in the reef to anchor off the town.

Darwin was not impressed with the town, to put it mildly. In his journal, he says: 'It is in all parts disgusting, the streets are narrow, ill paved and filthy.' If that were not enough, he goes on to say, 'the people are sullen and unfriendly'. Even remembering that this was towards the end of the voyage, when he was becoming very anxious to be home, it was not exactly a glowing report.

Darwin was particularly upset about the slavery which was still very common in Brazil at this time. A woman in Rio had shown him the thumbscrews that she used to keep her maid up to the mark. He had seen children horsewhipped and adults too cowed by their 'masters' to ward off blows. Now, here in Recife, he heard the screams of people being tortured. This was to be his last port in Brazil, and he wrote, 'I am happy to leave the country, and hope never to return while slavery survives.'

About fifty years after Darwin left, Recife had another distinguished nautical visitor – Joshua Slocum. This was a few years before he made the single-handed circumnavigation for which he is remembered. At this time, in 1888, he was Captain of the trading ship *Aquidneck*. He had the misfortune to lose the ship on the reefs off the city, but he, his wife and children survived.

Transport in those days was not as easy as it is now. The only way he could get himself and his family back north was to build a boat and sail them home. He designed and built the junk-rigged *Liberdade* on the beach right there in Recife. To fasten the wooden planks, he cast his own nails from melted coins. After his wife, Hettie, had made them a suit of sails, he traded her sewing machine for an anchor, about the only thing he felt unable to make. They sailed north and, a couple of months later, safely reached home.

In contrast, once we reached Recife, the Boss and his friends were able to take a taxi to the airport and fly back to Spain the same day.

The first part of our passage down to Recife from Fernando was not very comfortable. When we left the shelter of the island, the trades were blowing hard, and a big swell was running. The boat was crashing and jumping about. Just as Lana was getting ready to serve up dinner, an extra big lurch almost dumped the whole lot on the deck.

Through the night even Nick complained that he could not sleep, and it takes a lot to keep him awake. When it is rough, it is very hard to sleep. Despite having a canvas lee-cloth to stop you falling out, you are rolled from side to side in your bunk, and then every few minutes the boat falls off a wave with a bang loud enough to waken the dead. Fortunately the wind eased around dawn and became, if anything, a bit too light for optimum speed. However, at least with the lighter wind the sea went down, and the motion was more pleasant, even if progress was not as fast.

As the wind dropped, the heavy mainsail began to slat and bang about. As usual we had a preventer rigged to stop the boom from crashing around, but as we went to lower the mainsail, off the entrance to Recife, we discovered that its slatting had cracked the aluminium boom. That was going to have to be mended before we went much further. For once the telex machine was a blessing – I was able to send a telex off to the spar-makers in Holland before we even got ashore.

As we entered the harbour we found that a naval exercise was just about to begin, and ten or twelve big warships were getting ready to leave the harbour. As we passed each, Jeff dipped the British Ensign in salute, as is the proper custom. The first two were slow to respond, but then somebody must have got on the radio to warn the other ships that some foreign yacht was going to salute the fleet, because all the rest saluted us smartly as we passed.

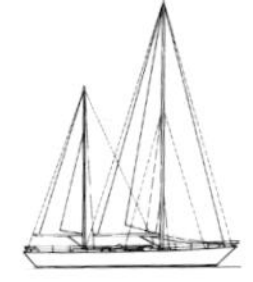

We spotted an empty wharf and tied up alongside. We had not been there five minutes before somebody came to tell us that we could not stay there, as a ship was expected soon. The only obvious alternative was to go and anchor in an open area at the south end of the harbour. Unfortunately the bottom was thin silt, and the anchor just could not get a grip. After four attempts we gave up, and almost in desperation tied up alongside a very rusty derelict ship that did not look as if it would ever sail again.

We were no sooner settled there when somebody else came round and said we should not stay there. Fortunately this man spoke English. He was not an official, just a concerned yachtsman. He told us that this side of town was dangerous, and if we stayed there we would certainly be robbed.

By now my opinion of Recife was if anything lower than Darwin's, but our new-found friend, Hermano, told us that all was not lost. He suggested that we tie up in the middle of town, alongside the wall of a small ornamental park. There we would be much less likely to be attacked. He jumped back into his car, and drove round to catch our lines. We were finally secured, at the seventh attempt.

Hermano not only found us the best spot to tie up, but he also introduced us to the Brazilian phenomenon of the *churascaria*. After we had waved goodbye to the Boss and the would-be film makers, I suggested to Lana that we eat ashore that evening to give her a break. I did not want to leave the boat unattended, so we would have to go in shifts. Lana asked Hermano to recommend a restaurant, and he suggested that if we collected his wife he would take us to a *churascaria*.

We drove across the city to his house. After he had gone through the third traffic light on red, and virtually stopped at the only green one we saw, I felt compelled to say something. He told us that traffic lights were a favourite place for muggers to lie in wait, and warned us that if we rented a car in any Brazilian city, we should never stop at a red light. The reason for stopping at the green one was because he knew people would be coming through the other way against the red light. This was not a place I would like to live!

We safely crossed the city to his house, met his wife and a very large pet toucan that ate whole bananas, skin and all. Once the toucan had finished its supper, we set off for the *churascaria*

A *churascaria* is a sort of barbecue restaurant. One gets the basic salads, vegetables and bread, usually from a buffet, then waiters bring round great slabs of meat, each of which is impaled on a sword. They rest the tip of the sword on one's plate, and cut off slices of meat. The meat is cooked over an open flame, so just the outside is cooked.

As they slice bits off and it starts to get a bit rare, they throw it back on the fire and grab another swordful.

The serving method is very clever. They start serving the cheapest items like chicken livers and sausages first, hoping the customers will fill up quickly, before they serve the more expensive cuts of meat. Those in the know refuse the first six or eight offerings to save room for the better stuff. There was beef, pork and chicken, and the waiters kept coming with more and more until we begged for mercy.

Once Chris and Nick discovered the *churascarias*, there was never a problem in getting them to eat ashore while we were in Brazil. For one fixed, and remarkably low price, they could eat until they could hardly move.

Once the Boss and his team had gone, there was no reason to linger in Recife, so we set off the next day towards the *Beagle*'s next anchorage, Salvador, some 400 miles to the south. This was *Beagle*'s first stop on the mainland.

After an easy passage down the coast, with mostly light winds, we found that it was much easier to find a spot to anchor at Salvador than it had been in Recife. There was plenty of room off the town, in the lee of the big breakwater.

Salvador is at the mouth of a very large, island-studded bay, which rather reminded us of the Chesapeake Bay in the USA. The bay is rather unimaginatively called Bahia, which in Portuguese means simply 'bay'.

Salvador is a very old city, indeed one of Brazil's oldest. It was founded in 1549, and was the capital when Brazil was a Portuguese colony. The Dutch held it for a brief period in 1624, but otherwise it remained Portuguese until the Brazilian war of independence in 1823.

The city is unusual, if not unique, in that it is built on two levels. The lower part is virtually at sea level, while the higher one is on a rocky bluff over 200ft above it. There are a few roads connecting the two, but the principal mode of transport between them is several gigantic lifts that climb up and down the cliff face.

As usual, Lana made a beeline for the market, which was conveniently situated right at the water's edge. It was kept well stocked by a non-stop procession of local boats, which kept arriving all day long, laden with fruit and vegetables of all descriptions. Chris took the dinghy right to the edge of the market to collect Lana's purchases. It was as well that he could get the dinghy so close, because she had bought far more than the two of them could possibly have carried. If only provisioning was always that easy.

Chris was less enarmoured of the city than we were. He wanted to change some money, and when he was offered about 50 per cent

Local dugout canoes in Salvador, used for fishing and bringing produce to the waterfront market. Although the harbour has been improved since Beagle*'s visit, the local boats are still the same.*

more than the usual black market rate, he thought it was too good to be true. It was. He handed over his $50 to one of a pair of men who had offered the deal. One took the money, ostensibly to change it, leaving the second as a kind of hostage. Of course he never came back, and after about fifteen minutes Chris and Nick began to smell a rat. Suddenly the second man took off down the side streets, and without pausing to think of the consequences, the boys set off in pursuit.

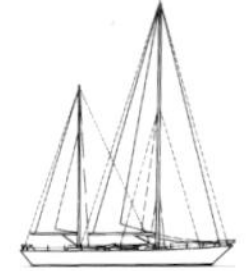

Fortunately they could not catch him, and only lost the $50. Had they had a confrontation up some little back alley, it is possible they could have lost a lot more. They did not even have the satisfaction of reporting the incident to the police, because what they were doing, changing money on the black market, is in fact illegal.

The town was very noisy. Preparations were in full swing for carnival season. Usually the boys were all for the bright lights and action, but after the money-changing episode they lost interest in the town. They were happy enough when I suggested that we look for a more secluded anchorage on the other side of the bay where we could hopefully find a bit of peace and quiet for a day off.

Thalassi *anchored off the island of Itaparica in Bahia, for our well earned day off.*

We found a wonderful anchorage, which we had to ourselves, behind the island of Itaparica. There was a beautiful little palm-fringed beach, with, as we discovered, an icy cold waterfall tumbling down the rocks behind it. Had *Beagle* been anchored here, it would have been easy for them to top up their tanks with the cool clear water. There was deep water almost right up to the beach, so they could have got the ship in very close.

We had heard from some cruising boats that there was another spring a bit further up the bay, which produced unlimited supplies of fizzy water. It was claimed to be every bit as good as Perrier. Apparently it was a popular spot for the cruising boats to visit, armed with every empty bottle they could scrounge. We did not get a chance to look for it, however, as our time was limited by the Boss's schedule for us to reach Rio, still another 700 miles to the south. One realises what a big country Brazil is, when one sails along its coast!

Meanwhile, there was a day off to enjoy. We were happy enough with our own little waterfall, even if it was not fizzy. We explored the beach soon after we arrived, and Chris, in a fit of machismo, shinned up one of the overhanging coconut trees. Even though it was leaning over, which made it easier than most to climb, it was a tall one and he did well to reach the top.

He was going to throw down some coconuts to us, and had the first one in his hand, when a machete-wielding man emerged from the jungle and started yelling at him. We were all a bit surprised, as we had thought we had the place to ourselves. We could not understand a word the man was saying, but got the message loud and clear – he did not want Chris to remove any of what were presumably his coconuts.

Chris was perhaps the most surprised of all of us, and promptly slid down the length of the tree. He came down a little faster than was wise, and since he was only wearing a thin pair of shorts, he skinned his chest and his knees, and a good part of everything inbetween.

For the official day off, it was decreed that no boat work would be done – a rare occurrence. We had a leisurely breakfast in the cockpit, watching one of the local sailing boats, heaped high with fruit, trying to work its way through the lee of the island. She was obviously headed for the market, but with the foul tide and light breeze, it was slow going.

As we watched, they made a few yards, then as the current became stronger than the wind, one of the crew heaved a kedge anchor over the bows so that they would not lose their hard-earned distance. The second crew stoked up the little open fire burning near the stern, and on went the kettle for a cup of tea.

Once the tea was finished, the anchor came up with the next puff of wind, and a few more yards were gained. As the breeze died again, so the process was repeated. Anchor, kettle and a leisurely cup of tea. It must have taken them seven or eight cups to clear the island, but they did not seem to be perturbed.

I guess it was watching their peaceful progress that inspired Jeff. He suggested that we launch the pulling boat and, using oars and sails only, see how far we could get up the river that we could see at the head of our anchorage. That did not offer enough action for the boys. They thought they would rather water ski the day away. Lana wanted to catch up on her letter writing, and then do some gentle windsurfing.

That was fine. Everybody could do their own thing on their day off. Jeff and I packed a picnic and some suntan cream, and feeling a bit like Darwin himself, set off for the river.

We hoisted sail and made quite good progress – for almost 100yd. Then we ran aground on the unseen bar that blocked the entrance to the river. We were still in sight of *Thalassi*, and our pride could not allow the major expedition to end there. Lowering a tentative leg over the side into the warm, chocolate-brown water, we found that the mud, although it was very soft, was only 3 or 4in deep. We would wade and skid the dinghy over the bar, and hope that the river itself would be deep enough for it to float in.

We had covered 10 or 15ft, when Jeff let out a shriek, and jumped almost clear of the water. He had trodden on something that had wriggled under his bare toes. I was still calling him a wimp, teasing him that it was probably a little piranha, when I trod on one. It was a horrible feeling – some unknown creature wriggling about underfoot, with what we called the primeval ooze squeezing up between our toes. If we had had any sense, we would have gone back to the boat for shoes.

Squealing like a pair of schoolgirls, we covered the next 50yd in as many seconds. Then the water became a little deeper and we both leaped back into the boat, almost capsizing it in the process.

I feel certain that Darwin would have captured whatever it was that we were treading on, and identified it as to genus and species, but we were just happy enough to be back in the boat, and hoisted sail once more to continue our voyage of exploration.

We had no idea where we were going. The chart showed the entrance to the river, but only as a dotted line, which suggested that

---

(Opposite) Chris up the coconut tree at Itaparica. He came down much quicker then he got up, when the owner of the tree arrived.

it was unsurveyed. Even the dotted line went for only half a mile or so before becoming a blank space on the chart.

The river became narrower, and because of the high mangrove trees, the wind was becoming more fitful. What little there was, was basically blowing down the river, against us. Undaunted, we furled the sails, and shipped the oars. We had two pairs of oars, and with both of us rowing, we made good progress.

We had covered perhaps 4 or 5 miles when we came to a clearing on the river-bank, and there was a group of Indians busy washing clothes. We paused in our rowing long enough to wave to them. They seemed a bit perplexed to see two white people rowing up their river in the middle of nowhere, and nobody waved back. Their heads just swivelled in unison as they watched the apparition pass them.

We carried on for another couple of miles, but the river showed no sign of ending, so we pulled the boat up on a handy sand-bank, and ate what bits of the picnic we had not already devoured on our way up the river. If we were to be back at *Thalassi* before dark – and neither of us fancied wading back across the bar in the dark – then it was time to start back down the river.

The current was with us now, so spells of rowing were interspersed with periods of drifting and listening to the birds that remained largely hidden in the mangroves. We reached the river entrance just as dusk was falling, to be met by Chris and Nick in the big dinghy. They had been sent to look for us by Lana, who was anxious not to lose both skipper and engineer at the same time. The tide had come in enough for us to sail across the bar dry-shod. We refused Nick and Chris's offer of a tow and sailed back down the bay on the last of the evening breeze. It had been a fine day.

One could spend weeks exploring the bay, but for us it was not to be. It was time to head for Rio.

Darwin actually enjoyed the trip south from Fernando to Salvador. They had light winds for the whole passage, and he was getting his sea legs at long last. He did suffer a bit from the heat, and often took to pacing the decks in the cool of the night. He was fascinated by the new and strange constellations of stars that appeared each night as they headed south.

He marvelled at the fact that just six months before he had not even thought of the possibility of making such a voyage. Now he had seen

the sun pass north of him at noon, and was about to set foot in the 'New World'. He was contented enough, but still a little astonished to find himself there.

I can understand his feelings. When things are going well for us, I sometimes find it hard to believe that we are being paid for doing what we do. Then we get a spell doing a refit, a long passage in bad weather or a charter with difficult guests and we know that we are not paid nearly enough. It is an emotional roller coaster.

Despite his euphoria, Darwin was feeling a little homesick. Although he was still looking forward to the rest of the voyage, he was already looking forward to it being over, and anticipating his return to England.

Eight days after leaving Fernando, the *Beagle* anchored off Salvador. Darwin wasted no time in getting ashore to start his studies. He collected botanical and entomological specimens and then, strange for a naturalist, had a day on a shooting expedition with some of the officers. Still eager to expand his newest interest of geology, he spent some time examining one of the big granite outcroppings, many of which are found up and down the Brazilian coast. He could not understand how they had been formed.

He also took his first walk in the jungle. Loud insect noises could easily be heard from on board the ship when it was anchored in the bay, yet once he got deep into the jungle, he found what he called a 'universal silence'; it was so quiet it was eerie. He was fascinated by the many parasitic plants, such as orchids, and the general profusion of vegetation. It was all beyond his previous experiences.

Most of his time was spent in the jungle, and he largely ignored the shore and its plants and animals. He devoted just one afternoon to exploring the beach. He spotted a puffer fish swimming close enough to be caught, and spent the next hour or two tormenting the poor thing, making it puff up like a spikey football, both in the water and out. He was curious to discover how it managed to inflate itself.

Fitzroy wrote his first homeward reports, and praised Darwin as 'a very sensible, hard-working man, and a pleasant messmate'. Darwin also had a high opinion of his Captain, both personally as a man, and for the care and sympathy he had shown him when he was seasick. He admired him too for his seemingly limitless mental and physical energy.

Yet it was here in Salvador that they had a violent argument, which almost caused Darwin to leave the ship. Even though Darwin had yet to experience it at first hand, he was most strongly opposed to slavery. By contrast, Fitzroy, with his Tory upbringing, would defend slavery to anyone, in the name of property rights.

One evening, they entertained a Captain Pagett from another naval ship in the anchorage. He brought up the subject, and Fitzroy became irritated at having to defend his position on board his own ship. After their visitor had left, Fitzroy continued the conversation, and told Darwin of comments he had heard from slaves he had met. Darwin queried the validity of such statements if the slaves had made them in front of their master, of whom they were probably frightened. At this Fitzroy exploded, saying that if Mr Darwin doubted his word, then he would never sleep under the same deck as him again.

Darwin was actually beginning to pack, ready to leave the ship for good, when the officers of the gunroom asked him to move in with them. Fitzroy exhausted his anger upon the luckless Lieutenant Wickham, who just happened to walk in at the wrong time. Once he had finished with him, Fitzroy went to Darwin and apologised completely and sincerely.

Although such outbursts were not common, it was not an isolated incident. As much as anything else, it was probably an indication of the pressures of living so close together. We had discovered for ourselves how difficult it can be when it is impossible to get more than a boat length away from people, sometimes for weeks at a time. Nick's grouchiness and withdrawal symptoms probably would not have appeared nearly so bad on our crossing if we, or he, had been able to go off for a long walk, or maybe to spend an evening at the pub.

Although Fitzroy usually seemed calm and in control, he was actually under a lot of pressure. It is worth remembering, that at this stage in the voyage he was still only twenty-seven years old. Sometimes the tremendous responsibility weighed him down, and he felt he was not achieving the ideals that he set for himself. For a while he was very close to a nervous breakdown, and several years after the voyage he ended his days tragically, cutting his throat in a fit of depression.

Beagle did not linger in Salvador – they too were in a hurry to get to Rio. The whole crew was eager to see the city, whose reputation for partying, even then, had reached England.

Chapter 8

Towards Rio

Our disappointment at leaving Bahia largely unexplored was somewhat tempered by the prospect of sailing to Rio de Janeiro. Who would not be excited by the thought of sailing to Rio? The boys were also hoping to find *the* girl from Ipanema. Moreover, Christmas was fast approaching, and our Christmas mail was supposed to be waiting for us in Rio. It can be a bit frustrating getting mail only every six or eight weeks, but we were doing a lot better than the *Beagle*. They often went as long as a year without mail, or indeed any news from home. On *Thalassi*, as on *Beagle*, the arrival of mail is very important and long anticipated.

About halfway between Salvador and Rio, there is a small group of reef-strewn islands called Dos Abrolhos. The Boss, who was not with us for the passage (he was still back home in Spain), had asked us to stop there and take some photographs. We thought it a little peculiar, but much later we found that he liked to be able to say of some remote spot, 'My boat has been there', the inference being that he had been there too. I did not mind. By sheer coincidence the *Beagle* had stopped there on her way south, so it was another anchorage we could share with her.

We were told that Dos Abrolhos colloquially translates as 'two wide open eyes'. Despite making our landfall soon after dawn, there were ten very wide open eyes on *Thalassi* as we gingerly felt our way in through the reef. The chart was vague as to the location of the reefs, and even had a warning printed on it that they might be in positions other than those indicated. As we closed the western of the two main islands, Lana spotted the wreck of a good-sized yacht on the beach – a salutory warning to go carefully.

We passed south around the island, and anchored to the east of it, in the lee of the larger one. The only sign of humanity was the lighthouse on the latter. We were not sure whether it was manned or not, but decided not to go over, in case there were officials there who said we should not be there. We contented ourselves with exploring the smaller, uninhabited island.

There were hundreds and hundreds of birds, which were totally

Once through the reef, we found a good anchorage at Dos Abrolhos. Beagle, *without an engine, could not get into this anchorage. They hove-to offshore, while Darwin and some of the crew went ashore.*

unafraid of us – probably because very few people visit the islands, and they have yet to learn to be afraid.

We walked over to the north side of the island, to take a look at the wreck. She was a ketch of about 45ft, and the waves had thrown her well above the high-water mark. What a desolate spot to get shipwrecked. I wondered whether they had hit the island in the dark? Perhaps the lighthouse was not working. And did the crew survive?

Back in the anchorage we all went snorkelling. The coral was a bit disappointing, but we did see a lot of fish, including several very large

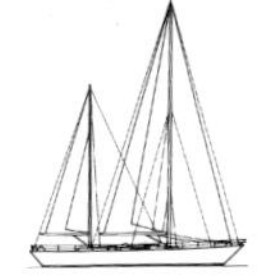

blue and yellow angel fish. Chris had been trying to persuade me to let him try diving with the scuba gear. He had watched the film crew with a mixture of envy and scorn, and was very keen to try it. I am a firm believer that potential divers should be taught by professionals but, for the sake of a happy ship, I finally gave in and said I would take him on one dive, on the firm understanding that this was a one-off, and if he wanted to go again, he would have to find somebody to teach him properly. I made it very plain that he and Nick were not to go off diving together on the strength of this one experience. The last thing we needed was a corpse or two on our hands.

We spent half an hour or so on deck, going through the basics, then I made him take off and replace his face mask under water. Finally we strapped on tanks and went down the anchor chain to the seabed. We stayed down about half an hour, exploring the area around the boat. He did very well, and was quite relaxed in the water. He thoroughly enjoyed the experience, and said he would make sure he became certified.

I broke my own resolution a bit later. I let Chris dive again in Rio, when we had to scrub the weed off *Thalassi*'s bottom. I did not see why he should get out of helping, just because of my stubbornness.

The day slipped by all too quickly. I wanted to be well clear of the reef before dusk, so we weighed anchor soon after 3 p.m., while the sun was still high enough for us to see the coral heads. The southern passage out was a little easier than the way in from the north had been. Soon we were in deep water, and could set sail again.

The second part of the passage was not as comfortable as the first. The breeze had picked up, and we were rolling a bit in the beam seas. In these stronger winds, the watch routine was altered to include a regular inspection of the cracks in the boom. Jeff had drilled holes at the ends of the cracks to try to stop them getting longer. They did not seem to be getting worse, but to be on the safe side, we kept the mainsail well reefed down to reduce the strain. Despite not being able to use full sail, we were making good progress, averaging around 200 miles a day.

Lana's equatorial promises to King Neptune were forgotten. We caught two fish. One was a good-sized tuna, but it escaped just as we were pulling it over the guard rail. The second was not so lucky. It was a 16lb male dorado, a brilliant blue and gold. He was in the oven within ten minutes of hitting the deck.

One reason why we had resumed fishing again was the lack of meat to buy in the shops. Although there was no shortage in the restaurants, as our visits to the *churascarias* showed, it was near enough impossible to buy meat at the retail level. We eventually dis-

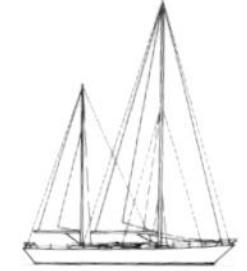

covered that there was a farmer's strike. The Government, in an attempt to control the country's galloping inflation, had fixed the retail price of meat, eggs, dairy products and, for some reason, beer. The producers said they would not sell at these prices, so refused to supply. There was a black market trade of course, but for outsiders that was harder to penetrate than the currency one. Supplies continued to be hard to find in Brazil, so a supper of fresh dorado was very welcome.

Our dawn landfall off Rio was spectacular. Rio is one of the few harbours we have visited that actually look as good in reality as in the tourist brochures. From the harbour you do not see the dirt, poverty or crime of the *barrios*, just the city nestling at the foot of high, tree-covered mountains. It is guarded on one side by the Sugarloaf Mountain, and on the other by the even higher Corcovado, topped by a gigantic statue of Christ.

It was easy enough to find space to anchor among the many yachts in the southern part of the harbour, but what turned out to be much more difficult was to find a place to get ashore. We went into the yacht club and got a very frosty reception. Later we discovered that the crews on one of the round-the-world yacht races had celebrated too hard there one year. Things had got out of hand and the party had finished with the riot police being called. Their solution was to teargas everybody, members and rowdy visitors alike. The yacht club in Rio has wonderful facilities, and the members pay dearly for privilege of using them. To see the place being abused by a bunch of drunken foreigners did not go down well, so the members voted to exclude all visitors, unless they had a personal introduction from a member. As so often happens, the few had spoiled it for the many. We were not allowed even to land there with the dinghy, and they could not offer any other suggestions.

We returned to the boat and the telex machine. With the Boss's help we managed to find a member of the club who had been at the races in Spain. With his help and introduction, we eventually got permission to use the club's dinghy dock, and to pass through their gates. We were not to use their bar, restaurant or swimming pool, and for some reason Lana and I were to use the main gate, but Jeff and the boys had to use the tradesman's entrance. Nick was incensed by this, taking it as a slight against Australia.

The most important job was to get the boom mended. The spar makers had sent us drawings showing how to repair it, and told us to get it welded locally. Through an unlikely string of contacts arranged by the spar-maker, we were introduced to Fernando Duarte and his son Paulo, who were the local fixers of things nautical in Rio.

Rounding 'The Sugarloaf' at dawn, to enter the harbour of Rio de Janeiro. From the seaward side, it does not have it's characteristic shape, nor did it seem very big. The landfall was not as spectacular as we had imagined.

Paulo arranged for a welder, and offered to translate our needs to him. All we had to do was get the boom ashore.

Thalassi's boom is over 30ft long, and weighs about 300lb, so it is not feasible just to pop it into the dinghy and run it ashore. Paulo got permission for us to take *Thalassi* alongside the fuel dock at the yacht

club, and for a truck to take the boom to the welders. It was easy to lift it off the boat with two halyards, straight onto the truck. Everything went remarkably smoothly, and with the promise that it would be returned in three days, the boom vanished into the city.

I did not want to leave the boat unattended, so we staggered our time off. Nick and Chris were sent off for their day first. I think they spent most of their time on the beach at Copacabana, watching the girls with their backless bikinis. They did manage to tear themselves away long enough to take a trip up the Sugarloaf, and returned well contented with their day.

Jeff spent most of the day with Paulo, in the never-ending quest for bits and pieces for the engine room. I tried to find out what had happened to our expected consignment of parts from Britain, including the replacement part for the centreboard, which was still being held in the 'up' position with a piece of rope. Even with Paulo's help, it took four days to trace it, and then a couple of bribes to get it through Customs.

Despite all these problems, Lana and I managed to take our day off to play at tourists. We left Nick and Chris to varnish the toe-rail round the edge of the deck, and Jeff came with us to go up the Sugarloaf. We walked to the base of the mountain, glad of the chance to stretch our legs, then took the cable car which goes to the top in two stages. And what a spectacular view we had from the top. We could look down onto *Thalassi*, which appeared to be lying almost directly beneath us, 1300ft below. Through one of the coin-in-the-slot tourist telescopes, I could see the boys stretched out on deck, sunbathing, all thoughts of sanding and varnishing apparently forgotten.

Whenever any of us go ashore, we carry a portable VHF radio, and the ship's radio in the cockpit is left tuned to a relatively quiet, little-used frequency. Thus, when we are ready to be collected, we can call up whoever is on board. Feeling just a little evil, I turned on the portable radio. 'This is your conscience speaking. Don't you think you'd better get on with the sanding?' We could see them jump up and look around in surprise. Nick went back to the cockpit and asked us on the radio where we were – he was a little bit put out when I said we were keeping an eye on them from the top of the Sugarloaf.

We recuperated from our trip up the Sugarloaf by having lunch on the beach at a *churascaria*. We had intended to walk up the Corcovado in the afternoon, but as we could hardly move after our big lunch, we went by taxi. It is probably as well that we did, as the mountain is 2300ft high, and the walk would probably have been too much for our legs which, because of all the time spent at sea, had not had much use recently.

Looking down on 'The Sugarloaf' and Rio's harbour, from the Corcovado.

The statue on the top of the mountain is enormous, almost 100ft tall, and the views from the Corcovado are even better than those from the Sugarloaf. To the north we could see the bay and the city, while to the south we looked down on the beaches of Ipanema and Copacabana. On the far side of the bay was the little blue speck which was *Thalassi*. It is hard to describe such views without digging out all the old clichés.

The days were slipping by. We got the boom back and repainted then refitted it. We got our spare parts on board, and Lana provisioned as best she could with the continuing strike. The Boss had agreed that we could stay there for Christmas Day, but then we were to go to the Falklands as quickly as we could. He was to join us again there, and our hearts sank a little when he told us that Paco and Wacko would be coming again, to make another film.

Christmas Eve dawned, and brought two events of momentous

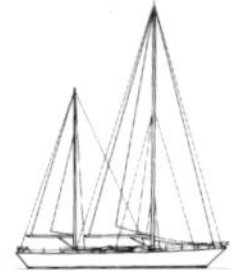

importance. We finally received our long-awaited mail, and I found that the mast was cracked.

I always go aloft and check the rig before an offshore passage, and since we were about to venture into the Southern Ocean, I was giving *Thalassi*'s rig an especially good look. I had started at the top of the mainmast and was making my way down, inspecting every fitting on the way. When I came to the top spreaders, which hold the cap shrouds away from the mast, I noticed a crack in the paint where the spreader fittings join the mast. I scraped away the paint and then the filler, and found that the weld itself was cracked.

I called down for Jeff to come up and take a look. Nick fetched the second bosun's chair, and pulled Jeff up on another halyard to join me. Together we scraped the paint and filler off all the joints, on both sets of spreaders. Of the eight welds, six were cracked.

That was a setback, to put it mildly. I was certainly not going to venture into the Roaring Forties with cracks in the mast. A quick telex to Holland found the mast-maker about to close for the Christmas holiday. He wanted photographs of the cracks before he would comment, so Jeff was back up the mast with a camera, then over the road to a one-hour processing place in the nearby shopping centre. We sent the photographs by courier so the mast-maker would have them when he reopened immediately after Christmas. While Jeff was doing this, I was on the telex trying to track down the Boss to break the news.

Everything in and around Rio shuts for the week between Christmas and the New Year, so nothing was going to happen until January. Paulo told us about a big shipyard at Angra dos Reis, further south, which had one of the few cranes tall enough to lift out *Thalassi*'s mast. A quick phone call revealed that they were already closed for the holidays.

After a rash of transatlantic telexes, it was decided that we would go down to the shipyard to see if they could do the job when they reopened. If that was possible, then the mast-maker would send out one of their engineers. He would bring the correct welding rod, and would help us unstep and restep the mast as well as supervise the repair.

Suddenly we were no longer in rush. What a change – we could enjoy Christmas and, much to the boys' delight, New Year's Eve in Rio. They had heard about the New Year's Eve fireworks and beach parties, and had already been asking if we could delay our departure. Now their wish had come true. The boys produced a Christmas tree from somewhere, Jeff rigged up some lights and Lana made lots of decorations. The boat took on a festive air.

Christmas morning dawned overcast and rainy. Although the wet season was officially over, we were getting more than our fair share of rain. Fortunately it cleared up soon enough to let the Christians among us go to church while the heathens slept in. Then Lana cooked a proper Christmas dinner, with turkey, stuffing, bread sauce and roast potatoes, followed by the obligatory Christmas pudding. Nobody could do much after that, except digest it. After a suitable pause, we opened presents and felt a bit homesick. It was a nice Christmas.

For the next few days, we did a few maintenance jobs on the boat, but it was all pretty low-key. Nick and Chris went off for a few days with Paulo to help him sail a friend's boat down to Angra dos Reis with his family. It was good for them, and for us, to have a break for a while. However well everybody gets on, there are inevitable irritations from living together in close quarters, and a spell away from each other does wonders. Darwin was very lucky to be able to spend several long periods ashore, including one in Rio. We were envious of the time he was able to devote to exploring on land; just to be able to spend *some* time off the boat would have been nice.

Although we had been happy to see the boys go for a few days, we were pleased to see them back in time for New Year's Eve. We were starting to feel rather like a family, and indeed the boys often jokingly called us Mum and Dad when they thought we were fussing over them unnecessarily.

The boys had been trying to talk me into taking *Thalassi* round to the beach off Copacabana for the fireworks. I did not fancy being out there in the dark, with speedboats racing about with drunken drivers and fireworks shooting off around us. We had enough boat problems already, without risking any other damage. They were a bit put out, but Lana and I offered to do the anchor watch, and I told them they could leave the little dinghy at the yacht club, and get themselves back any time they wanted. That mollified them a little.

Jeff must have had enough of parties, because he surprisingly decided to stay on board with us. We did our celebrating at 9 p.m., which was midnight GMT. We listened to the BBC World Service, and heard the chimes of Big Ben. As far as we were concerned, the New Year had begun, and we could have an early night.

At midnight local time we were woken up. All around us boats were hooting and we could hear the crash of fireworks from the beach. It was impossible to sleep – at least we thought so, but Jeff seemed to be managing.

We got up again to see if we could watch any of the fireworks, but the hills to the south of the Sugarloaf hid most of them from us. We were heading back to bed, when Lana spotted a lot of lights down on the Botofogo beach, off on our starboard side.

Through the binoculars we could see a group of people launching model sailing boats into the harbour. Each boat had candles in it. Some of the bigger ones had a dozen or more flickering away. The gentle breeze wafted them out into the bay, like an armada of tiny fireships.

Hand in hand we stood on deck, watching them sail off into the distance, on their infinite voyage. One by one the candles began to burn out, as if they were memories of the old year fading. Finally the bay was dark again. We kissed each other Happy Brazilian New Year, and retreated to a still warm bunk. It was a much more peaceful way to welcome the New Year than with noisy fireworks and rowdy parties.

On New Year's Day, Lana and I left the boys sleeping and went off on a last little expedition. We wanted to see the Botanical Gardens that Darwin had visited. Unfortunately, when we reached the gates, we found that the gardens were closed for the day. Not wanting to go back to the boat, we went for a long walk on the interconnecting beaches of Copacabana and Ipanema. Along the beach, there were people sleeping off the excesses of the night before, amid signs of the mayhem that we had missed. We enjoyed the walk, munching first on ice cream and then on corn on the cob sold at little stands along the beach.

On Copacabana beach we saw a group of people looking at something in the surf which was breaking on the beach. As we walked by we saw it was a dead man, wearing nothing but a plastic bag over his head. Was it suicide, murder or the result of a drunken prank? We would never know, but feeling like doting parents, we were glad the boys had arrived home intact the previous night. Rio can be a tough place.

We finally got the word that we were to head to the shipyard at Angra, who would do the repairs. We motored for eleven hours down the coast, on a hot and windless day, to the Verholme shipyard, which is about 5 miles from the town of Angra. Despite the presence of the enormous shipyard, the biggest, they claim, in the southern hemisphere, the area was one of the prettiest we had ever seen. There were many small bays off the main one, separated and surrounded by high, green, wooded hills, with only the occasional house peeking out.

The shipyard itself is at the head of one bay. The whole complex covers several square miles and employs over 2000 people. Indeed, we were to discover that it is like a small city itself, with its own

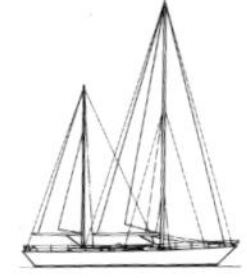

housing, shopping and recreation centres for the employees. As well as the company store, there is a company school, company bank and company church, all within the compound.

On the ways there was an enormous bulk carrier that they were building, which was nearing completion. Close by were three gigantic drilling platforms which were being repaired. Yet right in front of the yard was a pristine white beach, and the water where we were anchored was crystal clear. In stark contrast to the harbour in Rio, there was absolutely no sign of pollution at all. We swam from the boat every day – what a nice change.

Before we could start work, there were the obligatory visits to Costumes and Intimidation. Once that was out of the way, we could begin to get ready to take the mast out. This is not a quick or easy job on an eighty-three footer, with a 100ft mast. The first job is to take off all the sails. The lightest weighs almost 200lb, so it was lucky that we did not have to shift them far. We folded them as best we could, and stacked them on deck. Then comes the task of unpinning and slackening all the rigging, which is perhaps the most time-consuming part of the job.

The most complicated part, however, turned out to be getting the Dutch engineer, Jan, from the airport in Rio, almost 100 miles away, down to the boat. Nobody hired cars locally. After exploring many possibilities, the plan we came up with was to get a bus to Rio, then take a taxi from the city to the airport, where we could meet Jan. There we would be able to hire a car to drive back to the boat, and hopefully at the end of the project Jan could return the car and himself to the airport. I co-opted Jeff for moral support, and off we set. It all went surprisingly smoothly, although four hours on the local bus was a bit gruelling. We were back on the boat with Jan by about 1 a.m.

Early next morning we set the jet-lagged Jan to work, and by lunch time the mast was out of the boat and safely on the ground. The actual welding went a lot more slowly. They could only weld an inch or two at a time; then Jan insisted that they stop to let it all cool down, so as to avoid distorting and possibly bending the mast. Even the cooling down was slow, because the air temperature was close to 100 degrees. We built a little tent over the welding area to give some shade, but it was still hot. Any metal tool left in the sun for more than a minute or two became too hot to pick up. Flip-flop sandals had to be left face down, otherwise they were too hot to put back on.

We all swam a lot, but even that did not cool us down very much. The sea water off the shallow beach where we were anchored was as hot as a warm bath – well over 90 degrees.

Lana and I did get one chance to cool off. The Boss had told us to hire a surveyor to keep an eye on the repairs, which was how we came to meet Arthur. He was the resident surveyor from the American Bureau of Shipping, who was watching the bulk carrier being built. One day he invited Lana and me to visit his country home, with our swimming things. He had a surprise in store: his favourite swimming hole in the river, under what felt like the world's coldest waterfall. We were all goosebumps and chattering teeth in an instant, but it felt wonderful to be cold.

Arthur helped in another, more serious, way by introducing Lana to the intricacies of the provisioning black market. He managed to track down long-life milk, and to the boys' delight and relief, beer. Lana had not been able to buy either of these on her own. Then he produced some beef and some chicken. The only thing that was proving really difficult was butter. He solved that by going back to the shipyard and telling them they had better keep the surveyor happy if they wanted to launch their ship on schedule! Soon afterwards, somebody came down the dock with a 5lb block of butter, compliments of the company store. We were reprovisioned!

As a final favour, Arthur took the whole crew to see over the new ship. We all donned hard hats and followed him through the bowels of the ship. It was enormous. Jeff envied the air-conditioned control centre for the engine room, but the boys were glad not to have to scrub a deck that big.

By the end of the week, the welding was complete and we managed to step the mast before the yard shut for the weekend. Jan left us to set up the rig and bend on all the sails again. He was anxious to get back to Holland.

For trials and tuning, we sailed up and down the big bay a couple of times, and then across to Isla Grande at the mouth of the bay. Arthur had suggested a nice anchorage there, and I thought a last day of 'R and R' before the long sail south would do us all good.

The island is beautiful. It is about 10 miles long, hilly, wooded and not too developed. There is one small hotel, a few houses and, at the southern end of the island, a prison. Arthur warned us that prisoners escaped on a fairly regular basis, and usually hitch a lift ashore on a passing yacht. He said that if an escapee came to the boat, we should take him over to the mainland and drop him off; then we would have no problems! But we stayed away from the prison, and the prisoners stayed away from us. Lana and I walked over to the beach on the windward side to swim and snorkel. Jeff vanished into the hills for the day, and the boys looked in vain for waves big enough to surf. We all enjoyed our last days in warm waters. It was going to be a long

time before we were in weather this warm again.

Soon after leaving Bahia, *Beagle* sailed through a red tide – great areas of the sea stained a brownish red colour. As might be expected, Darwin took samples and found the colour was caused by plankton. There were literally millions of microscopic cylindrical animals. He did not know where they had come from, nor why they should have reproduced in such vast numbers, and he was not alone. Even now, I do not think that anybody has come up with a satisfactory explanation of what makes the plankton that cause the red tides suddenly multiply and bloom. What is well known is the damage they can cause. A red tide can kill other sea life or render them poisonous to humans.

For most of the passage down to Rio the weather was fair, and Darwin found the easy sailing quite pleasant. For once he was not seasick, and he began to hope that perhaps it was a thing of the past. He settled into, and began to enjoy, the shipboard routine. Breakfast was served at eight, and when that was over he would usually work on his specimens. It took many hours to identify them all and record their details. The chart table in the poop cabin would often be covered by his bits and pieces, and he would fight for space with the fortunately good-natured Lieutenants Stokes and King, the navigating officers of the forenoon watch.

The midday meal was much more formal than breakfast. It was called dinner, and was in fact the main meal of the day. The officers were served at 1 p.m., and Darwin usually ate with Fitzroy in his cabin. In the afternoons, Darwin either worked with his collection again or retired to his hammock to catch up with his reading. What they called tea was the last meal of the day. It was served at 5 p.m., so that all could be cleared away before dark. When we are at sea, we also try to eat our last meal of the day before dark. It is easier and more pleasant when we can see what we are eating. Unless the weather is bad, we like to eat in the cockpit rather than below, where the heat and cooking smells can sometimes stifle even the strongest appetite.

On *Thalassi*, there is virtually unlimited electric lighting. The generators run so much for the water maker and freezers that there is a surplus of electricity for lighting. The *Beagle*, of course, had no electricity. The officers had a lantern in their accommodation, but for

the crew before the mast, the stub of a candle was as much as they could hope for. As the voyage progressed and fuel supplies dwindled, even the officers would be discouraged from burning a lantern unnecessarily.

If he could get a lantern, then Darwin would sometimes work again or read in the evening. More often, however, he would just pace the deck, sometimes chatting with the officers of the watch. He seemed to get on well with all of them.

During the passage, they sighted a waterspout, caught a shark, and one morning Lieutenant Sullivan hailed Darwin. 'Come quickly. There's a grampus bear swimming off the port side.' Darwin abandoned his specimens, and rushed up on deck, to find the whole crew laughing at him. It was 1 April, and the Flycatcher had been caught.

Although he agreed to stop at Dos Abrolhos, Fitzroy quite rightly decided not to take the ship in through the reef. If we had not had a big, reliable engine, I would certainly not have taken *Thalassi* in there either. It is not an anchorage to try to sail into, or indeed out of.

They hove to off the islands and launched one of the whale-boats to take Darwin ashore. His time was limited, because Fitzroy wanted to be clear of the land before dark – there was no lighthouse there at that time. Darwin dashed about collecting samples of every plant he could find ashore; once again there was no mention of his looking at the coral or the sea life. Almost the only time he ever seems to have studied sea life was when they were at sea and he had no terrestrial life to observe.

They reached Rio a couple of days later, and anchored off Botafogo, which he describes as a pretty little fishing village. He would not recognise the place now; his pretty little village has become a series of high-rise apartments and shopping centres.

Waiting for them in Rio was their first mail from Britain, and probably only a long-distance sailor can fully understand how important that was for them. Darwin felt a little homesick, reading the letters from his family. The feeling was not to last long, because ashore he met an Englishman who was about to ride out to an estate he owned. It was about 100 miles to the north, near Cabo Frio, and he invited Darwin along for the ride. Of course Darwin did not need asking twice, and he set off with the Englishman and his five companions. It took them five days to reach the estate, and they passed through a wide variety of landscapes along the way. Close to Rio much of the land was cultivated, but as they moved out into the country, this soon gave way to thick forest, interspersed with swampy areas surrounding a series of lakes.

Most nights they found an inn to stay at, but Darwin described

them as basic, invariably dirty, and with owners who were not very friendly. They often had to go out and kill, then cook, their own supper. Riding for ten hours a day was hard on both riders and horses, but the horses suffered the most. At night, they were often bitten by vampire bats. Apart from the blood loss, the bites had a tendency to chafe and fester for days afterwards. Darwin, of course, had to catch one of the vampire bats to study it and add it to his collection.

On the third day, they reached a plantation belonging to a relative of one of the group. Darwin found the estate to be somewhat of a paradox. The furnishings in the main house were very ornate – gilded chairs and sofas – yet the rooms containing them had rough whitewashed walls, and no glass in the windows.

The main crop of the plantation was coffee, but a secondary cash crop was manioc, or cassava as it is also known. Cassava is a curious plant: its root is poisonous until cooked. The fresh juice is said to be strong enough to kill a cow. It makes one wonder how people discovered that it was safe to eat when cooked, if they had already discovered that it was poisonous when raw. All parts of the plant are used. The leaves and stalks are fed to the horses, and the roots are ground to a pulp, dried and baked to make farinha. We first came across farinha in the West Indies, where it is still commonly eaten, usually with stews or other juicy meals. The usual way to eat it is to pull a piece off the pile and roll it into a ball – it has the consistency of uncooked bread dough – then dip the ball in the stew and eat it with the fingers.

The plantation kept a few cattle for milk as well as for meat. They also grew beans and rice for food. In the surrounding forests, there was an abundance of deer and game birds for the taking, so nobody on the plantation went hungry. In fact, Darwin suffered from overconsumption. They sat down to a prodigious meal that evening and he thought it would be impolite not to try everything that was offered. He was just about at bursting point, and was congratulating himself on having managed to taste a bit of each dish, when the servants brought in a roast suckling pig, and a gigantic stuffed turkey!

Although he was most strongly opposed to slavery, he did grudgingly concede that the slaves on this plantation were not badly off. They only worked five days a week for the plantation, and the other two for themselves. He did not see any of the physical abuse that he knew was common. But the slaves were not free to leave, nor were they paid.

The party headed north the next day, towards the Englishman's plantation. When Darwin asked him how big the estate was, the

owner replied, 'I know it's about 2½ miles long, but I don't recall the breadth!'

The roads, such as they were, were very overgrown in places. Often somebody had to walk ahead of the horses, using a machete to cut a path through the vines and creepers that were blocking their way. Progress was slow, and Darwin had plenty of time to gather more bugs and plants for his collection as they travelled.

After a few days on the estate, they headed back to Rio. *Beagle* had gone back to Bahia Salvador to survey the bay, so Darwin moved into a rented house in Botafogo. I cannot help but feel that he would have found more of interest on the survey expedition around Salvador, but he seems to have been happy enough to be ashore. Perhaps it also did him good to escape the confines of shipboard living for a while.

During his stay ashore, he concentrated mainly on insect collecting. His usual programme was to spend one day collecting and the next studying and cataloguing. Between his collecting and his studying, he did manage to leave some time for his social pleasures too. He was invited to most of the naval events, and attended the Admiral's inspection of HMS *Warspite*, which was the social event of the month.

Darwin's house faced the Sugarloaf across the bay, and from his back garden he could see the Corcovado. He spent many hours watching the clouds form just below the peak of the Corcovado, which they did almost every afternoon. He did not get to the top of either peak. Of course at that time there was no cable car up the Sugarloaf, nor had the road been built up the Corcovado, so it would have been a fairly serious expedition to get up them.

His favourite time of the day was the evening. He enjoyed sitting out in the garden with a drink, and liked to watch the sun go down and the night come racing across from the east. In the tropics, nightfall is the signal for the tree frogs and cicadas to start up with their noisy chorus. The noise they make between them is surprisingly loud. The curious chirp that the tree frogs make is, for me, very evocative of tropical evenings spent in a quiet anchorage.

It goes without saying that even in these moments of relaxation, Darwin still had to satisfy his curiosity and track down and capture one of each of the noise makers. I am not sure whether he was surprised when he caught his first tree frog, but the first time I saw one, I was amazed that such a little creature could make such a big noise. They are tiny – only an inch or so long – and almost completely transparent. On the end of each toe they have a disproportionately large sucker, and can defy gravity by walking up vertical surfaces, even those as smooth as glass.

The other creatures that caught his attention, and suffered the inevitable consequences, were fireflies. He was fascinated by their bright flashes as they darted around his garden every evening. Under closer scrutiny he found that the flash comes from two bands around the body of the insect. Then he discovered that if he decapitated an insect, the bands stayed lit, often for as long as twenty-four hours. From this he deduced that the glow itself was involuntary, and the insect controlled the flashes by switching the glow off. (A sailor might say that the fireflies do not in fact flash, but rather occult.)

Darwin enjoyed his visit to the Botanical Gardens which we had tried in vain to see on New Year's Day. He was amused to see what he termed 'useful' trees growing there. It was the first time that he had seen cinnamon, camphor, clove and other aromatic trees growing. Then he found mango and breadfruit trees, important for their fruit, as well as timber trees such as mahogany and teak.

He spent some time studying spiders, comparing the ways in which they caught and devoured their prey. He also enjoyed watching the tiny humming-birds darting from flower to flower. There was much to occupy his mind, his days were full, and the time passed quickly. One morning, he awoke to see the *Beagle* anchored out in the bay once more. It was time to move back on board. It was time to head south again.

Chapter 9

South to the Falklands

Beagle sailed south for the River Plate, which was to be its base for the next stage of the surveys. On the second day out they sailed through a gigantic school of dolphins, which obviously excited Darwin. He was fascinated by some that came to play in the bow-wave of the ship, but mainly he was overwhelmed by the sheer numbers in the school, which took several hours to pass.

We often see dolphins when we are sailing, but usually only in small groups. Only once, about twenty years ago in the Pacific, did I ever see a school approaching the size that Darwin describes. I wonder if such big schools still exist, or whether we have killed so many of them that only the small schools survive?

Fitzroy decided to base their operations at Maldonado, in the wide estuary of the River Plate. It is on the Uruguay side, close to the entrance. As they sailed into the estuary, Darwin was intrigued to see how the muddy fresh water from the river seemed reluctant to mix with the clear blue sea water. Their wake left a swirling band of blue across the surface of the brown water, which was only a few inches deep, floating on top of the denser sea water.

Although they were based at Maldonado, they did sail up to Montevideo at one stage. Darwin, however, dismissed it as a dull and dirty town. Another day they sailed across to the Argentinian side, to visit Buenos Aires. Political tensions were running fairly high at the time, and when Fitzroy failed to heed a warning shot, they were fired upon by an Argentinian warship. Fitzroy retreated in an almost blind fury. His anger, for once, was shared by Darwin. Fitzroy sent a message to the Argentinians. 'If I had known I was entering an uncivilised port, I would have had my broadside ready for answering.' Of course *Beagle*'s few guns would have been no match against those of a full-blown warship.

They sailed to Montevideo, and there Captain Fitzroy asked the Captain of a British frigate to go over and demand an apology, or sink the offending vessel. Perhaps fortunately for all concerned, cooler heads prevailed and the incident was eventually forgotten.

Darwin was very busy writing letters home, and getting the first of his collection ready for shipping to Professor Henslow back in Cambridge. A fast packet-ship was getting ready to sail to England, and it would carry mail back for them.

Darwin had already collected several hundred samples, and there would have been even more if it had not been for the time he had spent on his meticulous notes. He had written some 600 pages in his journal by this stage, and that was increased to over 2000 by the end of the voyage.

His journal and geological notes were in fact to prove more valuable, in many cases, than the samples themselves. It turned out that he was a better note-taker than dissector, which is not surprising considering his lack of training. Some of his biological samples were so mutilated, and his drawings so poor, as to be almost valueless, but his descriptions were generally full and accurate.

In a covering note to Professor Henslow, Darwin apologised for the fact that the collection was not larger, but he protested that he had not been idle. I do not think anybody could argue with that. He said, 'Anybody who complains that my geological samples are small, should try carrying rocks for a mile or two under the tropical sun.'

From the River Plate, *Beagle* made a foray south for a month or two, to start the survey work. The weather was rough, and Darwin was very unhappy to find that once more he was desperately seasick. He spent much of his time at sea in his hammock, but whenever they stopped he was usually first ashore, reaping his usual harvest.

At Punta Alta, some 400 miles south-west of Maldonado, he found an enormous number of fossils embedded in an outcropping of soft rock. The fossils were from all kinds of beasts. One was of the skull of a creature that looked like a rhinoceros, but the real puzzler was what he was sure was a horse's tooth. It was generally acknowledged that horses were a modern introduction to the continent of South America, yet here was proof that they, or a very close relative, had existed there for thousands of years. What, he was often to ponder, had caused their extinction?

To help the survey work along, Captain Fitzroy hired two local schooners. He put two of his officers aboard each, and retreated north once more to Maldonado, leaving them to their work. Darwin complained from time to time that the *Beagle,* seemed to spend more time in port refitting than she did at sea. I know the feeling well! It seems to me that boats require at least two hours of work for every hour spent sailing.

Darwin had a bad case of depression while they were there. He began to wonder whether he could in fact endure the coming months and years. When he was ashore, and the ship confined in port, he was longing to be at sea, moving on to the next adventure. Yet once the ship was sailing, and seasickness reared its ugly head yet again, he wished fervently to be ashore. It is easy to criticise him, but we should remember that he was still only in his early twenties. It was hard for Lana or me to imagine 'our own' Nick or Chris taking responsibility for such an undertaking, or having the skill and patience to collect and describe all the specimens that he did.

While the ship was in port or surveying, Darwin did manage to make several long trips inland. We often envied the fact that he had the time for these expeditions. He rode and lived with the gauchos, the cowboys of the plains, for several weeks at a time. They carried no food on their travels, but ate whatever they could catch – armadillo, ostrich and puma. The puma, Darwin said, compares favourably with veal. Imagine the furore now, if one of the popular television naturalists sat down to a plate of puma and chips!

When the gauchos were out on the plains herding cattle, he found that they lived on a diet of beef, and nothing else. When the time came to eat, they would kill a cow and eat it. Darwin noted that 'like any other purely carnivorous animal, they were able to go for long periods between eating, without apparent discomfort'. Three days between meals was common. Compared to our crew, that was truly amazing – it was hard for them to go three hours without eating! Maybe Lana should have fed them more meat!

While he was with the gauchos, they had several of what he called 'skirmishes' with the Indians, all of whom were generally hostile, apart from a 'tame' colony near Punta Gorda.

When he could not find gauchos to ride with, the ever restless Darwin organised his own expeditions. For one such trip he hired two men and a team of twelve horses. This cost him the princely sum of $2 a day, which in those days amounted to about 8 shillings (40p). On meeting his guides he was a bit perturbed by the assortment of pistols and sabres they were carrying. They positively bristled with weapons, and he felt they were overdoing it a bit for what he saw as a little ride into the country. He changed his mind, however, when, just as they were about to leave, reports came in about a traveller found on the Montevideo road with his throat cut.

They spent their first night at a small country house, about 30 miles from Maldonado. After supper, while planning their next day's route on the map, Darwin's little pocket compass caused great astonishment. The locals were amazed that this gringo-stranger knew in which direction the next settlement lay without having been there before. His reputation as something of a sorcerer preceded him, and from then on, everywhere they went, he had to produce and demon-

strate his compass. At one settlement, he was summoned to the bedside of a very sick woman, to 'show her the compass', in the hope that it might cure her.

Just as the compass was a source of wonder for the locals, Darwin was equally amazed by what he perceived as the ignorance, not of the peasants but of wealthy owners of huge estates, with many thousands of cattle. They treated him as the fount of all knowledge, and he was stunned by some of the questions they asked: 'Is it the sun or the earth that moves?', 'Where is Spain?', 'Is it hotter or colder in the north?' He was quite put out when he discovered that most people thought that North America, England and London were different names for the same place. One such owner, better informed than most, knew that North America and London were countries close beside each other, and he was equally certain that England was a town in London. And that was just over 150 years ago, only four or five generations.

While staying at one of these ranches, Darwin went out before breakfast to the water pump beside the house. He filled a bucket with water and washed his face. This caused great consternation, and he was closely questioned about the curious practice. Somebody said that they had heard Muslims did such a thing, but none of them had witnessed it before!

He spent one night at a particularly large and wealthy estate belonging to gentleman who was actually called Don Juan. It covered many square miles and he owned thousands of cattle, which were tended by several dozen gauchos. He was obviously a wealthy man by any standards, yet his house had a packed earth floor, a few rough chairs and tables for furniture, and no glass in the windows. Darwin was appalled at the evening meal, which consisted of two gigantic platters heaped high with beef. One pile was roast, and the other boiled, so their guest could have a choice! There were a few bits of pumpkin added more or less as an afterthought, but no other vegetables or bread. Everybody drank from the communal water jug in the middle of the table. For a young man with his strict upper-middle-class upbringing, it must have seemed truly barbaric.

On his rides with the gauchos, he became fascinated by their skill with *bolas*. The *bolas* are made with two, or sometimes three, balls joined together with a leather thong, and are used to catch animals. The method is to hold onto one ball, and whirl the whole thing around your head to get it spinning. Once up to speed, it is thrown into the fleeing animals' legs. Because of the spinning motion, the balls and thongs became entangled in the legs and with each other, effectively tying up the animal by remote control. The gauchos use

balls of different sizes and of different materials, depending on the animal they are chasing. Stones are often used to make heavy balls for bigger animals, and wood for the lighter ones.

The gauchos showed amazing dexterity at throwing the *bolas*, and naturally Darwin had to try to learn. He found it was easy to use them while standing still, but it was a different matter altogether when galloping fast over rough ground. On one of his attempts on horseback, he caused great amusement. He was galloping along, and got the balls swinging successfully around his head. Just at the crucial moment, as he was about to let go, one of the balls touched a bush they were passing, which upset the rhythm. The ball ricocheted off the bush and into the horse's legs. The entanglement was swift and comprehensive. Horse and rider were instantly stretched out on the ground. The gauchos almost died laughing. They said they had seen many animals successfully caught by *bolas*, but they had never seen anybody capture themselves so effectively. Luckily no more than his pride was hurt. He might easily have broken his neck, and then who knows when we would have been introduced to evolution.

When he got back to Maldonado, political tensions had eased a little, so he was able to take a short trip to Buenos Aires. He does not offer much description of it, save to call it a big city of 60,000 people. What would he make of it now, with a population well over 3 million? A big change in a comparatively short time. Will it be fifty times bigger again in another 150 years? I am glad I will not be around to find out!

Finally, and to Darwin's barely concealed relief, Fitzroy announced that they were ready to head south again. On 6 December they left the River Plate for the last time, or as Darwin eloquently put it, they 'were never again to enter its muddy stream'.

He was anxious to press on south, as he now saw Cape Horn as the 'gateway to further adventures'.

We left Isla Grande on 17 January. For the first couple of days the sailing was pleasant – a beam reach, with the wind staying around 15–20 knots. Because by now my faith in the rig was close to zero, and because the mast was still liable to bend alarmingly despite our best efforts at retuning the rigging, we kept a permanent reef in the mainsail. Even so we were ticking off around 200 miles a day: an average speed better than 8 knots. The sun was shining, and all was well with the world.

I had hoped to be able to stop in Punta del Este, in Uruguay. This is where the round-the-world races now usually stop, since making themselves unwelcome in Rio. It is the port for Maldonado, and is fairly close to Montevideo. It would have been interesting to sail up the River Plate and take a look at Darwin's 'muddy stream". Unfortunately, time was passing by all too quickly. We were already past the middle of the southern summer, and if we were to have time to explore Patagonia, we had to press on. For once we were as eager as the Boss to hurry. He was still planning to meet us in the Falklands, ostensibly with his film crew, so we steered a direct course for Port Stanley.

The good conditions could not last. We knew we were heading into one of the stormiest areas in the world, but that did not stop us enjoying the fair breeze while we could.

We had our first taste of what lay in store when we were passing the entrance to the River Plate. The pilot book warns of the strong squalls that can come down the river valley from the high plains. I thought that by staying about 250 miles off the coast we would avoid them. I was wrong! The squall came out of nowhere, at about tea time. There were no dark clouds, no warning; the wind just increased from about 15 to 50 knots in a matter of milliseconds. Fortunately we had the precautionary reef in the mainsail, but even so we had far too much sail set.

It was Nick's watch, but I was in the cockpit with him. We ran off before the wind. Lana came to take over the steering while Nick and I went forward to get the mainsail reefed some more. Jeff heard the commotion and got on deck in record time. Without waiting to be told, he rolled up most of the jib, then came forward to help us. Nick and I struggled to pull the mainsail down. The wind from astern was pressing it against the rigging, making it very hard to drag the sail down. The wind was really howling, but it had increased so suddenly that there had not been time for the waves to build up. The tops were blowing off the waves in a continuous sheet of spray, which made it hard to see where we were going.

The main came down slowly. Although Nick and Jeff were only inches away, I had to yell at them to be heard. 'Don't stop at the second reef. Let's keep going for the third one.' I did not dare look up the mast to see how much it was bending. As Nick and I dragged the sail down, Jeff was winching in the reefing pendant at the leech of the sail as fast as he could. The boom was flailing about as the sail flogged, when suddenly there was a bang and the after end of the boom hit the deck with an almighty crash.

The hydraulic vang had burst. This type of vang not only holds the boom down against the force of the sail, but also supports it when the sail is being lowered. Now it had collapsed and there was nothing to hold the boom up until we got the reef pendant tight. It was just good fortune that nobody was beneath the boom when it crashed down. We already knew how heavy it was, having had to lift it off for the welding in Brazil. Had it landed on somebody's head, it could well have killed them.

Jeff kept winching in the reef pendant, and slowly the boom returned to its horizontal position. As luck would have it, by the time we had tied in the reef points along the foot of the sail, the squall had passed, and the wind was back down to a pleasant 20 knots. Those three reefs stayed firmly tied in, however, until we were well south of the River Plate. We were not going to be caught by any repeat squall.

Once we had passed the River Plate, the night watches became distinctly nippy, and we dug out various woollies that had lain dormant in the bottoms of lockers for many a month. The water temperature had fallen by about 25 degrees Fahrenheit since leaving Brazil, showing that we had reached the cold Falklands current, which flows up from the Antarctic, around Cape Horn. Not only was it making things colder for us, but it was running against us at almost 2 knots, which meant we had to sail an extra 50 miles a day.

Nick and Chris became excited as we crossed the fortieth parallel. We were now in what the old sailors called the Roaring Forties, named after the number of gales encountered in those latitudes. We were lucky, however, for us they were the Whispering Forties. The wind stayed mostly light, and to keep to our schedule we motorsailed in the calm patches. Although the wind never blew really hard, we had a couple of very uncomfortable days when it went well south of west, and we were beating into the wind and weather. Every time *Thalassi* came off the top of a big wave, she slammed; it felt as if she was being dropped from a great height onto solid concrete. Under these conditions it was difficult to eat, harder still for Lana to prepare the food, and almost impossible to sleep. Not much fun.

Just past the halfway mark we had another good day's sailing – a beam reach with 25 knots of wind, and not too much sea. Despite keeping an extra reef in the mainsail, we did over 9 knots all day long. Everybody started to be a bit more optimistic about our arrival date in the Falklands, hoping that these conditions might hold for the

---

(Opposite) Our downwind rig. A following breeze was all too rare, it was usually on the nose. A headwind was bad enough for us, but would have been almost impossible for the Beagle.

AMERICAN RIVER COLLEGE

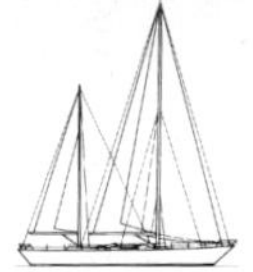

last 900 miles.

It was wishful thinking. That night the wind went back round to the south again, right on the nose. I did not want to sail *Thalassi* too hard, not only for the comfort of the crew but also to try and keep the rig intact. We reefed the sails right down, and used the engine as well. The motion was awful. The best speed we could make was about 5 knots. Any more and she would start slamming so hard into the confused sea that Chris was convinced that the motion was going to shake the fillings out of his teeth. With the Falklands current also slowing us down, we made only about 40 miles in the next twenty-four hours. If the wind stayed like this, it was going to take us weeks to reach the Falklands. Jeff was becoming concerned about the amount of fuel we had used. We did not have enough to motor all the way to the Falklands, so we had to hope for a change in the weather.

Fortunately the wind co-operated and went back into the west, and life on board once more assumed a degree of normality. Everybody caught up on their sleep and began to take a bit more interest in the surroundings.

We saw a large sea-lion, which was investigating a big patch of seaweed. It gave us a whiskery grin as we passed. Our first albatross had visited us a day or two before, and now there was scarcely a moment when there were not at least one or two circling the boat. Darwin made no mention of the albatross visiting them while *Beagle* was at sea; he only described the nesting and feeding habits of the birds ashore. Perhaps because the Forties were roaring for the *Beagle* and Darwin was confined to his hammock, he missed seeing them circle the ship. We made the very Darwinian observation that almost without exception they circled us in a clockwise direction. Was this to do the Coriolis effect, which determines the direction in which bathwater goes down the plughole in each hemisphere? Unfortunately albatross are not found in the northern hemisphere, otherwise we might have been able to confirm that they circled in an anticlockwise direction there.

When the first albatross came to visit us, we were a little disappointed. It did not look as big as we had expected, just like a big seagull. Because they are so well proportioned, and there is nothing to scale them against, they really do not look very big when they are flying. Only when one comes face to face with one ashore, does one realise just how enormous they are. The biggest species have a span of up to 11ft.

Some types of albatross will spend five years or even more at sea without ever touching land, so we should not have been surprised to

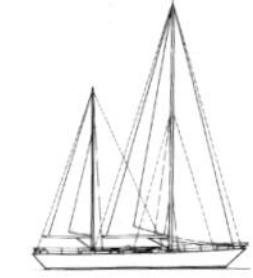

see them 600 miles from shore. It was fascinating to watch them glide, apparently effortlessly, often for minutes at a time.

An albatross will swoop down into the trough between two waves, often actually touching the breaking crest of the wave with one exploratory wingtip. The air being pushed along by the wave gives them enough momentum to enable them to bank sharply round up the face of the wave, and then soar up high enough to complete at least one complete clockwise circuit of the boat, all without a single flap of their long slender wings. They appeared to be able to repeat the process, without effort, *ad infinitum.* When it was rough, we kept waiting to see one dumped by a breaker. They flew so close to the waves that it seemed to be only a matter of time before a breaking wave would catch one, but it never happened. The rougher it became, the easier it was for them to soar.

The only time we ever saw an albatross struggling was in flat calm weather. It is very difficult for them to take off from smooth water, as their long wings hit the water. They run along the surface with their big feet, trying to get up enough speed for take-off, but if there is no wind to help them, they more often than not, flop back into the water, exhausted, after 100yd or so. By contrast, when it is windy and there is a good sea running, they can take off with scarcely a flap. They sit, bobbing about in the water, then by timing the spread of their wings to the arrival of the crest of a wave, they take off. By swooping down into the trough to gain momentum, they can start their endless soaring without a single flap.

For the same reason, an albatross will not willingly land on flat ground. With its long wings and short undercarriage, it may not be able to take off again. They will always nest at the top of a cliff, so that by stepping off the edge, they are airborne with no effort. It is almost as if it is 'nonU' in the albatross world to flap one's wings.

If we had not expected to see the albatross so far from land, what came as an even bigger surprise was a group of penguins swimming along when we were still some 500 miles from the Falklands, the nearest land. At first we thought they were seals when Lana spotted them in the distance. Having nothing better to do, we hardened up and sailed over for a closer look. There were half a dozen small penguins bobbing along, heading north, even further away from land. Were they lost? Were they migrating? Were they going back whence they came? Even allowing for the favourable current they would have had from the Falklands, it seemed a very long way for a penguin to paddle with its short, fat legs.

Every day now, we were seeing more and more birds, including tiny storm petrels, which looked too frail to be out there among the

waves. The old sailors called them Mother Carey's chickens and it is easy to see why: they appear to run about among the waves rather than fly. They look just like inquisitive chickens poking around in a farmyard. Why these little birds are not drowned by each passing wave is one of nature's secrets.

Being able to watch the wildlife made the daylight watches pass a little quicker, but it was a little spooky at night, as the eternally circling albatross kept flying through the glow cast by the navigation lights.

We had 350 miles to go, and a bit of a race was developing. On the maps we were receiving from the weather fax, we could see a very deep low approaching Cape Horn. Would we reach the Falklands before it did? Neither Nick or Chris had experienced a bad storm at sea, and nothing that Jeff, Lana nor I could say would convince them that the experience was to be avoided at almost any cost. They were excited at the prospect of the impending gale; we were scared.

I came on deck just before dawn. Jeff and Chris had the watch, and we were roaring along at over 10 knots. It was comfortable enough, and at this rate we would easily beat the gale to the Falklands. As the sky started to lighten, we could see the high cirrus clouds or mare's tails, a sure sign of an approaching front. I went forward to take a look up the mast. It was bending too much. I waved for Jeff to come and help me pull down another reef. At first he tried to talk me out of reefing. 'Don't be a wimp,' he said. 'She's going fine. Let's get in before this gale.'

I did not say anything. I just pointed up the mast. He leaned over, sighted up it and without saying another word started uncoiling the reef pendant. It was frustrating not being able to sail the boat properly, just because the mast could not take it, but to lose the mast at this stage would be disastrous.

With the third reef down, we were doing 8 knots, perhaps still fast enough to beat the storm. The conditions stayed pretty much the same all that night, although the wind may have picked up a little more. We were making excellent progress, and it began to look as if we would win the race.

Then at dawn, quite unexpectedly, the wind dropped, leaving us slatting around in a confused sea. We did not waste time trying to sail; on went the engine. Was this the calm before the storm? Did we have enough fuel to motor the last 180 miles? Maybe, but it would be close.

We motored all day, at what Jeff judged to be our most economical speed. He was monitoring our fuel consumption very closely, using a dipstick to measure what fuel was left, since the gauges were already reading virtually empty. The wind stayed light, and we motored all night.

We sighted land at dawn, and as we motored down the east coast into the lee of the land I breathed a huge sigh of relief. As soon as we were in the calmer water, we hoisted the main anchor up out of the forepeak and shackled it onto the chain – before leaving Isla Grande, we had cleared everything we could off the deck in anticipation of the Roaring Forties. As we reached Port Stanley, we rounded up into the wind to drop the sails, and with almost literally the last bucketful of fuel we motored through the narrow entrance into the harbour.

Over the radio, the Harbour-Master directed us to tie up at a very ramshackle-looking jetty, more or less in the middle of town. It would be convenient enough, but the way the barometer was heading, I

The anchorage off Port Stanley, in the Falklands. We were happy enough to get in before this gale struck, even though it was too rough to get ashore.

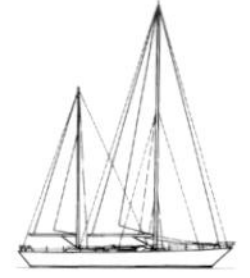

thought there was a good chance of us pulling the whole thing out by the roots as soon as the wind got up. When I expressed my concern, he told us that we could anchor in the harbour if we preferred. The only proviso was that we would have to go and fetch the man from Costumes and Intimidation, and bring him out to the boat to clear us in. No problem.

The anchor and the big dinghy hit the water at about the same time. Nick and Chris zoomed to the shore, while Jeff paid out the chain. We were in about 20ft of water. Thinking about the forecast, and since there was plenty of room, I had Jeff let out some 200ft of chain. The harbour is long and narrow, and its only design fault is that it runs east–west. Every Cape Horn gale blows from the west, and where we were anchored there would be a fetch of at least a mile. If only the bay had formed running north–south, it would have been perfect. Even as it was, it looked a lot better than being out at sea with a big gale on its way.

The boys were soon back, bringing a very helpful and friendly gentleman who was to do all the official business. We settled him down in the saloon, with all his papers and a drink, but he seemed to be in a hurry, and suddenly announced that he had done enough for now; we could finish the rest ashore later. As we came back on deck I realised why he was in such a rush. He had sensed that the gale was all but upon us, and he wanted to get ashore before he was stranded on board, perhaps for the night. The boys drove him back in, and by the time they got back, the wind had arrived and was already blowing over 50 knots. It was howling.

We brought a second anchor up on deck, shackled it onto its rode, then made several abortive attempts to drop it up to windward using the dinghy. I did not want to motor *Thalassi* forward to drop it, for fear of letting the boat fall back onto the main anchor chain with a jerk, which might make the anchor drag, or even snap the chain. We struggled ineffectually for about half an hour. The second anchor weighed 140lb and the dinghy was bouncing around – somebody was going to get hurt.

I called a halt. The best we could do was to drop the second anchor under the bows of the boat and then carefully let out another 100ft of chain on the main anchor. That meant 300ft of chain in 20ft of water. If we dragged or the chain snapped, then at least the second anchor was ready, even if it could not share the strain yet.

We retired below to a well-earned lunch that Lana had prepared. Even the boys agreed that we had been lucky to get in when we did. They conceded that they would rather be here in Port Stanley than still out at sea. If we had been at sea, we would have been hove to by now. Progress against this wind would have been impossible, particularly with our suspect rig. We would have been losing ground to the east, and then be faced with a long beat back after the gale had passed. It felt good to be well anchored in a secure harbour. The wind was gusting well over 60 knots now, almost up to Force 12 on the Beaufort scale. We had been lucky. Welcome to the Falklands!

Government House at Port Stanley. A timely surrender by the Governor saved it from getting flattened by the Argentinian invaders.

Chapter 10

The Falkland Islands: In and Around Port Stanley

The *Beagle* made several trips to the Falklands during her stay in the south. She zigzagged through Patagonia, and to and from the Falklands. She retreated there more than once for a bit of wound licking and repair after the boisterous conditions off Cape Horn. Once again, rather than follow their adventures in a chronological order, I will do it geographically, relating their adventures to our progress along their route.

Captain Fitzroy was becoming almost as frustrated as Darwin about the lack of progress. The survey work was going much more slowly than he had hoped and expected. They were still using the two chartered schooners, and now he bought a third, slightly larger one out of his own pocket. He was hoping to be reimbursed by the Admiralty, but for the time being he was happy enough to pay for her himself so that the survey could be speeded up. Remembering the ship that had accompanied *Beagle* on her first voyage, he renamed her the *Adventure*, and sent her off to look for the other two schooners, which were still surveying the east coast of the mainland.

On her first visit, *Beagle* spent five weeks anchored off East Falkland. Darwin describes this as a dismal time. It was March, pretty much at the end of the southern summer. If he had been there a month or two sooner, perhaps his eye would not have been so jaundiced. He describes the land as 'having a wretched and desolate aspect, being barren and treeless, with only a few miserable inhabitants'. After his book was published, Darwin received a letter from Captain Sullivan, who had been one of the lieutenants who had stayed on in the Falklands to complete the survey after *Beagle* had left. Sullivan told Darwin that he had painted a falsely bleak picture of the climate and the islands, a fact which Darwin acknowledged in later editions of his book.

The general mood on board the *Beagle* was not improved when the Captain's Clerk, Hellyer, was drowned while on a shooting expedition. The funeral further depressed the ship's crew.

Darwin made a foray ashore with one of the shooting parties, but he found that his blood lust had left him. Geology was now more interesting to him than killing birds or animals for sport. In the last batch of mail they had received before leaving Montevideo, he had received another geology book, which had just been published in Britain. He read it from cover to cover on the sail south. The book expressed the very latest thinking in geology. Indeed the whole consignment of mail was very up to date – it had reached them in what Darwin felt was the remarkably quick time of five months.

He was treating geology as a mental exercise as much as anything else. He enjoyed taxing his brain trying to answer the various puzzles that he discovered during his geological forays.

Darwin took a six-day ride across East Falkland, escorted by two gauchos and six horses. Without the geology to hold his interest, he said, the ride would have been boring. For most of the time they were riding over undulating moorland, covered with light brown, withered grass interspersed with a few small shrubs. The soil was mostly a springy peat, except for the rocky hills they crossed in the middle of the island. These were barren, rocky, and difficult for the horses to cross.

In the valleys between the hills, they saw some geese and a few snipe, but not many other birds. Once they crossed the hills to the southern plains, they spotted several herds of wild cattle. According to the gauchos, these had once been more numerous, but were now declining – hardly surprisingly, because that day the gauchos killed a cow for a single meal for the three of them.

They found a small herd of cattle, and one of the gauchos separated the chosen cow from the herd. Using his *bolas* and a lasso, he managed to bring it down, and then with some difficulty killed it with a knife. They cut out the meat that they needed and carried it to the place where they had decided to camp for the night.

Darwin was fascinated by the way the gauchos were able to make a fire, even though it had been raining for most of the day. They scrabbled around beneath small bushes and tufts of grass to find two or three small, fairly dry twigs. They rubbed these into fine fibres, then surrounded them with other twigs, rather like a bird's nest. Then they produced a small piece of rag from a saddlebag, and sparked it with a tinder box. The rag with the glowing spark was laid over the centre of the nest, and the whole thing held up into the wind. It soon began to smoke, then quite suddenly burst into flames. They put it back on the ground, and built a fire round it.

There are virtually no trees on the Falklands, but the gauchos showed Darwin how well beef bones burned as fuel. Older bones burn better, but even fresh bones, with the meat picked off, will burn well enough. They also pointed out one particular shrub which will burn reasonably well even while it is still green.

To cook the slab of beef, they did not bother to skin it. They laid it out skin side down, and roasted it on the embers of the fire. It was moulded into the shape of a saucer to contain all the gravy. The gauchos called it *carne con cuero* – meat with skin. Darwin thought it was about the best beef he had ever eaten, saying it was 'a delicacy fit to serve to a London Alderman'. He did not seem to have any pangs of conscience about killing such a big animal for a single meal for the three of them.

It was mainly the cows that were killed, presumably because they were an easier prey. As a result there were disproportionately more bulls than cows, often roaming in small groups of three or four. The conditions on East Falkland obviously suited them, because they were much larger than any cattle Darwin had seen before. The gauchos were wary of the bulls, saying they could be very fierce. They warned Darwin that a bull would sometimes charge a rider and horse, often with fatal results.

On their long ride, they met a big bull while they were trying to cross a small stream. The bull stood its ground, even when the gauchos tried to chase it away. For its pains, the gauchos decided to emasculate it, supposedly to take the fire out of it and prevent it from making trouble in the future. One suspects, however, that it was more a matter of Latin macho pride, to prove that they were braver and stronger than the bull. The gauchos ran the bull down and caught it with their *bolas* and lassos. After a bit of a struggle, they were able to tie it up sufficiently for them to do the dirty deed. Once again, Darwin did not seem to be concerned about these antics, or if he was he kept his feelings entirely to himself.

They came across a herd of wild horses near the southern end of the island. These had been brought there by the French in 1764 and, according to the gauchos, had proliferated. They had no natural enemies, yet after a while their numbers stabilised, and then began to decline. Now only a few remained. Why this had happened was a mystery. Had some sickness decimated the herds? Had they eaten all the good grazing?

There was another paradox concerning the horses for Darwin to ponder upon. The cattle had grown to be larger than usual yet the horses, under the same conditions, were becoming smaller and smaller with each generation. Now, they were almost like Shetland ponies. Why?

There were a lot of rabbits, which had also been introduced and had prospered. For some reason the gauchos did not bother to eat them; it seems they preferred to kill the cattle for food.

The animals the gauchos liked to kill for sport were foxes. They were the only native quadrupeds, and by the time of Darwin's visit, the gauchos had all but wiped them out. They killed them by holding out a piece of meat for them in one hand, while holding a knife at the ready in the other. Darwin noted in his journal that the activities of the gauchos was likely to reduce the fox to the level of the dodo, but he did not seem to be too worried. What was one species more or less?

Another aspect of the fox did concern Darwin, however, and he had a long and passionate discussion with Fitzroy about it. The fox on the islands was similar in many ways to the Patagonian fox of the mainland, yet different enough to be distinct. Darwin was convinced that they were different species. Fitzroy was equally certain that they were the same species, but had changed through successive generations because of the modifying influences of climate, food and habitat in the two different places. In other words, Fitzroy felt they had evolved, but Darwin dismissed the theory. The way had been shown to him, but he had ignored it.

For much of his ride Darwin was to concentrate on geology. In fact he noted in his journal that there was little to say about the zoology of the islands, a comment I find hard to understand in view of our own experiences there; but more of that shortly.

He mentions seeing hawks, carrion vultures and owls, but few other land birds. He does say the waterfowl were numerous, and spent considerable time watching a cormorant playing with a fish it had caught. Eight times it let the hapless fish go, and eight times it caught it again. He likened it to the way a cat might play with a mouse before killing it. He had seen an otter do the same thing with a fish, but otherwise such actions are rare enough in nature. Most hunters kill their prey quickly; few will torment and play with them.

He describes the upland goose, which is commonly found in pairs or small flocks. It is a big bird, which does not migrate. It nests on the outer islands, presumably to escape the attentions of the foxes, and is a vegetarian, eating mainly grass. They are hunted even now, not for the pot – they do not taste very good – but because of the amount of grass they eat. Most of the farmers today rear sheep. The grazing is poor enough, and it is said that a full-grown goose will eat as much grass as a sheep.

There is a smaller goose called the rock goose, which lives exclusively on the beach areas. Then there is the bird which amused us on many occasions, the steamer duck. It gets it name from its peculiar

method of locomotion. It cannot fly, and rushes across the water in a cloud of spray like a desperate little paddle steamer in a hurry. Its wings and legs move at a furious rate, much like a farmyard duck's when it is being chased across a pond by an excited dog. It seemed to Darwin – and to us – that it uses its wings alternately, like somebody swimming crawl, rather than together, as other birds do when flying, or even swimming. No doubt someone has by now discovered whether this is true, perhaps with slow motion photography. However they do it, they always seem to be in a hurry, and they are fun to watch as they bustle about in their own furious way. They cannot dive very deep, so feed exclusively on the shellfish that live among the kelp which is found in the tidal zones.

Magellanic penguins at Cow Bay. Where Darwin reported seeing the odd one or two penguins, we found them in their thousands. Have they increased, or did he just not visit the areas where they live?

The only other bird that Darwin describes, is a solitary Jackass penguin or Magellanic penguin. It gets its nickname from the fact that its call sounds for all the world like a donkey that is being tormented. I find hard to understand that Darwin did not see, or if he did see, did not record, more penguins. Apart from the Jackass, we saw Gentoos, Rockhoppers, Macaroni and King penguins – not just a few but, with the exception of the kings, many thousands of each. I doubt whether they can have proliferated so much in the last 150 years. Perhaps he was just very unfortunate in the choice of areas where he went ashore. Maybe he got so involved in his geology that he largely ignored the shoreline, but the huge flocks of penguins we saw would have been impossible to ignore.

Surprisingly, the other bird that he appears to have missed was the albatross. We saw great colonies of these birds nesting on the cliff tops, so unafraid of us that we could walk among them.

What caught his attention geologically, and what I think are possibly unique to these islands, are what he called the 'streams of stones'. From a distance they do indeed look like mountain streams, tumbling down the sides of the valleys. When one gets close to them though, one finds that they are made of jagged, angular rocks that are too sharp ever to have been rolled and polished by flowing water. The individual rocks are quite big: the smallest are usually at least 1ft across, and many of them are as much as 10ft or more. They are not thrown up in heaps, but spread out in level streams – there really is no other word to describe how they look. The streams vary in width from a few feet to perhaps as much as a mile across. Darwin talks about crossing one such stream, jumping from rock to rock for at least half a mile. Some of the rocks were so big that when it started to rain, he had no difficulty finding a rock big enough to shelter under.

The crevices between the rocks are not filled with sand, which suggested to Darwin that the streams had been formed after the land had emerged from the sea. And although the rocks themselves obviously had not been part of a river-bed as such, at several of the streams Darwin could hear water running far beneath them. How deep down the water lay he could not tell, as he lacked the time and equipment to move the rocks. He was also frustrated at not being able to ascertain how deep the rocks themselves went. He had to content himself with measuring the angle of the slopes down which the streams appeared to flow.

Because of the size of the rocks, this was difficult enough to do. It was obvious that few of the streams were steep enough for the rocks slide down; most slopes appeared to be about 10 degrees, and some were almost horizontal. He followed one stream up a valley, to the crest of a hill, where he found rocks, some as big as houses, seemingly poised to begin their journey down the valley.

What had caused the streams? What had propelled the rocks down the shallow inclines? He was to ponder this long and often. Perhaps his most plausible theory was that they were streams of lava which had solidified before being broken to fragments by some cataclysmic upheaval. Has anybody come up with a better theory?

Had he not been so interested in these streams, had the weather been a little kinder and had Captain Fitzroy put him ashore in an area with more wildlife, perhaps the Falklands would have interested him at least as much as the Galapagos were to do. We certainly found them and their wildlife more interesting. We shared Captain Sullivan's opinion: Darwin failed to do the Falklands justice.

Although we were happy enough to be safe in the harbour, it was a little frustrating to be anchored off Stanley but not able to get ashore. It had become far too rough to risk venturing out in the dinghy. We had to content ourselves with minutely studying the town through the binoculars. The wind howled all that afternoon and most of the night.

By the time we woke up the next morning, however, it had finally abated and the sun was shining. The world looked like a different place. After a quick breakfast we all piled into the dinghy and headed ashore. Lana made a beeline for the Post Office to look for our mail, while I went to visit the Harbour-Master.

He was every bit as friendly and helpful as the man who had come out to the boat, and gave me a lot of useful local information. He told me that the population of Stanley was about 1500, with about the same number living on outlying farms, or 'in the camp' as he put it. Additionally, there were still some 3000 British troops stationed there, mostly living in a new base built at the recently completed airport, near the centre of the island.

The most important thing he wanted to give me, however, was a minefield map. Although the war with Argentina was already a fading memory, the legacy of that war will be with the islands for ever. All of the land has been graded to three levels with regard to the risk of mines. The first grade is deemed to be safe. This land has been minutely searched, and there are no mines or other unexploded ordnance. Such areas are close to Stanley and the other settlements, as well as areas where there was no fighting, such as some of the offshore islands. The middle grade covers most of the island. These areas are thought to be safe, but no guarantees are given. They have not been closely swept, and people go there at their own risk.

The third grade, shaded in red on the map, covers known minefields that have not been, and probably never will be, cleared. Some of these areas are around Stanley, others along potential landing sites where the Argentinians thought attacking troops might land in any attempt to retake the islands. In many cases the Argentinians had made no effort to record the positions or even the numbers of the mines, and the modern plastic one are difficult to sweep for without setting them off. These minefields will be there for many years to come.

Known minefields are well marked, both on the map we were given, and around the perimeter. Some of the minefields will never be cleared, because of the difficulty of finding the plastic mines.

Formalities completed, I met up with a rather downcast Lana. There was no mail at the Post Office yet. We walked down the road to the Company Store, where she was a bit happier at what she found. This is the general store run by the Falkland Island Company, and it is about the only shop in town.

We learned that much of the land, and almost all of the commerce, in the Falklands is controlled by the Falkland Island Company. The main business for the islanders is ranching sheep, some on land owned by the company, some on private property. The company, however, seemed to have a monopoly on collecting the wool from the farms and shipping it to Britain to be sold. Its ship makes a regular run between Port Stanley and the outlying farms. In the shearing season the ship collects the wool, and the rest of the year it delivers supplies to the farms. These goods are usually ordered by radio from the Company Store, with payment offset against wool collected and sold. We were to find that many of the people living on the outer islands visited Stanley only once or twice a year. The rest of the time all their shopping, and most of their socialising was done by radio.

Every farm has a radio, and it is very important to the way the community survives. Not only is most business done this way, but it is also the medium for gossip. There are twice-daily sessions reserved just for idle chatter. Other periods are for school work. Many of the children are educated at home, using the radio to talk to the teacher, and for class discussions. The doctor also has a period reserved for him. Each remote farm has a standard medical box, with all the medications numbered. In non-serious cases, or if the weather prevents him from flying in for a house call, the doctor discusses the symptoms with the patient, and then prescribes by numbers – perhaps 'three Number 18 every six hours.' It must be difficult sometimes, discussing personal illnesses with the doctor, knowing that half the population of the islands is probably also listening. An ongoing illness could probably be a fair substitute for the TV soap operas that have yet to arrive here.

In the Company Store, Lana found all sorts of canned and packaged goods from Britain – Branston Pickle, digestive biscuits and Marmite, things we had not seen for months. There was a small amount of frozen food, but no fresh vegetables or meat. We discovered that everybody grows their own vegetables, but fruit is virtually unknown because it is too windy for the trees to survive. The only meat the islanders ever eat is lamb or, more accurately as we were to discover, mutton. The locals jokingly refer to mutton as 365, because they eat it every day.

While we were at the store, Jeff had found out which jetty we could come alongside to get fuel. We did not have enough money to fill up, as we were waiting for a transfer of funds from the Boss. We had enough to get 150 gallons, but Jeff was worried that if we used the generator much more, there would not be enough fuel to get the boat to the dock, our fuel was so low, so he had arranged for us to go to the fuel dock right after lunch. Nick and Chris had toured the town and discovered the southernmost fish and chip shop in the world.

As we went back down to the dock where we had left the dinghy, we saw that the company supply ship had come in and tied up across the end of the dock. She was a happy-looking little green ship called *Monsunen*. Perhaps she was a little past her prime, but she looked capable enough and well cared for. The skipper saw us looking at her, guessed we were from *Thalassi* and invited us aboard. George was obviously proud of his little ship. He gave us a guided tour and a lot of useful local knowledge. There can be few people who know these islands and the anchorages as well as George does.

He offered to allow *Thalassi* to lie alongside *Monsunen* for a few days, until his next trip. That would be much safer for us than against one of the other rickety docks, and a lot more convenient than having to go to and fro in the dinghy all the time.

There are half a dozen docks sticking out into the harbour from in front of the town. Some are more substantial than others, with the company dock, where *Monsunen* lay, being the biggest. George explained that the docks have all been built by sinking old ships, filling them with rocks, and boarding over the top with planks.

There are numerous hulks of old sailing ships scattered around the harbour, one or two looking almost intact and still partially rigged. Others have been built up with wooden structures to make small warehouses. Then there are all the ships that were sunk to become jetties. When I asked about the wrecks, I was told an interesting tale. In the days of sail, ships would often struggle through appalling conditions, trying to round nearby Cape Horn against the prevailing westerlies. All too often they would suffer damage and run back to what the skipper might perceive to be the safety of Port Stanley.

Unfortunately for the ship owners, the local Lloyd's adjuster was also the only shipwright. If a damaged ship which came in for repairs had the misfortune to be insured, this gentleman (using the term loosely), would metaphorically put on his Lloyd's hat, inspect the damage, and insist on a quote for repairs. He would then put on his shipwright's hat and proceed to give an absolutely outrageous quote for repairs. Back once more in his Lloyd's persona, he would assess the value of the ship, find that the quote for repairs exceeded the insured value and promptly condemn the ship. There was nothing

One of the many wrecks in Port Stanley. This one is at the eastern end of the harbour. Disabled ships seeking shelter were often condemned by the Lloyds Surveyor, and they provided a ready source of timber in a place where virtually no trees can grow.

the captain or owners could do. The hapless ship would become a storage hulk or a jetty, or even be broken up for the timber, which was always in short supply in the treeless islands.

One ship to suffer such a fate was an American clipper by the name of *Snowsquall.* She had become part of the jetty next to the main company dock. She and four or five other ships had been tied side by side and sunk to form the foundation. Now a group of people from Maine were working on her, trying to cut off and salvage about 35ft of her bows that stuck out from the side of the jetty. They claimed that she was the only surviving American clipper ship, although to say that she had 'survived' is perhaps stretching the point.

The cold water that had preserved her timber so well, made it difficult for the divers who were trying to saw through her salt-hardened timbers. We watched their progress daily, and shared their excitement when the bow section finally broke free. It was lifted on to a specially made cradle on board a big container ship, which was eventually going to carry it back to a museum in Maine.

Our first evening ashore was to be a cook's night off. We reconoitred the one and only hotel, the Upland Goose, which George had recommended. Much to our surprise, they said they were fully booked for the next several nights. So instead we ended up at Emma's Guest House, which happened to be where the *Snowsquall* people were staying. We had a good meal, and enjoyed chatting with the divers.

The waterfront of Port Stanley is dotted with jetties leading out to grounded hulks of old sailing ships, which are used as ready-made warehouses.

We thought we had completed a full and interesting day, but it was not to be. The boys wanted to stop for a drink at a bar called the Globe. Lana and I were feeling like tired little sailors, but finally agreed that we would stop for just one drink before heading back. The boys could drink the night away if they wanted, but we were ready for sleep. The pub was rather noisy, very smoky and quite busy. The clientele looked like about an equal mix of islanders and soldiers – who was whom was immediately apparent by the haircuts!

We were about to leave when we saw a young soldier come in and start to assemble his bagpipes, so we decided we would stay a few minutes more. He played one short skirl, then started to pack the pipes away. Lana went over to ask him why he was not playing more, and he explained that the barman had told him he could not play in there. He went on to tell her that there was a folk club meeting in the Town Hall that night, and he was going to be playing there.

Lana was keen to go and investigate – by now she was getting her second wind. Off we set, back down the road to the Town Hall, thinking that the piper was right behind us. When we got there, we found the show had already started. Two soldiers were singing with a local girl, accompanying themselves on guitars, and they were good. The piper was supposed to perform for the second half, but did not show up, so members of the audience filled in instead. Midnight was approaching, and we had just about given up on the piper when he and his friend stumbled in. They were both so drunk that they could hardly stand. A minor problem like that was not going to stop him from playing, however, and play he did. He was amazing. His equally inebriated friend accompanied him on the accordion. We later learned that the piper had won the Scottish National Championship two years running. It was an excellent end to a busy day.

The next few days were almost as busy. We had had word that the Boss was coming in a week's time. After he had learned the price of the air tickets, he had abandoned the film crew, and was coming on his own, which would make the provisioning and catering a little easier. There was plenty of cleaning and polishing to do before his arrival, but we were determined to do a little exploring as well.

Jeff and I were keen to go up into the hills overlooking Stanley, where the fiercest battles of the war had been fought. I do not want to dwell too much on the war, but it did obviously have a great impact on the islands, and has changed, perhaps for ever, the way they are perceived by the rest of the world. After a longstanding dispute over sovereignty, the Argentinians invaded the Falklands on 2 April 1982. The British sent an almost unprecented task force of 100 ships 8000 miles to fight them, and the combined cost of the war was 1000 lives.

Argentina surrendered the islands once more on 14 June.

During the war, while we were living and working in the Virgin Islands, we had listened regularly to the BBC World Service, following the progress of the fighting. Now it was a very moving experience to walk over the sites of the battles, and visit the places that, for a short time at least, had become household names.

The Argentinians had built a defensive horseshoe around Stanley and the harbour, fortifying all the high ground, from Wireless Ridge across Mount Longdon, Tumbledown Mountain and Sapper Hill. Jeff, Nick and I set out to walk this ridge line. The first mile or two was easy enough, along the road to the western end of the harbour. We had our first glimpse of the war when we found the ruins of the Moody Brook Barracks, which had been levelled in a mortar attack during the first assault.

From the barracks we headed north for Wireless Ridge. As soon as we left the road, we realised that the going was not going to be easy. The land is mostly peat bog covered in a wiry, coarse grass. For the most part we were able to keep our feet dry, but every now and then, usually with a loud curse, one of us would break through a particularly boggy bit and squelch into knee-deep muddy water. It was hard going. The struggle we were having brought home to us just how fit the marines had been who force marched some 26 miles across the island in the dark, carrying full kit. The fact that they were able to surprise the Argentinians by arriving behind them suggests that the Argentinians too had thought the feat would be impossible.

Huffing and puffing, we scrambled up onto the ridge. On the pretext of admiring the view of the harbour below us, I suggested a pause, and sat down on the driest spot I could find. All around us were craters in the peat from mortars and shells that must have literally rained down on the defending Argentinians.

Jeff, lighting a cigarette, joined me. Nick, ever the restless one, was roaming about along the ridge. He called us over to see what he had found. We ambled over, to see him poking at something sticking out of the side of the crater. He was scraping the mud away from a brown cylindrical object, about 18in long. Nick reckoned it was a fire extinguisher, and was all for digging it out and taking it back as a souvenir. Jeff pointed out that fire extinguishers do not have fins on the end, and started to back away in a tactical retreat. It could have been an unexploded shell of some sort. We were in one of the areas thought to be safe, but not closely swept, so it was entirely possible. We gathered a few stones and a couple of sticks to mark the spot, and decided that we would report it when we got back down to Stanley. Let the experts decide what to do with it.

We struck off westwards along the ridge, towards Mount Longdon, trying to be careful about where we trod. We had been grumbling about stepping into mud holes on the way up, but it would be a lot worse to tread on a mine! As we struggled up the flank of Mount Longdon, there were ever-increasing signs of the battle. Dozens of slit trenches had been cut into the hill, and even though the battle had been fought several years before, there were many things inside left by the surrendering troops. We found mess kits, bits and pieces of clothing and boots galore. Inside one, wedged in a niche in the rocks, Nick found a comic book in Spanish. Many of the Argentinian troops had been teenage conscripts. We could just visualise a cold, wet, homesick, young kid, huddled in the trench, probably scared out of his mind, seeking solace from his magazine. The war suddenly took on a personal touch. Real people had fought and died here.

The slopes of Mount Longdon were closely covered with trenches, many of them still connected by wires from field telephones. All around them were craters, big and small, where falling shells had exploded. It must have been truly awful to have been there, for soldiers on both sides.

On the top of Mount Longdon, 600ft above the harbour, was a small memorial and some wilted flowers. Fairly recently, somebody had taken the trouble to climb all the way up there to leave flowers. Sad. We ate lunch, and nobody talked much.

We scrambled back down to the road, skirted a well-marked minefield, and began the hardest climb of the day, up the rugged side of Mount Tumbledown. It is aptly named – the top is little more than a heap of gigantic boulders. It is steep enough to make the climb hard work. We reminded ourselves that we were doing it on a summer's day; the troops attacking the mountain had done it on a winter's night, carrying weapons and fighting kit, with people trying their hardest to shoot them. After a struggle we reached the top, and found another memorial and a magnificent view down the harbour and across the town.

On the mountain were the remains of quite intricate bunkers, built in among the rocks. Some were connected by passages, some were out on their own. Again there was still a surprising amount of abandoned personal gear in the bunkers. Real people had been hiding here as well.

After catching our breath, and waiting for my pulse to go below 200, we made our way down the eastern flank, towards Sapper Hill. This was the last high ground before Stanley, although it was much lower than the other hills. Much of that was still fenced off with minefield markers, so we skirted the edge and dropped down into Stanley.

A bunker on the top of Tumbledown Mountain, that has now become a memorial. Looking down the length of Port Stanley harbour.

The next morning Jeff and I went to report the 'fire extinguisher' that we had found on Wireless Ridge. We met Captain King, who was in charge of the bomb-disposal crew. He asked us to describe the thing and as soon as we mentioned two yellow stripes, he said they would have to go and attend to it. Yellow stripes, he explained, are the international symbol for high explosive. As the Boss's arrival was increasingly imminent, I explained that we did not have time to walk all the way back up there. He laughed and told us that he was not going to walk either; we would all drive.

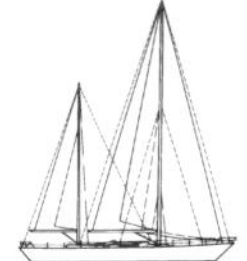

The Captain said we could take the rest of the crew, so Jeff ran back for the others and we all piled into a very curious vehicle. It looked like a small tank towing a trailer, but in fact it was all one vehicle, articulated in the middle. The part that looked like a trailer had tracks like the front section, and both sets of tracks were driven. Lana and I got the last two seats in front with the bomb crew while Jeff and the boys were put in the back where, the soldiers warned them, the ride was much rougher. We trundled off down the road.

At the foot of the ridge, the driver just turned off the road and headed straight up the hill. Boggy peat or jagged rocks all seemed the same to this vehicle. We went straight up the side of the hill that we had stumbled up with so much effort the day before, and found the 'fire extinguisher' without too much effort. The boys emerged from the back of the vehicle looking a little pale. It was rough enough for us in the front, but apparently in the back they had been well shaken about.

One quick look by the bomb crew confirmed that it was an unexploded Argentinian mortar shell. Captain King tied a long piece of wire round the tail and, from what he deemed to be a safe distance, pulled it out of the mud. It did not go bang, so with what was perhaps

Captain King examines the unexploded mortar shell we found. He decided it was too rusty to take back to their depot, so blew it up on site.

a touch of bravado, he picked it up. It was pretty rusty, so he said it was not safe to defuse and take back to Stanley, which was fine by me; I would not have wanted to ride back down that bumpy mountain inside a tin box with a live bomb!

He decided to blow it up right there on the ridge. He put it into one of the deeper craters to minimise the chance of shrapnel flying about. Next he stuck a piece of plastic explosive and a detonator on the side. We needed no encouragement to stand back. It went off with a surprisingly loud bang, and the crater where it had been sitting was now about 4ft across. We tried to imagine what it must have been like to be hiding in a trench with these things raining down all night long. Awful.

Back on the boat, the preparations continued. *Monsunen* left to do her rounds, so we had to move out to anchor. Her place on the dock was taken by one of the British Antarctic Survey ships, the *John Biscoe*. Somehow we managed to get ourselves invited on board for a cocktail party, and her Captain, Chris, offered to let *Thalassi* lie alongside as she had done with *Monsunen*. He also told us some fascinating tales about his many trips into the Antarctic, supplying the various bases.

Monday was a festive day. It was Nick's birthday, and Lana found our mail at the Post Office. Our excitement at getting the mail was somewhat overshadowed when we opened our bank statement. We had not been paid for the last three months. That would give us a good opening conversation with the Boss when he arrived.

We celebrated Nick's birthday with lunch at the southernmost fish and chip shop in the world. It was fortuitous that we did, because Lana found out that the owner of the shop also imported fruit and vegetables, and he was expecting his monthly shipment that very night. She went back at 4 p.m. to find she was at the back of a long queue. By the time she had worked her way up to the front, there was not much left, but she did get some apples, a few grapefruit and a big bag of onions.

The butcher came to *Thalassi* to deliver Lana's order. Ostensibly we got lamb chops, legs of lamb and several pounds of lamb mince, as per Lana's request. It was only after the butcher had been paid, and we were chatting over a drink in the cockpit, that he explained the economics of sheep farming. In the Falklands sheep are reared primarily for their wool. They will produce good wool for four or perhaps five years, after which the quality falls off, so the animals are killed. That is when the butcher gets his hands on them. Young lambs are not killed for meat, because they are too valuable for their five years' worth of wool. So we had just filled the freezer with what turned out to be very tough five-year-old sheep. When Lana roasted the first of the legs, it looked and smelled delicious, but it blunted the sharpest knife and defied the strongest teeth. The expression 'tough as an old boot', could be rewritten as 'tough as an old sheep'. It was like rubber. The only way we could eat any of it was minced up as lamb burgers.

The second BAS ship came in. She was newer and bigger than the *Biscoe*, and was painted the same striking red colour. Her name was the *Bransfield*, and it did not take us long to be invited on board for a tour. She had much more modern equipment than the *Biscoe*, and I was especially fascinated by a TV display which gave a real-time picture from a satellite above. They used it mainly for spotting big icebergs, but it was equally valuable for looking at what sort of weather was coming. The cloud lines of approaching fronts were clearly visible. I wanted one!

During the tour, we met a young doctor, Tony. He had just been picked up by the ship after spending a winter with fifteen others at Halley Base, deep in the Antarctic. Apart from looking after the health of everybody on the base, he had been doing various experiments. Now he had several months to wait until his samples reached Britain before he could complete his projects. He asked if we needed any more crew. The timing was fortuitous. Chris was waiting to hear about a date to go back to a job in the 'real world', so we were casting around for another crew member to replace him. Since the insurance company insisted on five crew, I thought it better to have one extra for a few weeks than to end up one short in Patagonia. We told him to come over to *Thalassi* for a talk.

I let him talk to Nick and Jeff first. They could explain to him about the martinet skipper, the cantankerous cook and the wayward owner, and then if he was still interested, he could talk to Lana and me. We took an instant liking to him. He was extremely intelligent, quick on the uptake, and had a good sense of humour. Jeff liked him and Nick seemed ambivalent. Chris was a bit put out that we would even consider replacing him with somebody who had never sailed before. I said that I felt he could learn the sailing, but what he already had was the ability to rub along with other people in a confined space. If he could live underground in the big plywood tube which was Halley Base with fifteen other people for a year, then he would probably manage to fit in with us.

It was agreed, and we signed him on. He would join us just in time for the Boss's arrival.

Chapter 11

In and Around the Falkland Islands

The day of the Boss's arrival dawned. We all made an early start to finish off the last bits of cleaning and polishing. Just before breakfast, we received a message that he had missed one of his flight connections, and the next plane was not due for another four days. Suddenly the pressure was off. The boat was near enough ready, so we could take a few days to play with a clear conscience. We could do a bit of serious exploring. Jeff decided to celebrate by going back to sleep. It was agreed among the rest of us that we would have a lazy day in Stanley, then make a short expedition to one or two of the nearby islands for a couple of days.

A couple of hours later I received another interesting piece of news on the radio. While we are travelling, I try and make daily contact on the ham radio with a couple of friends. One lives in Michigan, near Lana's family, and the other is in Ireland. We had a house in Baltimore, in west Cork, where we spent some time when we were not sailing, and our friend Neilie lives a few miles away in Skibbereen. I am still not sure quite how he managed it, but Neilie had unearthed an old newspaper cutting about Conor O'Brien, and the building of a boat in Baltimore for the Falkland Island Company in 1926. Neilie asked us to enquire about the boat, called the *Ilen*, and see if we could find out what had happened to her.

After the radio contact, I went back up into the cockpit and scouted around the harbour with the binoculars. I had noticed an old green ketch anchored behind us, only because she was the same colour as the *Monsunen*. Sure enough, as she swung on her anchor, I saw the name *Ilen* on her stern. Lana and I went ashore to ask in the company office if we could go on board. No problem, they said, so off we went. That she was still in commission after more than fifty years in these stormy waters is surely a tribute to her builders. Her engine has been replaced, but otherwise she is as built.

Conor O'Brien had stopped in the Falklands in the course of a circumnavigation. People from the company had admired his boat, the *Saoirse*, and tried to buy it. He refused to sell, and instead offered to build a new boat and deliver it the 8000 miles from Baltimore. The

The Ilen, *built in Baltimore in West Cork, where at the time we had our home. She was sailed out from Baltimore by Conor O'Brien in 1926, and is still in regular use.*

result was the 56ft ketch *Ilen.*

She had no sails bent on when we saw her, but they do still regularly use her under power for short-haul deliveries, mainly running supplies out to the fishing boats anchored in the bay outside Stanley. In the wheelhouse, the builder's brass plaque naming Baltimore made us feel intensely homesick.

Tony moved on board *Thalassi*, and was happy enough to find that he would have a few days to get to know his way around the boat before the Boss arrived. It was all new to him, but it was uncanny how quickly he was able to learn things. Nothing ever had to be explained twice.

The anchorage recommended in the Admiralty Pilot Book, in the centre of St Peter and St Paul's Rocks. Darwin landed at this spot from Beagle*'s whaleboat, so it must have been calmer for him than it was for us. The only way we could get ashore was to swim.*

Swimming with the dolphin at Fernando. Darwin never mentions swimming, let alone diving. What would he have made of swimming underwater with the dolphin? We loved it.

Waiting for a breeze. Local boat becalmed in the lee of Itaparica, on her way to the market in Salvador.

Above: Any time the penguins got fed up with us following them, they would head into the sea, with a look as if to say 'Are you going to follow us now?'

Right: The skipper out on the end of the pole, checking for chafe; a common enemy that we shared with the Beagle.

It was only when we got close to the albatross that we realised how big they are. They were totally unafraid of us, and it was the size of their beaks that made us keep a respectful distance.

The fluffy albatross chicks sat on their pedestal-like nests waiting to be fed. Their feathers are not yet developed enough for them to fly. Neither they nor their parents minded us getting close to them.

Once they had enough of us photographing them, the King penguins walked down into the breakers and swam out to sea, confident that we would not follow them into the icy water.

Going ashore at Keppel Island. Many of these farms are so remote that the inhabitants only get to visit Stanley but once or twice a year. They rely on George and the Monsunen *for all their supplies.*

Thalassi *sailing past the Romanche glacier in the Beagle Channel – the blue of the ice almost matching the colour of her hull. This was the first big glacier we saw, and it was probably on the beach opposite the glacier, that Darwin and crew nearly perished when an icefall sent a wave across the channel which almost washed their boats away.*

Off the Garibaldi glacier, where we spent a worrysome night in the worst anchorage we found in Patagonia.

Thalassi *moored in 300 feet of water in front of Glacier Asia. We did not need to anchor – the ice held her snugly.*

Estero Peel, near Glacier Asia.

Thalassi *anchored off the beach at Puyuguapi, waiting for Jose to join us.*

Our first little expedition, and Tony's first sail, was up the coast a few miles to Cow Bay. We anchored in the bay and dinghied over to the beach. It was a bit of a scramble up the low cliffs to get to the grassy meadowland that overlooked the bay. We could hear the Magellanic penguins well before we got to the top. They sounded uncannily like a herd of donkeys. After hearing all this noise, we were surprised when we saw how small they were, only about 18in tall. Instead of the solitary bird that Darwin described, we found a colony of hundreds, maybe even thousands. There were a few sheep grazing unconcernedly in among the penguins. They were very shy of us, and ran off if we walked anywhere near them, but the little penguins were much braver. They would stand their ground as we walked up to them.

Magellanic penguins at Cow Bay. They were quite unafraid of us, unless we got too close, when they would dive into the nearest burrow, often to the digust of the occupant.

Magellanics are unusual in the world of penguins in that they live in burrows, just like rabbits. In fact the only other birds that I can think of which live in burrows are puffins, but there may be others.

Although the Magellanics are remarkably brave little birds, there are limits to how near they would let us come. If we got too close, then they would panic, and bolt into their burrows. Sometimes, in its haste, one would dive down what was obviously the wrong burrow. A cacophony of donkey noises would then accompany it as it came flying out backwards. It would usually give us a reproachful look before dashing off to try its luck down the next burrow.

Some of the penguins liked to stay and watch us from the safety of their burrow entrances, seemingly as interested in us as we were in them. They did not seem to be able to look straight ahead, but swivelled their heads from side to side as they studied us, first with one eye, then the other. If we stood over their burrow, their heads would turn round through 180 degrees to look at us. When they stood watching us like that, it looked as if they had their heads on back to front. Kodak shares must have gone up at least ten points in the hour or two we spent there.

From Cow Bay, we walked a couple of miles along the shore to Victory Beach, a wonderful white beach, that really *was* pristine. It stretched unbroken for at least half a mile across a shallow bay. We climbed down to it, and spotted half a dozen King penguins among many hundreds more Magellanics. They are the biggest, and least common, of the five types of penguins found in the Falklands. They are at least 3ft tall, and strut about imperiously among their lesser subjects. They are better groomed than the Magellanics, some of which have a tendency to look a bit scruffy. The Kings dress in smooth grey-blue coats, very white shirts and smart yellow cravats.

The Magellanics, when they are dashing about on the land, often use their wings like front legs; nothing so ungainly for the kings. When they had finally had enough of the paparazzi and their clicking cameras, they walked slowly and majestically down the beach into the surf. With a last royal look at us over their shoulders, they took off through the waves, as if daring us to follow.

Our second expedition was to Kidney Island, a very small island a few miles from Stanley. Kidney is interesting for two reasons. Probably because it is so small, it has never had sheep grazed on it, and so it still has the original vegetation of tussock grass. The locals had also told us that there was a colony of fur seals living there.

We found a nice anchorage to the south of the island, and took the dinghy in to the stony beach. Across the front of the beach there was a broad band of kelp, thick and rubbery seaweed which seemed designed to tangle propellers on outboard motors. I stopped the engine just before it ground to a halt, and Nick and Chris paddled the last few yards to the beach. There were two large male fur seals, together with three smaller females, at one end of the beach. The males were growling, roaring and puffing up their necks as we approached, so we diplomatically chose the other end of the beach to make our landing.

Tony, our new resident expert, told us about the differences between seals and sea-lions. He explained that the first things to look at are their ears. Most seals do not have external ears, and all these so-called earless seals swim by using their back flippers for propulsion and their front ones for steering. The back flippers have become well adapted for this, almost fusing together to form a single tail. Whilst this tail is very good in the water, it is not much use on land. When these seals come ashore, they have to more or less flop along in a rather ungainly manner.

A baby fur seal on the north side of Kidney Island. We didn't want to get too close, in case Mum or Dad were watching. A big fur seal is an intimidating proposition.

The seals with external ears, which include the fur seals, and sea-lions, move in a different way. They swim by using mainly their forward fins for propulsion, and the back ones for steering. On shore, they are able to swivel the rear flippers forward, to make them effectively four-legged. As a result, Tony warned us, they can move very quickly on land, and as they have big, ugly teeth, he suggested we treat them with the utmost respect. That was fine by me; I was happy to watch them from the other end of the beach.

Nick was not going to be intimidated by some old seals dressed up in fur coats – at least not at first. He wanted a close-up photograph. With his Australian bravado, he marched up to the watching seals. The two males were some 8 or 9ft long, and by Tony's estimate weighted about 600lb apiece. The biggest made eye contact with Nick, who swears he saw the seal lick its lips before letting out a gigantic roar. Without breaking his stride, Nick did a 180-degree turn, and beat a reasonably dignified retreat.

We decided to try to cross over to the other side of the island, where the main colony of seals were said to live. The beach was fringed with the tussock grass which used to cover all the islands before man introduced cattle, horses and sheep, and allowed them to run wild. From a distance the grass looked pretty much like any unkempt meadow, with the grass growing in little tufts. When we came close, however, we found that it was more than 6ft tall, and one could easily walk between the tufts. Feeling a bit like Gulliver in the land of the giants, we set off along the paths between the gigantic tufts of grass.

Tony explained that the paths had been made by the seals, and we should make a noise so as not to surprise one. Nick was elected as the bravest, and certainly the noisiest, and was sent on ahead, armed with a dinghy paddle. At first he started shouting a warning to any hidden seals, 'I'm bad. Don't mess with me. I'm bad.' After the first little rustle of the leaves, however, his chant became 'I'm scared, you don't need to mess with me.'

He retreated to the back of the line. We took a vote on who was dispensable enough to be put at the front. We could not do without the cook, so Lana was safe. We would need the doctor if anybody did get bitten, so Tony off the hook. Chris already had his ticket to fly out from Punta Arenas, so he could not risk it. Only Jeff could prevent complete mayhem from developing in the engine room. Nobody, however, seemed to feel the skipper was needed at all, so I found myself unanimously voted to the front of the line.

It was unnerving poking along through the giant tufts of grass, expecting at any moment to be attacked by an enormous seal.

Lana and the tussock grass of Kidney Island. We were very wary of meeting a fur seal in among the grass.

Whether it was Nick's continuing noise that did the trick, or just that no seals wanted to use the path at that time, however, we safely crossed to the other side without even a glimpse of a seal.

It was worth the adrenalin. We found ourselves at the top of a rocky ledge, overlooking a whole family of seals, about 15 or 20ft below us. There were three little pups, looking friendly and fluffy, with the mother and maybe her sister lying beside them. They were all being watched over by big, ugly father. We did not try to get close, but satisfied ourselves with watching them from the cliff top.

The way back through the grass was not nearly so traumatic, at

least not for me, as Jeff went first. Going back never seems to take as long as getting there anyway. Back on the beach, we found that the two big male seals had moved much nearer to the dinghy. I wondered whether they were going to give us problems as we tried to drag the dinghy back into the water. I had recently read an account of some people who had visited the Antarctic, and had left their black rubber dinghy pulled up on a beach. A big, myopic fur seal had spotted it, not recognised it for what it was, and tried to make love to it. When it failed to respond to his amorous advances, he had bitten it. After it burst, he had ripped it to shreds, leaving the people stranded on the beach with an over-sexed, frustrated seal. We were luckier. We got to the dinghy and although we got ugly looks and a few growls as we dragged it back down the beach, the seals did not try to eat us, and the dinghy retained its virginity.

Back in Stanley, the *Biscoe* had moved off the dock to let *Monsunen* back to her normal spot. As we came into the harbour George very kindly waved for us to come back alongside him.

The Boss finally arrived at lunchtime the next day. I went out to the new and enormous airport at Mount Pleasant to meet him. Before they were allowed to leave the airport, all the new arrivals had to sit through a short lecture about the danger of mines, and they were each given a mine map.

He wanted to sail the next morning, but the wind was howling out of the north-west, effectively pinning us to *Monsunen*'s side. So although he would have happily had us set off to sea, fortunately we could not move the boat with the wind pressing her so hard against the *Monsunen*. We took him on a tour of the harbour area, showing him some of the old wrecks, but he showed only a cursory interest; he was anxious to be off.

That evening we told him about our bank statement, and the missing pay. He was a bit flustered, but explained that he was reorganising his financial affairs, and since he had lost track of how many standing order payments were being made from his various accounts, he had stopped them all! He promised to sort it all out when he got back, and assured us that we would be paid. When we told Jeff, he decided that he had better contact his bank and see if his pay was arriving. It turned out it was not. The only crew receiving any money were Nick, Chris and now Tony, as Lana paid them on board, from petty cash.

The wind eased a little that evening, so we moved out to anchor, so that we would not be pinned on again if the wind freshened in the morning.

Freshen it did. It was so fresh it was howling again. It was blowing over 30 knots, but that was not going to stop the Boss, so off we set. I suggested that we go to Kidney Island again. I knew that the anchorage there would be snug in the north-wester. That was not far enough away for the Boss, however, he wanted to get to Salvador, halfway along the north coast of East Falkland. He scorned the radio forecast of strong gales and extremely rough seas, and insisted that *Thalassi* could take it. Perhaps she could, but I was less than sure that the mast or the crew could!

It was not too bad in the lee of the land, but when we turned the corner and felt the full strength of the gale, it was awful. There must have been a good current against us, because after three hours of hard sailing, bashing and crashing to windward, we had only made about 8 miles. As tactfully as I could, I pointed out to the Boss that there was no chance of getting to Salvador before dark – at the present rate of progress it would be about lunch time the next day. Reluctantly he agreed to let me turn round and run back and look for another anchorage for the night. Volunteer Beach was the nearest anchorage that would give us reasonable protection, but even that was a couple of hours away.

It turned out to be a snug enough anchorage, but we could not go ashore as the beach was shown as one that was mined. It cannot have been too thickly mined, however, because on the beach there was a big fur seal, which weighed a lot more than a person. If he did not set the mines off then nor would we, but nobody, not even Nick, wanted to take that chance.

We watched the fur seal stalking a big goose. It looked rather like a big cat, sneaking along, low to the ground. When it was about 15 or 20ft away, it pounced. The speed was amazing for such a big beast. It caught the goose totally by surprise. After catching it, the seal batted it about, just like a cat toying with a little bird or a mouse, before finally settling down to eat it. I vowed not to get within 20ft of a hungry fur seal!

Fortunately the wind eased again during the night, and we traversed the north coast the next day without too much trouble. By mid-afternoon, we were anchored in San Carlos Water. This is a good-sized bay off Falkland Sound, which is the strait that separates the two main islands. We were struck with another pang of homesickness. With the cool misty weather, rolling green hills and rugged, rocky shore, we could just as easily be anchored off our house in west Cork, Ireland.

San Carlos was where the main British assault force landed to retake the islands. Several ships were sunk in the sound, and many men died in the landing. We went ashore at the settlement, and

walked up to visit the stone-walled cemetery, where many of them lay. It was terribly moving. We saw the grave of Colonel H. Jones, who led the assault. What was most upsetting were the graves of some of the young soldiers. Many were still teenagers when they died. On most of the graves were personal letters sent out by parents, brothers, sisters and sometimes wives and children. It was not just the cold wind that made my eyes water. It was sad. We asked ourselves, why?

The British Cemetery at San Carlos, where, amongst others, Col 'H' Jones is buried. It is very moving to read the personal family messages affixed to many of the graves of the young soldiers.

After a few quiet moments in the cemetery, we walked over to the nearby farm. Sheep shearing was in full swing, and we were invited into the shed to watch. Each farm has its own shearing shed, but in most cases the actual work is done by a group of itinerants who travel from farm to farm. Some come from as far away as Scotland or New

Zealand for the seasonal work. They use electric clippers, and it is incredible how quickly they remove each fleece. It was funny to see the bemused, newly shorn sheep emerge from the shed, shivering in the cool breeze. The foreman showed us how the wool is sorted by grade and then, using a very old manual press, squeezed into bales of some 500lb each, ready for George to collect with the *Monsunen*.

Over the next few days we made our way steadily west. The weather was like the little girl with the curl. When it was good, it was very very good, and when it was bad it was bloody awful.

We had a very pleasant sail to Keppel Island, then had to hole up there for an extra day while the next depression rattled up from Cape Horn. While we were at Keppel Island, we went to another penguin colony. This time they were gentoos. Again they were there in their thousands, living in apparent harmony with hundreds of ducks.

Perhaps the most exciting wildlife encounter, however, was our first visit to an albatross colony on Saunders Island. Saunders is quite a large island, but it is farmed by a single family. The farmers, David and Susan, had few enough visitors, and were proud to show us their island and its wildlife. They invited us all up to the house for tea, then we piled into two ex-army Land Rovers and they drove us over to the western side of the island.

Along the cliff tops was a colony of albatrosses. The young were some three months old, and already about the size of a full-grown chicken. They were covered in a fluffy grey down, and it would still be several weeks before they would be able to fly. Until that time they were destined to sit on their nests, being fed by their parents. The nests are curious pedestal-shaped structures, about 12in high. They seem to be built of seaweed and grass, cemented together by mud or perhaps the albatross's own droppings. One chick stands purposefully on each pedestal. As a parent swoops in to land beside the nest, the chick starts clacking its beak. The parent sticks its own beak far down the chick's gullet and regurgitates the food for it.

The chicks showed no fear of us. If we went very close to them they would start clacking their beaks, not from fear but, I think because they were hoping for us to regurgitate some food for them. Not even the adult birds were frightened of us. If we sat quietly beside a nest, one of the parents would often come swooping in, to land within inches of us and proceed to feed the chick. I think we were more wary of them than they were of us. At least to begin with, it was a little unnerving to make eye contact with such big birds at such close range. Their curved beaks are at least 4 or 5in long, and they were often pointed in our direction, from perhaps 1ft away. Never once, however, did they show the slightest sign of aggression, or

Many of the albatross nests were perched on the edge of the cliffs. While this was precarious for the young, it made it easier for the parents, who just had to step off the cliff to be airborne. Even parents with their young were happy to let us get as close as we wanted to.

indeed of fear.

When the parents want to take off, they nonchalantly stroll over to the edge of the cliff and step off into space. Just by spreading their wings, they soar away in the air currents blowing up the cliff. They do not give even a single flap with their wings. It is totally effortless.

Far below us, on the lower portions of the cliff, we could see our fourth kind of penguins, the comical little rockhoppers. It was so funny to watch them pop out of the water like small missiles, to land unerringly on a rock with a sort of 'Who me?' expression.

Leaving Saunders Island, we had our first look at krill, the shrimp-like creatures that abound in the southern ocean and form a major link in the food chain that supports all the wild life. We caught them in a very un-Darwinian way. As we were getting ready to hoist the anchor, the ever-vigilant Jeff spotted that the engine was running a little hotter than normal. He stopped it to investigate, and found the filter for the cooling water intake was blocked with half a bucketful of krill. I was surprised at how big they were; for some reason I had imagined them to be some microscopic form of plankton, but they were the size of small shrimp. The Boss wanted Lana to boil them up for lunch, but I persuaded Jeff to 'accidently' dump them, as we had no idea how long they had been in the filter. They were well and truely dead, and some might have been there for a day or two.

At each island we visited, we received an equally warm welcome ashore. On these outer islands, the people rarely get into Stanley, and generally their only visitors are George on the *Monsunen* or the other

Chris makes his first, slightly wary encounter with the Carcass Island Sea Elephants.

supply ship, the *Forest.* A few of the farms have bulldozed out an airstrip, and some of them offer R and R accommodtion to the soldiers from Mount Pleasant. Without exception, they seemed pleased to see visitors, and took a proprietorial interest in showing us 'their' wildlife.

Rob on Carcass Island took us to see his sea elephants. What monsters they were. The males can exceed 20ft in length, and more than 7000lb in weight, but it is not just the size that has given them their name. The males have a curiously shaped nose, remarkably like a somewhat shortened elephant's trunk.

He showed us several sea elephants on a beach, stretched out in the sun. Then he took us along a path through some tussock grass to where a family group of half a dozen were lying. Rob told us that they were ashore for moulting, which they do annually at the end of the breeding season. They were snuggled together in a muddy little hollow, sighing, burping and making smells in total satisfaction. I told Nick that with the noises and smells they were making, they reminded me of him relaxing after a big meal. He did not think it was funny.

We could get pretty much as close to them as we wanted, for as long as we could stand the smell. The biggest, and presumably the oldest, male was a bit protective, however. If anybody ventured a little bit too close, he would growl and burp until we retreated. Despite their bad breath (from both ends), their mouths looked pink, clean and soft. They had big, weepy-looking eyes which Lana found appealing.

In the area around the sea elephants, there were literally thousands of seabirds. Rob identified some of them for us. He pointed out kelp and dolphin gulls, heron, black-browed albatross, kelp and upland geese, more Magellanic penguins and, flying amongst them all, cariacara hawks. There were not just one or two of each species, but, with the exception of the hawks, hundreds if not thousands. As we walked along the northern point of Carcass Island we could easily imagine that we had stepped into Hitchcock's movie, *The Birds.* There were birds everywhere, and the noise was quite deafening.

My favourite island was West Point. Roddy and Lillian, the owners, were as welcoming as everybody else, and we were soon invited up to the house for the obligatory cup of tea. Lillian is a keen gardener and, against all odds, she has cultivated a wonderful rose garden in a sunken, well-screened area that Roddy has built for her. The whole farm is spick and span, and very well organised.

Roddy drove us across to their albatross colony. It was even more extensive than the one on Saunders. There were hundreds of fluffy

Compared to the King penguins, the Rockhoppers looked decidely scruffy, but they provided an endless source of entertainment, watching them literally hopping up and down the steep rocky cliffs.

grey chicks, all clacking their beaks as we walked past them. Once more there were Rockhopper penguins living below the colony. None was swimming, so we could not watch them doing their trick of popping up out of the water, but we did see them hopping up surprisingly steep cliffs. They seem to be unable to waddle like the Gentoos or Magellanics; they appear to hop everywhere they go. These penguins have a distinctive fringe of spiky yellow feathers over their bright orange eyes. We graded them better dressed than the scruffy Magellanics, but nowhere near as smart as the kings or even the Gentoos, who were voted into second place.

As we made our way back to the boat, Roddy gave Lana two enormous cabbages, and three lettuces which were nearly as big. All were fresh from the garden, and Lana was munching away on the lettuce before she was even out of the dinghy. In the bay, Tony identified our first oystercatchers for us. They were poking about on the beach with their long red chisel-shaped beaks.

Our departure from West Point was slightly delayed by another bucketful of krill in the filter, and an enormous ball of kelp round the anchor. When the anchor came up, it was lost from sight in a tangle of kelp some 4 or 5ft across. Nick was lowered over the side with the bread knife, and it took him several minutes to cut away the rubbery kelp so that we could stow the anchor.

Our last Falkland stop was to be at New Island, at the western tip of the group. This island is privately owned, and is being kept as a nature reserve. The owners were away in Stanley, but we managed to get permission by radio to explore it. Next to the landing spot, I was excited to find a Jarvis brace winch, still in working order. This winch is what revolutionised the last days of commercial sail, and allowed the ships to sail with much reduced crew. It consists of a pair of conical drums, which haul in the brace from one side of a sail's yard while letting out the other. The geometry of the thing is very subtle, since the rate at which the rope is hauled in varies as the sail swings round during a tack or gybe. Here was one, bolted to the end of a concrete ramp, used now for hauling dinghies out of the water. What ignominy.

Nobody else shared my interest or enthusiasm, and I was soon escorted off to the next penguin colony. I have to say that this was one of the best. We were able to walk right down among the rock-hoppers, which were so thick on the ground in places that we had to be careful not to tread on them. Sometimes it was even necessary to push them gently aside to gain a foothold.

During our last day at New Island, we made our preparations for the passage to Cape Horn. We took off the large jib and stowed it below, leaving the smaller Number 2 jib in place. The storm jib and trysail came out of their stowage, and I got the crew to try hoisting each in turn. It was easy enough in the quiet calm of a sheltered anchorage, but I hoped that we would not have to set them in a Cape Horn storm.

After we had finished our chores, Chris and Tony dared each other into going for a swim. The water temperature was just 9 degrees above freezing. It was funny watching their reactions as they hit the water: I would say their swim should be entered in the *Guinness Book of Records* as the world's shortest. We did not think it was possible for two people to come up the ladder at the same time.

Lana baked an extra supply of bread and cooked a giant pot of stew. It all went into the freezer ready in case conditions became too rough to cook.

I was sad to be leaving the Falklands. We had only scratched the surface of this wonderful cruising ground, but at least we had done better than Darwin. How could he have missed so much?

It was time to visit new places. As Darwin had said a 150 years before, Cape Horn was now to be the gateway to further adventures.

Chapter 12

Cape Horn

As *Beagle* was making her way south into Le Maire Strait, Fitzroy chose to hug the shore of Tierra del Fuego, trying to gain some shelter from the endless westerly gales. In his journal, Darwin described the days as cold, gloomy and gusty. Off to the east they could see the forbidding sight of Staten Island, with its inhospitable rocky shoreline and snow-capped mountains.

Despite the bad weather, and another bout of seasickness, Darwin was thrilled to be visiting Tierra del Fuego. He was looking forward to some serious exploring of what he described as 'a country never before traversed by Europeans'.

Tierra del Fuego was discovered by Magellan in 1520, when he sailed through the strait which is named after him. It is a large island, over 28,000 square miles. To the north it is bounded by the Straits of Magellan, and to the south by the Beagle Channel. For the 300 years from its discovery to the beginning of the *Beagle*'s survey, it was rarely visited, and little was known of the land or the people who lived there.

In 1881, forty-eight years after Darwin's visit, the territory was divided between Chile and Argentina, with Chile getting the western two-thirds. The remaining islands to the south were arbitrarily allocated to the two countries at the same time. Nobody seemed to care much until oil was discovered in 1945. Ever since then, who owns what has been a serious bone of contention between Chile and Argentina.

Of course Darwin could not know anything of this, nor did he know that Tierra del Fuego's highest peak would be named after him. Mount Darwin is 7999ft high. If only we had had the time, I would have loved to go up and put another rock on top to make it up to 8000ft.

Working their way down the Fuegan coast, always on the lookout for new anchorages, Captain Fitzroy spotted a good sheltered bay, so they pulled in for the night. The bay was almost completely surrounded by comparatively low, rounded mountains. The slopes were thickly wooded, with the trees coming right down to the water's edge. The landscape was like nothing Darwin had seen before, and he was hoping to be able to explore it.

That night a gale sprang up. Heavy squalls came down from the mountains, making the *Beagle* tug at her anchor chain. They could see huge waves running past the entrance, but their bay stayed calm enough. Everybody was glad to be at anchor – it was not a night to be at sea. They named the anchorage Good Success Bay.

When they first sailed into the bay, a group of Fuegans had stood on the point watching them, waving their ragged capes and shouting. As soon as the wind began to ease in the morning, Captain Fitzroy sent a group ashore to talk to them. Darwin went of course, together with the three Fuegans they had on board.

To Darwin's disappointment they could not communicate at all. The three Fuegans from the ship could understand those on land no better than anybody else. To Darwin's ear their language was a barely articulate series of grunts. Captain Cook, on his visit, described it as sounding like a man clearing his throat.

This seems to be the first time that Darwin took much of an interest in the three Fuegans on board the *Beagle* – at least it is the first time he mentions them in his journal. It is surprising to me that he seems to have largely ignored them until then, especially as it was ostensibly to take them home that the voyage was being undertaken at all.

All three of them had become reasonably good at speaking and understanding English, but the girl, Fuegia Basket, was the linguist of the trio. Not only was her English the best, but she had picked up a fair smattering of Spanish and Portuguese on their voyage south. The younger man, Jemmy Button, who had been swopped for a pearl button, was the favourite with the crew. He was almost always cheerful and laughing. When Darwin was seasick, he would come to visit him, saying 'Poor, poor fellow', while at the same time laughing at him, as he could not believe that a bit of rough water could make somebody ill.

Jemmy was short, thick and fat, yet exceedingly vain. He wore his hair very short, and loved to study himself in a mirror. He almost always wore gloves, and would be very irritated if his highly polished shoes got scuffed.

The surviving adult was called York Minster, not after the cathedral itself, but after a large rock near his home, which in 1768 had reminded a homesick Captain Cook of it. He was a short but powerful man, who tended to be a bit reserved, even taciturn.

Despite the fact that all three were fairly good at English, Darwin had found it quite difficult to get information from them about the

way they had lived before coming on the *Beagle*. Sometimes it seemed to him as if the Fuegans thought in a different way to the Europeans, and they were often overwhelmed by the apparent complexity of what Darwin took to be a simple question. He did manage to understand that the living was difficult, and times could be very hard. Jemmy described how, in periods of famine, they killed the old women of the family by suffocating them to death in the smoke of a fire, and ate them. When Darwin asked him why they did not kill and eat the dogs, Jemmy looked at him in utter astonishment. He explained, as if to a child, 'Doggies catch otters. Old women, no.'

So despite his contacts with these three, Darwin was ill prepared to meet the Fuegans on the beach. He thought that they seemed 'like troubled spirits from another world'. They were a 'curious and interesting spectacle'. The only clothing they wore was a cape of guanaco skin, worn with the woolly side out. The guanaco is an animal that looks a bit like a llama. It used to be very common in much of South America, but it has been hunted for its skin almost to the point of extinction.

The Fuegan faces were painted with red, white and black stripes. The remainder of their skin was a reddish, coppery colour. They looked very fierce, and Darwin said that he could not believe 'how wide is the difference between savage and civilised man. It is greater than that between wild and domesticated animals.'

He and Fitzroy had another of their long philosophical discussions, and agreed that these people must be of a different species to themselves, and surely lacked the same high potential. Fitzroy refused to believe that he could be even remotely related to the Fuegans. This time Lieutenant Sullivan took the more sympathetic view, and suggested that the Fuegans were victims of the harsh surroundings in which they found themselves, and were perhaps just adapting to them. Darwin and Fitzroy remained unconvinced.

The Fuegans certainly seemed to have adapted to the cold. The crew of *Beagle* were to see naked mothers suckling bare children, apparently oblivious to the snow falling on their bodies. Most of the Fuegans wore just the cape, which sometimes, as a concession to a particularly cold wind, might be swivelled round and worn on the windward side of their bodies.

Fitzroy was anxious to press on and return Jemmy, Fuegia and York to their own territory, west of Cape Horn. They sailed south in gentle conditions, and rounded the Horn on Christmas Eve, which was a calm, bright evening. They had an almost unprecedented easterly breeze.

Captain Fitzroy felt a bit smug, the crew were all congratulating

themselves on an easy rounding of the Cape, and Darwin wondered what all the fuss was about Cape Horn. Their thoughts were an hour or two premature. Before they could reach an anchorage, the easterly wind vanished and a gale sprang up from the west. They were unceremoniously driven back past Cape Horn. It now looked as forbidding as its reputation. Low, black clouds scudded along and enormous waves broke against the ominous black rocks, throwing spray over the cliffs which are more than 200ft high. Rain and hail was mixed in with the icy cold spray.

Our landfall on Cape Horn itself. Nick and Chris were disappointed not to be rounding in a gale, but the rest of us were happy to take advantage of the brief spell of good weather.

They ran back into the lee of the land, and were fortunate to make an anchorage in a snug little cove in time for Christmas dinner. They dropped three anchors and rode out the gale without any further problems.

It was New Year's Eve before the wind abated and they could sail again. While they were waiting, Darwin tried to explore the area around the bay, but with limited success. Almost all the trees were a kind of beech, with unusual brownish yellow leaves, which Darwin says made the place look gloomy. He soon found that it was not going to be easy to explore, as the underbrush was extremely thick and virtually impenetrable. The only progress he could make was by crawling up the bed of a stream – what devotion to duty!

When *Beagle* set sail again, the wind was still in the west, and quite strong, but they made reasonably good progress. At least Fitzroy thought it was reasonable; Darwin was in the grip of seasickness yet again, and felt it was anything but reasonable.

They weathered the Horn again, and were within a couple of miles of the anchorage at Waterman Island, where York Minster lived, when the wind increased considerably. They took in sail and reefed as the wind got up, until they were down to just the topsails with five reefs in each. They kept beating, but could not make the final few miles. Slowly and inexorably they lost ground, and were swept back past Cape Horn again.

The gale increased to a full storm. Fitzroy reckoned it was the strongest that he had ever seen. They stowed and secured the topsails and set the storm trysail, close reefed, and the forestaysail. Under this rig they lay virtually hove to for two days.

The ship was labouring in the huge seas. The noise of her creaking and groaning could be heard even over the shriek of the wind. The crew were getting tired. Everything they owned was wet, and there was no way to dry their clothes. Even their bunks were wet, and at the end of each watch they turned in 'full standing', without even bothering to get out of their wet oilskins.

Unperturbed by it all were the albatrosses. Even at the height of the storm, Fitzroy recorded that they were swooping and circling around the ship. Darwin was past caring.

One wave, bigger than all the rest, came roaring out of the mist. It stopped the *Beagle* dead in the water. Before she could gather way enough to answer the helm, a second wave hit her. That threw her round, beam on to the waves. The next one broke right over the struggling ship, and pressed her down until the lee bulwarks were several feet under water. One of the whale-boats, which was stowed on deck, filled with water and was swept away.

The two men on the wheel did not need to hear the command to put the helm down to run before the wind. They knew that if another wave hit them now, the ship would probably give up the struggle. It seemed an eternity before she answered her helm and began to turn. Slowly, ever so slowly, she began to turn and come back upright. The water was streaming off her decks in torrents. She was going to live to sail another day.

That turned out to be the last fury of the storm. It was almost as if the wind had tried its best, failed, and had now given up. The wind dropped quite quickly, and despite the large sea that was still running, they crowded on sail, and set off westwards once more.

Cape Horn was passed for the fifth time. This time, Captain Fitzroy decided not to try and go west to Waterman; instead he ducked in under False Cape Horn, and anchored in a small but very deep bay. They anchored in 47 fathoms (282ft) of water. The extra weight of the chain, reaching down to those depths, caused it to run out so fast that sparks flew off the new patent windlass. It was going to be a good test for the windlass to recover all that chain.

At last they were anchored west of Cape Horn. They had made good 30 miles to the west after twenty-four uninterrupted days of cruel beating.

We were hoping for a leisurely breakfast followed by an unhurried departure from New Island, for our attempt on Cape Horn, but we had reckoned without the Boss's impatience. He could not sleep, whether from excitement or fear we did not know. Before dawn he was pacing the deck, banging on cabin doors, anxious to go. He was not even interested in waiting for a proper breakfast. We had to make do with a rushed snack before hoisting the anchor at first light.

We stood out into a blustery south-westerly Force 7 – 30 knots of wind, right on the nose. Not a happy prospect. All day we crashed along. Lana had the worst of it, trying to cook a hot lunch to make up for the abbreviated breakfast. Things were flying off the cooker and going everywhere. Even Nick, with his cast-iron stomach, was off his food.

I was nervous. My confidence in the mast was close to zero. I gave strict orders to all the crew that I was to be called before shaking out any reefs, or at the slightest suggestion of an increase in wind, or if

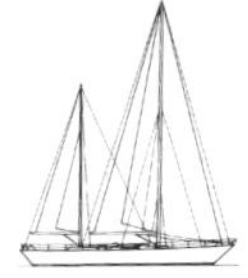

anybody saw an approaching squall. If it was like this now, on what really looked like quite a 'nice' day, what would it be like off the Horn if we were caught?

Dinner was not much easier than lunch had been. Chris was complaining because it was too rough to run the dishwasher, and he had been seconded to help clean up in the galley.

Fortunately the wind eased as darkness fell – just about the time Lana finished stowing the galley, it fell away to almost nothing. I did not hesitate or consult the Boss. On went the engine. I did not want to hang around. We rolled up the jib and motorsailed through the night, with just the reefed mainsail set. With the engine's help, we could lay our course, and we made excellent, if rather uncomfortable, progress. By early morning we were passing down the east coast of Staten Island.

We could have followed *Beagle*, and we would have saved a few miles by going through the Le Maire Strait, between Staten Island and the mainland. But that was Argentinian water, and we had been advised that a British-flag vessel bound from the Falklands would not be welcome in Argentina. Rather than risk a diplomatic incident, I decided to stay outside the island.

We were close enough to see the iron-bound shore that Darwin had described. It looked very forbidding, guarding the snow-covered mountains. A couple of months later, in Chile, we met an old man who was in his nineties. He had been shipwrecked there as a boy. He had sailed from Hamburg on a ship in the nitrate trade. They had been caught off the Horn and swept back to be wrecked on the south side of the island. He had swum ashore, and vowed never to go to sea again. He stayed in Chile for the next seventy-five years. Having seen the waves breaking on those cliffs, even on a gentle day such as we had, I can only think he must have been exceptionally strong or very lucky.

The wind stayed fairly light, and crept slowly round to the north. The barometer was rising and on the weather map the nearest depression was still well west of the Cape. I was not tempted to stop the engine, however. Our big jib was below decks, so we would not be able to set enough sail in the light wind to keep up our speed. We were making good progress as we were, and the good weather would not last long.

By dawn we were some 80 miles off the Horn. The wind was still light, about 10–15 knots, and it had gone right to the north. The Boss was now becoming anxious that it would be dark when we came to pass the Horn. As far as he was concerned, that would not do at all – he had not come all that way to go past it in the dark. He wanted

me to slow down and wait until the next morning.

I did some sums and talked to Jeff. We reckoned that if we increased the revs a bit, and increased the pitch of the propeller a little more, we could probably get there late afternoon, in time for the Boss to get his photographs. Jeff shared my feelings. The sooner we got into a secure anchorage the better. The longer we stayed out, the more likely we were to be clobbered.

We shook out one reef from the main, and set the jib. Together with the help from the engine we were flying along, averaging close to 10 knots. Cape Horn was abeam at tea-time, and Lana opened the obligatory bottle of champagne.

The bleak and barren landscape was pretty much as we expected. We already knew that Cape Horn itself is a fairly nondescript little island, but what did surprise us was the miserable little lighthouse. We had expected a monumental stone tower at the very least, but instead found a very rusty, insubstantial structure, built right down on the beach on the south-eastern shore. We closed to within about 200yd of the cliffs, and spoke to the navy lookout on the VHF. He invited us ashore. It would have been calm enough to land on the beach with the dinghy, and that would certainly have been a exciting thing to do, but darkness would soon be approaching, and we still had to find an anchorage for the night. The Boss was insisting that we anchor somewhere to the west of the Horn for the night, so we could round it again the next day.

These islands are no place to be poking around in the dark – in fact they are no place to be poking around at all. In my opinion they are a place to visit if you must, before going north quickly, into more sheltered waters.

We found a promising-looking bay on the eastern side of Hermite Island. It would shelter us from the existing north wind, and from the westerly which must surely come soon. The barometer was still high, but it was already beginning its descent. On the weather fax a row of low-pressure systems were lining up across the Pacific, waiting their turn to give us a blast. The bay was deep, but nowhere near as deep as the 47 fathoms where *Beagle* had lain. We dropped the anchor in about 18 fathoms and let out all the chain. We dropped a second anchor as well, and despite a bit of complaining from the boys, we brought a third anchor up from below, together with its rode, and got it ready in case we had to drop it in a hurry.

By the time we were all cleared away, it was getting dark. Cape Horn looked as if it was crouching in wait for us. We went below and found that Lana had supper ready on the table for us. We had rounded Cape Horn – hard to believe, really.

Heading into Hermite Island for the night. I found it intimidating to be anchored for the night in sight of Cape Horn.

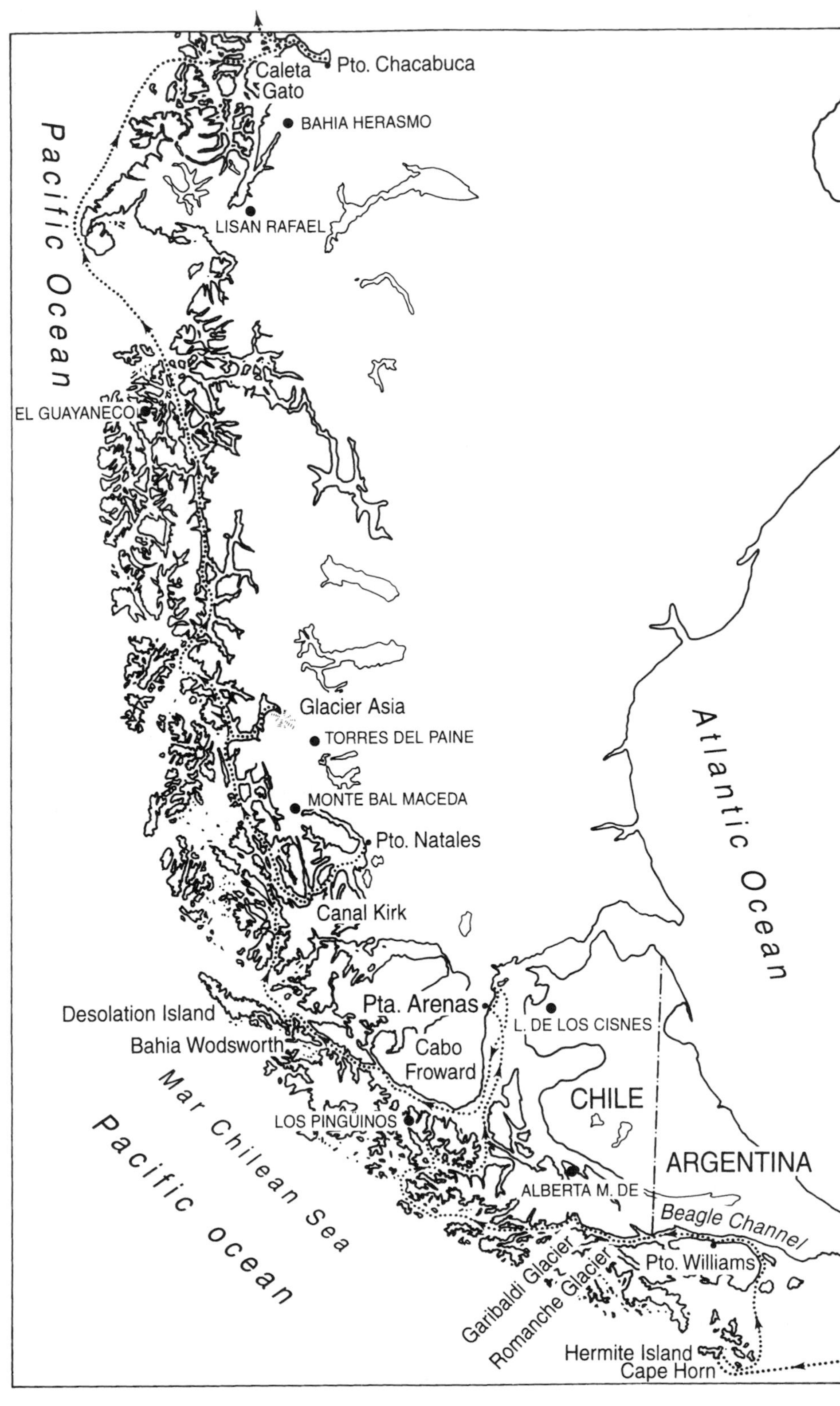

Pto. Chacabuca
Caleta
Gato
BAHIA HERASMO
Pacific Ocean
LISAN RAFAEL
EL GUAYANECO
Glacier Asia
TORRES DEL PAINE
MONTE BAL MACEDA
Pto. Natales
Canal Kirk
Atlantic Ocean
Desolation Island
Pta. Arenas
L. DE LOS CISNES
Bahia Wodsworth
Cabo
Froward
Mar Chilean Sea
CHILE
LOS PINGÜINOS
Pacific ocean
ARGENTINA
ALBERTA M. DE
Beagle Channel
Garibaldi Glacier
Romanche Glacier
Pto. Williams
Hermite Island
Cape Horn

Chapter 13

Tierra del Fuego and the Beagle Channel

Fitzroy was anxious to get the three Fuegans home, but after the twenty-four days it had taken them to weather the Horn, he was not anxious for *Beagle* to leave the anchorage. He decided to mount an expedition westward through the Beagle Channel, using the yawl and three whale-boats. They could take the Fuegans home and survey the channel at the same time.

The carpenter fitted a temporary wood and canvas deck on the yawl, which they loaded with supplies for the expedition. Although it could sail quite well, it was too big and ungainly to row when there was no wind or the wind was ahead. When that happened, the three whale-boats would have to tow it.

Twenty-four crew from the *Beagle* set off, including Darwin and Fitzroy. Then there were the three Fuegans, and Mathews, a missionary who was hoping to convert the natives to Christianity. With all the necessary provisions, the four boats were heavily laden. They were open and offered no protection from the elements for the crews, but they did carry tents for shelter at night.

Darwin and Fitzroy were in the yawl. Despite the fact that it was the biggest of the four, it was carrying the most cargo, so it was pretty cramped for the occupants. All the crew were pleased to be ashore each night, if only to stretch their legs.

Fitzroy decided to begin his exploration by running back downwind to enter the Beagle Channel at the eastern end. This, I think, was in itself something of an act of faith, considering the struggle that *Beagle* had endured to get as far west as she had. It would seem to me that they ran a significant risk of not being able to beat back to the ship. Fitzroy, however, obviously weighed up the odds and decided that they would manage.

After leaving the ship, they sailed eastwards through the islands to get to the Beagle Channel itself. They found a snug little cove for their first night's stop. Darwin paints an idyllic picture of the place. Imagine a small bay, surrounded by low hills, with the four boats anchored off the beach. The water is glassy calm. Trees are growing right to the water's edge and actually overhanging the beach in places. Their tarpaulin tents are suspended over crossed oars, and in front of each a campfire is burning. The smoke is drifting up through the trees, curling up into the wooded valley.

Darwin, and one assumes the others, were supremely content. It had been an easy day, followed by a pleasant evening and a good night's sleep. Unfortunately, that campsite was not typical. Their first night was to be one of the few peaceful ones they were to pass on the entire expedition.

The Beagle Channel runs more or less directly east–west, with a fork towards the western end. The prevailing wind, of course is from the west, so it usually comes howling down the length of the channel, which is about 120 miles long and a fairly uniform 2 miles wide. It was likely to be a tough beat for the boats to make their westing.

As they entered the channel proper, conditions were still mild, and they enjoyed some more pleasant sailing. The channel reminded Darwin of the valley of Loch Ness, which he had visited on several of his trips to Scotland. It was easy sailing, augmented by a bit of rowing when the wind dropped light.

Parts of the channel are so straight that the water disappears over the horizon, between the lines of fringing mountains. Most of the mountains bordering the channel are over 3000ft, rising straight up from the water. The lower parts of the slopes are covered in the same dusky-coloured beech trees that Darwin had seen in the east. They exist only below about 1400 or 1500ft. Above that height there are no trees, and the cut-off line is remarkably sharp and well defined. As Darwin commented, it looks just like the high tide mark on a beach.

It was not long before they came across the first group of Indians. Like those they had met on the east coast, these were naked, with long straggly hair. They had perhaps never seen white men before, and their surprise at seeing four boats go sailing by could not have been greater had they seen ghosts. They waved, yelled and shook the sticks they were carrying.

At night the sailors could see fires burning on virtually every point. Were the fires for warmth, for cooking, or for passing along the word that these strange apparitions were coming? Earlier explorers had witnessed the same phenomenon, and hence the name they had given the island, Tierra del Fuego – Land of the Fire.

That night, a group of Fuegans approached the expedition's camp. Fitzroy was not sure whether their overtures were hostile or not, so he passed out gifts to try and encourage them to be friendly. The most popular item was red tape, which the Indians tied round their heads. Jemmy was visibly embarrassed by these people. He kept reassuring Fitzroy that his own tribe was better. He was to be proved woefully

wrong.

Fitzroy was concerned that the Fuegans, as a race, were hard to intimidate. They seemed unable to grasp that guns were dangerous. Even when one of the sailors shot a bird or animal, the Indians seemed unable to accept that the bang from the gun was connected with the demise of the distant creature, since they were not able to see anything pass between the two.

As the boats progressed westward, they passed into an area of neutral territory between Jemmy's tribe and their neighbours. Jemmy himself was well aware of the strength of the expedition. He knew exactly what the guns were capable of, but he had still been very nervous about landing in his neighbours' territory. The respect each had for the other's fierceness was perhaps indicated by the broad no man's land which separated the two tribes.

The expedition stopped for one night close to the beginning of Jemmy's tribe's territory. They were to the west of Navarino Island and found a sheltered bay where a peaceful family of Fuegans were living. After a short period of mutual uncertainty, they shared the camp peacefully. *Beagle*'s crew set up their tents and lit their fires. They handed out some biscuits to the Fuegans, who after a nervous nibble or two gulped them down. Despite being clothed as warmly as the Royal Navy knew how, the men from *Beagle* had to sit close to the fires to try to keep warm. It was a chilly autumnal evening. In contrast, the naked Fuegans were sitting well back from the fire, and Darwin was surprised to see perspiration streaming off them from the roasting they considered they were getting.

As the expedition progressed ever further west, Jemmy began to recognise landmarks. They finally met up with his tribe at the settlement called Woollya.

His father had died while he had been away, but his mother and brothers came to meet him. He had been gone for five years, and Darwin expected a certain amount of excitement at the reunion. He was disappointed, however. He says that the meeting was as interesting as that between a horse turned out into a field when he joins an old companion. There was no display of affection at all. His mother stared at Jemmy for a moment, and then returned to attend to her canoe. Perhaps she was worried that she was going to have to return the button she had received in payment for him.

It transpired that Jemmy, never a gifted linguist, had forgotten most of his own language. Darwin found it rather pathetic listening to him trying to converse with his brother first in English, then in Spanish, and becoming angry when nobody could understand him.

The women of the tribe paid more attention to Fuegia than they did to Jemmy, even though she was not from their tribe. York, who had firm designs on Fuegia by this time, decided that they might settle right there. There was a reasonable amount of flat land next to the settlement, which is a rare enough commodity in this mountainous area.

Mathews the missionary had been casting around for a place to set up his mission, and decided that Woollya would suit him too. So the *Beagle*'s crew set to work. They built three wigwams, dug two gardens on the flat land, and planted seeds enough to give the whole tribe food in the spring.

Although Fitzroy and the men had given the Fuegans many presents, it seemed that they always wanted more. The first word that a Fuegan would utter on meeting a stranger was *yammerschooner*. This, York explained, meant 'Give me.'

There were some 120 members of the tribe living in and around Woollya. The women worked hard, doing all the domestic chores, while the men lounged around watching and *yammerschooner*-ing. The whole tribe was fascinated, and most of them came to watch, when any of the crew washed themselves in the little stream that bordered the camp. Like the gauchos in Argentina, they had never seen such a curious thing before.

It was all very peaceful and relaxed. Darwin and one or two of the officers took long walks in the bush surrounding the camp. Everything seemed fine and friendly, until one day Fitzroy noticed that all the women and children had vanished. Neither York nor Jemmy knew why. Fitzroy became very nervous. He wanted to avoid a confrontation because he knew that his men would kill many of the Fuegans if it came to a fight. He decided to move his camp that night, to another bay a mile or two down the channel. Mathews, however, decided to stay put.

The night passed uneventfully, and when they returned to visit Mathews the next day, all was well with him too. Fitzroy therefore decided to leave him there and carry on with the survey. He sent the yawl and one of the whale-boats back to the *Beagle*, and carried on west with the two remaining whale-boats.

That day was hot and sunny enough to cause some sunburn among the crew. Beagle Channel was looking at its best, with the brilliant white snow outlining the mountains against the deep blue sky. The water between the mountains was almost as blue as the sky. A group of whales swam, puffing and spouting, ahead of them. The light wind meant that the sailing was pleasant, and Darwin was not the only one to wish that it would always be so.

They sailed all day and just before dark found a good campsite. It was a beach of well-rounded pebbles. Rather to his surprise, Darwin found that that was one of the most comfortable nights he spent on the whole expedition. Peat was cold and damp to sleep on, while rocks were usually jagged and sharp. He did not like camping on a sandy beach, as sand always got into the food and into his bedding. He discovered that a sleeping bag on a pebble beach was heaven at the end of a long day in an open boat.

Even though they were moving away from the settled areas, they kept a watch all night. Darwin took the watch from midnight to 1 a.m., and there was just the occasional distant bark of a dog to remind him that they were not alone on the planet.

Their luck, and the good weather, held the next day too, and they passed the fork in the channel. Fitzroy decided to explore the northern arm first. The mountains on the northern shore, that is on Tierra del Fuego itself, towered some 4000ft above them, and several peaks were considerably higher. The tops of all of the mountains were permanently covered with snow, and all along the shore were streams and waterfalls fed by the melting snows, plunging down through the woods.

After a mile or two they came to their first glaciers. They found several of them reaching right down to the water. Darwin was surprised at their blue colour, as we were when we got there. He described it as beryl-like. The contrast between the blue ice of the glaciers and the white snow above is striking.

They stopped for lunch on the shore opposite a big glacier. From Darwin's description of the place, it seems to have been the Romanche Glacier. They pulled the boats up onto the beach and settled down to eat lunch. While they ate, they admired the ice cliff facing them on the other side of the channel. A few small bits of ice broke free and splashed down into the water. They were hoping to see some bigger pieces fall in, and their wish was fulfilled with a vengeance. Suddenly, with a crack like a cannon shot, a great section of ice fell off the face. The gigantic splash it made sent a large wave racing across the channel towards them. Everybody dashed to save the boats. One seaman reached the water just as the first wave arrived and was tumbled about in the breakers, although fortunately he was not hurt. The boats took a bit of a pounding, but were fortunately not holed. Fitzroy was shaken. All their provisions and weapons were in the boats, and if they had lost them they would surely have died. They were more than 100 miles from the ship, and of course since radios were yet to be invented, they had no way of summoning help.

Just before the wave came, Darwin had been prowling about the beach. He had found some boulders that appeared to have been

The Romanche Glacier, with meltwater running off from under the ice. All the glaciers are retreating, and we have seen photos only about fifteen years old, of the glacier reaching right down into the water.

moved recently, and he had been wondering who or what could have moved them. Now he knew.

At the western end of the Beagle Channel, they found many desolate, uninhabited islands. The weather had turned more characteristically miserable. In many places the coast was too steep and rugged to find room for the tents, and they would have to row extra miles in the dark searching for a campsite. One night, the only place they could find to sleep was on top of two big boulders. When the tide came in, their perch became smaller and smaller, until they had to move back into the boats.

The furthest west they got was Stewart Island, about 150 miles from the ship. Finally even Fitzroy had had enough, and they turned round and headed back.

With the wind behind them the going was easier and quicker. They sailed back along the southern arm of the channel, and soon arrived back at the settlement at Woollya, where Mathews told a sorry tale. He had been systematically robbed of everything he possessed, and then several times threatened with violence. One group had tried to keep him awake for several consecutive nights by making loud noises beside his head whenever he lay down.

Darwin felt sure that they had arrived just in time to save Mathews's life and Fitzroy decided that he should not stay, but should return to the ship with them. Mathews did not protest too much. Jemmy was sad to see what was happening. After five years of civilisation, he had come to enjoy some of the habits he had acquired. Now he was finding them impossible to keep. Even his own brother had robbed him of some of his clothes.

Rather than go all the way back to the eastern end of the channel, which would leave them with a long beat back to the ship, Fitzroy decided to go to the west of Navarino Island and take the outside route downwind to the ship. Although they had used a lot of their supplies, the whale-boats were still low in the water. Darwin does not dwell on the passage, but says that it was a rough and dangerous voyage – surely an understatement. He makes no mention of seasickness, so perhaps he could handle the motion of the small boat better than the ship itself.

After 300 miles and twenty days in open boats, they were all pleased to get back to the comparative comforts of the *Beagle* once more. Fitzroy and his officers spent a couple of weeks surveying the area around the anchorage, then after waiting for yet another gale to pass, they retreated to the Falklands for one of the recurring refits and then sailed back north to Montevideo for the worst of the winter.

They returned the following summer, 1843. *Beagle* once again anchored near the eastern end of the Beagle Channel. Perhaps it was the memory of the thrashing they had taken the previous year, but Fitzroy decided to try to beat westwards down the channel with the *Beagle* rather than face the Horn again. It would be hard enough to do this with a modern yacht, but with a ship such as the *Beagle* I would have considered it impossible. Since a square-rigger is not very efficient when going to windward, they would end up sailing about 3 or 4 miles for every 1 mile made good. They would have to zigzag up the channel against the wind, and at every tack there would be a tremendous amount of pulling and hauling for the whole crew, as the

heavy yards had to be swung round and the sails trimmed.

On the rare days when the wind went light, Fitzroy ordered the crew to launch the whale-boats, and with ten men rowing in each, they towed the ship. We were spoilt. A touch of a button, and with a roar of the Mercedes we could do an effortless 9 knots, under the same conditions. Sailing or rowing, it was exhausting work for them, but they managed to get the *Beagle* up the channel to Woollya. They were escorted for the last few miles by a dozen canoes. The Indians had no understanding of why the *Beagle* was tacking, and so followed her every zigzag instead of just paddling a direct course up the middle of the channel.

On board the ship, Darwin felt more comfortable, physically and psychologically, than he did ashore. He felt that not even the boldest Fuegan would try and attack something as big as the *Beagle*.

When they reached Woollya, the place looked deserted, but then a canoe appeared. It was Jemmy, although to begin with nobody recognised the thin, gaunt, naked savage with the long scraggly hair. They had left him plump, clean and well dressed. He was obviously ashamed of the way he looked, and most of the time he kept his back to the ship. Fitzroy invited him on board and gave him a big meal. Jemmy told them that he had lost all his possessions, but had gained a wife. Fitzroy offered to take him back to England, but he declined. This was where his wife was and where his life lay.

He told them that he had relearned quite a lot of his old language, but when they eventually met his wife, and some other tribe members, Darwin and Fitzroy were amused to hear that they all had a smattering of pidgen English. York and Fuegia had left the settlement. York had built a canoe, and they had last been seen paddling westwards.

As the crew of the *Beagle* said goodbye for the last time, and sailed southwards out towards the open sea, Jemmy lit a signal fire in farewell. *Beagle* headed back to the Falklands yet again, and that was the last time she would be in the channel to which she gave her name.

We kept an anchor watch through the night, but did not have even one squall. It turned out to be a snug, calm anchorage, but I did not sleep well. An overactive imagination had offered various scenarios of what a 100-knot squall would do to us. At the first sign of dawn I got up, and when a very gentle tap of the barometer resulted in the needle jumping markedly downwards, I sent Nick to wake everybody. For once I was as impatient as the Boss to get moving. The wind was back in the west, and it did not take a meteorologist to forecast that we were in for a blow.

We had a quick breakfast and then recovered both anchors. Left to my own devices, I would have stayed in the lee of Isla Hoste, and passed between it and Navarino to get into the Beagle Channel. But that would not do for the Boss. We had to 'round the Horn' again. I suppose Nick and Chris were pleased enough. They had been disappointed to motor round on a sunny day. At least now we had a bit more breeze, about 30 knots, and the passing rain squalls made the Horn look a bit more fearsome. As we sailed past for the second time, the Boss got enough photographs of the Horn looking tempestuous to satisfy him.

We turned north to pass Lennox Island, and entered the Beagle Channel east of Navarino. This was the route Fitzroy had chosen for the boats to get into the channel. Once we were in the lee of Navarino, I began to feel a bit more relaxed. We entered the Beagle Channel at lunch time, and started motoring against the moderate west wind towards Puerto Williams.

I had automatically assumed that we would be stopping there if only to enter Chile officially, but as we got closer, the Boss told us that he had been there on a previous trip, and in his opinion it was not worth stopping. He wanted to keep going. We had a small mutiny. I wanted to do the right thing with Costumes and Intimidation, and Lana was keen to see if there was any fresh food. The boys were anxious to have a run ashore and Jeff was hoping to top up the fuel tanks. When the Boss found that he had no support he backed down, and we anchored for the night in a well-sheltered bay close to the west of the town.

The bad weather passed in the night, and the next day dawned as what they would call in Maine a 'sparkler'. There is no other word to describe it. The clear, deep blue sky, the brilliant white snow on the mountains and the bright red roofs of the buildings ashore were all in happy contrast with each other.

By 6.30 the Boss was pacing to and fro, anxious to get ashore. He had suddenly decided that he had to make a phone call, and when we found that the surrounding high mountains made it impossible to do so by radio, he was in a rush to get ashore to find a telephone. Lana managed to persuade him that nothing would be open at 6.30, and that we should at least have breakfast before going in. As it was we were ashore by 8, only to be told that nothing opened until 10. So we had time to explore a bit before starting what turned out to be

the rather lengthy process of clearing into Chile.

Puerto Williams is a very small settlement. It claims to be the southernmost town in the world. I would not question latitude I but I wonder whether it deserves the status of a town. It is really little more than a naval base. The navy rules the southern part of Chile, mainly because there are no roads or railways, so everything moves by ship. Puerto Williams really only exists because of the navy and their perceived need to maintain a presence on the island of Navarino. The islands to the south of the Beagle Channel all nominally belong to Chile, a claim that has long been disputed by Argentina, which controls the eastern section of Tierra del Fuego. Each country jealously patrols its shore of the Beagle Channel, and the gunboats seem to be almost glaring at each other as they pass. Politics and the British flag kept us from the Argentinian side, but there was more than enough to see in Chilean waters.

Puerto Williams – the southernmost town in the world. We made our official entry into Chile here.

The Chilean entry procedures were long and complicated, but they were completed, I thought, in a friendly manner. The Boss finished his phone call and was anxious to go. The navy Commandant offered to allow us to come into their dock for fuel, and knowing that the Boss liked to go everywhere at 10 knots, and that the next settlement was Punta Arenas, almost 300 miles away, I insisted that we took the time to top up the tanks. I felt that it would be a mistake to pass up the opportunity of a fill-up, especially in an area such as this, where the chances are few and far between.

The Boss was almost apoplectic by the time we got under way at about 2.30. He reckoned that we had wasted a day, and was determined to reach the Romanche Glacier that afternoon. As the glacier still lay some 65 miles to the west, we were going to have to burn a fair amount of our newly purchased fuel to get there before dark.

We had been under way almost an hour when the radio burst into life. It was the Port Captain from Puerto Williams. Evidently I had omitted to get somebody to stamp one of the many papers I had been given. They wanted us to come back. I thought the Boss was going to die – he was so angry he looked as if he was about to have a heart attack. He was determined to ignore them and carry on. I was even more determined to play by their rules. It was we who would be left trying to sort out the mess, possibly long after the Boss had flown out from Punta Arenas. So we did a U-turn, and as we got close to Puerto Williams, the boys put the dinghy over and I zoomed in to get the required stamp on the necessary bit of paper.

We did not get to the Romanche that day, but we did find an excellent anchorage for the night. It was a little cove off the channel, completely surrounded by trees. We had the place to ourselves, with no sign that anybody had ever been there before. Although the weather was looking settled for once, we lay to two anchors and ran a rope ashore to one of the trees. This was to become our Patagonian routine; whenever we could, we ran a rope or two ashore in addition to setting at least two anchors. We knew the weather could change in a flash, and I did not want to be dragging round some little anchorage in the dark if a big squall came.

Our little bay was so quiet, it was almost spooky, and we found ourselves talking in whispers. We were already probably 25 or 30 miles from the nearest people, and about to move further away. Although we were close to where Jemmy had been returned home, there were no signs of any Indian settlements. Sadly it seems that all the Indians have either died or moved to the towns. While we were in south-western Patagonia, we often went 100 miles or more without seeing a house, a boat, a navigational aid or even a puff of smoke.

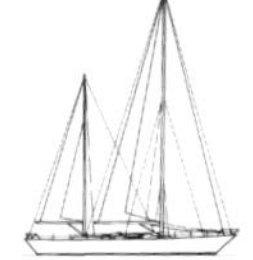

We seemed to have the world to ourselves.

We were blessed with another spectacular dawn. Although we probably had our fair share of bad weather, we did have a number of truly superb days. This was going to one of them. The water in the Beagle Channel was like glass, reflecting the snow-capped mountains that climbed straight up out of the water. The pale dawn sky was tinged with green and pink. It was almost overwhelming.

We carried on up the channel, arriving at the fork that Darwin and Fitzroy had struggled to reach in their open boats. What had taken them almost two weeks, we had done in a day and a half. We passed the mountain which is now named after Darwin.

Every few hundred yards along that part of the Beagle Channel, there is a waterfall tumbling over the sheer cliffs and splashing into the channel below. Glaciers are visible in the distance, winding their way down the mountains from the snow cap, but seeing them from afar had not prepared us for meeting one face to face as it were. It was a bit of a shock, therefore, when we came up to the Romanche Glacier, which empties, if that is the right word, directly into the Beagle Channel.

Although we had all read that glaciers are blue, none of us had expected them to be quite so blue. The colour almost matched *Thalassi*'s topsides. There was some ice in the water in front of the glacier, and remembering what had happened to Darwin and company here, we did not linger close in front of the glacier for long – not that it was the Boss's habit to linger anywhere for long.

All too soon he was ready to press on to the next one. I was anxious to find an anchorage for the night, but the Boss was determined to 'do' another glacier first. He wanted to visit Garibaldi, and assured me that he had been there before, and that there was an excellent anchorage right beside the glacier.

What could I say? We motored up the long fjord, through ever-increasing ice. Obviously Garibaldi glacier was a lot more active than Romanche. We had to pick our way round the larger bits of ice, many of which were the size of a car, with a few bigger, house-sized pieces mixed in with them. Because of the ice, our progress was slow, and dusk was creeping up on us by the time we got to the head of the fjord. We would have to anchor soon, but as we got closer to the end, the Boss became increasingly vague about where this safe, secure anchorage lay. His previous trip had been seven years before, and now he admitted that nothing looked familiar, and he was beginning to wonder if we were even up the same fjord that he had been thinking of.

All fjords tend to be deep. Most of the Beagle Channel is between

400 and 500ft deep. Canal Messier is reported to be an astonishing 4000ft. Although the fjord at Garibaldi was nothing like that deep, we were struggling to find anywhere less than 100ft. It was too late to go back through the ice to the Beagle Channel; like it or not, we were there for the night, and just had to make the best of it.

After doing a fairly comprehensive survey, we found a spot on the north side. It was a little indentation, not big enough to pass for a bay, and it was still over 100ft deep, but that would have to do us. There were a couple of stunted trees ashore that we could tie on to, so we layed our main anchor towards the face of the glacier and ran a line ashore to the strongest-looking tree.

We were much too close to the face of the glacier for safety. If a big piece of ice came off we could have been in trouble from the waves. During the night, as the temperature dropped, a katabatic wind started up. The cold air dropped down from the snow plain, and came howling out through the fjord where we were anchored. It was unnerving seeing the creaking rope vanishing into the dark and knowing that it was tied to a rather questionable tree. The anchor was not doing much – every time I tried to put a bit more weight on it it dragged, and if we pulled much more we would pull it home. So it was all down to the tree. As we listened to the waves on the rocks behind us it was an anxious night, and Lana and I stayed on deck for most of it.

As soon as the sun rose enough to warm things up, the katabatic effect was lost and the wind dropped. It was the third sunny day in a row. The Boss had slept through the night, and was convinced that it had been a snug enough anchorage. He took the boys off in the dinghy to poke around the glacier, and I went to sleep while Jeff kept an eye on things.

Chris brought back a piece of glacier ice and made an interesting discovery. The ice was probably several thousand years old, and it was so hard and compressed that it would hardly melt in a drink. One lump would suffice for at least three drinks. A piece he left in the cockpit for several days also refused to melt, despite an air temperature well above freezing.

Once their exploration was over the Boss was ready to go, so we picked our way back through the ice, down to the Beagle Channel. He had picked out a spot off Burnt Island, in Canal O'Brien, where he wanted to spend the night.

I should explain that the Patagonian 'canals' are not in any way man-made, or even man-improved. They are an intricate network of interconnecting fjords, and are, for the most part, as natural as the day God made them. The term simply derives from the Spanish for channel.

Canal O'Brien is at the western end of the Beagle Channel. When he made it his planned destination, the Boss had not reckoned on the westerly gale that was now howling down the length of the channel. *Thalassi*'s 200 horse-power kept us moving into the teeth of the gale, but only slowly. After about 20 miles or so, even the Boss had had enough. We spotted a reasonably sheltered-looking cove, and pulled in for the night.

On the chart, only the main channels have soundings marked to show the depth of water. Whenever we left these main thoroughfares, we were on our own. The big dinghy was fitted with a depth sounder, and we often sent it ahead to investigate for us. Before anchoring, we always sounded around the bay to check depths, either from the dinghy or by circling round with *Thalassi*. I wanted to be sure that there were no hidden rocks for us to swing on to if the wind changed or the tide dropped.

As we were getting ready to anchor in our unnamed, possibly unsurveyed bay, we did the usual circuit, checking the depths. The centre of the bay was about 150ft deep, but there was a handy little shelf to the north, with only about 30ft on it. That is where I tried to anchor. We had four attempts, all to no avail; the anchor dragged every time. It was getting dark, so we were more or less committed to staying in that bay for the night. More in frustration than any real hope of success, I dropped the anchor right in the middle of the bay. It was 148ft deep where we let go. Normally we like to put out chain at least five times the depth of water, but here it was far too deep for that – we had little more than twice the depth. Much to my surprise the anchor held at the first go. Once the main anchor was dug in, we let the second one go, and it too held.

Eventually after a few similar episodes, we realised that in these rocky little bays, it was best not to look for a shallow spot because they were invariably rocky. If we dropped in the deepest part, we always found good holding. Whatever silt found its way into these bays migrated to the lowest point, and however rocky a bay was, there was always a pocket of good sand or mud in the deepest part. If ever I venture back in these waters, the main anchor will have at least 500ft of chain – more if there is room to stow it.

We kept an anchor watch, just to be sure that we did not drag in the night. Squalls were rattling down off the hills all night long; the spell of fine weather had broken.

The wind was still howling when we left the next morning. In the Beagle Channel it was a steady 40 knots. I was glad we were not in an open boat with Captain Fitzroy. On board *Thalassi*, whoever was off watch was able to get warm and dry, sitting in front of an electric fire. I was able to do almost all my navigating from the comfort of the chart table, using the satellite navigator and the radar to identify each headland or island as it loomed out of the rain. The person actually on watch did get wet, but at the end of the watch they could throw their clothes in the tumble drier, so they were dry to put on before the next one.

Although it was not too uncomfortable, it was not much fun. We felt we were missing all the scenery, but the Boss had his schedule. We finally reached Burnt Island, our target from the previous day, and as it was getting late, we called a halt. We were getting towards the western end of the channel, and it was becoming much more exposed, and noticeably rougher. We anchored in Caleta Ancha, off Burnt Island.

There were a few stunted trees growing down by the water, and after a bit of searching the boys managed to find one big enough to be worth tying to. Since it did not look any too strong, they also found a large rock, round which they passed a chain to make a second, rather stronger securing point. With two anchors down and two lines ashore, I felt reasonably happy for the night, but we still kept a watch, just in case.

The wind did not let up all night, but early the next morning the Boss was making his usual 'let's go' noises. Lana expressed what everybody else was feeling. She had been watching the wind-speed indicator hovering close to 50 knots and said, 'It'd be really stupid to go out there now.' The Boss knew better than to argue with the cook. But after lunch, he had another go at encouraging us to leave. Although the wind had eased, it was still gusting up to 40 knots. It was also bucketing down with rain, and the visibility was about 20yd. The looks the crew gave him were enough to persuade him to stay put until the next day.

I think he would have gone crazy if we had had to stay another day, but fortunately the gale blew itself out in the night and we were able to get under way for Punta Arenas, which is about halfway along the Magellan Straits. To get into the strait we had to duck out into the open Pacific for a few miles. Even though the wind was down, there was still a big sea running. I thanked my lucky stars that we had not tried to come out there in 50 knots of wind. The coast was so exposed, so windswept, that there were no trees, indeed nothing growing at all. The granite cliffs have been polished smooth by the perpetual onslaught of wind and waves from the westerly gales. Even on this relatively calm day, the spray from the waves was being thrown 100ft or more up the cliffs – not a place to be shipwrecked.

We managed to sneak round the corner into the south-western

entrance to the Magellan Straits before the wind could get up again, and within a few miles we were back in the shelter of the islands and canals again. I had plotted a route which followed the main channel up to Punta Arenas. This seemed to be the obvious way to go, but the Boss had other ideas. He had been studying the chart and had spotted a narrow little canal that wound its way between two islands. It would admittedly save us 3 or 4 miles on our 60-mile passage, but no soundings were shown on the chart for that canal, nor was it mentioned in the pilot as an alternative route. The Boss, however, was anxious to press on after the delay, and determined to reach Punta Arenas that night. He was sure it would save us some time, and insisted that we take his short cut.

We turned into the canal, and within a mile or two the cliffs began to close in on us from each side. I slowed right down, in case it suddenly became shallow as well as narrow. We had gone about 12 miles up the canal when our way was blocked by a series of rapids. Fortunately the water was flowing towards us so it was easy to stop, just stemming the tide while the Boss was summoned to study the situation. To my amazement he said that we should just motor against the stream, and go up the rapids. At first I thought he was joking, but he was serious. Before I would even agree to try, we put the dinghy over and Nick and Chris went to reconnoitre.

From on board *Thalassi*, we could see the dinghy bucking and bouncing as they drove up through the rapids. We hardly needed their report when they came back. 'No bloody chance, mate,' said Nick, as they started to hoist the dinghy back on board. 'It's deep enough all right, but that sucker's running at 20 knots.'

Since *Thalassi*'s best speed under power is a little over 10 knots, we did not have to argue any more. There was no hope of us going against 20 knots, so we turned round and retraced our steps back to the main channel.

Because of the time we had wasted it was a race to reach Punta Arenas before dark. Jeff turned up the wick on the engine, and we set the jib and mainsail. By motorsailing as hard as we could, we got there just at dusk, and anchored off the town for the night, to a collective 'Phew' from the crew.

Chapter 14

The Straits of Magellan and Northwards

After her visit to the Falklands, and the trip back to Uruguay, *Beagle* returned to Patagonia for the last time. On this occasion she sailed into the eastern end of the Straits of Magellan; no more attempts on Cape Horn for Captain Fitzroy.

Having managed to beat through the Beagle Channel to Woollya, he was confident that he could manage to get *Beagle* through the Straits of Magellan. Although much of the strait is wider than the Beagle Channel, which would let them sail longer tacks when beating, there are a couple of narrow parts where the tide roars through at 8 knots or more. Despite the fact that *Thalassi* was a lot easier to handle than the *Beagle*, I would not have fancied trying it without being able to use the engine.

Their first anchorage was at Cape Gregory, where they met a group of the fabled Patagonian giants. Darwin was a little disappointed to find that they were not really giants. They were certainly taller than the likes of Jemmy's people, but far from the size he had imagined. Most of them, including the women, were around 6ft, with a few slightly taller. The way they dressed made them look taller. They wore full-length sweeping capes made of guanaco skin, and had long, flowing hair. Over the years, they had had numerous contacts with the European seal hunters who regularly worked in this area, and many of the them had at least a smattering of English. Darwin found them to be friendly and classified them as being at least 'half civilised'.

In contrast, when they later anchored off the settlement at Port Famine, they were once again pestered by Fuegans, all of whom were *yammerschooner*-ing. It got to the point where Fitzroy ordered the ship's guns to be fired to intimidate them. The guns were aimed low, and when the shots splashed into the water, the Indians threw rocks in retaliation. The fact that the ship was about ½ mile away did not seem to deter them. If the 'rocks' from the ship could all but reach them, then surely their rocks would reach the ship.

On their first visit to Port Famine, Darwin had ventured ashore to climb the nearby Mount Tarn. At 2600ft, it is the highest mountain in that locality. He and a couple of officers set off at 4 a.m. to try to reach the peak. As soon as they passed the high tide mark, however, they found themselves struggling through almost impenetrable forest. No landmarks were visible through the trees, so they had to lay a course with Darwin's trusty compass. After a couple of hours, they had made only 100yd or so. At that rate there would be no chance of reaching the summit that day. They almost gave up, but then they stumbled, literally, into a ravine. The going was still tough, but at least they could go a little faster.

The wind that had been whistling through the trees did not penetrate into the ravine and it was deathly calm. It was so cold, damp and gloomy, that not even fungi, moss or ferns could grow there. The bottom of the ravine was filled with a tangle of fallen and rotting tree trunks which they had to climb over and under. When Darwin, pausing for breath, leaned against one tree, the whole thing disintegrated and fell down, it was so rotten.

By way of the ravine, they finally reached the treeline. A row or two of stunted trees was the demarcation line, and above this, the ridge was bare rock. From there it was an easy walk to the summit. From the top they had a good view down the strait, and across the fjords and inlets. To the north lay row after row of snow-capped mountains separated by deep dark valleys.

The wind was bitingly cold, so despite the view they did not linger. They went down much quicker than they came up, because, as Darwin pointed out, every time they fell, it was in the right direction.

Most of the trees were beech, some of gigantic proportions. Darwin measured the girth of one as 13ft. Many of them had big lumps of fungus growing on them. Darwin found that one type grew only on a particular species of beech tree, and another type of tree was host to an altogether different kind of fungus. There was never a mixing of the two. The Fuegans ate this fungus in large quantities. Indeed it was about the only vegetable that they did eat.

There were few animals, and even fewer birds for him to study, so for once Darwin focused his attention on the sea and the tidal zones. He became interested in the kelp, the long rubbery strands of seaweed that fringed every rocky area here, just as it had in the Falklands. He managed to pull up one strand that was over 350ft long, and felt sure that there must be longer strands in even deeper water. He speculated that kelp is probably the longest plant on earth.

Along the shoreline, he spent hours pulling up kelp plants and shaking out the creatures that were living among the fronds. There were several kinds of shellfish, which he discovered were collected and eaten by the Fuegans. In fact these and the fungus formed the major part of their diet. In the kelp, he also found crabs, cuttlefish, starfish and sea urchins. Growing on the fronds themselves were a variety of coral-like polyps. He decided that there was more life to be found in the kelp than in any terrestrial forest.

Fitzroy wanted to leave the Straits of Magellan by the newly reported Magdalen Channel, which lay to the south of the more usual route. The weather did not treat them kindly, and Darwin was disappointed to be missing so much of the scenery in the overcast and foggy conditions. He caught tantalising glimpses of blue glaciers, high, rugged peaks and spectacular waterfalls. *Beagle* anchored one night in thick weather near Mount Sarmiento, but its 7000ft peak remained hidden in clouds that reached down almost to the water. On the beach they could see the remains of a long-deserted wigwam, a reminder that people did visit the area, although they had not seen any settlements for many miles. Early the next morning, the clouds parted long enough for them to see the whole mountain. Above the treeline it was completely covered in snow. On its flanks were several big glaciers, which Darwin described as 'frozen Niagaras'.

HMS Beagle *in the Straits of Magellan – Mount Sarmiento in the background.*

After a long day, *Beagle* reached the western end of the strait just before dark. It was too late to navigate their way out through the mass of islands, and the water was too deep to anchor. One small cove offered a possible anchorage, but Fitzroy decided to give that to the *Adventure*, which was following close behind them. *Beagle* would stand off for the night. Winter had arrived, and there were fourteen hours of darkness to suffer through.

There was an area of about 4 square miles in which it was safe to sail. During those fourteen hours, they criss-crossed it in every direction. Fitzroy decided to keep a good press of sail on the ship, and keep her moving. She was much more manoeuvrable when sailing at a reasonable speed than when sailing slowly or hove to. He also felt that the crew would be more alert working the ship than if she herself seemed half asleep.

For the first part of the night they had to beat hard, just to hold their own against the incoming flood tide. Later, when the tide turned, they had to bear away and run back east, as the ebb tide tried to draw them out into the offshore islands. It also rained almost all night, and squall after squall came racing in from the west. To sail to and fro for fourteen hours, in such confined water, with no lighthouses or buoys for bearings, knowing that a winter gale could arrive at any moment, must have given Fitzroy more than one grey hair.

Darwin noted the night's activities in his journal, but did not seem to be concerned. What impressed him more, as they sailed out at dawn, was an area they passed called the Milky Way. This is an area of shoals, reefs and jagged rocks, where the sea always breaks white. He said, 'One sight would be enough to make a landsman dream for a week about shipwrecks, perils and death.'

Beagle got safely clear of the land, and turned north. That was to be their last sight of Patagonia.

Punta Arenas is the capital of southern Chile. Darwin did not visit the town for the simple reason that it did not exist when he was in the area. It was to be another fifteen years before the first settlement was established there, in 1849. As steamships began to reach and pass through the strait, Punta Arenas became an important coaling station, and it rapidly increased in size and importance. It is now a city of over 100,000 people.

The Boss was ashore almost at first light, trying to meet a friend from his previous visit, and to organise his flight out. It was also time for Chris to fly back to reality, so he too was off visiting the travel agents. For the rest of us, there were plenty of chores to do on board the boat. We hoped to get our chance to explore the town once the Boss was on the aeroplane.

He was gone all day, and arrived back in the evening with his friend Julio, Julio's brother Jorge, and their respective wives. Julio runs a TV and radio repair shop and a small coast radio station to enable ships to make telephone calls by radio. His brother Jorge is a dentist. He rather reminded us of Wacko the film-maker.

It was a bit difficult for us to entertain them unannounced. Lana had not been shopping for three weeks, and provisions were getting low. The Boss, living as he does in a hotel, could never grasp the logistics of trying to feed unexpected guests.

During the course of the evening's conversation, the Boss let us in on the next stage of the plan. We were to go to Puerto Natales, about 100 miles to the north-west, to pick up some Chilean guests to whom he had given the use of *Thalassi*. The chart showed that our route would involve some 300 miles of twisting and turning channels, yet the Boss had decided we could do it in two days, regardless of what the weather might be. He thought I was being very pessimistic when I expressed some doubts.

The Boss and Chris were both booked to fly out the next afternoon. In the morning we hired a pick-up truck and started on the provisioning. Driving in Punta Arenas was very strange at first. Every street in the town is one way, with alternate streets going in opposite directions. There is no two-way traffic anywhere in the town. Later we were to discover that this was by no means unique to Punta Arenas; many towns in Chile have a similar system. Indeed, Chile seemed to us to be a land of one-way streets.

Jorge took the Boss to the airport in his car, while Chris came with Lana and me in the pick-up. They had both checked in, and we were sitting in the lounge waiting for their flight to be called, when the Boss dropped one of his bombshells. Quite casually he mentioned that Julio and his 'family' would be moving on board the next day to sail to Puerto Natales with us.

This was our twenty-fourth day in succession with the Boss, and while some of it had been fun, we were physically and emotionally exhausted. Lana and I had been looking forward to at least a day to ourselves. We looked open-mouthed at each other and at him. He seemed oblivious. For once even Lana was struck dumb. I stood up and said, 'We'd better get busy then.' We walked out of the airport without another word. When we broke the news to the others, I

thought for a moment that we were about to be left crewless.

Julio had told them about Mother Teresa's bar, grill and whorehouse, and they were determined to visit it – just for the food, they assured us. They were unanimous that they were going nowhere until they had paid their respects to Mother Teresa.

The breeze was picking up, and the anchorage off the town is not very well protected. I cannot understand why the main dock was built where it was, in a totally exposed position. We moved the boat a mile or so up the coast, to anchor in a well-sheltered little bay, surely a better place for them to have built the port. Lana drove the truck round to meet us.

We split into two teams for the evening's entertainment. I did not want to leave the boat on her own, so Lana and I went out first and had a nice, peaceful dinner ashore in one of the hotels. By the time we got back, the second contingent was all spruced up and ready to make their foray. We did not ask where they got to, but it was the wee small hours before they returned.

The next day Julio came down and told us that it would be just him and his brother sailing with us. Neither wife could go. That was better than we had feared. We had imagined four adults and a clutch of kids. What was even better news was that they could not leave until the next day, so we had a day's reprieve.

We needed the extra time. Jeff was tasked with locating fuel, and failed to find anybody who would deliver it. In the end he found or borrowed a couple of 50-gallon drums; we took the boat alongside the dock and ran a shuttle service with the trusty pick-up. It was easy enough, but it took a lot of time, syphoning each drumful into *Thalassi*'s tank.

I set about trying to sort out Costumes and Intimidation. It was not easy to get permission to put Chilenos onto our crew list. Eventually I had to get Julio to come and help. He sorted it out fairly quickly, and I suspect a little money changed hands.

Lana seconded Nick to the grocery shop and the market. They came back with the pick-up sagging on its springs. Not knowing when the next chance would come, Lana had done some serious shopping.

She and I managed to squeeze in a quick trip down to the naval shipyard. The hulk of a big iron sailing ship was lying on the beach, forming a breakwater for the little patrol boats. She was the *City of Glasgow*, the ship that Stanley had chartered to search for Dr Livingstone in Africa in 1871. On a later trip round the Horn, she had fallen into the trap of visiting the Falklands for repairs. Like so many of the others, she had been condemned; and had lain there for a

The wreck of the City of Glasgow *in Punta Arenas. This is the ship that Stanley chartered to try to bring back Doctor Livingstone from Africa. We were allowed to board the wreck, but not allowed to photograph it for 'security reasons'.*

number of years before somebody had tried to salvage her. I believe that her new owners were hoping to tow her to California, but as they were passing Punta Arenas a gale arrived. The towline snapped, she was swept ashore and there she lay, condemned for a second time.

We received permission to board her, but the puzzled navy people could not understand why we would be interested in a wreck. Although we tried to explain in our phrasebook Spanish, they thought we were on some clandestine mission. They let us on board, but forbade us to take any photographs. She was largely intact, with a fair amount of her deck gear still there. It would have been an interesting project to record it all, but bureaucracy and the Boss's schedule precluded it.

We got Julio and Jorge settled aboard, and bade adieu to Punta Arenas. It was a beautiful, sunny, windless day, another sparkler. As we rounded Cape Froward, the southernmost point on the South American mainland, we decided it looked much more as Cape Horn should have done – a big, bold headland with a large cross on top. Julio told us that the cross is regularly blown down, but somebody always goes back up to install another.

An effortless 113 miles were reeled off, and we found a reasonable enough little bay in which to anchor for the night. We were hoping that it was all going to be that easy, but of course it was not. The next day dawned wet and windy – back to normal! We made an early start, mainly because Julio woke us all up yelling for his brother – he had seen a flying saucer. I got up to investigate, and found that he had in fact seen Venus, which appeared to move past his hatch as the boat swung at her anchor in the breeze.

By the time it was light we had breakfasted and were ready to leave. Outside the shelter of our little bay it was a bit ugly – damp and drizzly and blowing about 30 knots on the nose. Thank goodness we did not have to beat, tacking to and fro as the *Beagle* had been forced to do. The engine pushed us easily into the wind, but as we approached the end of the strait, it became a bit rough. *Thalassi* started to slam into the waves and take heavy water on deck.

By late afternoon we had reached the aptly named Desolation Island, a forbidding piece of land. Even the trees looked as if they were huddling down to try and escape the perpetual wind. On the chart, we spotted a very promising-looking inlet on the island, called Bahia Wodsworth. It is a fairly long, twisting fjord, and the twists and turns promised us complete shelter from the swell. When we reached the inner end, we found a perfect little pool just big enough for *Thalassi* to anchor in.

There was not room for her to swing if the wind changed, so we dropped the anchors at the entrance of the pool, then as I turned and backed down, Nick and Tony ran two lines ashore with the dinghy. We were completely landlocked, surrounded by tree-covered hills around 1500ft high. The bay was so small that not even the squalls could reach us; it was glassy calm. What a contrast to what we had been suffering outside. A spectacular waterfall poured over the cliff, to crash onto the beach close on our port side. It was a truly beautiful spot, with no sign of habitation. In fact there was probably nobody within 60 or 70 miles of us that night. It was a privilege to be there.

Jeff and I decided that there must be a good-sized lake at the top of the cliffs to feed such a waterfall. We thought we would pop up and take a look before dark. However, what looked like a few bushes

The superbly sheltered anchorage at Bahia Wodsworth at Desolation Island. Thalassi *well secured with two anchors down and a line ashore, our typical Patagonian anchoring routine.*

on the hills turned out to be virtually impenetrable jungle. From the boat it was impossible to judge the size of the trees ashore; there was nothing to give a sense of scale. We struggled through the undergrowth for an hour, much as Darwin had done near Port Famine. We had gone only a small fraction of the distance by the time dusk approached. Neither of us fancied being caught in the jungle after dark, so we gave up and headed back to the boat.

Back on board, we found Tony engaged in a chess match with

Julio. During his winter in the Antarctic, Tony had played many chess games via the radio, mainly with Russians wintering at another base. In those games they had made just one move a day, so they had had plenty of time to think about it. It was a bit of a novelty for Tony to have a 'live' opponent, and he felt a bit rushed, not having twenty-four hours to consider each move.

Jeff and I had hoped to make another attempt on the waterfall at first light the next morning, but when we woke, the rain was pouring down, so we had a long and lazy breakfast instead.

From Desolation Island our route took us across the Straits of Magellan for the last time, before entering the smaller and generally more sheltered canals that go northwards. The canal that leads up to Puerto Natales is Canal Kirk. It has a formidable reputation, and we received several warnings to treat it with respect. The problem is that Puerto Natales is in a gigantic shallow bay. The enclosed area is perhaps a couple of hundred square miles, and the only connection to the open sea is Canal Kirk. As the tide rises and falls, a prodigious amount of water must pass through the canal. To make matters worse, there is a very narrow section, and here the current regularly exceeds 15 knots. The Port Captain in Punta Arenas had told us to attempt the passage only at slack water, and then only if it was not too windy. The narrows are called Angostura Kirk, but we renamed them Angustia Kirk – *angustia* being Spanish for grief!

When we left Desolation Island, we were reminded just how sheltered our anchorage had been. As soon as we stuck our nose outside into the Magellan Straits, we found it was blowing 30, gusting 40 knots. It was rough enough as we crossed the strait, and we were all glad to get into the comparative shelter of the canal on the north side. We passed the wreck of a big freighter. It had been tossed up on the land, almost clear of the water. I did not want even to imagine the conditions that could have done that. *Angustia.*

As we approached the entrance to Canal Kirk, the wind increased and heavy squalls came funnelling down out of the mountains. These sudden bursts of cold wind dropping out of the mountains are called 'williwaws'. As they raced across the canal towards us, they picked up the surface of the water. An area, in some cases the size of a football field would suddenly lift up in the air, to be blown away as spray. What would happen to us if we were in the middle of one of these mini-tornados? Luckily we did not find out, but trying to avoid them kept things interesting for us.

The Admiralty tide tables are a bit vague for this area, but as near as I could tell, slack water at the narrows was at 2.30 p.m. As we approached the narrows, I tried calling the Port Captain at Puerto

Natales for confirmation. Nobody answered my calls, so Julio called up his own radio station, and got them to telephone the Port Captain for us. There seemed to be a bit of hesitation, before he finally told us that he thought it would be about 5 p.m. He did not say it with any degree of conviction, however, so I decided to stick with the earlier time. If we were too early we could wait, but if we missed it, there would be a 15-knot current against us, and we would have no chance of pushing through against that.

As soon as we turned the corner into Canal Kirk itself, we seemed to leave the williwaws behind, much to my relief. We were still a mile or two from the narrows when Julio spotted a fishing boat. We went over to ask them for a bit of local knowledge. As we pulled alongside, Julio saw bags of scallops in the boat, and immediately started bartering for some. It was only after he had made his deal that I was able to remind him to ask for the fishermen's advice about the narrows. For a six-pack of beer and half a case of Coke, Julio got a sack of scallops, a bucket of mussels and the suggestion that we would be all right to pass through the narrows right away.

There was a bend in the canal just before the narrows, and even as we came round the corner, the current, which was pushing us along, increased dramatically. We had probably already passed the point of no return, as the current was already going faster than we could, and we could neither turn round nor stop. Ready or not, we were on our way through the narrows.

The narrows really *are* narrow, and just to complicate things, there is a big rock in the middle of the channel at the tightest part. There are range markers showing that the rock should be left to port. As we passed it, we could see a waterfall ahead. The drop was probably only a foot or so, but as we raced up to it, it looked like the brink of Niagara Falls itself.

I kept our speed through the water at about 6 or 7 knots, to make it easy to steer. With the speed of the current and our speed through the water, we were doing close to 20 knots over the ground. It all happened very quickly, so I did not have to hold my breath for too long. *Thalassi* was squirted out of the narrows into the wide bay which leads up to Puerto Natales. Although the wind was howling again, it was a relief to escape from the confines of Canal Kirk.

For once we actually had a following breeze, so we set the jib and a bit of mainsail and sailed up the bay to Puerto Natales. The closer we got to it, the stronger the wind became, until it was blowing a steady 45 knots. The Port Captain must have spotted us, because he called us on the radio to say that the port was closed because of the bad weather. It did not really affect us, as I would not want to tie up to their rather exposed dock in that wind anyway.

We anchored in the lee of a low bank to the west of the town, and were perfectly snug. The wind was howling in the rigging, but on deck everything was relatively calm. Julio called his wife on the radio to find out how best to cook the scallops and mussels. While Julio was relaying instructions to Lana in the galley, Jorge kept us all amused by making us guess which singer or actor he was trying to impersonate. He had quite a repertoire, which increased with each drink he took. It was a pleasant evening, rounded off by an excellent meal of fresh seafood. What could be nicer?

Julio and Jorge were to leave us here, and we were to await the next visitors. The Boss had given the use of *Thalassi* to a gentleman called Klaus, from Santiago, in the hopes that he would ask the Boss's boatyard to build him a similar boat. Julio had offered to help with the logistics of getting Klaus and his friend to Puerto Natales to join us, and also offered to take all our exposed film back to Punta Arenas, get it developed, and send it back with Klaus. Both offers were eagerly accepted. Nick took him and Jorge ashore the next morning to catch the one and only bus back to Punta Arenas, and came back looking like a drowned rat. It was still pretty rough.

Julio and Jorge had been good if exhausting company, and we needed some quiet time, to get ourselves ready for the next visitors. The day was declared a no-work day, so we explored the little town, and ate ashore to give the cook a break.

Puerto Natales is a real frontier town. It looked like something out of the Wild West – slightly ramshackle, clapboard buildings lining unsurfaced roads. Jeff, Tony and Nick rather lost interest when they failed to find a single bar. The town appeared to be dry.

We had a couple of days to get organised before Klaus was due to arrive, or so we thought. When the wind dropped we brought the boat in to the dock for the usual routine of topping up the fuel again – the never-ending quest. This time Jeff had managed to find a tanker which would deliver right to the door. Apart from the fact that the nozzle on the tanker's hose was about twice as big as our filler, the operation went quite smoothly, and we were soon back at anchor.

Lana visited every shop in town and bought what provisions she could. She had just arrived back on board when the VHF radio crackled to life, and we heard the unmistakable sound of Julio's voice. We knew that he must be close, because that radio has a range of only 20 miles or so. What on earth was he doing back here, when our guests were due the next day?

I went in with the dinghy to meet him. He had met Klaus and his friend, another Jorge, at the airport. Rather than leave them in a hotel

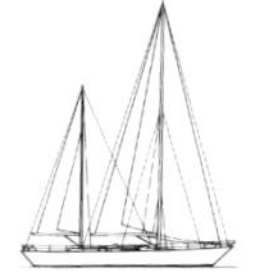

for the night, he had decided to help by driving them 150 miles to deliver them to us, albeit a day early. A big panic ensued. Since we were not expecting the guests until the next day, their cabins were not ready for them. And as it was getting dark, we could not send Julio off to drive back; he would have to stay the night too.

Lana's consternation was softened a little by getting all her photographs back, plus a new batch of mail, and a great big box of chocolates from Julio and his brother, addressed to their 'fair lady'. She managed to rustle up a scratch meal for eight – no small feat, since we had been planning to have a 'last supper' ashore for the crew before the guests came. It was a rather hectic start to Klaus's visit.

Chapter 15

Torres del Paine and North from Patagonia

Having once negotiated the dreaded Canal Kirk, it no longer held the terror that it had the first time, but we still gave it a healthy dose of respect. After we had waved goodbye to Julio again, we safely negotiated the narrows at slack water, more by luck than tide tables.

The plan was to take Klaus and Jorge to Puerto Aysen, some 500 miles to the north as the condor flies. However, the zigzags and little detours would probably add at least another hundred, so we had quite a distance to cover. The Boss had told us we would be doing it in a week, which would have been hectic. Fortunately he had also told us that the most important thing was to give them a good time, in the hope that Klaus would buy a boat.

Both Klaus and Jorge were delightfully laid back, and seemed more than happy to do the trip at a slower pace. They were both interested in exploring, and Klaus especially was an absolute fount of local knowledge. He knew one of the admirals in the southern Fleet, and on Klaus's chart he had marked all their secret fuel dumps in the area we would be crossing. Apparently the navy has established dozens of 'secret' bases where their submarines and patrol boats can refuel in the event of war with Argentina. Klaus had been given *carte blanche* to raid these supplies if we needed to. We never had to, but it was reassuring to know that extra fuel was available. This was but a small example of the doors that Klaus was able to open for us. Nick and Tony took to calling him 'Mr Chile', not entirely flippantly.

A couple of calls on the radio rearranged their flight schedules, to give us a more realistic timetable for the passage. The only real pressure for them to get back came from Jorge's wife, who was intensely jealous that she was not able to leave her travel agency business long enough to join us.

It was Klaus's opinion that the best area to explore was around the extensive national park, Torres del Paine. When we heard the words 'national park', we pictured hot-dog stands, souvenir stalls and tourist day-trip boats, but there was none of that. We saw the occasional fisherman, but otherwise we had the park, and sometimes it seemed the world, to ourselves.

We did 81 miles the first day, and 89 the second, which brought us to the edge of where Klaus reckoned the good part started. We stopped for the night in the aptly named Puerto Bueno. It was very *bueno* indeed, with good holding for the anchor, pretty scenery and hundreds of wild flowers ashore. Despite its name, it was like no other port we have been into. It was as nature had designed it, and it did not look as if anybody had ever been there before us. So we learned that the term *puerto* on the chart did not necessarily mean that there was any settlement there, but that it was likely to be a good anchorage. Jorge gained points with the cook by collecting a large bunch of wild flowers for her.

The next morning found us well into glacier country. There were at least a dozen coming down the mountains on the mainland side, all shining that strange, almost iridescent blue. There were several pieces of ice floating by, broken off from glaciers that came right to the water's edge. We turned into the entrance of Estero Peel, and immediately found much more ice in the water. By the amount, we guessed that there must be a more active glacier in this fjord. There was a bit of a dog-leg to the fjord, and as soon as we came round the bend, we could see two glaciers coming down at the end.

We often found it impossible to judge distances in Patagonia. I am not sure if this was because on a good day the air was very clear because there is no haze-making pollution, or whether it was just because there were no man-made objects to give us a sense of scale. Whatever the reason, we regularly underestimated distances, usually by a factor of two or more. So when we sighted the two glaciers, Jeff got everybody to guess how far away the nearest one was. The estimates varied from a low of 1 mile to a high of 3. He measured the distance on the radar, and found it to be almost 10 miles. It took us a couple of hours to cover that 10 miles, dodging lumps of ice along the way. We anchored in Caleta Amelia just as Lana announced that lunch was ready.

Klaus and Jorge were happy enough to spend the afternoon exploring the area. If the Boss had been with us, we would have had to do another three glaciers before tea time. Klaus chose a beach in front of the northern glacier to visit. This was much the smaller of the two glaciers, but it finished right on the beach. Jeff and I decided to go for the big one. Jeff had an ambition to stand on a big glacier, and this one seemed to be only a mile or so up the valley. We would have done well to remember our distance-judging efforts of the morning.

The expedition to the little glacier was the popular one, perhaps because it was less energetic. Jeff and I had no takers for ours. The others dropped us off at the beach near 'our' glacier *en route* to theirs. We took a portable radio so that we could call for a pick-up when we arrived back. Just as we were landing, a guanaco appeared on the beach. It was very shy, and after it realised we were coming ashore, it ran off. That was one of only three of these small deer-like animals that we saw in all the time we were in Chile.

One of only two guanacos that we saw. They used to be plentiful but have almost been killed off for their meat and skin. This one watched us land on the beach for our assault on 'Jeff's' glacier.

The first part of our expedition went smoothly enough. We walked up the valley floor, which consisted of gravel that had been crushed by the glacier. All the glaciers in that area are retreating, and where we were walking would have been under at least 100ft of ice a few years before. We could see great gouges in the cliffs on either side of the valley, where the ice had scraped by.

The first snag we came to was the river. Because it was summer, there was a steady flow of melt-water coming off the glacier. The river did a big zigzag from the cliff on one side of the valley to the one on the other. There was no way round it. The cliffs were too sheer to climb. We could either cross the river or go all the way back down to the beach and look for another route. Ever a man of action, Jeff pulled off his jeans and waded across. The water was just about at freezing point – an hour or two previously it had been ice. The river was just shallow enough for Jeff to avoid getting his underpants wet, but when I followed him over, I discovered that even on tip-toes, my legs were about 6in shorter than his – a rather crucial six inches from my perspective. I got no sympathy from Jeff.

All went well for the next couple of miles. It was easy walking on the valley floor, although we were beginning to realise that we had been hopelessly optimistic about the distance. Eventually we reached the face of the glacier – or at least we almost did. At the bottom of the face was a big pool of water, stretching right across from one cliff to the other. It was too deep to wade across, and far too cold to swim in.

We were disappointed, but not yet totally thwarted. We had passed a section of the cliff that had fallen into the valley. It was only ½ mile back, so perhaps we could climb up there to get up out of the valley, and reach the glacier from above. We hurried back, and sure enough, we managed to scramble up to the top of the cliff without too much serious climbing. There was not much vegetation along the cliff top, so we were able to walk back to the area of the glacier fairly easily. Now the problem was to get down to the ice itself. We were a good 100ft above it, but having come this far, Jeff was determined to walk on the thing.

After a couple of false starts, we found a route down, and finally reached the glacier itself. Because it was melting, the surface was fairly smooth. There was a surprising amount of dirt embedded in the surface – we were rather surprised that the whole thing looked rather grubby. As the ice melts, any dirt trapped in it is left on the surface. Because this glacier is hardly moving at all, the dirt we saw could have been hundreds, even thousands of years old.

We walked about on it quite casually, until we found our first

Looking down onto the glacier that Jeff was determined to walk on.

crevasse. Down on hands and knees, we peeped cautiously over the edge. The crack was quite long, but only a foot or so across. It really did look bottomless, going down and down into inky blue darkness. That did it for me. I decided I had seen enough and headed straight back to terra firma.

The climb back up to the cliff was a bit of a struggle, but we managed it. I was very keen to avoid the river on the way back, so we stayed out of the valley and made our way back along the cliff tops. A mile or so from the glacier, we came to a patch of very fine gravel, almost like coarse sand. Right across the middle of it was a row of gigantic footprints, each about 25 per cent bigger than Jeff's size eleven, and not quite the right shape to fit a shoe. I have always been sceptical about the tales of 'yetis' and 'bigfoots'. But having come across those footprints in the wilds of Patagonia, I must now at least concede the possibility that they exist. Whatever had made them was very much bigger than us, and we hoped that we would not meet it face to face on the way back.

Having gone further than we had anticipated, we had a small race against the darkness to get back to the beach. It was almost a dead heat. Nick came to pick us up, just in time for a hot shower and a good dinner. The others had enjoyed their less strenuous expedition, and everybody was happy. It had been an excellent day.

The weather became better and better. A rare but welcome high came and sat over Patagonia, and we were blessed with three perfect days for exploring glaciers. There was no wind to blow the ice about, the sun was warm all day and the sky was the clearest blue it is possible to imagine.

The best glacier was Glacier Asia – at least that was what it was called on the Chilean charts. The British had it down as Calvo, but the Chileans placed Calvo further south. Whatever it is called, it is spectacular. It was the most active glacier we found, and there was so much ice cooling the water, that the open stretch in the approaches was starting to skin over with ice. We met some fishermen who warned us that it would freeze solid for the winter with the next cold spell. *Thalassi* was breaking ice all the way up the fjord. Remembering what had happened to the *Beagle*'s crew, when they ate lunch too close to a glacier, I stopped the boat about ½ mile short of the face and I turned her round to face the way out before the ice

The mysterious footprints we found on our way back from the glacier. Do these belong to a yeti type creature? Not even Darwin saw one of those, but many people attest that such a creature lives here. Having seen the footprint, I am prepared to believe it.

Near Glacier Asia there was so much ice in the water that it was often hard to see a way through. Often we had somebody up the mast looking for the best way. We could break the thinner ice, but I did not want to hit any of the big lumps.

we had broken could freeze again. The water was about 300ft deep, but we did not need to anchor; *Thalassi* was held quite snugly in the ice.

The glacier itself is huge – a little over ½ mile across the face. Doing a bit of a Fitzroy, we calculated the height of the face by taking a sextant angle and measuring the distance off with the radar. It was 375ft above the water, give or take an inch or two. If the ice went down to the floor of the fjord, it could well be over 600ft thick in total – a lot of ice. The northern side was the most active. A steady stream of bits were falling off. Every now and then a larger piece, about the size of a car, would come crashing and splashing down.

We had heard that noise can sometimes start an ice fall, so Nick, always happy to make a noise, started hooting away with *Thalassi*'s foghorn. There was no noticeable reaction. Ever since Brazil, Jeff had been trying to teach me to play the bugle, so we got our bugles out and blew as hard as we could. There were a few rumbles, but no splash. Lana thought she would show us how to do it. She took my bugle and gave a rather off-key toot. Instantly, a piece the size of a house fell in. Jeff and I were convinced that we had loosened it for her.

Jorge was anxious to get closer. I did not want to risk puncturing the inflatable on some ice, so we launched the fibreglass pulling boat, and Tony, Nick, Jorge and Jeff tried to paddle it to the shore. They did not get more than about 6ft; the ice was too thick to let them row or even paddle effectively, but it was also much too unstable to walk on. We decided to see how the outboard would cope. I passed it down to Jeff, and he fired it up. It pushed the boat along quite well. Most of the time there was clear water under the stern of the boat, but if any bits of ice got in the way, the motor worked like a blender making pina coladas, and ground it up with no apparent difficulty, or harm to the engine.

There was a big rounded rock close up to the ice face, towards the southern edge. Jeff landed the others there and came back for Lana and me. That part of the glacier was not nearly so active as the northern side, but there were enough big pieces of ice lying about from previous falls to make us more than a little wary.

The glacier was always making a noise, sometimes a gentle creaking noise, at other times a rumble like distant thunder. Then a sudden crack and an avalanche would come roaring down the face. It was almost as if it were alive.

We reluctantly left it to go and look for a safer anchorage for the night. We found one of the best ever, off Estero Calvo. It was an almost totally landlocked little bay which we shared with a camp of fishermen. A very large rock in the middle of the entrance ensured perfect shelter once we were inside, but made the entrance itself very narrow. *Thalassi* had only 3 or 4ft to spare on either side as we squeezed gently in. Once inside there was plenty of room to anchor, with a couple of lines ashore to stop us swinging. No ice could get in and bother us in the night, and even if the wind came, we would be perfectly sheltered.

The fishermen came over to see us. They had built a camp on the beach and had two boats from which they went diving for scallops. Their diving technique was somewhat unorthodox. For air they used motor-driven spray-paint compressors connected to a length of garden hose, with a scuba second-stage regulator on the end of it. They were diving under the ice, in considerably more than 100ft, and

Nick trying to develop a new sport, which he called Windberging.

staying down for much of the day. Nobody had told them it could not be done, nor that they should all have died from the bends years ago. They had not even heard of decompression.

Klaus proved to be as adept at striking a bargain as Julio had been. The fishermen traded an enormous sack of scallops for two bottles of wine, a packet of Jeff's cigarettes and one of Nick's rude magazines. Klaus and Jorge spent most of the next day cleaning what looked to me like a lifetime's supply of scallops.

We were almost settled down for the evening when something happened that I had not bargained for. An extra big lump of ice had floated across the fjord and stopped right in the entrance of our little bay. There was immediate panic. As pretty and snug as the bay was, none of us fancied staying there for the approaching winter. If the tide went out and left the iceberg stranded there, or if a cold snap froze it in place, we could find ourselves in what a friend of ours would describe as 'Dicky's meadow'.

The others looked at me as though I was mad when I said that we should go and move it before it got stuck. Tony was trying to work out how many tons it might weigh, and by the time Jeff and I had launched the big dinghy, he was into the thousands. Lana, Jeff and I motored the dinghy over to the unwelcome iceberg. We put the bows against its side, and started pushing with all the 55 horse-power that the outboard could muster. For a while it looked like a hopeless task, but then we realised that it was moving – only slowly, but it was moving. Lana scrambled up onto the top to tell us which way to steer, and we kept pushing for about ten minutes or so. By this time we had moved it about 50yd, which I hoped would be far enough for it not to come back. We recovered Lana and retired back on board.

The scallop fishermen of Estero Calvo, with their supply boat.

From *Thalassi* we watched the iceberg. Although it was barely moving fast enough to see, it had enough momentum to keep it moving against the general flow of all the smaller ones, knocking them out of the way. We watched it until it was too dark to see, by which time it had gone at least a mile down the fjord. It may have taken us a long time to get it moving, but it was not going to be easily stopped.

Three sunny days among the glaciers must have used up our ration of good weather. It soon returned to normal, but it was time to move on anyway. I could easily spend a whole summer just in that one area, walking, exploring and glacier spotting, but even Klaus's laid-back schedule was ticking by. We set off northwards once more. Even though the canals here were basically running north to south, the wind always seemed to be on the nose and we had to motor a lot.

Lana in command of the iceberg that we had to move because it was blocking our way out from the anchorage. She guided our efforts, telling us which way to push the berg clear with the dinghy.

Our regret at leaving the glaciers was tempered a little by finding a wonderful anchorage off the Paso Brassey. The weather was cold and rainy, and as Darwin had said, we were missing a lot of the scenery. Fortunately the rain stopped as we approached our chosen anchorage, a perfectly landlocked circular little bay at the end of its very own tiny canal. There were no soundings on the chart, so we did not know whether the approach would be deep enough for us. We launched the big dinghy, and Lana, Tony and Nick went ahead, doing a rapid survey for depth. They zigzagged to and fro across the channel, telling me on the radio where the deepest water lay.

The channel was very narrow, only about twice as wide as the boat, with steep, rocky cliffs on either side. It made a dog-leg about halfway along, which made things very tight. The dinghy team had done a good job checking depths, and assured me that there was plenty of water right up to the cliff, but none of them had looked up above. As we came round the corner, I was horrified to see a tree sticking out over the water. It was growing on the top of the cliff, but there was a big branch sticking out into the middle of the channel, just about level with the upper spreaders. Almost on the end of the branch, there was a large bird's nest. I could not see how we could miss it, but a big push with the bow thrutcher got the main mast round it. Then I swung the stern as far over to port as I dared, and the mizzen rigging just brushed by the nest. Had the branch been a foot longer, there would have been a homeless bird or two that night.

Our effort was rewarded by a superb anchorage, as snug as can be imagined. There were high hills all around, usually a sign of nightly williwaws, but the bay was so small that they passed over the top of us. The water was completely calm. A waterfall at the head of the bay was pouring over a cliff that was more than 400ft high. The anchorage was given eleven out of ten. The chart gave it a Spanish name, but we logged it as Bird's Nest Bay, and that is what we will always remember it as.

Jeff and I were getting beckoning signals from the waterfall, saying 'Come and climb me', but unfortunately, once more we had to press on.

In the Canal Messier, the main north–south route, we had a reminder not to become complacent. The water was consistently between 200 and 300ft deep, and we were chugging along quite happily, watching the scenery go by. In the distance we spotted a ship – the first we had seen since leaving Puerto Natales. It took a long time for us to reach it; it seemed to have stopped right in the centre of the channel. As we got closer, we could see that it was a wreck. It had run up onto a rock, right in mid-channel. The rock must

stick up like a spike, in water over 200ft deep. 'MV *Leonides*' had ended her days there, and if she had not been marking that rock, it might have been us instead of her that hit it.

The dreaded Golfo de Penas lay ahead. The well-named Gulf of Pains has a fearsome reputation. It is a bay some 70 miles across, wide open to the west winds of the Roaring Forties. A sailing ship such as the *Beagle* could easily be embayed in heavy weather, unable to beat out past either headland, eventually to be swept ashore on to the jagged rocks.

On the northern headland, Taito Peninsula, the Indians had a portage, an area where they could carry their canoes over a narrow neck of land. Using this, and the smallest canals, they only had to be in exposed water for 10 or 15 miles. Obviously we could not follow their route, so we had to go outside for about 170 miles before we could get back in behind the next chain of islands. A hundred and seventy miles of lee shore in the Roaring Forties did not sound like much fun.

Nick was still feeling that he had been robbed of a Cape Horn gale. Tony said he would be interested in seeing the big waves he had read about. He seemed to forget that to see them he would have to feel them. Jeff was with the rest of us – fingers, toes, arms and legs crossed that we would have an easy passage.

The weather map showed a small high-pressure ridge building, which should give us light winds, so we made a dash for it. The wind stayed light through the night, but there was still quite a big sea running. Poor Klaus lost his dinner, I came close and even Nick refused second helpings. But it was probably due as much to anticipation of what might have been as to the waves themselves. Once again the Forties failed to roar, and as far as I was concerned, that was perfect. We found a sheltered little cove in time for tea, followed by a good night's sleep.

North of the gulf, the terrain and the weather were noticeably softer. There were many more trees, growing on low, rolling hills. For the first time in a long while, there were no snow-capped mountains in sight, and when the sun came out, it was warm enough to sit out on deck. We had a couple of easy days, sailing in sheltered waters. The weather was being gentle, and we had less than 100 miles to go to Puerto Aisen, where Klaus and Jorge would leave us, and three days to do it in.

Klaus was determined to make the most of the last few days. In one small bay, in among the Chonos Islands, he led Jorge, Tony, Nick and Jeff on a little expedition to reach a waterfall that we could see from the boat. Jeff told us later that the going was pretty tough, with

The wreck of the MV Leonides, *in Canal Messier. It might just as easily have been us that hit this pinnacle of rock which was not shown on our chart. If I ever go back, we will have a forward-looking echo sounder to spot such dangers.*

very dense undergrowth. Klaus was undeterred, however, and pressed on in the lead. He led them, one might say, up a gum tree. It was not really a gum tree, it was actually a dead beech tree, but he got everybody up it. It was a very big tree which had fallen over. In the thick undergrowth it afforded a handy path, so he scrambled up onto it, and walked along the trunk. The vegetation was so thick that he did not realise that the tree had not fallen all the way down. When

The anchorage at Caleta Gato, or Pussycat Bay as Jorge not quite literally translated it.

they got to where the branches made it difficult to continue, and Klaus was about to jump off the trunk, they suddenly realised that they were about 30ft off the ground!

Back on terra firma, he decided to take them along the bank of the river. His luck was still out. Part of the bank collapsed, and Klaus fell headlong into the river. Jeff was stripping off to go in after him, with visions of what might happen to us if we drowned one of Chile's most important industrialists. But while he was still teetering on the brink, he realised that Klaus was all right, and laughing his head off. Klaus thought it was a huge joke and swam back to the boat, leaving the others to struggle back through the jungle.

Our last night with Klaus was spent in Caleta Gato, 'Pussycat Bay' in Jorge's not quite literal translation. It had rained most of the day on the way there, but in the late afternoon the weather cleared up. The bay was quite a bit bigger than most of those we had been wriggling into, but it was just as well sheltered. Tree-covered hills surrounded us once again.

Klaus wanted one last expedition. He had been here a couple of years previously, and remembered a lone fisherman who lived nearby. The fisherman lived by catching *centollo*, gigantic crabs, and shipping them off by a cargo boat that kept a monthly schedule. He thought that if we could find the fisherman, we might be able to have crabs for dinner. Jeff said his nerves could not stand keeping an eye on Klaus for another of his expeditions, so Lana, Tony and I went with him and Jorge.

The harbour at Chacabucco, which is the port that serves Puerto Aisen, which is too silted up to be a port. We dropped-off Klaus and Jorge here, and fuelled up for our passage north.

Klaus found the camp without any problems, but it was deserted. The wooden house was open and obviously abandoned, although there were a few home-made tools lying about in a workshop beside the house. The garden was running amok: everything was overgrown, and obviously nobody had tended it for several months. It was so sad. Somebody had put in an enormous amount of work to clear the area, plant a garden and build the house. Now it had all been left, and the jungle would soon reclaim it. Lana and I were suffering from a real dose of melancholy when Klaus started yelling.

He was down on his hands and knees, scrabbling about with something. He had discovered potatoes, lots and lots of potatoes, and he was digging them up. He said they would only go to seed if we did not take them. Feeling a bit guilty, even though it was all but certain that the place had been abandoned for good, we joined him. We dug up as many potatoes as would fit in Tony's hat. Lana cast around the overgrown garden with a more culinary eye. She soon found carrots, cabbages, a clump of chives and a little bush of thyme. Then she found a patch of lettuce which unfortunately was just about to go to seed. We had more fresh vegetables than we had seen since Punta Arenas, and we had a very big and very healthy meal that night.

The next day, April Fool's Day as it happened, we dropped off Klaus and Jorge. Although Aisen is termed a *puerto*, it has become so badly silted as to be effectively closed, so we anchored off Chacabucco, letting them complete their trip by taxi. They promised that they would see us again when we got close to Santiago, which was still the best part of 1000 miles north. We looked forward to it; they were both fun people and had been good shipmates.

Chapter 16

Patagonia to Valparaiso

After *Beagle* stood out to sea from the Magellan Straits, they ran into some awful weather. Although it was unwelcome it should not have been entirely unexpected, since it was by now the middle of winter. I would not have liked that at all. Apart from the added risk of bad weather, the winter days are very short, and the nights correspondingly long. A gale by day is infinitely less frightening than one at night, when the helmsman cannot see the waves coming.

Leaving the Milky Way and the coast of Patagonia behind them, they had to beat to windward to get themselves off the lee shore. Poor Darwin succumbed to the seasickness once more. For more than two weeks he made no entries in his journal, and for much of that time lay flat out in his hammock.

It took them eighteen days to make good the 800 miles to Chiloe. Because they were beating and tacking, the distance they actually sailed was a lot more than that, and every mile of it was hard going. The crew were cold, wet and miserable. Every squall or increase in wind sent them aloft to reef or furl the sails. Rain and spray wet their clothes, and with no heating and little ventilation below decks, there was no chance to dry them. The clothes actually began to rot

I wonder how long our crew would have lasted under those conditions. Nick liked to put his socks in the tumble drier as he came off watch so that he always had warm, dry ones to put on for the next one. Jeff usually managed to organise generating time while he was off watch so that he could keep the electric fan heater running in his cabin while he slept. I think only Tony might have coped. He seemed oblivious to the cold. I do not know whether it was because of his Irish ancestry or the past winter in the Antarctic, but he never once complained about being cold. In fact he was becoming worried about how he would handle the heat when we got further north.

The day before the *Beagle* reached the island of Chiloe, one of the crew died. Darwin does not say whether it was an accident, illness or just plain fatigue, but the entry in his journal expresses his feelings. He writes: 'It is an awful and solemn sound, that splash of the waters over the body of an old shipmate.'

When they reached Chiloe, they anchored off the town they called San Carlos. From Darwin's description, I think it must be the present day Quellon. The schooner *Adventure* caught up with them a couple of days later. Her passage north had been no easier; although she sailed to windward better than the *Beagle* did, she was considerably smaller and suffered even more in the bad weather.

Both ships lay anchored off the port for two weeks, and Darwin was soon fit enough to take some walks ashore. He enjoyed beating his own path through the lush vegetation, which reminded him of Brazil. During that first visit, he spent much of his time studying his geology books. His mind was struggling to cope with the almost unbelievably long epochs that are suggested in geological history, compared to the relatively short periods that people, and indeed all animals and plants, have existed.

They sailed north from Chiloe in easy conditions. As they arrived in Valparaiso, Darwin reports that after the rigours of Patagonia, the climate felt quite delightful. They arrived in the dark, and when Darwin got up in the morning, he marvelled at the view. The soil was very red, contrasting starkly with the whitewashed houses and their tiled roofs. It reminded him very much of Santa Cruz in Tenerife, where the health authorities had denied them permission to land what now seemed like a lifetime before. The sky was blue, with not a cloud to be seen. The atmosphere felt wonderfully dry, and he says 'all nature seemed sparkling with life'. One gets the feeling that he was glad to have stopped sailing for a while.

Fitzroy's plan was to spend several months in Valparaiso, doing the inevitable refit on the ship and bringing all their survey records up to date. Darwin was looking forward to using that period to sort out his own collection, and hopefully to ship the next lot of samples back to England.

Darwin describes Valparaiso as consisting of a long straggling street running along the beach, joined by houses built on either side of ravines running down from the low hills. What would he make of it now? It has expanded to house over 300,000 people, and a series of funicular railways, elevators and zigzag roads connect the original lower parts of the city with the various levels that have been built above it in the hills.

When he got ashore, Darwin was delighted to find a group of English-speaking academics, with whom he was able to have long and involved discussions. He was also excited to receive a batch of mail with up-to-date news of England, which had taken less than eighteen months to reach them. In the mail was a letter from

Henslow, praising him for the collection that he had sent from Montevideo. It seemed to Darwin that all was well with the world.

By coincidence he found that one of his school friends from England was now living in Valparaiso, and he arranged to move in with him for the duration of *Beagle*'s stay. He was happy to escape the confines and routines of the ship for a few weeks.

If all was well with Darwin, the reverse seemed to be the case with Fitzroy. He had worked himself up into a state of nervous tension, and had opted out of all the official functions and shore duties, sending Lieutenant Wickham in his place. Fitzroy spent all his time plotting and planning what to do next, and his schemes were becoming more grandiose by the day. He started to talk of a return to Tierra del Fuego, to survey the coast of western Patagonia, all of Chile and Peru. Then on their way across the Pacific he thought they might well survey New Zealand as well as the Pacific islands themselves. Whatever his officers felt, naval protocol prevented them from commenting. Darwin began to worry that the voyage would go on for ever, but he comforted himself with the thought that since the ship was made of wood and iron, it could not last for ever, so the voyage would have to end eventually.

Fitzroy's plans took a severe blow when he got word from the Admiralty that they would not authorise the purchase or even the hire of the schooner *Adventure*. This was not only a blow to his plans, but to his pride and his pocket as well. So far he had paid all of the *Adventure*'s expenses himself.

Darwin considered leaving the *Beagle* then and there, but his fascination, almost obsession, with the geology of Chile made him stay. He knew he was unlikely to return, and he could not bring himself to leave without taking a look at the geology of central Chile and Peru.

Eventually Fitzroy got a grip of himself, but his attitude was permanently changed. Perhaps even he was becoming a little homesick. He wrote that he could no longer bear the thought of such a long separation from his country, yet he had always made light of being away for long periods, and had shown little compassion for those who were homesick. After his change of heart, he announced that they would complete their survey of Chiloe and the Chonos Islands, then sail north to Peru. From there they would cross the Pacific and head for home. Everybody was relieved about that. The mood among the officers improved at once.

Just before they left Valparaiso, Fitzroy and Darwin had another of their rows. All the officers had been well entertained ashore, and Fitzroy was grumbling about having to throw a reciprocal party on board before they left. Darwin suggested that if it was such a problem for him, then perhaps it was best forgotten. Fitzroy roared at Darwin that he had always thought him to be a man to take favours without feeling the obligation to repay them. Darwin left without saying a word, and went to stay with his friend ashore. When he returned a few days later, Fitzroy received him cordially, and the matter was never referred to again. It was probably just another example of the pressures brought about by close living. We can sympathise.

Adventure was discharged, and *Beagle* returned south to survey Chiloe and the Chonos Islands. When they reached Chiloe, *Beagle* once more lay anchored off San Carlos. While they were there, on a rare clear day, Darwin watched Mount Osorno and two other mainland volcanoes smoking.

A month or so later, they had grandstand seats for an eruption of Osorno. It happened at night, and *Beagle*'s lookout, who first spotted it, thought it was a star rising. The light became steadily brighter, until it was obvious that it was something other than a star. Suddenly flames and lava shot up into the air. Even though the volcano was more than 70 miles away, they could see the streams of red-hot lava running down the side of the mountain. Darwin was fascinated to find out later that several other volcanoes, some as far away as 3000 miles, had all erupted at exactly the same instant.

Witnessing the eruption increased his geological interest still further, while the damp, drizzly weather dampened, literally and metaphorically, his biological ardour. He decided that Chiloe's climate, which he described as being detestable in the winter, is only a little better in the summer.

Fitzroy wanted to survey the whole coast of the island. It is quite large, over 90 miles long and about 30 broad, so he decided that he would take the *Beagle* down the exposed west coast, while Sullivan could survey the sheltered east coast from one of the whale-boats.

Darwin chose to go with the whale-boat. He rode overland to join them at the north end of the island, where they were to start the survey. He found that, because the ground was so damp and boggy, a wooden road had been built from squared-off logs. Because the forest was so difficult to clear, only one road had been built. Boats were the main form of transport for both people and goods, even when going from one part of the island to another.

The climate is the main reason why the islanders found it so hard to clear the forest. The regular and almost continual rain prevented them from burning areas of trees, either for road building or for agriculture. After felling, the trees all had to be cut up into small pieces and carried away. The soil is certainly very fertile, which is why the

The island of Chiloe – after the rugged barren south, the patchwork fields of Chiloe looked soft and inviting. Where we found fields, Darwin had found almost impenetrable forest.

trees grow in such abundance, but the climate makes it virtually impossible to grow anything which needs the sun for ripening. The staples for the locals were potatoes, pigs and of course fish. Little fruit, and almost no grains were being grown.

Once Darwin joined the whale-boat, they worked their way south along the length of the island, camping on the beach each night. They aroused considerable curiosity. Strangers were rare enough on the island, and several people approached them, asking if they were soldiers who had come to liberate the island from the patriot government of Chile. Chiloe had been one of the last strongholds of Spanish Imperialism, and Spain had relinquished control of the island only eight years before.

Darwin was fascinated to find that most of the inhabitants of the island wore home-knitted garments, a tradition that continues to this day. They not only wear knitted sweaters, but often knitted hats and ponchos as well.

The survey team paid a visit to Castro, which is now the capital of the island. Darwin called it a forlorn and deserted place. Under Spanish rule it had obviously been a bigger, more important town, because they could still see the quadrangular arrangement of disused Spanish streets. In the remains of the plaza, and indeed on many of the roads, a fine green turf had grown, and where the *señoritas* had once paraded their charms, sheep now grazed.

Darwin visited the wooden church, and describes it as having 'a picturesque and venerable aspect', but they found the whole town to be very poor. Because none of the 200 inhabitants could afford a watch or a clock, an old man, who was said to have a good sense of time, was employed to ring the hours on the church bell by guess-

Inside the wooden church at Castro, on Chiloe. This was where Darwin found a man paid to guess the time and ring the bell, as nobody had a clock.

work. I have no doubt that Darwin will have timed him, but unfortunately he does not record whether the chimes were accurately rung or not.

As they worked their way south, Darwin was intently studying the rock formations. He concluded that granite was the 'fundamental rock' of the world; at that time it formed the deepest layer of the earth's crust that man had been able to penetrate.

When the whale-boat crew rejoined *Beagle* at the southern end of the island, Darwin went ashore where some of the officers were taking bearings for the survey. He saw a fox, of a species which is unique to this area and extremely rare. It was so engrossed in watching the surveyors that Darwin was able to creep up behind it, and whack it on the head with his geological hammer. It eventually ended up stuffed and mounted back in London. It did not seem to worry Darwin that he had killed one of the last of the species, perhaps contributing to its extinction.

He accompanied the survey team in an attempt to reach the summit of one of the hills. They ran into the same problem as Klaus had. The trees were so densely packed and tangled together that he reckoned they sometimes went ten minutes or more without touching the ground. At one stage they found themselves so far above the ground that some of the seamen, in jest, started calling out the soundings.

They also explored and tried to survey the Chonos Islands. It was not easy: the weather stayed bad almost the whole time. One day, while they were anchored in the Chonos, they had one particularly strong gale which Darwin felt was worthy of Cape Horn. The water was white with flying spray, and sheets of dark rain drove past them. At the height of the storm, the sun peeped out through a brief break in the clouds, and they saw a very bright rainbow. As they stood on deck looking at it, the wind picked up enough spray from the sea to complete the rainbow's circle.

Christmas came and went, and was recorded by Darwin as a dreary occasion. For one so young he was rapidly becoming a bit of a curmudgeon. A couple of days after Christmas they discovered a new harbour, which of course had to be surveyed. Much to their surprise, they saw a man on the beach, waving furiously. A boat was sent ashore, and they found a group of six men who had run away from an American whaler. They had absconded with one of the ship's boats, but had lost it in a storm and were now marooned. It was their greatest good fortune that *Beagle* had stumbled upon them; otherwise they would certainly have perished.

The new year, 1835, was ushered in with yet another gale. The weather obviously intended to start as it meant to go on. Darwin was looking forward to leaving this coast before the end of the year, and wrote that he was looking forward to crossing the Pacific, 'where a blue sky above tells one there is a Heaven – a something beyond the clouds above our heads'.

The survey of the Chonos continued with difficulty, as gale after gale swept through. Darwin made a few sorties ashore, and on one of them discovered a lot of wild potatoes. The potato as we know it is derived from those which the Spanish explorers found growing in several areas of South America. It is thought that the Indians in some areas have been cultivating potatoes since before the time of Christ. Darwin dug up some of them and was a little disappointed that when they were cooked, they were not as good as the home-grown ones he was used to. He found them a bit watery and almost completely tasteless.

He did not find many animals to study. There were a lot of seals, which always seemed surprised to see visitors, and he also saw several sea-otters and a capybara, a creature that looks like a large rat.

When the survey of the islands was finished, they headed north again for the last time. They stopped briefly in Chiloe once more, then anchored close to Valdivia, on the mainland. When he rode inland to the town itself, Darwin discovered that it was almost awash in apples. The trees virtually engulfed the town, and everywhere he went, there were apples. The soil and climate were so suitable for the fruit that a branch cut off a tree would root, sprout and even sometimes bear fruit if it was just stuck in the ground.

He spent a few nights there, and commented that his first night ashore was often a bit restless, as he was not used to the tickling and biting of the fleas. Although *Beagle*, like all ships of her time, was infested with rats, the fleas seem to have been kept under control. I wonder whether rats eat fleas?

While he was ashore, Darwin experienced an earthquake at first hand. He was sitting in the forest, taking a breather, when the ground began to shake. He leaped to his feet and found that he could stand, although the swaying of the ground made him feel giddy, almost like being back at sea. The trees swayed and the leaves whispered. He found the experience more interesting than frightening. Fitzroy and some of the officers were in Valdivia where not many of the wooden buildings fell down. As the houses shook, however, the planks creaked and groaned, and people came running outside in terror. It was the general panic that made it seem more frightening there than out in the forest where Darwin was.

On their way back north, they found that Concepción and

Talcahuano had been all but levelled. A tidal wave had come roaring through Talcahuano to complete what the quake itself had started. The wave reached a height of 23ft above high water, and when it receded, little more than a single row of bricks remained where the houses once stood. A schooner had been thrown up into the ruins of the fort, and left 200yd from the sea. When he saw the damage, Darwin tried to visualise the effect that such an earthquake would have on London. It was beyond his imagining.

The earthquake heightened his geological interest. He saw that the land around Talcahuano had risen by 2 or 3ft above the sea, and at an island a few miles north, rocks that they had recently surveyed as being under water now stood 10ft clear. It was fine to theorise about geological upheavals, but to see it happen at first hand was fantastically exciting. In Concepción, he studied the way in which walls had fallen. He noticed that the walls running along the line of the shock wave had often stood intact, while those running across the line, had almost invariably fallen. He may have felt a little guilty that his compassion for the inhabitants had been overshadowed by his geological interest. He wrote that this was the most exciting thing he had seen since leaving England.

Back in Valparaiso they had a final refit, to get the *Beagle* ready for crossing the Pacific.

The last word we had received from the Boss had been for us to get to Talcahuano as soon as possible after dropping Klaus. We did the usual fuelling and provisioning, and started north. We were coming to the part of Chile that Klaus knew best, and before he left he went through the charts with us and marked on a few suggested stops.

On the first day, we covered an easy 58 miles and stopped in a long narrow bay called Puerto Amparo. Perhaps it was the low grassy hills that reminded Tony of his native Ireland, but something inspired him to try his luck at fishing. 'This looks like grand salmon country,' he said as he, Nick and Jeff went off in the dinghy to try and capture supper.

While they were gone, two fishermen stopped by *Thalassi*. They wanted to trade fish for cigarettes. I stole a packet from Jeff's supply, and got two big, ready-cleaned hake in return. When the boys came

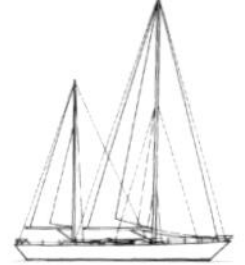

back empty-handed, I rather smugly showed them what I had 'caught'.

Our next anchorage was rated a 'do not miss' by Klaus. It was a little bay about halfway up a long fjord. At the head of the fjord was a little town called Puyuguapi – pronounced as near as we could get it as 'pooyoowappy'. The bay where he had told us to stop was a small fishing resort. Normally we shy away from known resorts, but we were glad we had heeded Klaus's advice on this one.

The hotel was a very low-key little place. It was in the process of closing down for the winter, so there were no guests. When they did have guests, the resort's speciality was to fly them to the lakes, high in the mountains, in a small float plane. This way their guests could fish otherwise inaccessible lakes. But, although most people came to Puyuguapi for the fishing, what Klaus had told us to investigate were the hot springs.

There were three pools at different levels down the side of the hill. The lowest was the hottest – too hot for any of us to get into. The middle one was a small swimming pool, but our favourite was the top one, a little rock pool set into a grotto-like cave. It was just big enough for the five of us to get into. It was very hot, but just bearable if one eased in gently. Once in, it felt wonderful. Across the fjord were the last of the snow-capped mountains, just visible through the trees from the pool. Lana had had the foresight to pack a cooler full of beers and Cokes. To lie in the steaming water, sipping a cold drink, surrounded by dripping ferns and flowers, gazing across the fjord at the snowy mountains was just about the most sybaritic experience one could imagine. Wonderful.

Afterwards, five wrinkled prunes finally staggered back to the boat, to face another bombshell – a message saying that an engineer from the boatyard, José was arriving to join us the next morning, in Chacabuco. The Boss had arranged for him to come and sail with us for ten days so that he would see what problems still existed with the boat and hopefully learn from our experiences when building the next one. That was fine, except that the Boss had forgotten to tell us, and we had left Chacabuco two days previously. We were now over 120 miles away, and there was no way we could get back there in time for José's arrival.

I tried calling the boatyard in Spain, but it was Friday night and the place was closed for the weekend. I called Julio, back in Punta Arenas, and asked him to help us sort things out. He got Klaus involved, and we managed to get a message to Santiago airport, where José would have to change planes *en route* to Chacabuco. Julio had discovered that there was a bus from Chacabuco to Puyuguapi,

In the hot springs at Puyuguapi. To soak in the hot pools while looking across at the snow covered mountains was wonderful.

so I decided that we would stay put and let José come to us. It would be much quicker than for us to sail south to collect him and then have to come all the way north again to resume our journey to Talcahuano. At least that is what we thought, but that was before we had experienced Chilean public transport. In the meantime, we reconciled ourselves to having to spend another day in the hot pools, waiting for José and the Chacabuco bus to reach us. Life can be so trying!

The bus was due to arrive late the following afternoon, so after soaking the day away, we dinghied into town to look for José. There was no bus, no José. A policeman saw us wandering around, and asked us if we were looking for José. When we said we were, he told us that the bus (there was only the one it seems) had broken an axle and would not be running for several days. Somehow the policeman had found out that José was coming by boat, and would arrive the next morning on the Chacabuco ferry.

When José did eventually arrive, he was almost out on his feet, having been travelling for about four days. He did not seem to be in any state to sail so, out of consideration to him, another lazy day at the hot pools was forced upon us. By the time we left the following morning, we must have been the cleanest crew of yachties ever to set sail!

We made 88 miles in very light winds that day, to reach Tictoc Bay. Klaus had promised us some resident killer whales there, but it was not to be. We cruised around searching the bay, but all we found was two groups of sea-lions. Compared with their Falkland cousins, they were wimps. They dived into the water without even a growl as soon as the dinghy came anywhere near them.

It was Lana's birthday the next day. Nick undertook to get up early (a serious sacrifice for him) and to cook breakfast. He insisted that Lana was served hers in bed. By the time the resulting mayhem in the galley was cleaned up, we were a bit late getting underway, so I decided to make a fairly short hop of about 50 miles, to the southern end of Chiloe, *Beagle*'s landfall after her eighteen-day passage up from the south.

It was a grey and rainy day. It was not a howler, but the wind was fresh enough as we crossed the open Golfo Corcovado. Poor José was looking distinctly green; he had not found his sealegs yet.

About halfway across the gap, Lana went into our cabin to fetch something, and found hydraulic oil pouring out of the deckhead, all over her bunk and a fair number of her clothes. Happy birthday! Jeff and I started to take down the panelling to see where the oil was coming from. Lana went up into the cockpit and we could hear her roaring at poor José: 'You built the stupid boat, so you go and stop

the oil pouring onto my bunk.'

José came down and took a brief look, then hastily retreated, preferring to face Lana's wrath rather than the smell of hydraulic oil in the bouncing cabin. Meanwhile Jeff and I were getting close to losing our breakfasts, which Nick had laboured over for so long. The heavy motion and the stink of the oil were a powerful combination. We traced the leak to the seal under one of the hydraulic winches. There was nothing we could do about it until we stopped. No more oil would come out if we did not use that winch, but there was plenty of oil still to be cleaned up.

Lana had another go at José. She gave him a bucket and some paper towel and sent him back down to help. 'It's the boatyard's fault that all my things are covered in oil – the least you can do is help them clean it up.' He appeared dutifully at the cabin door, clutching his roll of paper towel and bucket. He took a look and a sniff at what was going on, and a moment later his breakfast was in the bucket. Lana finally relented, and he was allowed to retreat before he made a bigger mess for us to clean up.

No sooner was our cabin back in reasonable order than Jeff found that the stern gland was leaking again, even worse than before. We hove to for a while so that Jeff could tighten his makeshift lashings. José was openly relieved that Jeff did not make him go into the engine-room bilge to take a look. We were hoping to haul the boat in Talcahuano and replace the whole gland, so Jeff contented himself with grumbling at poor José all the way to Chiloe.

By the time we got into the lee of the island, everybody had had enough. We anchored in the first sheltered spot we came to, off the town of Quellon. Nick and Tony were sent ashore to try and find a restaurant where we could take the cook out for a birthday dinner. They did well, and a nice meal ashore put everybody in better spirits.

Quellon is a sleepy little town that still has a fair amount of horse-drawn traffic. The green hills, the scattered cultivated fields and the damp drizzly weather reminded us of Ireland. The invention of the chain saw has resulted in the demise of a fair amount of Darwin's dense forest. There are now quite big areas patchworked with fields, and a network of roads cover the island.

When we got to Castro, about halfway up the east side of the island, we found it to be bigger and a bit more bustling than Quellon. The houses along the waterfront are all built on stilts, with water lapping around them at high tide. Almost all the buildings, including the big church that Darwin visited, are wooden. Most of the houses and shops seem to be made of some kind of pine, but the church appears to be built of cedar.

I am not sure whether the church we saw is a new one, or the original one which has been refurbished, but it is all in extremely good condition. The inside is spectacular – all vaulted ceilings and arches. Everything is of wood, even the massive pillars, which are built in sections and reach up to the high ceiling. The whole church smells like a cigar box. I was somewhat surprised to see four confessionals, each of them a two-seater. The people of Castro must be either very sinful or very pious.

There is still a thriving woollen industry in Chiloe. Many of the locals wear home-knitted garments. Lana received a sweater from me and a knitted poncho from the boys for her birthday.

From Castro, we coast-hopped up to the north end of the island. It seemed that every mile we went, the land became more and more cultivated. Big tracts of forest had been cleared, to be replaced by cultivated fields.

From the north end of Chiloe to Talcahuano is about 300 miles. There are no more off-lying islands or sheltered canals, so I decided to do it in one shot. It was getting close to the time when José was due to fly out anyway, and he did not relish another journey by Chilean public transport – he was anxious that we deliver him to Talcahuano itself in good time for his flight. On the second night out, we crossed the fortieth parallel – we had escaped the forties without getting seriously roared at.

A couple of hours before dawn, Tony spotted a red flare off to the east. Jeff, who was on watch with him, came to wake me. On the radar we could see a small echo about 5 miles away. We motored over to investigate. As we came close, we could see that it was a small fishing boat, in total darkness. Although Jeff's Spanish is quite good, we decided to roust out José, and let him do the talking.

I was distinctly nervous about going too close to an unknown vessel in the dark. We had read about pirate attacks and dope smugglers who steal yachts. Were we being set up? I am basically opposed to guns on boats, and I was not happy when I had found that the Boss had four guns and several thousands rounds of ammunition on board. On this occasion, however, it gave me some comfort to have his .45 revolver in my pocket.

The crew of the fishing boat told José that they could not start their engine, and had flattened their battery in the process of trying. They asked us for a tow. I really did not want to tow them the 50 or 60 miles to port, so we used the radio and managed to raise another vessel in their fleet. He agreed to come and do the tow. We gave them our position and turned on our deck lights so that they could find us. We stood by, a discreet distance off, until the second boat came into sight, and then continued on our interrupted journey northwards.

Klaus had warned us that Talcahuano could hardly be considered the garden of Chile, but we were entirely unprepared for the dirt, pollution and general squalor of the place. The little town that Darwin described is gone forever. Talcahuano is now a city of over 250,000 people, and Chile's main naval port. The anchorage close to town is dirty and extremely smelly. Ashore there is a fish-processing plant and a slaughterhouse, and neither of them appear to be too careful about what they allow to run into the water. As we walked past the slaughterhouse, there was a row of big vultures sitting on the fence, licking their beaks, waiting for lunch. The fish plant was even more depressing – great truckloads of fish being tipped into the grinder to make fertiliser.

Costumes and Intimidation took a good part of the day, then we walked up to the big shipyard, where the Boss had assured us that we would be able to haul the boat. It was well past time to renew the anti-fouling paint on the bottom, and we had to do something about the now permanently leaking stern gland. It turned out that the yard had no equipment for lifting yachts, and never had had. All they could offer was to put us into the dry dock for big ships. If we went in with another ship, then we would have to stay as long as it did, which might be anything from a week to a month. If we went in alone, the charge would be the same as for a big cargo ship. When we sent the Boss the quote for that, the telex almost smoked with his reply. The gist was that we were to haul the boat elsewhere, but he offered no further suggestions as to where.

We waved goodbye to José, and hoped that he would not have to suffer another four days' travelling to get home. If the twenty-five-page report (that he took back with him) helped the yard improve their product, then his journey would have been worthwhile.

Lana, in her foray ashore, had found a Chinese restaurant, and everybody was keen to go there for dinner. Since I did not want the boat to be left unattended, we went in shifts. Lana and I went first, and had a reasonable meal. The only problem we had was with the street children begging. They were pestering and jostling us, and I even caught one with his hand in my pocket. Threatening to break it off did not seem to worry him. We got back without being robbed, and then the boys set off. As usual, they took a radio and said they would call me when they were ready to be picked up. It would not be safe for them to leave the dinghy tied up ashore unattended; if our experience with the children was anything to go by, it would be stolen in a flash.

I settled down with a good book to await their call. Midnight came and went. By 2 a.m. I was feeling like an anxious parent, and by 4 a.m. we were downright worried. Had the radio broken down or been stolen? Were they stretched out bleeding in some gutter after being mugged? There was really not much we could do in the dark. I was not going to go wandering round town on my own looking for them. If it was a radio problem then surely they would think to go to the Port Captain or even a fishing boat, and use their radio? We decided to wait until 9 a.m. before taking action.

I was just finishing breakfast when a cheery sounding Jeff came on the radio, saying that they were ready to be picked up. I found three somewhat hungover but giggly crew standing on the dock. They started to tell me that they had decided to spend the night in a guest house that they had found. The guest house must have been very busy, because they had each had to share a bed with a total stranger – three girls as it happened. I was furious. It was the only time on the whole trip that I yelled at them, and all became a bit sheepish when they realised how cross I was. If they had called on the radio I would not have minded at all, but I had missed a night's sleep, and Lana and I had worried unnecessarily, just because they were to idle to call.

Back on board they all found jobs to do, and went straight to work. It must have hurt them not to be able to sneak off to bed, but to be fair to them, they did not try.

Luckily none of us bore grudges, and everything was back to normal the next day. Their night ashore was to come back to haunt them, though – but more of that later.

Our mail arrived, together with a replacement stern gland from the boatyard – unfortunately the wrong size. The other bit of bad news was that we still had not been paid. Nor had Jeff, and he was absolutely furious. 'The Boss's not going to get away with this,' he said. I do not think I have ever seen Jeff so angry. 'I'm going to get a writ put on the boat, so that we cannot move until he pays up.'

Lana, ever the practical one, tried to calm him down a bit. 'If we do get the boat arrested, then let's find somewhere nicer than Talcahuano to stay in.'

She and I had a family conference, and decided that we had had enough. We sent the Boss a telex giving him three months' notice to find a new crew, and in the meantime, asked him to bring Jeff's and our salaries up to date. We were feeling a bit as Fitzroy did when he heard that the Admiralty were not going to repay him for the *Adventure*'s expenses. He did not understand why he should have to pick up the bill for doing part of the Admiralty's survey, and we did not see why we should be subsidising a millionaire's yacht.

Since we were not going to haul the boat at the shipyard, there was

no reason to linger in that smelly harbour. That morning, when I had gone into the cockpit, I had come face to face with two vultures, sitting on the mizzen boom and looking down the hatch. They are such ugly birds close up, especially as these looked as if they had just come from breakfast at the slaughterhouse. Vultures have no feathers on their heads or necks, so that if they stick their heads into some rotting carcass, there is nothing to catch and stop them pulling it back out. I went back below to tell the others so that they could come and look. 'I recognise them,' said Nick. 'They are the Boss's accountants who came to the boat in Spain.' After he had pointed it out, we all agreed that there was indeed a strong resemblance.

Klaus had given us an invitation to visit his yacht club at Algorrobo, about 15 or 20 miles south of Valparaiso. The plan had been to go there in three or four weeks' time, after our supposed haul and refit, but the vultures decided it. I went ashore to call Klaus, to ask if we could head up there at once, and do our bits of work in prettier, less smelly surroundings.

He seemed a little hesitant, and asked if we could delay for a couple a days. If we could wait until the weekend then he would be able to meet us there and guide us in. I did not want to be too pushy, but told him we had had enough of Talcahuano, and were going to leave that day regardless. I said we would be more than happy either to anchor outside the club's marina until the weekend or, if that became too exposed, to go up to Valparaiso for a day or two. Anything would be better than another night in Talcahuano.

We had a couple of hundred miles to go, so it was going to be an overnight journey. As we left the bay of Talcahuano, we ran into thick fog. There were all kinds of little fishing boats messing about, and some of them did not show up too well on the radar, so we set the foghorn going, hooting every two minutes. Fortunately the fog cleared enough a few miles offshore for us to turn it off, otherwise nobody would have got any sleep.

On the way up the coast, Jeff started teasing Tony unmercifully. 'You think you're a sailor now, just because you've done 2000 miles on the boat. You've been round Cape Horn (twice by the Boss's reckoning) but you've still got the real test to come.

Tony was looking a little nervous. 'What's that?'

'You've never been into a marina yet,' said Jeff with a self-satisfied smirk. 'That's really going to test your mettle.'

We found the club without difficulty. The marina was a very small artificial harbour, protected in part by a large rock – or perhaps I should call it a small island. On the rock/island was a colony of penguins. We thought we had left them far behind, but then realised that the cold current which flows up the coast there is the same one which affects the climate of the Galapagos, and of course there are penguins there too.

I was about to anchor just north of the marina entrance, where it looked as if we would be sheltered from the swell, when somebody ashore spotted us. There was a lot of whistling, yelling and waving. They wanted us to go in. The entrance was very narrow – like Bird's Nest Bay all over again. They directed us along the end of the harbour, where it became apparent why Klaus wanted to delay us: they were building a floating dock specially for us to tie up to.

It turned out that when Klaus called it 'his' yacht club, he was not exaggerating. He was the founder and the main mover behind it. He had been planning to build a dock big enough for his dream ship, and our visit had brought that building forward. He told the club staff to build his dock now so that we could use it! They were mortified that it was not quite finished.

The club was a much nicer spot than where *Beagle* lay in Valparaiso, and infinitely better than Talcahuano. It turned out to be a great place to get our jobs done, and thanks to Klaus and Jorge, a good spot to do a bit of sightseeing from as well.

The vultures on the boom at Talcahuano.

Chapter 17

In and Around Valparaiso

During the *Beagle*'s two stays in Valparaiso, Darwin managed to do a fair amount of exploring and collecting. On their first visit, he made a fairly serious foray into the foothills of the Andes. Along the way, he found several signs that many of the mountains had been under the sea at one time. There were old seashells at a height of over 1300 ft – not just one or two shells, but great banks of them, enough for the locals to burn them to make quicklime. He tried to imagine the forces that must have been involved to lift the whole range of mountains bodily upwards for over a 1000 ft.

On his various trips in the mountains he noticed a comparative lack of animals. He sought to explain this by saying that perhaps none had been 'created' since the land had risen up from the sea.

The dry climate suited Darwin well. He felt that the last of the Patagonian dampness was being driven from his bones. The prevailing summer winds are mostly offshore and very dry. It is usually only during the three months of the winter that any rain falls at all. The dry climate determines what vegetation can grow. Trees are few and far between, but he found many species of wild flowers. He had noticed that in a dry climate, plants often tend to have a stronger smell than those in damper regions. During the course of his walks, his clothes picked up the scents of plants he brushed against.

He visited the hot springs at Cauquenes, which are still used as mineral baths today. He measured their temperature, and pondered the puzzle that the water in the springs is not only hotter but more plentiful during the dry summer months. What he does not record is whether or not he enjoyed a soak, as we did in Puyuguapi.

Towards the end of his first expedition, he went down with a mystery illness. It laid him up for three weeks, and although he never did find out what it was, he blamed it for his subsequent bad health. It may just have been a bad case of 'traveller's tummy'. When visiting new places, we sometimes fall prey to some 'bug' to which the locals are completely immune. Curiously enough, in the cold dampness of Patagonia, none of us had so much as a chill, yet once we got to the kinder climate near Valparaiso we, like Darwin, all developed various ailments.

From *Beagle*'s anchorage off the city, they could see the Andes, and the peak of Aconcagua. This is the highest peak in the Andes, indeed in the western hemisphere. By a series of triangulations, the *Beagle's'* officers measured it to be 23,000 ft. That is remarkably close to the figure 22,834 ft that today's cartographers have arrived at.

One can begin to understand just how narrow the country of Chile is when one realises that from the coast one can see Aconcagua, which is well within Argentina's borders.

If Darwin perhaps looked wistfully at the mountain, he must have accepted that it was beyond their resources to climb it. It was to be another fifty years before a serious attempt was made, and it was not until 1897 that it was first climbed, by Matthias Zurbriggan. Even though Darwin did not climb Aconcagua, he did make a trip high into the mountains, to cross to the Argentinian plains. He travelled first to Santiago, Chile's capital, but did not linger, preferring to spend his time in the mountains. He had two local companions, and a train of eleven mules.

He was fascinated by the way one mule, termed the *madrina*, or godmother, controlled the group. Wherever she went, the others followed, like obedient children. Her sole task was to lead the troop; she was never ridden, nor did she carry a load. The *madrina* wore a small bell, and when it was time to get under way in the mornings, all that was required was to find her and ring her bell, and the troop would form up in line astern. On level ground each mule could carry more than 400 lb of cargo, but on a mountainous route this was reduced to around 300 lb. Of the ten mules they took, not counting the *madrina*, six were intended for riding, and four for carrying goods. They were rotated in their tasks during the expedition.

Because it was late in the year, and there was a risk that they might be snowed in somewhere, they took extra food with them.

As they made their way up the valleys into the mountains, Darwin studied the shingle terraces that they passed. It occurred to him that the shingle looked exactly the same as the material which a mountain stream deposits when it is suddenly checked in its course by flowing into a lake or the sea. Finally it dawned on him that perhaps these banks had been formed in exactly that way, as the mountains were slowly thrust upwards. The banks would have formed first near the head of the valley, at what was then sea level. As the mountains rose, successive banks would form lower down.

This was radical thinking, because until that time the popular view was that the mountains had been formed by some vast cataclysmic upthrust, not a comparatively gentle, slow rising. The further he went, however, the more signs he saw and the more convinced he became that his theory was correct.

They crossed the ridge at about 14,000 ft, and even the mules were finding it difficult to breathe. They would stop every 50 yd for a few seconds to catch their breath. Then they would restart of their own accord, such willing beasts were they. Darwin says he felt a slight tightness across his head and chest, and likened the feeling to that of leaving a warm room and going outside to run on a frosty day. The Chilenos called the feeling *puna*, and did not understand that it was related to altitude and the air becoming thinner. They thought that wherever there was snow there was *puna*, and they were convinced that the only cure was to eat a lot of onions. Darwin found that the best cure for him was finding fossil seashells at the top of the ridge – he was so excited that he completely forgot about the *puna*.

The other effect that the altitude had was on the cooking. They carried a big iron pot in which they boiled their potatoes on a campfire. Because of the reduced pressure, the water boiled at a much lower temperature than at sea level – just the opposite to a pressure cooker. The boiling point is reduced by 1 degree Fahrenheit for every 500 ft of altitude. So at 14,000 ft, the water was boiling at 184 degrees Fahrenheit, or about 84 degrees Celsius. Despite leaving the pot on the fire all night, with the potatoes boiling all the time, they were still too hard to eat in the morning. Darwin overheard his two companions discussing the matter. He knew that they both firmly believed in *puna*, and now he heard them say that the pot, which had been newly purchased for the expedition, was cursed. It had obviously decided not to cook the potatoes.

After their potatoless breakfast, they carried on over the ridge and began their descent to the plains of Argentina. Darwin was at once struck by the difference in vegetation between the two sides of the mountain chain. He found similar differences between the animals, and concluded that the mountains had been there, as an impassable barrier, longer than the animals and plants had existed.

As they reached the valley floor, they came to an outpost, where an officer and three soldiers were stationed to check passports. So Costumes and Intimidation were in full operation even then. One of the men was a pure-blooded pampas Indian. His job was to track anybody trying to sneak past the outpost. The officer in charge told Darwin that a few years before, somebody had tried to get past them by taking a long detour over a nearby mountain. The Indian, by chance, crossed his track. He was able to follow the track over dry and stony ground for a whole day before finding the fugitive hiding in a gully. It strikes me the Customs could use more agents like him today to catch the drug smugglers and illegal immigrants.

When Darwin and his companions eventually arrived back at Valparaiso after some three weeks in the mountains, they found that the *Beagle* was almost ready to continue her voyage northwards. Darwin wanted to investigate the geology of the land further north. Fitzroy agreed that he could go overland, and be picked up at Copiapo, about 420 miles north of Valparaiso.

For transportation Darwin bought four horses and two mules, for the princely sum of £25. At the end of his journey, he sold them for £23. Since rain was so infrequent, they usually slept under the stars, so all in all, it turned out to be a cheap journey for him. He set off along the coast, accompanied by one of the guides from the mountain trip. They had not gone many miles north before the few remaining trees gave way to scrubland. He found the coast road more or less barren, and singularly uninteresting. He took a few detours inland to visit one of the gold-mining areas, and to do a bit of geological work.

They reached Coquimbo and had a brief rendezvous with the *Beagle*. Fitzroy came ashore to dine with Darwin at the guesthouse where he had taken a room. The meal ended in chaos, as another earth tremor shook the house. The locals all fled in panic, anticipating the worst. As it happened it was a mild tremor, and no damage was done.

Darwin went to examine the shingle terraces above the town. They were narrow and fringe-like, rising one behind the other. On the highest, over 250 ft above the sea, he was delighted to find the shells of existing marine species. This strongly reinforced his theory about the land being slowly uplifted.

On another day he was taken into the foothills to visit a silver mine. The thing he found most remarkable about this trip was that the bedroom he stayed in at the silver mine had no fleas. Where he was staying in Coquimbo, there was a swarm of them. At the silver mine they were at about 3000 ft and it was a littler cooler, but not very much. Yet there was not a flea to be seen or felt. He was very curious to know why. Was it the altitude? Could fleas not get up to 3000 ft?

While they were in Coquimbo it rained for the first time for seven months. It was a light rain, and hardly seemed to wet the ground, yet to Darwin's amazement the whole area, which the day before had been as bare as the road, grew a green fuzz almost immediately. We have seen a similar thing in the West Indies, when the first rain of the season turned a brown hillside green overnight.

Darwin, his companion and the animals carried on northwards to Copiapo, which is on the edge of the Atacama Desert. This is the driest desert in the world, and rain has never been recorded in some parts. The Andes form a barrier for the north easterly trade winds, and the cold Humbolt Current makes a temperature inversion, holding cold, dry air close to the surface. It is no wonder that the words sterile and barren frequently occur in Darwin's account of the last part of the journey.

Beagle arrived at Copiapo soon after Darwin did. He sold the horses and mules and said goodbye to his riding companion. He seemed happy enough to be back on board the *Beagle* as she left to sail north the next day.

For the passage up the Peruvian coast, Lieutenant Wickham was temporarily in command. Fitzroy had heard that another naval ship, HMS *Challenger*, had gone aground south of Talcahuano, and had set off to organise her rescue. When he got there, he had a blazing row with the officer in charge, who was actually his superior. Fitzroy thought he was dragging his feet, and threatened him with court martial. He then proceeded to take control of the whole operation. Perhaps it was fortunate for him that the ship was safely refloated. The jaunt did him good, and he was in fine form when he eventually rejoined the *Beagle* in Callao, the port for Lima.

Darwin had not had such an exciting time. They stopped at the small town of Iquique, which was then in Peru, but is now well and truly inside Chile. He did not think much of the place. It is totally isolated by desert to the north and to the south, and he thought life there was no better than that on board a ship. Everything, including water and food, had to be brought in by boat. The town existed because of a saltpetre mine, which Darwin of course had to visit. These deposits of nitrates are what sparked the war between Chile and Peru in 1879. In the battle of Iquique, on 21 May, the Peruvians suffered the loss of their best battleship, the *Independencia.* This allowed the Chilean forces to land, and they eventually captured Lima. Under the terms of the peace treaty, the southern section of Peru, including all the nitrate beds, became part of Chile, which they are to this day.

The road to the mines was remarkable for the number of mule skeletons. The mules had all perished making the same trek, and now lay beside the road. Other than vultures, which were constantly circling above as if waiting for Darwin and his companions to join the mules, he saw neither bird, quadruped, reptile nor insect for the whole journey.

Darwin was happy enough to leave Iquique, and sail north to Callao. At least he was happy until they got out to sea. Strong following winds made the ship roll, and soon put Darwin back in his hammock. The weather was overcast for much of the time. When he

had been in the Atlantic, he had longed for the Pacific. Now he fondly remembered brilliant days, cool evenings, glorious skies and bright stars; the Atlantic had all the virtues.

Darwin did not think much of Callao either. The whole town was filthy, and he said that the inhabitants were drunken and depraved. He felt the whole country was on the brink of anarchy. From stories we heard from other yachts, it seems little has changed in the last 150 years.

Lima he liked, however. He said that the dark-eyed women, their tight gowns showing off their firm, full figures, were better to look at than all the churches and buildings in the city.

Although the ship was there for six weeks, awaiting the return of Captain Fitzroy, Darwin spent most of his time on board, writing up his diary and his geographical notes covering the preceding six months. He was anxious to get out into the Pacific proper. He wanted to visit a coral atoll. The current thinking was that the circular atolls only grew on the rims of submerged volcanic craters. Now Darwin began to wonder, if the whole of the South American continent was being slowly lifted up, as he had seen, what was to stop equally large areas of the seabed from sinking? If this was the case, then the reefs could easily be growing up around the edges of sinking mountains. We now know this to be the case. Before even seeing his first atoll, Darwin had solved the riddle, but he was anxious to go and see if he could find proof.

Fitzroy finally returned, full of the joys of life after his adventure. He went out and bought another schooner, and sent it back to Chile to continue the survey. The *Beagle* set off towards the Galapagos, taking Darwin towards his greatest discovery.

Our stay in Algarrobo was a delight. The town is small, clean and prosperous. It is one of several popular coastal weekend destinations for people from Santiago, Chile's capital. It did not take Lana long to discover that there were numerous little restaurants within a few minute's walk of the marina.

Ajoining the marina compound was a tree-filled park, with a series of paths zigzagging through it. We instituted an evening get-fit jog, to try and get rid of some of the fat we had all gained from the general lack of physical activity. Spending so much time at sea had taken its toll on our waist-lines.

What really made our stay memorable – and pleasant – was the hospitality shown to us by Klaus and Jorge. Jorge brought his parents down to visit *Thalassi*. He gave them the tour of the boat, and then invited us all to go to his parents' weekend cottage for a barbecue lunch. Fortunately it was only a few miles away, because it was a squeeze to get everybody into two cars.

The weekend cottage turned out to be an old farm of about 200 acres. The original stone house had been most beautifully restored, and a section of the garden is now a dedicated barbecue area. There is not only the normal barbecue pit, but also a separate spit and a traditional Chilean stone oven. Tables and benches are arranged in the shade of big, droopy flowering trees. Pisco sours, Chile's national drink, which the crew were managing to drink all too easily, were followed by an excellent lunch of grilled sausages, steaks and a variety of vegetables. Everybody ate too much.

Jorge told us the tale of how his grandfather, whom he brought to visit the boat later, had swum ashore on Staten Island after being shipwrecked seventy-five years before. He had forsaken the sea and his native Germany, and had chosen to settle in Chile. He had started making and mending things, and this had slowly grown into the steel construction company that Jorge and his father now ran.

While we were trying to digest the lunch, Jorge showed us the rest of the farm. The only part that was run with any commercial sense was a big barn with some 300 angora rabbits which were being bred for their wool. The rest of the land was slowly being turned into an enormous garden. He told us that his mother had already planted over 20,000 trees and shrubs.

At the end of the tour, Jorge's father asked if any of us played golf. Tony and Nick both fancied themselves as golfers. 'Is there a course nearby?' asked Tony.

Jorge's father gave him a slightly puzzled look. 'We have one,' he said. He sounded as if he thought everybody had their own golf course at their weekend cottage.

We walked beyond the trees behind the barbecue area, and there was a fully fledged golf course. Jorge was a bit apologetic that it was only nine holes; they had not got round to building the second nine yet. The greens should have been called browns. In the dry climate short grass cannot survive, so the greens were hard-packed sand. Jorge said that when it rains in the winter, flowers spring up all over the greens, and they have to be cut.

Jeff, Lana and I are no good at golf; I find I can throw the ball further and straighter than I can hit it. So Jorge produced a couple of motorbikes for us so that we could tour the rest of the farm while he and his father soundly thrashed Nick and Tony. It was a fun day.

To complete a lazy weekend, Jorge arrived on Sunday morning to take us for a drive to Santiago. It took Darwin a whole day to reach the city by mule. An hour or so up the motorway in Jorge's car and we were there. Santiago has, of course, grown since Darwin passed through. It now has a population of some 4½ million.

Jorge took us to the main shopping area, and Lana was drooling. Fortunately for the bank balance, she did not get much encouragement to shop, being with five men. She was somewhat appeased when we stopped in a little café for a drink. For the first time since arriving in Chile, she was able to buy real coffee. Nescafé seems to be the national hot drink of Chile. If one asks for coffee, even in a fancy restaurant, one is given a cup of hot water, a spoon and a tin of Nescafé. Lana really likes her coffee. She bought three month's supply of coffee beans, and on the strength of that voted the whole expedition to Santiago worthwhile.

Jorge then took us on a walk through the old part of the city, pointing out the various buildings, and explaining where the action had occurred when Pinochet overthrew Allende. All over the city, but especially near the government buildings, there were soldiers to be seen, all with machine-guns dangling.

Once we had finished being tourists, he took us back to his apartment to meet his wife, Maresol, and her parents who were visiting them. We went out *en masse* for a Chinese meal, and ended up overeating yet again. After the meal, Jorge told us that they had decided to lend us their second car for the two weeks that we anticipated being in the marina, doing our repairs. It was very generous of him, and certainly made life much easier and more pleasant for us.

Our only worry was getting back to the marina from the centre of Santiago. Jorge escorted us to the outskirts of the city and, with Jeff at the helm, we set off down the motorway to the coast. We hit a small snag at the toll booths. The soldiers checked our papers and became very excited because Jeff did not have a Chilean driving licence. It took a bit of sweet talking, but eventually they let us continue, and we finally arrived back at the boat.

We now faced two weeks of pretty concentrated work, trying to get the boat in shape for the next part of the trip. The Boss came to see us, just for the day – he said he was too busy to stay longer. Klaus collected him at the airport and brought him down to the boat. He was a bit sour with us for having given notice, and concentrated on persuading Jeff to stay on. Like us, Jeff had not been paid for over four months, and he laid into the Boss saying that the money, and interest for the delay, had better be in his bank within seven days, or he would have the boat arrested. The Boss assured us that it was all an administrative error and that we would be paid at once.

With that out of the way, he gave us the new plan. Up until this point, we were supposed to be heading west across the Pacific. Now he wanted us to get back to Britain as soon as possible. His racing boat had been chosen to represent Spain in the Admiral's Cup races, and since the professional racing crew would not let him sail in any of the races, he wanted *Thalassi* back there so that he could at least watch. He promised us all a bonus if we got the boat back in time.

At first that sounded quite reasonable; Britain was about 8000 miles away, and the races started in approximately twelve weeks. After we had agreed it was possible, however, the Boss said that he was planning to meet us in Panama and again in the West Indies, for two small cruises. A week in each place would effectively give us just under ten weeks. The two weeks of planned work in Algarobo reduced it to eight. A thousand miles a week was still possible, but left no room for delays or bad weather. But having set the schedule, the Boss disappeared back to Spain.

When Tony heard about the new plan, he decided to leave, and fly back to Britain. He had been looking forward to visiting some of the Pacific islands, but a virtually non stop sail to England did not appeal. We could hardly blame him. It did not appeal to us much either. However, we felt that we had to see it through to complete our obligations, and it was probably our only chance of getting our outstanding four months' pay. Tony agreed to stay long enough to help us prepare the boat for our long journey. We were very sorry to lose him. His personality, medical knowledge and helpful attitude were going to be missed.

We thought that if we made a big push with the work, we might get away a few days early. Our course north to Panama would take us close to the Galapagos, and the Boss had told me I should stop there, since Lana, Jeff and Nick had never been there. That would have been very generous of him, except that he had not allowed any time in the schedule for a stop. If we could shorten the refit without compromising the boat, there might be a few days for a little expedition. I had certainly enjoyed my previous visit there, and Lana was determined that we were not going to sail past without stopping.

Unfortunately the work schedule suffered somewhat as one by one we all fell sick. Tony was the first to go down. He contracted food poisoning from a little restaurant we visited. It is a poor situation when one's doctor is sick. He did not want anybody to tend him, and steadfastly refused to take any medication. He wanted to suffer alone, and heal in his own time.

He was just about back on his feet, when the boys' night out in Talcahuano came back to haunt them. One of the trio discovered that he had a small problem. He has begged, pleaded and threatened that he should remain anonymous so as not to spoil his future chances with the ladies, so let us just call him crew. He had contracted what might be termed a communicable disease, as a direct result of the night ashore. At first I laughed, but then I realised the seriousness of it. Of course the other two members of the trio started sweating and counting the days for the incubation period to pass. Were all three going down? It would have been poetic justice. I realised that it was not a laughing matter when said crew could hardly walk the next day. Obviously something had to be done. He could not go to sea in that state.

I did not feel that I could discuss the matter with our hosts. There we were, in Chile's fanciest yacht club, and one of our crew had the clap. I had the feeling that they would not be thrilled to know that. The next problem was that our Spanish dictionary was light on medical terms, and ignored all symptoms and organs below the waist. Then I had a brain wave. Valparaiso is a very big port, and since all too many sailors go down with various diseases of this ilk, I felt sure there must be a special clinic there. It was only a question of finding it.

We drove into Valparaiso, found the docks easily, and a parking place with difficulty. We walked down to the main gates of the docks – at least I did, my companion was hobbling along in a manner bound to invoke sympathy. At the gates was a young, machine-gun-toting guard. He watched us a little suspiciously as we approached him, my friend with his curious bow-legged gait. Surely the guard would know where to send us.

In our best fractured Spanish we told him that my friend had *un problema abajo* – a problem down below – and pointed a little south of his belt buckle. We needed a *clinica especial* to take care of the problem. Slowly his puzzled expression was replaced by a grin of comprehension. Yes, he knew where there was a special clinic that could take care of the problem. Leaving me to hold his machine-gun, he drew a complicated little map. At the end of the trail he marked, '*Clinica Especial*'. Feeling rather as if we had solved the last clue on a treasure hunt, we sallied, and hobbled, forth.

We eventually found the clinic, but found that our soldier had been deceived by my companion's curious walk. He had sent us to a foot doctor! Fortunately the foot doctor could speak good English and knew all the more graphic medical terms in both languages. He directed us to the right clinic.

It turned out to be a rather seedy little place, and I felt glad it was not me being treated. After the walk, however, crew was beyond caring, and collapsed into a grubby chair. They took care of him in short order, and within forty-eight hours he was pretty much back to normal. I kept a note of the address, in case either or both of the others went down with the same problem. Fortunately for all concerned they did not. The incubation period eventually passed, but they certainly sweated it out.

Next to go down was Lana. Perhaps foolishly, we went back to the same restaurant where Tony had been infected. He figured that it would be alright since he was the only one of the five of us to become ill, and we had all enjoyed the food. Again the rest of us were fine, but Lana was ill for about three days. To have the cook laid up with food poisoning severely cramped our culinary style. When we all took turns at trying to cook, we realised how much she had spoiled us over the previous months.

One of the most important boat jobs was to replace the stern gland. We had finally persuaded the yard in Spain to send us the right one; all that remained was to fit it. The gland is a waterproof seal that fits over the propeller shaft and the tube which it passes through. If the boat were out of the water, it would be an easy enough job. The propeller shaft is disconnected from the engine and slid back far enough to allow the old seal to be taken off and the new one put on – no problem.

Our problem was that there was nowhere that we could haul the boat. Jeff and I discussed whether we could change it in the water. At low tide *Thalassi*'s keel was almost touching the bottom, so I thought we would be safe enough to have a go. We did not know how much water would come in when we took the old seal off, but at least at low tide, if we did have a problem, the boat would not sink without a trace.

Jeff got the coupling, and the control gear for the variable pitch propeller disconnected. Before we could push the shaft back, however, somebody would have to go into the water to remove an anode off the shaft. It was a hot sunny day, so I was happy to jump in and have a go. I had forgotten about the Humboldt Current. The water was icy – it took my breath away. I could not dive down to touch the shaft, never mind work on it. Jeff called me a wimp, and put on his wet suit. With the benefit of this protection, he managed it with no problem. Before the tide rose, the new seal was in place. Hopefully that would be the end of a longstanding leak.

Finally the jobs were all ticked off the list. We waved goodbye to Tony, and did an enormous three-month food shop. Then it was my turn to be sick. I caught flu and postponed our departure. A day later, I was still feeling grim, but decided we should go anyway. To clear out from Chile we had to take the boat round to Valparaiso; Costumes and Intimidation had said I could not drive there, the boat had to come. Klaus and Jorge and an assortment of family and friends sailed round with us. When we got there, they came with me to help with officialdom.

The clearing was a long draw-out affair. They wanted to know our exact route along the coast, and I was told to call in with our position each day while we were in Chilean waters. It all seemed terribly complicated, but eventually it was all done. Nobody came out to the boat, so we probably could have got away with driving over, but at least Klaus, Jorge and friends had had a bit of a sail out of it. We were sorry to say goodbye to them; they had certainly made our stay memorable.

After an early night, we were ready to leave the next morning. We motored out of the bay after breakfast, and ran into thick fog and a stiff southerly breeze. We made sail, and headed straight out to sea, to get clear of all the fishing boats we could see on the radar. Fortunately, as before, the fog thinned a few miles offshore, and the visibility improved to about a couple of miles. We altered course to the north, and steered towards the Galapagos.

The *Beagle* made a pit-stop in Peru, and that would have been interesting for us, but we had heard horror stories from southbound yachts about boats being arrested, detained and fined on the flimsiest of pretexts. Peru has been going though a long period of civil unrest, and even if the Boss's timetable had been a little less demanding, I think we would have chosen to give it a miss.

We were just settling down into our seagoing routine, when we heard a call on the VHF radio: 'Northbound blue sailing yacht, this is Chilean warship calling you.' We were blue, and heading north, but we could not see any ship that could be calling us. On the radar the nearest vessel was about 10 miles away – much too far for them to be able to see us – so I ignored the call. The warship was persistent. In the end I called them back, said we were a northbound blue yacht and gave them our position. I explained that I did not think we were the vessel they were hailing, because we had no warship in sight.

The voice on the radio came right back to me at once. 'Yes it is you I am calling. What is your destination and last port?' After getting the answer, he asked more questions about the boat and about us. I gave him all the information, and then asked him where he was, as we still could not see a warship. He replied, 'Under the sea,' and signed off. We were being escorted from Chile by a submarine. What would

Captain Fitzroy have thought of that?

We thought afterwards that we should have turned on the big depth finder. In addition to the normal one *Thalassi* had a huge depth sounder with almost unlimited range. If we had turned it on, I felt sure that they would have been able to hear it, whereupon we could have said, 'Oh yes, we see you.' That would have given them as much to talk about as we had!

All day the breeze blew. In fact it picked up as the day progressed. We were roaring along, making excellent progress, averaging around 10 knots, but the motion was not very pleasant. The boat was rolling around in the following sea. I was still feeling grim, and had managed to pass the flu onto Lana, so neither of us was enjoying the sail at all.

There was nothing on the weather maps to show where the breeze was coming from, and the pilot chart showed the expected average wind to be about 10–15 knots. The wind ignored all the charts and forecasts, and stayed strong. It blew between 25 and 30 knots for four days. We were nearly half way to the Galapagos, well into the tropics once more, when it stopped. One moment it was blowing 30 knots, then the next, it was down to almost nothing. We started motoring, but the motion was still uncomfortable, as the swell continued to make us roll. It was another day of light winds before the motion eased enough to be called comfortable. The sun came out, Lana's flu started to get better, and Jeff had a birthday. Things were looking up.

The wind stayed light, and the engine ran for three days. Jeff and I started doing some calculations regarding the fuel. The Galapagos are close to 1000 miles from the Panama Canal, in an area renowned for light winds. I wanted to be certain that we had enough fuel to motor from the Galapagos to Panama if necessary. The Boss's schedule did not allow for us to become becalmed. I sent a telex to our agent in Britain, asking him to contact the Ecuadorian Embassy to find out whether fuel would be available to us anywhere in the islands. I knew from my previous visit that finding it would not be easy.

After three days of flat calm, we got a bit of wind. It tended to pick up a little during the day and die away at night. We sailed whenever we could, and motored when we had to, in order to keep our average speed above 7 knots.

One particular dark night, Lana called us up to watch a spectacular light show. The bioluminescence – sparkling plankton – shining in our wake was exceptionally bright. For some reason the plankton only switches its light on when it is disturbed by a wave or a wake. Our wake was a silver shining ribbon stretching to the horizon. Four dolphins had come to play around the boat, and each of them was leaving a shining zigzag trail through the water. They criss-crossed

under the bows, weaving an intricate pattern of light. Lana wondered if they could see the sparkling trails they were making. Were they also enjoying the pattern?

Less than 50 miles short of the Galapagos, the engine broke down. At least, Lana heard it change note and stopped it so that we could investigate. It was 3.15 a.m. and there was not a breath of wind. It took Jeff about one minute to discover that the drive belt for the cooling water pump had snapped. As it came off, it had taken two more belts with it, so now the engine had no cooling water and the alternator was not charging the battery. Jeff devised a jury rig which was good enough to get us into port. To fix it properly would involve removing the hydraulic pump from the front of the engine, and that could wait until we were anchored.

We made our landfall on San Cristóbal, the easternmost island, just twelve days after leaving Valparaiso. We had averaged 181 miles per day, and were almost three days ahead of schedule!

Wreck Bay, San Cristóbal Island, our port of entry for the Galapagos. We were careful not to leave the dinghy in the water unattended, in case it became home to a sea-lion. Almost every unattended boat had its resident sea-lion.

Chapter 18

The Galapagos

Although it was his observation of the wildlife of the Galapagos which was to make Darwin famous, he concentrated on the geology first.

From his reading on board *Beagle*, he knew that there are ten main islands, five of which are rather larger than the others. In addition there are numerous smaller islands, some little larger than rocks poking up from the seabed. They straddle the equator, and are a little over 500 miles from the mainland of South America. They are owned by Ecuador.

All the islands are formed by volcanic rock, and all the larger ones are studded with craters, some of which are enormous, the rims rising in some cases more than 400 ft. The flanks of the big craters are peppered with smaller craters. Darwin estimated that there are approximately 2000 craters in the archipelago. He had hoped to find an active one to study, but although he saw wisps of smoke coming out from one or two, he could not find one that had bubbling lava in it, nor one that was spewing out rocks or even ash. It was a bit of a disappointment, but he did manage to study several of the dormant craters.

He found that there are two basic sorts of crater. Some are formed by jagged lava rocks, thrown up in jumbled heaps. The others are composed of finely layered material called tuff, which looks rather like sandstone. These were made by eruptions of volcanic mud, without any lava being present.

He examined twenty-eight of these tuff craters, and found that without exception, the southern sides were much lower, some even broken down altogether. This suggested to him that they had formed while standing in the sea, and that the waves and swells from the trade winds had erroded the sides. The fact that they were now above the sea was strong evidence that the land had risen up in a similar way to the places he had looked at on the mainland.

The Galapagos had a reputation among early navigators as being hard to find. Indeed one name often given to them was the Enchanted Islands, because on some days they seemed to have vanished. Ships would often sail to where the islands were supposed to be and search

for them in vain. The reason for this elusiveness is that near the islands the skies are often overcast. They are in the area known as the doldrums. This region, between the trade winds, often has grey and squally weather. If the sun and the stars were obscured by clouds, then the navigator could not take sextant sights to fix his position. Under these conditions he would have to rely on what is called dead reckoning, plotting the course and distance made good, and calculating where the ship had got to. Unfortunately, often there are also strong and variable currents near the islands, and these would upset the most careful of calculations. So it was not a case of the islands not being where they were supposed to be, but more that the ship was not where the navigator thought it was.

Beagle's passage over from the mainland was uneventful. Captain Fitzroy managed to make his landfall as planned, on Chatham Island. Although he was a consummate navigator, he must have been relieved when the island appeared over the horizon on cue.

Perhaps I should explain about the names of the islands. Each island has two names, one given to it by the early explorers and surveyors and the other which Ecuador has bestowed upon its possessions. I will use the old names throughout Darwin's narrative, and the modern ones in ours. To avoid confusion, the first time an island is mentioned, I will give both names.

Beagle anchored off Chatham Island, which is now called San Cristóbal, in the bay which has come to be called Wreck Bay. Darwin was soon ashore, but was disappointed with what he found. He said that nothing could be less inviting than the first appearance of the island. He found broken black lava thrown into waves, which were crossed by great fissures. Walking across it was very difficult. The only plants he could see was the occasional stunted, sunburnt brushwood, which showed little signs of life. Fitzroy described the landscape as 'fit for Pandemonium', while one of his officers compared it to the cultivated parts of Hell.

Undaunted, Darwin set off under the noonday sun to go collecting. The air felt like the blast from an oven. The sun quickly heats up the black lava to the point where it becomes uncomfortable to walk on, even when wearing thick boots. He soon discovered that the brushwood, which appeared lifeless from a short distance, was actually in full leaf, and in some cases even in flower. The leaves and flowers were extremely small so that not much water would be lost by evaporation. The commonest bush was a kind of acacia. The only other plant big enough to cast any shade at all was a big prickly cactus. He returned to the ship hot, sweaty and weary. Although he had been searching for botanical samples, he described the few that

he found as 'weeds, that would have better become the Antarctic than an equatorial flora'.

It rarely rains in the Galapagos, but the higher elevations are often shrouded in clouds. The lower parts of all the islands are for the most part dry and barren, but as Darwin was to find on later walks, above about 1000 ft, the clouds keep the climate damp and there is reasonably luxuriant vegetation, especially on the windward side. Moreover, many of the craters hold water, and in them the growth is as thick as in any jungle.

Darwin's second trip ashore on Chatham was a little more rewarding. He found an area where there were sixty miniature volcanos, each with its own little crater. These craters were formed by red slag, which appeared to have been cemented together. None of the cones was much over 50 ft high. The surface of the entire area was pierced like a sieve. The lava had been blown into bubbles just as it was setting, and this had left thousands of circular, steep-sided pits. The regular uniformity of the pits and the cones gave the area an artificial, man-made appearance. He remarked that it reminded him of the potteries of his native Staffordshire. Do we detect a twinge of homesickness?

On his way back to the ship, Darwin came across a pair of the giant tortoises after which the islands were named. They were quite big ones; each must have weighed at least 200 lb. Darwin was enthralled. One was eating a cactus plant, and as Darwin crept closer, it kept a beady eye on him but continued munching. The other proved to be more timid. As he came closer, it suddenly gave a hiss, and retracted everything into the safety of its shell. Darwin sat fascinated. The whole scene caught his imagination, with the big reptiles surrounded by the jet black jagged lava, the virtually leafless shrubs and the prickly cacti. It all seemed so primitive to him as to be antediluvian.

As he sat there quietly watching, he saw a few dull-coloured birds, which cared for him no more than they did for the tortoises. He in turn took little notice of them. Although it was these finches that were to make his reputation, for the moment it was the tortoises that held him enthralled.

Beagle spent a week at Chatham. Darwin explored and collected, Fitzroy and his men surveyed the shores of the island. At the end of the week, they sailed across to Charles Island, now called Santa Maria. It was, incidentally, not named after Darwin, but after the King of England. Like several of the others, it had long been visited on a regular basis by buccaneers and whalers, but only six years prior to *Beagle*'s visit, the first permanent settlement had been established. Some 300 people, whom Darwin describes as 'being of colour,' had

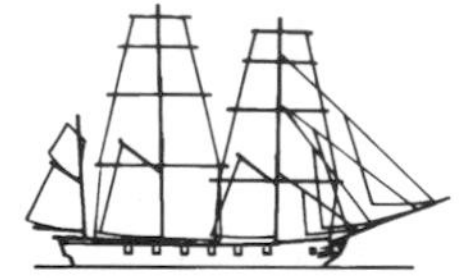

Wild tortoises – much more satisfying than seeing them in the zoo at the Darwin Institute. Our guide found them by following a trail of fresh droppings.

been sent out from Ecuador, mostly as punishment for political crimes. They were condemned to live in this remote spot for the rest of their lives.

Darwin set off almost at once to visit the settlement. He thought it strange that it was not on the coast, but over 4 miles inland, and at an altitude of 1000 ft. As he climbed up the steep rocky path, however the reasons for choosing the site became apparent; the higher he climbed, the greener the land became. When he finally reached the highest ridge, Darwin found a cooling southerly breeze and fairly big areas of cultivated land. Most of the fields were devoted to sweet potatoes and bananas.

The natural vegetation was mainly a mixture of ferns and coarse grasses. He puzzled over the fact that there were no palm trees, as he knew that Cocos Island, so named because of the abundance of coconut trees, was only about 350 miles to the north.

The villagers told him that there were wild goats and pigs roaming in the woods surrounding the settlement, but most of the locals preferred to kill tortoises for meat; they were easier to hunt than the swift goats and pigs. The numbers of tortoises had been greatly reduced by hunting, not just by the locals but also by visiting ships. Even so, there were still enough to provide a week's supply of meat for a family after an average day's hunting.

Sailors and buccaneers had long ago found that the tortoises could be kept on board their ships for long periods without food or water, and they were a convenient source of fresh meat in the days before refrigeration was invented. When the islands were first visited, a single ship might take as many as 700 tortoises. Even just a year or two before *Beagle*'s visit, the crew of a frigate managed to collect over 200 in a single day.

The Vice-governor of the settlement, a gentleman by the name of Lawson, talked to Darwin at length about the tortoises. He said that they differed so much from one island to another that he could tell at a glance where any tortoise came from. Darwin did not recognise the significance of these remarks for several days, and continued collecting specimens and mixing them with those collected on the other islands. Indeed, even when he did finally realise that there were specific differences between finches shot on the different islands, his own collection was hopelessly muddled. Fortunately Fitzroy had made his own collection of birds and, being methodical, he had noted where each had been caught. When they got back to England, Fitzroy's collection was used to help sort out Darwin's own, and prove that birds of the same type had evolved specific differences adapting to the local conditions found on each island.

Mr Lawson went on to tell Darwin that he had seen several tortoises so big that they required eight men to pick them up, and that one that size, when butchered, gave over 200 lb of edible meat.

Some tortoises live on islands where there is no standing water, or on the equally dry coastal plains of the bigger islands. The only moisture they take in is what they get by eating the succulent cactus.

Those tortoises that live in the higher, damper regions eat leaves, and they are very partial to a green lichen that hangs down from the trees. Despite their ability to survive long periods without it, the tortoises are actually very fond of water, and will often travel great distances to visit a small pond. Given the chance, a tortoise will drink vast quantities of water, and enjoy a long wallow in the mud. After spending three or four days drinking, they will return to their normal territory. Mr Lawson explained that after drinking, the tortoise's bladder is distended with fluid, and he thought that this is an extra store. After a period without drinking, the volume of fluid in the bladder decreases, and the fluid itself becomes less pure. He told Darwin that if the locals became thirsty down on the dry coastal plain, they would sometimes kill a tortoise to drink the contents of the bladder. Darwin, the devoted scientist, remembered that, and when he saw a tortoise killed, he tried drinking the fluid. He described it as being quite limpid, and with only a very slight bitter taste. I think I would have to be very thirsty indeed before I would want to drink tortoise urine!

The tortoises provided the inhabitants not only with meat, but also with oil, which they rendered from the fat. When they found a tortoise, it was common for the locals to cut a slit in the happless animal's skin, under its tail, to look inside the body. If there was a good layer of fat under the dorsal plate, then it was killed. If there was not much fat, it was actually freed, and the hunter looked for a better specimen. Mr Lawson assured Darwin that the slit soon healed.

From Charles Island they sailed for Albermarle Island. This is the largest in the group, and is now called Isabela. They sailed round its southern tip and beat up towards the channel between it and the smaller Narborough Island (Fernandina). As they neared the entrance to the channel, they ran out of wind, and lay becalmed for much of the day. Darwin spent almost the entire time on deck, gazing up at the peaks of the volcanoes which formed the two islands. The landscape was bleak – streams of naked, black lava, which had flowed over the rims of the great cauldrons to spread over miles of the coast.

Eruptions had been known on both these islands, and as they crept slowly up the coast of Albermarle, Darwin became very excited when he spotted a wisp of smoke curling out of the top of one of the craters. Although he had watched the eruption of Aconcagua in Chile, he wanted to get close to an active, bubbling crater.

Beagle finally reached her anchorage. The bay that Fitzroy chose was actually a flooded volcanic crater called Bank's Cove. It was one of the tuff craters, whose south-western side had been so eroded as to let the sea flood it.

Early next morning Darwin set off exploring. It was not enough for him that the ship was anchored in a crater, he had to climb up to another one. The crater he found was almost a mile across, and some 500 ft below the rim was a lake, in the centre of which, forming a little island, was a perfect miniature volcano. It was a very hot day.

The black lava was almost too hot to touch, and Darwin was very thirsty. The clear blue lake looked very appealing, and he swiftly scrambled down the cindery slope into the crater, expecting to drink his fill. When he finally reached the bottom, he found that the water was saltier than the sea.

On his way back to the ship, he paused to study some of the giant lizards, or iguanas, for which the islands are well know. He soon spotted that there are two types: a purely land sort that lives in burrows, and a marine kind, which seems equally at home on the shore or in the water. During their stay on Albermarle, he spent considerable time watching these marine iguanas, which are unique to the Galapagos. He caught several and opened up their stomachs to see what they had been eating. He found minced seaweed; they appeared to be purely vegetarian in their diet.

The marine species have flattened tails and webbed feet to help them swim, whereas the land-based ones have rounded tails and clawed feet. The preferred food of the terrestrial ones is cactus, the pricklier the better, it seems. The marine species are found in all the islands, but the land ones are limited to the islands around Albermarle; they are not found in the extreme eastern or northern islands.

Marine Iguanas blending almost perfectly with San Cristóbal's black volcanic rocks. If we got too close, instead of running away, they spat at us.

Although he does not record the exact moment of revelation, it seems that it was while they were at Albermarle that he finally realised that the finches he had collected were similar to, yet different from, those of the other islands. He wrote in his journal that it appeared as if one species had been taken and modified for different ends. The seeds for his theory of evolution had just sprouted.

From Albermarle, they sailed to James Island, named after another of the Stuart kings of England. It is now called San Salvador, or sometimes Santiago. On James Island, Darwin and Mr Bynoe were left ashore, together with their servants and a tent, while *Beagle* went off to look for water. They found a group of people, who had been sent over from the settlement at Charles Island to dry and salt fish and tortoise meat. They went off to visit the two tortoise catchers, who were living in a small hovel about 6 miles inland, and at a height of about 2000 ft. Although, as on the other islands, the coastal strip was dry and barren, high up at the camp the damp from the clouds supported fairly lush vegetation.

While staying in the upper region Darwin and his group lived entirely on tortoise meat. He does not appear to have had any qualms about killing and eating these unique creatures, even though he had already noted that their numbers were dwindling. His favourite way of cooking them was to roast the breast plate with the meat attached, in a similar way to the gauchos cooking their *carne con cuero.* Cooked this way, he thought the tortoise meat was very good. He also discovered that young tortoises make an excellent soup, but otherwise he declared the meat to be indifferent.

Beagle returned with her water tanks filled for the long voyage which lay ahead. Their survey of the Galapagos was complete, and it was time to leave for their next destination, Tahiti. As they sailed away, Darwin little realised the repercussions that would be felt around the world from his stay in the Galapagos.

When we anchored in Wreck Bay, off the island of San Cristóbal – Darwin's Chatham Island – there were about half a dozen other yachts there, together with several little local fishing boats.

Since Darwin's visit, a small town and a large airport runway have been built, so the place no longer has quite the desolate aspect that he described. The arrival of the town has meant officialdom, and

Costumes and Intimidation had to be sought out and satisfied. Jeff came ashore with me, to help with the translating. Although my Spanish was improving, his was still much better.

We launched the inflatable and headed for shore. On the way in we saw that a couple of dinghies and several of the open fishing boats had big sea-lions lounging in them. We never saw one get in or out of a boat, but I made a mental note not to leave the dinghy in the water unattended. I did not fancy trying to persuade one of the beasts to get out if it chose to sunbathe in our dinghy.

Ashore we soon tracked down the Port Captain, who was very friendly and helped us to get the paperwork sorted out. Since we did not have an official visa from Ecuador, the rule was that we could only stay for three days. It was going to be a rushed visit. The Ecuadorian government has tightened up on visiting yachts after several incidents of crews abusing the hospitality of the islands. One group of yachties was caught with a row of marine iguanas roasting on the barbecue grill. Now, without a visa and an authorised guide, we were limited to three days, and we could only visit Wreck Bay, and Academy Bay on Santa Cruz. On my previous visit a few years before, things had been much less regulated, and we had wandered through the islands more or less at will. Those days are probably gone forever.

The next setback was fuel, or rather the lack thereof. We had had no reply from our agent in Britain about the availability of fuel. If we were to have any chance of keeping to the Boss's schedule across the Gulf of Panama, with its fickle winds, then fuel was going to be vital. We did not have enough to get all the way to Panama if there was no wind. The Port Captain told us that there was none in Wreck Bay, and the only place where there was any at all was at Baltra, a little island which houses the main airport and the naval base. He explained that the navy controlled all the fuel, and they were not allowed to sell it without permission from the mainland.

As soon as we got back to the boat, I fired off another telex to Britain, asking again that the Ecuadorian Embassy be approached, to authorise fuel for us. All we could do then was wait and hope that we would get permission before our three days ran out.

After lunch and a short nap, we all set off ashore. Lana and Nick went to see what fresh food was available, while Jeff and I went back to the Port Captain again. We showed him the copy of the telex we had sent, and explained that we were asking the Embassy in London to obtain permission for us to buy fuel. He was suitably impressed. He seemed to think the telex said that permission had been granted, and we did not point out his mistake. He made a few phone calls, and eventually said that we could buy 250 gallons of fuel at Baltra. I was hoping for 350, but any was better than none. He had been so helpful and friendly that we invited him to come to the boat for a drink after work. He was pleased to be asked and we agreed to pick him up later.

We walked back into town, to find that Lana and Nick had been picked up by two small boys and escorted to their mother's restaurant and bar. Mother turned out to be a very busy and businesslike woman called Cecelia. Her bar, thanks in no small part to the hustling of her sons, was the place where all the yachties ended up. She was also the main money changer, and the general organiser and procurer of things. In the bar, she had two thick books of photographs, drawings and comments from yacht crews who had visited over the past few years. Over a cold drink or two, we thumbed through the books, recognising many old friends from anchorages past.

To give the cook a well-deserved night off, we booked dinner with Cecelia for a little later, and then headed back to give the Port captain his guided tour of *Thalassi.* The first thing he spotted when he came on board was the radio. It turned out that he was a ham, and he was keen to try out *Thalassi's* radio, which was bigger and more powerful than anything he had used before. I fired it up for him, and within a few minutes he was talking to some friends on the mainland. He was in ham heaven, and we had a firm friend.

After a beer or two, and several radio contacts, he settled down to tell us all about the Galapagos as he saw them. He was from the mainland, and sympathised with our desire to stay longer than three days. He could do nothing about it officially, but told us exactly where the patrol boat would be and when. He suggested that we could plan a visit to the outer islands around the schedule of the patrol boat, and avoid meeting it.

Although it was tempting, I did not feel we should risk it. The Boss already had a pretty low opinion of us, and it would be awfully hard to explain to him that his boat had been confiscated because we had made an illegal tour of the islands. When I explained this to the Port Captain, he seemed a little crestfallen. Then he had another idea. We could stay in Wreck Bay for our three days, and leave without clearing. We could then go to Academy Bay and clear in as if from Chile, and spend three days there. That seemed an altogether safer proposition.

We dropped the Port Captain back ashore, and went on to Cecelia's for an enjoyable dinner. We told her that we would like to drive round the island, and she promised to find us a taxi. What turned up next morning was not exactly a taxi, but it would do. What she had found

for us was a rather rusty, old, green pick-up truck with three lawn-chairs in the back. Lana was ushered into the cab with the driver, while Nick, Jeff and I climbed into the back and settled down into the folding chairs.

Cecelia's two boys jumped aboard as well, and we set off out of town, up the twisting road that flanked the side of the highest hill. As we passed the cemetery, the two boys crossed themselves fervently. We realised why on the way down. Only one brake on the truck worked, the one on the after port wheel. On the descent, the driver managed to keep the truck down to a reasonable speed by leaving it in first gear with the engine turned off. Any attempts to stop resulted in the one wheel locking, but since its tyre was bald, this had little effect on our speed. But as the truck ground its way upwards, we were oblivious to this problem; otherwise we too might have crossed ourselves.

Eventually we reached the end of the road, but not the end of the journey. The driver and our guides were determined that we should go up to the rim of the crater, which was shrouded in clouds. They seemed to be suspended permanently over the peak, and provided plenty of moisture for plants to grow. This particular volcano had obviously been long dormant, as it was completely covered in grass.

We scrambled up the steep slope, our legs protesting – they were as yet unaccustomed to walking, after twelve days at sea. When we reached the rim, almost 3000 ft above sea level, we could look down through the mist into the crater itself. Far below, we could see a lake. Birds were circling beneath us, deep inside the crater.

At first the coolness of the clouds felt pleasant after the heat down on the shore, but quite soon the cold and dampness began to seep into us. Before too long we were ready to head back down to the warmth, and began the perilous ride back to town. Once we were back down on the level streets of the town, we eased our white-knuckled grips and paid the driver. We gave him an extra tip, hoping that he would spend at least some of it on his brakes.

We celebrated having cheated death once again by having lunch and a cold beer at Cecelia's. Suitably fortified, we then set off on foot to the eastern side of the island to look for the marine iguanas that Cecelia told us were there. The first part of the journey was easy. We just walked along the gigantic runway that had been carved across the tip of the island, for a mile or more. Once we left our smooth, paved path, however, the going became a little rougher and soon degenerated into sharp, jagged black lava rocks. We skirted along the shore searching for the iguanas.

We came to a family of sea-lions, playing in the surf. They did not

A friendly seal on the beach at San Cristóbal.

seem to be as fierce as their Falkland cousins – they did not roar at us, but simply retreated if they thought we were getting too close. After we had photographed them from every possible angle, we were about to call an end to our biological studies and retire once again to Cecelia's when Lana spotted an iguana. We must have walked within a few feet of it; its colour and jagged profile blended perfectly with the lava rocks it was sitting on. If it had not moved, we would probably have walked past it again.

As we walked slowly up to it, we realised that there were several of them. The longer we looked, the more we spotted. There were at least half a dozen sunbathing on one jumbled pile of rocks. The marine iguanas are between 3 and 4 ft long, with their tails forming

almost half their length. With their spiked plume, scaly skin and E.T. smile, they look positively prehistoric, like miniature dinosaurs. If they thought we were approaching too close, they spat at us with unnerving accuracy, but apart from this they did not do much except grin at us.

Once we had used up what film was left after the sea-lions, we headed back for town, and a last drink with Cecelia. As we were getting ready to leave, she asked us if we had any old clothes that we could give them. We thought we could find something, so offered to take them all out to the boat. She produced a very pretty daughter, whom she had wisely kept hidden from Nick and Jeff, and we all went back out to *Thalassi*. We managed to find them a few spare T-shirts, and Lana produced a skirt for the lovely daughter. They seemed well pleased with their haul, and we deposited them ashore, at the end of a long and hectic day.

The fuel question was still hanging over us, so we set off early the next morning for Baltra and the navy base. We reached the island just before dusk, and anchored off it for the night. It was still uncertain whether our friendly Port Captain had arranged the fuel for us, and we might yet be denied. I composed a fake telex and sent it to myself, saying that the Embassy in London had assured us of an ample supply of fuel. I thought that it might help if we ran into problems.

Early the next morning, we launched the dinghy, and Jeff and I went in to see how the land lay. To my immense relief they were expecting us. Our friend in Wreck Bay had organised it all for us, and we could come alongside and get the fuel. As soon as we had tied up alongside the small dock in front of the naval administration building, we were met by the Commandant of the base. It transpired that this was the changeover day from one to the next, and it was the retiring Commandant who had agreed we could get the fuel. Since he was leaving, it would not matter to him if they ran out in a week or two.

There was no pump or even a hose. A gang of conscripts wheeled down a 50-gallon drum on a rather shaky little cart. The new Commandant told us that we could buy only five drumfuls.

When the first drum was in place on the edge of the dock, Jeff and Nick got a syphon running, and the fuel trickled slowly into the tank. The two Commandants sat in the cockpit, beers in hand, supervising the proceedings. While Lana and I kept them entertained, and their glasses full, Jeff was chatting to the four young conscripts who had been delegated to shift the fuel. He was even more anxious than me to get extra fuel, and unbeknown to the rest of us, he arranged a trade – a carton of cigarettes and some of Nick's girlie magazines for an

extra drum of fuel. All that remained to do was to get it past the Commandants. After the fourth drum was in, they all started saying loudly, Three down, two to go.' The new Commandant said he was sure we had four already. But everybody insisted it was only three, and when the retiring Commandant agreed with the men, he had to back down. So we got 300 gallons, and we were glad of every one of them.

When the last of the fuel was aboard, and the bill paid, we had an easy sail down to Academy Bay on the island of Santa Cruz, or as Darwin would have called it, Indefatigable. This is the second port of entry for the islands. It was obviously the more popular one, and there were about twenty other yachts anchored in the bay when we arrived. It is also the main port for the tourist boats which take people on escorted tours through the islands. Compared to Wreck Bay, it was positively jumping.

The anchorage at Academy Bay, on Santa Cruz island, home of the Darwin Institute.

We got the anchor down and set, and were sitting in the cockpit looking around the anchorage when we were surprised to hear somebody calling *Thalassi* on the radio. It turned out to be the manager of the hotel at the northern end of the bay, the Hotel Galapagos. He had been watching us through his binoculars, and invited us all ashore to visit the hotel for a complimentary welcome drink. It was too late to deal with officialdom that evening, so we needed no second asking. We launched the dinghy, and motored over to their dock.

The hotel has a fabulous setting. With several stone terraces looking out over the bay, each with its own colony of iguanas frolicking in the surf in front of it, it is a magical place. Ken, the manager, showed us around with obvious pride, and organised a round of drinks for us. It was a shrewd move, and he soon recovered the cost, as we ended up staying for dinner.

Early next morning we set off to explore the town and take care of the formalities. We got our pass for three days, and walked up to visit the Darwin Institute. This is a multinational affair, and is concerned with all the wildlife of the islands, but especially the tortoises, it seems. They have a programme of collecting the eggs from the various islands, hatching them, and letting the tortoises grow to a size that renders them safe from predators before releasing them back on their own island. We saw tortoises of every size, from tiny newly hatched ones to monsters which weighed several hundred pounds. One group of big tortoises was in a pen that we could walk into, right in among them. As they walked, the bigger tortoises creaked. Lana could not decide whether they had creaky knees or whether it was their thick, scaly skin that squeaked. They did not seem to be too good at steering. One would set a course for some distant part of the pen, oblivous to the fact that it was on a collision course with another tortoise. They bumped each other with alarmingly loud crunches, but did not seem to suffer any damage.

As we told Ken that night, it was interesting enough but it still felt like a zoo. When we said we wanted to see wild tortoises, he organised an expedition for us the next day.

We made an early start, in another pick-up truck/taxi. At least this one had operable brakes, even if it did not have the lawn-chairs in the back. It was a trade-off that we were happy enough to make. Ken had told us that it was obligatory to go and see the lava tunnels first, before going on the tortoise hunt.

Our driver therefore deposited us at the end of one of the tunnels, where we paid a fee and, in return, each received the loan of a torch with very second-hand batteries. With no more ado or instruction, we

were ushered off into the mouth of the tunnel and left to stumble our way through the darkness as one by one the batteries expired.

The tunnels were formed by rivers of lava that had cooled and solidified on the outside. The tunnel we were groping our way through was about a mile long, and by the time we reached daylight at the other end, we were down to one light, which was barely glimmering. We were a bit concerned that we were going to have to grope our way back through the tunnel to the beginning, when we spotted our driver. He had brought the trusty, rusty, pick-up round to collect us. We returned our lights, and continued onwards and upwards on our expedition.

Our next stop was a ranch with the unlikely name of Santa Rosa. It is in the south-west of the island, and high enough to be very lush. There were more trees here than we had seen for a long time. The plan now was to go on horseback into a nearby valley, where hopefully we could find some wild tortoises.

We sat in the shade, under a large tree, sipping cold drinks, while the horses were saddled for us. The equipment was, to put it kindly, basic. The bridles were made of rope and fencing wire, while the saddles were solid wood, carved from a gigantic log. The only concession to padding was an old sack as a saddle blanket which might have saved the horses from a little chafing, but did nothing for us. We sat directly on the rough wood.

Our guide, Roberto, set off at a good clip, and our horses ambled off in pursuit. Only Lana's seemed eager to keep up with our leader. Jeff's was the slowest, or perhaps the laziest. It kept falling so far behind, that eventually Roberto cut a large stick and told Jeff to keep hitting his horse.

Nick's horse was also strong-minded, and kept straying from the path. Its favourite trick was to walk under low branches to try and knock Nick off its back. When that failed, it took to walking close to every thorn bush it could find, scratching Nick's bare legs unmercifully. He threatened to turn it into kangaroo meat.

To begin with, the path lay through fairly open land, but as we progressed the trees became thicker, until after about an hour and a half, we reached virtually impenetrable jungle. Roberto leapt agilely to the ground and hitched his horse to a tree. He explained that from here on we were to go on foot. We slithered off our mounts a little less gracefully, and struggled to straighten our knees enough to walk. Roberto was hacking away with his machete, cutting a path through the jungle for us. He seemed oblivious to the fact that we could barely walk. The unaccustomed exercise and the wooden saddles had taken their toll.

The giant tortoises are being bred in the Institute, to ensure their survival. Once they are mature, they are released into the wild on the island their parents came from.

Fortunately the jungle was thick, so progress was slow enough for us to limp along with him. He led us down into the depths of the valley, which we assumed was a very overgrown crater. As we made our way ever deeper into the jungle, he told us about one group of tourists who had come into the valley without a guide. It took them a week to find their way out again. Hopefully Roberto knew where he was going and, more importantly, which way was back.

We had been hacking and stumbling our way along for about half an hour when we came upon a muddy track. Roberto became very excited. He bent down to pick up what was obviously animal droppings. He squeezed and shaped it like putty, then held it our for us to try. None of us was too keen, but we got the gist of what he was trying to show us. They were fresh, not yet hardened by the sun, so whatever had done them was close by. Motioning us to be quiet, he crouched down to follow the trail of droppings, and soon found us a tortoise, a genuine wild tortoise and quite a big one at that. While we crept up to peer at the beast, which was sitting placidly in a muddy puddle, Roberto cast around, and soon found us two more. We were well satisfied.

Having produced the tortoises for us, we thought Roberto would feel he had finished his job. Not a bit of it. Waving his machete wildly, he cut a path off in a new direction to show us what he called the *Láguna.* A lagoon it was not; it was a rather overgrown pond. Floating at one end was a group of what looked like very ordinary ducks. Roberto reached new paroxysms of excitement, pointing at the ducks. Why he was so excited, or exactly what sort of ducks we were looking at, we never did find out. We nodded and smiled gratefully at him for finding them for us, and then headed back to our horses.

We were pleased to find that all the horses were still there, even if our bodies were complaining as we climbed back on board; it was, we thought, better than walking back. By the time we got back to the ranch, however, I for one had changed my mind. I was of the firm opinion that I would be hurting less if I was carrying the horse than riding it.

There was a bit of a swell coming into the bay that night, and all the boats were rolling, but compared to the horses the motion was nothing. We all slept soundly.

We had only one day left, and that had to be given over to work. Jeff spent virtually the whole of it in the engine room, emerging only for meal-times and his cigarette breaks. Nick and I attacked the varnish work on deck while Lana did some last-minute food shopping, cleaning and stowing below, and made a Panamanian flag ready for our next landfall. We were going to take the short-cut back to Britain that Darwin had wished for by this stage. After the Galapagos, he became increasingly anxious to get back. The Boss's schedule might have suited him, but the Panama Canal was not even at the serious planning stage when he left the Galapagos. *Beagle* had to sail back the long way, across the Pacific.

Chapter 19

The Voyage Home

The *Beagle* was blessed with a fair wind as they left the Galapagos. She could have easily been becalmed for several days or even weeks, but the breeze quickly carried her down into the south-east trade winds, and they steadily ticked off 150 miles a day.

The sailing was almost perfect, with bright sunshine and deep blue water. The only clouds were the fluffy fair-weather trade-wind cumulus. They passed through the Tuamotus without stopping, but as they passed close to one of the atolls, sailing along close to the brilliant white, sandy beach, Darwin climbed up to the mast-head to look out across the enclosed lagoon.

Despite the idyllic conditions, however, he was feeling lethargic. He did little for the entire three weeks. He made only two entries in his journal during the passage, and did not even spend much time with his collections. He was still suffering from seasickness, but what was affecting him more was homesickness. He was growing more and more anxious to be back with his family.

Fitzroy also seemed to be anxious to get back, because they only stayed ten days in Tahiti. He had three tasks that had to be completed. The first and most time-consuming was to take the sun sights to check and rate the chronometers. Then there was the usual task of taking water on board. In Tahiti, which has good rainfall in the interior and many streams flowing down onto the coast, this was not difficult.

His third task was curious. Some two years previously a small ship, sailing under the British flag had been plundered in the Tuamotus. Since those islands came under the rule of the Queen of Tahiti, Fitzroy had been told to ask her for compensation, to the tune of some $3000. It turned out that the royal coffers were a little low at that time, but many of her subjects decided to chip in to pay the money. Fitzroy had a few pangs of guilt, that these people were paying for a crime committed by others, several hundred miles away. The local chiefs thanked him for his concern, but felt that since Pomarre was their Queen, they had to help her out of this embarrassment with the British Government. Somewhat to Fitzroy's surprise,

the money was soon collected.

While all this was going on, Darwin managed a three-day expedition into the interior. He took along his servant to carry his gear, and two local guides who had been given the task of not only leading him, but also supplying the food. They were very much amused at the thought of carrying food up into the mountains when there was so much already there for the taking.

When it was time to camp for the night, they quickly built a little house using bamboo and banana leaves. Then one of them dived into the nearby stream and, using a small net, soon captured enough fish and fresh-water prawns for the evening meal. Darwin watched with fascination as they lit a fire by rubbing a sharpened stick in a groove cut in another piece of wood. He insisted on trying this for himself, and was inordinately proud when he finally got a little glowing ember.

While Darwin was practising the art of fire-making, the Tahitians got their own fire going, and then heaped rocks over it. As the wood burned down, they began to cook the evening meal on the hot rocks. The fish, prawns and some bananas, both ripe and green, were wrapped up tightly in banana leaves and placed on the hot rocks. The food cooked in a very short time, and the banquet was served on a cloth of banana leaves. For dessert, the Tahitians dug up a root from a kind of lily. It was as sweet as treacle, and made a delicious end to the meal. Darwin was well content.

By the time he got back down to the ship, the watering had been completed and Fitzroy had invited the Queen out to the ship with what turned out to be about 200 of her closest friends. He regretted that he was not able to fire a royal salute from the cannons, but having just spent six days rating the chronometers, he did not want to risk upsetting them with the shock of the guns. Instead they put on a firework display with signal rockets. The Tahitians were excited by the display; they had never seen anything quite like it before.

The next day *Beagle* sailed for New Zealand, another long passage of just over three weeks without a stop. The highlight of the passage was crossing the Dateline, and Darwin was quick to note that now, every mile they sailed brought them a mile nearer to Britain.

Crossing the Dateline gave him a psychological boost, but the gale a few days later brought him down again with a bump. He wrote in his journal that he was now earnestly wishing for the termination of the voyage. He was tired, not just from the regular bouts of seasickness, but also from the months and years of labour without any sustained periods of rest. He had even had enough of new sights; he was longing for things familiar.

They sailed into New Zealand's Bay of Islands four days before Christmas, but Darwin could find little good to say about it. The country around the bay where they were anchored was difficult for walking. There were few birds and almost no animals. He described the local Maoris as dirty and treacherous, and most of the British inhabitants, he said, were the very refuse of society. The only place he had anything good to say about was the settlement of Waimate, where the missionary inhabitants made him welcome.

Christmas itself made him very depressed. Counting the first Christmas, in Plymouth, this was his fifth on board the *Beagle*, and he was fervently hoping it would be his last. They sailed from New Zealand on 30 December. Despite the fact that it was midsummer the weather was unsettled, and there was a gale in prospect. Darwin wrote that he would rather face any gale then have to spend another hour in New Zealand.

A couple of weeks later, the *Beagle* reached Australia and dropped anchor in Sydney Harbour. There were many other large ships at anchor, and big warehouses lined the harbour. As he walked ashore that first evening, Darwin was astonished at how much had been achieved in the relatively few years that Australia had been settled by the British, compared to what had been achieved over centuries by the Spanish in South America. As he surveyed the booming town with patriotic pride, he congratulated himself on being born an Englishman. Over the next few days, however, as he explored inland, his enthusiasm was tempered a little. He saw the convict associations as lowering, and he felt that there was little culture, and few economic prospects.

From Sydney they crossed to Tasmania, and spent ten days anchored in Storm Bay. A little of Darwin's former enthusiasm returned, and during their stay he made several expeditions into the interior, mainly looking at things geological once more.

They made one last stop in Australia, spending a week at King George's Sound before leaving the continent for good. As they left, Darwin wrote in his journal that he did so without sorrow or regret. He had also written to Henslow in Cambridge, saying that he was tired of seeing new places unless they held some special scientific interest.

By coincidence, he found this interest at their next destination – the Cocos Keeling Islands. After two mostly rough weeks at sea, the palm-fringed tropical beaches of the atoll looked particularly appealling. This was his first chance to study an atoll closely, and he spent considerable time investigating the reef, seeking confirmation for his theory that the atoll had formed around a sinking mountain peak.

They completed the crossing of the Indian Ocean to arrive in Mauritius where, for the first time since leaving Valparaiso, they found a measure of European culture. Darwin went for an elephant ride, and passed what he called an idle and dissipated time.

It was as well that he had a good rest in Mauritius, because the three-week trip down to Cape Town was a fairly rough one, and he suffered worse than ever with the seasickness. He did not think much of South Africa – to his slightly jaundiced eye he had never seen a less interesting country. His mood was not improved when he received his mail and found that Professor Henslow had already started to publish some of his letters. Darwin had intended to wait until all his thoughts and notes were complete before making anything public.

The one bright spot in the visit seems to have been the social whirl of Cape Town. He enjoyed dining out on several occasions, and was stimulated by the long intellectual discussions he was able to have with people such as the Astronomer Royal, whom he met there.

After leaving Cape Town, they had a fairly gentle passage north, and Darwin was able to spend much of his time writing. He was mainly trying to consolidate his geological notes. Fitzroy too was busy writing. He had decided long before that he would write a book about the voyage, just as Lieutenant King had done on the *Beagle's* previous voyage. Fitzroy had asked Darwin if he might use parts of his journal to augment sections of his own book. Darwin agreed, and read out passages to Fitzroy. Even at this late stage in the voyage, he himself had no real intention of trying to write a book. He was hoping to publish some scientific papers, but not a book for the general public. It may well have been watching Fitzroy at work that encouraged him to do likewise.

They stopped at St Helena for six days, which was the time it took to take the sun sights and rate the chronometers again. During this time Darwin moved ashore, and took several long walks. Although his house was close to Napoleon's tomb, he chose to ignore this aspect of the island's history, as it depressed him. He was not even very interested in the flora, after discovering that of the 746 types of plants known on the island, only fifty-two are indigenous; all the rest have been introduced. Once more it was the geology that concerned him. He spent many hours wandering in the hills, looking at the rock formations. He was sure that the island had existed for many thousands of years, yet here again were signs of upheaval and suggestions that at some stage the land had been lower or the sea had been higher.

For once he was almost sad to be leaving. He had enjoyed St

Helena and found it interesting. He seemed to be getting a second wind now that the end of the voyage was almost in sight. When they reached Ascension Island, his spirits had another lift. When he received his mail from home, there was a letter from his sisters saying that their father had heard from Sedgewick at the University that it was his estimation that Charles should take a place among leading scientific men. This was heady stuff for somebody still not yet thirty years old.

His elation was short-lived. As they were preparing to sail, Fitzroy suddenly announced that they would return once more to Bahia, in Brazil, to check the chronometers against their outward trip. Darwin was torn. At times he looked forward to a last walk in the tropical forest he had enjoyed so much, but at others he felt heartily fed up with the whole journey and longed to get home. He wrote that he now loathed and abhorred the sea and all ships which sail on it.

The old sailors had a name for this phenomenon of increasing homesickness the closer one got to home. They called it channel fever – a longing to be up the English Channel. The *Beagle* was still several thousand miles from home, but there is no doubt that Darwin had a bad case of channel fever.

When they reached Bahia in early August, he took long walks in the jungle around Salvador, trying, as he put it, to fix the impression in his mind. He knew that he would not be back. Then as soon as the sights and the chronometer rating were complete, they set off north once more. An ill-timed gale sent them scurrying for shelter into Pernambuco, or Recife as it is now called. He cared for neither the place nor the inhabitants, and when they finally sailed, he remarked that he was glad to be away from it, from them, and from Brazil.

They crossed the Equator on 21 August, almost at the same spot as on their southward journey. Since all the crew were shellbacks, little was made of the event, and they beat northwards against the trade winds.

Just nine days later they reached Porto Praya in the Cape Verdes for the second time. Once more they stopped for the obligatory six days for the chronometers before heading onwards for the Azores, their last stop. They anchored off Terceira, once again for just six days. It was here that Darwin fulfilled one of his wishes. He found an active volcano; it was a very small one, but at least it was bubbling with hot mud and larva.

The *Beagle* made a brief stop at San Miguel, hoping for mail, but there was none so Fitzroy decided to sail on. Finally, to Darwin's unutterable relief, they started the last leg of the voyage, to the English Channel. They had a quick passage of seven days, but the

weather was bad for most of it. Poor Darwin finished the voyage at least as seasick as he had begun it. The ship drove up channel with close-reefed topsails set, a blustery south-westerly gale blowing, and driving rain – a typical autumn day.

Just before dusk, on Sunday 2 October 1836, the *Beagle* dropped her anchor in the shelter of Falmouth Harbour. Darwin was weak from seven days of seasickness. It was late, the gale was still blowing and rain was pouring down. Nevertheless, Darwin was ashore that night to catch the night mail-coach heading eastwards. He had spent almost five years aboard the *Beagle*, and he was not going to spend another night on board if he could help it. It took him almost forty-eight hours to get home to Shrewsbury; the traveller had finally returned.

When the weather in Falmouth abated, Fitzroy took the *Beagle* up channel and eventually reached Greenwich. When he completed the last of his calculations, using the eleven chronometers that were still running, he found that an error of thirty-three seconds had crept in during the five-year circumnavigation. Although he was perhaps a little disappointed, perfectionist that he was, it was really a remarkable achievement, given the equipment they had to work with.

Darwin never travelled far again. He settled down to write about his experiences and the rest, as they say, is history.

I think that if the Panama Canal had been in existence when the *Beagle* left the Galapagos, they would have almost certainly come back that way; Fitzroy seemed just as anxious as Darwin to finish the voyage. Although there had been talk of building a canal since 1534, when the King of Spain commissioned a survey, it was not until 1880 that anybody tried to build it. The French, who made this first attempt, struggled for twenty years before giving up. Finally, in 1913, the Americans achieved what at one stage had looked impossible, and the canal was opened. *Beagle* was almost eighty years too early to take the short cut back to England.

After leaving the Galapagos, the first couple of days saw us sailing along in uncharacteristically fair breezes. It seemed as though our struggle to find fuel was going to prove unnecessary. We need not have worried, however. On the third day, true to form, the wind vanished and a persistent drizzle set in. We hoisted the iron topsail and motored steadily onwards.

As we approached the mainland, the skies began to clear and finally the rain stopped. At around 3 a.m. on the fifth day, a welcome green smudge of land appeared on the radar screen. By dawn, we were feeling our way in through dozens of anchored ships.

We anchored off the Balboa Yacht Club to complete the formalities and wait for permission to go through the canal. While there we were visited by the former President of Panama, a gentleman by the name of Aristides Royo, the man with whom President Carter had reached agreement on the handover of the canal to the Panamanians in the year 2000. He had been told about us by one of the Boss's South American contacts.

He came out on the yacht club launch, and leaped on board. I came up into the cockpit to meet him and introduce myself. He shook hands, tucked two gigantic cigars into the top pocket of my shirt and sat himself down. I was still standing there, rather open mouthed, when he waved his arm imperiously in my direction, and said, 'You may sit.' I sat down, for once completely at a loss for words. He then proceeded to invite us to join his family for a picnic on Flamingo Island the next day. He explained that a simple meal like a paella would suffice. I was vaguely nodding and grinning vacantly at him when it finally dawned on me that he was inviting the whole family to come on *Thalassi* for the day, and that Lana would be expected to cook a modest little paella for about fifteen people. We could do without that; we had work to do and an almost impossible schedule to keep.

Fortunately Jeff had been eavesdropping, and came to the rescue. He came breezing into the cockpit and told me that he had found the problem with the main engine, and hoped to have it running in a couple of days. Regretfully I explained to the President that the boat was immovable until Jeff fixed the engine, and much as we would have liked to take them all out for a picnic, we would have to postpone it until some future visit. Perhaps he realised that he was being conned, because he left almost at once, without even taking the tour of the boat we offered.

Eventually all the formalities were done, and the required certificates and permissions granted. The following Tuesday, we headed off through the canal. We had the obligatory pilot on board, and to bring the crew numbers up to the required five (the canal regulations require four crew to handle the lines in the locks, in addition to the helmsman) we took a young Canadian called Paul from a cruising boat. The pilot does not participate; he just issues instructions. Paul was happy to come for the ride, and to take a look before taking his own boat through later.

Going up through the three sets of locks was quite painless. *Thalassi* was moored in the middle of the lock chambers, and as she rose we tightened the four mooring lines using the hydraulic winches. It was all much easier than when I had been through a few years before in a much smaller boat. Most yachts have to take two days going through the canal, spending the night at Gamboa, about halfway through. But on *Thalassi* we were able to make enough speed to get through in a single day.

There was a slight hold-up as we came down the locks at the northern end, at Gatun. We were put into the lock ahead of a Japanese car-transport ship. The ship had only inches to spare on either side, and it was guided into the lock by eight powerful electric locomotives, which in canal parlance are termed 'mules'. Just as the ship was squeezing into the lock, and being drawn ever closer to our stern, there was a tremendous bang, and one of the mules all but disappeared in a cloud of smoke. It took them a long time to organise another one and finally get the ship far enough into the lock to close the gates. Despite the delay, we still managed to go all the way through, and be tied up at the Cristóbal Yacht Club before dark.

The twin cities of Cristóbal and Colón have long had an unsavoury reputation. We were firmly warned not to leave the yacht club compound on foot, but to go everywhere by taxi. We took the advice and had no problems. Jeff managed to organise a truck to deliver fuel to us, Lana topped up the provisions and Nick was sent off to get enough cigarettes for the Atlantic crossing. We did not want any chance of him running out again at sea.

That evening there were some riots in town and somebody was shot, so we decided to move out early the next morning. We had received word that the Boss had changed his mind, and was too busy to come to Panama. Instead he would meet us in Antigua in a couple of weeks. We left at first light, and motored out through the breakwaters into a stiff easterly breeze. The short, steep seas were very uncomfortable, and we were not making much headway, but I was determined to make our scheduled stop in the San Blas Islands, with or without the Boss to share it.

I had been there before, but none of the others had, and Lana especially had been looking forward to it. I felt it would do us all good to have a couple of days off after the hustle and bustle of Panama. Everybody had been working hard and deserved a short break.

All day the wind blew hard, at least twenty-five knots, and it stayed right on the nose. Progress was slow and uncomfortable. Finally, in the late afternoon, the islands came into sight. The San Blas group consists of literally hundreds of tiny, flat islands, each rising only a

few feet above sea level. When making a landfall there, the first things one sees are trees, which appear to grow out of the sea. One has to be quite close before the land itself becomes visible.

Although the wind was stronger than we might have wished for, at least the visibility was good. The charts for the area are not very good, and I was a little nervous as we felt our way in through the reef. Some close friends of ours had lost their boat trying to fetch this same anchorage. A rain-squall had come at the wrong moment, visibility had fallen to almost nothing, and in an instant they were on the reef. With an anxious eye to windward, therefore, watching for squalls, we found the pass through the reef, and soon anchored in the lee of the main island, Porvenire.

Within moments of the anchor splashing down, we were surrounded by at least half a dozen dugout canoes, each full of women and children. They were hoping to sell us the *molas* which have become synonymous with these islands. They are squares of cloth sewn together in layers. A pattern is formed by cutting through the various layers to expose the different colours – a sort of reverse appliqué. All the edges of the cuts are hemmed with minute hand-sewn stitches. The smaller and neater the stitches, the better the *mola*. For the local women, they form the front and back of the blouses of their very colourful costumes.

They climbed on board, and soon had the deck covered in a bright array of *molas*. If they were disappointed to find only four of us on board, they did not show it, but proceeded with the hard sell. Lana, who loves to bargain, was in heaven, and in no time had amassed a good collection of *molas*.

The women of the San Blas are very striking. They are small, all under 5 ft, and their features look rather Asian. What fascinated Nick more than anything else was the fact that each woman had a gold ring through her nose. Once the selling frenzy was over, they climbed back into their canoes, and returned from whence they had come.

I went ashore to Porvenire to hunt out Costumes and Intimidation. Although the islands are technically part of Panama, they are semi-autonomous, and so I was required to clear in with them. I found the office easily enough, but it was empty. I cast around and eventually found somebody in uniform at a little bar. He granted us permission to stay as long as we wanted – formalities over. By this time it was almost dark, so we saved the explorations for the next day.

After breakfast, I decided we ought to get the work out of the way before we went off to play. The bottom of the boat needed scrubbing again, so Jeff, Nick and I put on scuba tanks and scrubbed while Lana baked bread and did some varnishing. *Thalassi* never seemed

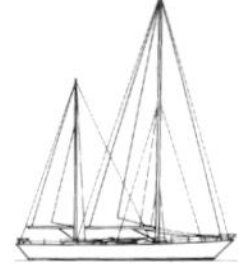

bigger than when scrubbing her bottom, but at least we were in clean, warm water. It took most of the morning to finish, so we agreed that lunch and a nap were in order; then the explorations could begin.

The first island we went to was called Nuala Naga. It is a very small island and almost completely covered with small, neat houses. The walls of the houses are made from bamboo, and the roofs thatched with palm fronds. As we peered in through the open doorways, we could see that in most cases the only furnishings were a couple of hammocks suspended over the beaten earth floor.

Lana thought that the whole village looked like a toy town. The houses were very small and packed together, yet everywhere was neat and tidy. There was no litter anywhere, and even the sandy paths between the houses looked as if they had recently been brushed. There were coconut trees squeezed in between the houses, but no signs of any gardens. All the fruits and vegetables are grown on the mainland, to which the men commute by canoe.

The next day we dinghied over to the neighbouring island, Whichub Huala. This was not quite as spotless and tidy as the other, but it was certainly much cleaner than an equivalent community in the West Indies. Once again there were *molas* being offered at every turn, as well as necklaces and beads. A young boy tried to sell us a toucan. The bird's beak was so brightly coloured that it almost looked as if it had been painted.

I had planned to leave after lunch, but a big rain squall came rattling through. When it was still overcast and squally at 4.30, our departure was officially postponed until the next morning. Although going out through the reef would be easier than coming in, I did not want to take a chance of making a premature end to the voyage.

From the San Blas, the logical route to Britain would have been to go north, pass west of Cuba, then ride the Gulf Stream north into the Atlantic. The second choice would be to pass between Cuba and Haiti, through the Windward Passage. Neither of these routes were for us, however. The Boss had said he would be waiting for us in Antigua. The fact that the island lay some 1200 miles dead to windward did not seem to enter his calculations at all.

We had a most miserable trip east. I did not want to get too close to the Colombian coast, as stories abounded of boats being attacked or confiscated in those waters. We stayed a minimum of 20 miles offshore, and battled strong headwinds and an adverse current. We motorsailed the whole time, slamming and crashing our way to windward.

The fuel was going more quickly than Jeff had expected, and it was obvious that we would not have enough to get to the West Indies in

one hop. I decided to pull into Curaçao for fuel, and to let us dry out. The thrashing to windward had shown us deck leaks that we had not even suspected were there. The eighteen-hour respite in Curaçao did us all good. Then, once the fuel tanks were filled up again, we set off once more. This time conditions were a lot easier. Since Venezuela is a lot safer than Colombia, we were able to hug the coast, clear of the worst of the current. Progress was much improved, and morale was even beginning to rise a little, when we got a message from the Boss He had changed his mind once more, and would not now be joining us in Antigua. We could have taken the easy route after all. A few choice words were uttered over dinner that night.

We were so close to the Grenadines now that I decided to stick to our original plan. Besides, our mail had been sent to Antigua, and we were not going to miss our first post since leaving Chile. We made our landfall on Union Island in the Grenadines, and met up with our long time friends Rick and Sue, who were working there. Nick and Jeff went off diving while Lana and I caught up on a few years' worth of Grenadines gossip.

From Union we had a good sail up to Antigua, making just a brief stop in St Lucia for Jeff to borrow a welding machine to fix something in the engine-room, and for me to see an old ham radio friend who was dying of cancer. Antigua was as busy as ever. We collected our mail and all went for a last tropical swim, before heading out across the Atlantic.

Our crossing to the Azores was quite painless, with very light winds for most of the way, so once more the Mercedes did sterling duty to help us stay on schedule. We arrived in Horta, Faial, thirteen days out from Antigua, and burned about the last gallon of fuel motoring across the harbour.

Like Darwin at this stage of the voyage, we were all getting channel fever; we were anxious to finish the trip. Lana and I had told the Boss that we would take the boat to Britain, but would then leave. He had organised a busy schedule of race-following, followed by a session in a boatyard putting in a new mast and we did not relish either prospect. In the meantime, we had work to do to ready her for the last leg of the trip.

Once the work was done, we took a last day off to enjoy Faial, our favourite island in the Azores. Lana and I decided to hire horses, and ride up to the volcanic crater at the top of the island. Jeff decided to come with us, but Nick opted out, saying that his rear end had barely recovered from the last horse ride in the Galapagos.

This time the horses were better equipped, and the ride up to the crater was very pretty, with hydrangeas and wild roses fringing the roads. Nevertheless, four hours in the saddle turned out to be a bit much, and we were all a bit bow-legged as we staggered back on board that evening.

It did not take long for the weather to turn cold as we sailed north. Blankets came out, and we took to wearing shoes and socks on night watch. Like the *Beagle* we had a quick passage. We too took a week, although we went a little further than the *Beagle*. We escaped the gale they had, but went barrelling up channel with a brisk south-westerly, under grey skies. We made such good speed over the last 100 miles or so that we actually sailed up the Lymington River one tide sooner than our schedule had dictated.

By coincidence, Darwin had arrived late on a Sunday night, as we did. But unlike him, we were not free to escape immediately. Clearing with Costumes and Intimidation took some time, especially when we showed them the Boss's guns and ammunition. They were a bit put out when I suggested that they would need a wheelbarrow to shift all the ammunition to their bonded store.

Lana and I stayed on board for a couple of days to clean the boat and make her ready to hand over to George, who would run her during the race-following period. He would then deliver her to Holland for the new mast. The Boss came down, and settled the outstanding bills. Much to our relief, we were all paid up to date.

Suddenly it was over. We finished the last of the packing, said our goodbyes, and retreated to our cottage in Ireland. It had been a good trip, but we were more than ready to stop, at least until the next adventure comes along.

After the hustle, bustle and civil unrest of Panama, the San Blas Islands seemed especially peaceful and tranquil.

Specifications

Thalassi was designed by Ron Holland, and built in 1986 by the Belliure brothers in Calpe, Spain.

Her length overall was 83 ft 7 in, but she has since been extended to 90 ft. Her beam is 19 ft 6 ins, and her draught, with the centreboard up, is 9 ft, and 16 ft with it down.

She is built of glass-reinforced plastic, with additional Kevlar strengthening in the bows. Her total weight is some 80 tons.

Her engine is a 250-horsepower Mercedes, which can give her a maximum speed under power of 11 knots. A more economical cruising speed is between 7 and 9 knots, and she has a range under power of about 3000 miles. She has two electrical generators, one of 16kW and the other of 10kW. The working sail area is 3680 square feet, and all the sails are controlled by hydraulic furlers and winches, allowing one person to set or trim any sail alone.

Her electronic aids include a Furuno 48-mile radar, Magnavox satellite navigator, a Furuno Loran C. and an Anschutz gyro compass. The instruments for wind direction and strength, as well as boat speed and heading, have read-outs on deck for the helmsman, and they are repeated in each cabin as well, so that while lying in my bunk I could open one eye to see if the wind had changed, or if we were still on course.

For communication, she carries an 800W Skanti radio, with telex capability. This let us talk to the UK on an almost daily basis.

Best of all was the autopilot, made by a German boffin called Mr Seeger. It was wonderful, and freed us almost completely from the chore of having to steer. It was worth at least half a dozen more crew.

Thalassi's watermaker is able to make 30 gallons of fresh water an hour from sea-water, so we never had to take on fresh water from ashore. There was always enough water for showering, washing clothes and for running the dishwasher in the galley.

The galley cooker is electric, powered by either generator, and we had two freezers, a fridge and a large walk-in cooler for storing fresh food.

In Patagonia, we carried five anchors: two CQR plough-type

anchors, two collapsible fisherman-type Luke anchors, and a very large Danforth. Our main CQR anchor was on 100 metres of chain, but we had rope rodes, with a short length of chain for each of the other anchors. The rope allowed us to set them from the dinghy if needed – chain would have been too heavy for us to handle. The anchors were recovered using the hydraulic windlass, an easy job for one person.

We carried three boats for getting ashore or exploring. The main dinghy was an 18 ft semi-rigid inflatable, with a 50-horsepower outboard. We also had a 14 ft pulling boat, built of Kevlar. This could be rowed, sailed or powered by a 6-horsepower outboard. Finally we had a 10 ft inflatable which was called the cook's dinghy, although Lana much prefered to use the big one!

We normally sailed with one person on deck and another on standby within earshot. So even when there were only four of us sailing the boat, we usually had twelve hours a day off duty – an undreamed of luxury for the *Beagle's* crew.

Beagle

Beagle was a Cherokee class brig, of which over a hundred were built between 1808 and 1837. She was built at the Woolwich Naval Dockyard, and launched on 11 May 1820. She stayed in naval service until 1845, when she became a Coast Guard watch vessel. She served in that role for fifteen years before being broken up in 1870.

By definition, a brig only has two masts, yet all illustrations of the *Beagle* show her to have three. The small mizzen mast, with its fore and aft sail was fitted for her first survey voyage, to make her easier to steer and handle in confined waters. Although this third mast makes her a barque, Darwin always referred to her as a brig.

She was 98 ft long on deck, only 15 ft longer than *Thalassi*, yet she carried seventy-four crew. In fair weather she could set as many as twenty-four sails, and each of these had to be hoisted, set, furled and trimmed by hand.

Although she was fitted with a new patent anchor windlass to replace the capstan, it was still powered by hand, and recovering an anchor from a deep Patagonian anchorage would have been hard work indeed.

She carried seven boats on deck, a 28 ft yawl, a 25 ft cutter, three 25 ft whale-boats, a 21 ft gig and the smallest, the dinghy. None was powered, they had to be sailed or rowed, and they covered many hundreds of miles while surveying.

Beagle of course had no electricity; the only light was from oil lamps or candles. She also had no engine; she had to be sailed or, if becalmed, towed by rowers in the whale-boats.

There were no facilities for cold storage. Meat was preserved in brine, or in the newly invented Kilner jars – the forerunners of canned food.

Water was always rationed, and they never missed a chance to top up the tanks. The amount of water they could carry effectively limited the time they could be at sea.

Life on board, especially in the cold of the southern ocean, must have been rough indeed. We had it easy by comparison.

Thalassi *sailing past the Romanche Glacier in the Beagle Channel – the blue of the ice almost matching the colour of her hull. This was the first big glacier we saw, and it was probably on the beach opposite this glacier, that Darwin and crew nearly perished when an icefall sent a wave across the channel which almost washed their boats away.*

Index

Index

Index

LINCOLN THE UNKNOWN

DALE CARNEGIE

★

Lincoln

THE UNKNOWN

DALE CARNEGIE & ASSOCIATES, INC.
NEW YORK

PRINTED IN THE UNITED STATES

To
My Father and Mother

HOW THIS BOOK WAS WRITTEN—AND WHY

ONE SPRING DAY, some years ago, I was breakfasting in the Hotel Dysart, London; and, as usual, I was trying to winnow a bit of American news from the columns of the "Morning Post." Ordinarily I found none, but on that fortunate morning I made a strike rich and unexpected.

The late T. P. O'Connor, reputed "Father of the House of Commons," conducted in those days a column in the "Morning Post" entitled "Men and Memories." On that particular morning, and for several mornings following, "Tay Pay's" column was devoted to Abraham Lincoln—not to his political activities but to the personal side of his career: to his sorrows, his repeated failures, his poverty, his great love for Ann Rutledge, and his tragic marriage to Mary Todd.

I read the series with profound interest—and surprise. I had spent the first twenty years of my life in the Middle West, not far from the Lincoln country; and, in addition to that, I had always been keenly interested in United States history. I should have said that of course I knew Lincoln's life-story; but I soon discovered that I didn't. The fact is that I, an American, had had to come to London and read a series of articles written by an Irishman, in an English newspaper, before I realized that the story of Lincoln's career was one of the most fascinating tales in all the annals of mankind.

Was this lamentable ignorance peculiar to me? I wondered.

But I didn't wonder long, for I soon discussed the subject with a number of my fellow-countrymen, and I discovered that they were in the same boat, that about all they knew about Lincoln was this: that he had been born in a log cabin, had walked miles to borrow books and then read them at night, stretched out on the floor in front of the fireplace; that he split rails, became a lawyer, told funny stories, said that a man's legs ought to be long enough to reach the ground, was called "Honest Abe," debated with Judge Douglas, was elected President of the United States, wore a silk hat, freed the slaves, spoke at Gettysburg, declared that he wished he knew what brand of whisky Grant drank so he could send a barrel of it to his other generals, and was shot by Booth in a theater in Washington.

Aroused by these articles in the "Morning Post," I went over to the British Museum library and read a number of Lincoln books; and the more I read, the more fascinated I became. Finally I caught on fire and I determined to write a book about Lincoln, myself. I knew that I had not the urge, temperament, training, or ability necessary to produce a learned treatise for the benefit of scholars and historians. Besides, I felt there was little need for another book of that kind, for many excellent ones are already in existence. However, after reading many Lincoln volumes, I did feel that there was a genuine need for a short biography that would tell the most interesting facts about his career briefly and tersely for the average busy and hurried citizen of to-day. I have tried to write such a book.

I began the work in Europe, and labored over it for a year there and then for two years in New York. Finally I tore up all that I had written and tossed it into the wastebasket. I then went out to Illinois, to write of Lincoln on the very ground where he himself had dreamed and toiled. For months I lived among people whose fathers had helped Lincoln survey land and build fences and drive hogs to market. For months I delved among old books and letters and speeches and half-forgotten newspapers and musty court records, trying to understand Lincoln.

I spent one summer in the little town of Petersburg. I went there because it is only a mile away from the restored village of New Salem, where Lincoln spent the happiest and most formative years of his life. There he ran a mill and a grocery store, studied law, worked as a blacksmith, refereed cock-fights and horse-races, fell in love, and had his heart broken.

Even in the heydey of its glory New Salem never had more than a hundred inhabitants, and its entire existence covered a span of about ten years. Shortly after Lincoln left the village it was abandoned; bats and swallows nested in the decaying cabins, and for more than half a century cows grazed over the spot.

A few years ago, however, the State of Illinois secured the site, made it a public park, and built replicas of the log cabins that had stood there a hundred years before. So to-day the deserted village of New Salem looks much as it did in Lincoln's time.

The same white oaks under which Lincoln studied and wrestled and made love are still standing. Every morning I used to take my typewriter and motor up there from Petersburg, and half of the chapters of this book were written under those trees. What a lovely spot in which to work! In front of me flowed the winding Sangamon, and all about me the woods and the hay-fields were musical with the call of the bob-white; and through the trees flashed the color of the blue jay, the yellowhammer, and the redbird. I felt Lincoln there.

I often used to go there alone on summer nights when the whip-poor-wills were crying in the woods along the banks of the Sangamon, when the moonlight outlined Rutledge's tavern against the sky; and it stirred me to realize that on just such nights, about a hundred years ago, young Abe Lincoln and Ann Rutledge had walked over this same ground arm in arm in the moonlight, listening to the night-birds and dreaming ecstatic dreams that were destined never to come true. Yet I am convinced that Lincoln found here at New Salem the only supreme happiness that he ever knew.

When I came to write the chapter dealing with the death of Lincoln's sweetheart, I put a little folding table and a typewriter in a car and drove out over country roads and through a hog lot and a cow pasture until I reached the quiet, secluded spot where Ann Rutledge lies buried. It is utterly abandoned now, and overgrown. To get near her grave, it was necessary to mow down the weeds and brush and vines. And there, where Lincoln came to weep, was set down the story of his grief.

Many of the chapters were written in Springfield. Some in the sitting-room of the old home where Lincoln lived for sixteen unhappy years, some at the desk where he composed his first inaugural address, and others above the spot where he came to court and quarrel with Mary Todd.

★

PART ONE

★

THERE WAS a woman in Harrodsburg—it was called Fort Harrod in those days—named Ann McGinty. The old histories record that Ann and her husband brought the first hogs into Kentucky, the first ducks and the first spinning-wheel; and they also declare that she was the first woman ever to make butter out there in the dark and bloody wilderness. But her real claim to fame rests upon the fact that she performed an economic and textile miracle. Cotton could be neither grown nor purchased there in the mysterious Indian country, and timber-wolves slaughtered the sheep. So it was well-nigh impossible to find any substance from which clothes could be made. Then the ingenious Ann McGinty found a way of spinning thread and making "McGinty cloth" from two substances that were both plentiful and cheap—nettle lint and buffalo wool.

It was a tremendous discovery, and housewives traveled as far as a hundred and fifty miles to sit in her cabin and learn the new art. And as they spun and wove they talked. And they didn't always talk about nettle lint and buffalo wool. Frequently the conversation degenerated into gossip, and Ann McGinty's cabin soon became the community's acknowledged clearing-house for scandal.

In those days fornication was an indictable offense, and bastardy was a misdemeanor. And evidently there were few other activities in life that gave Ann's shriveled soul more deep and abiding satisfaction than uncovering the story of some suffering girl's error, and then running to the Grand Jury with the news. The records of the Court of Quarter Sessions in Fort Harrod repeatedly tell the pathetic story of some unfortunate girl indicted for fornication "on information of Ann McGinty." Seventeen cases were tried at Harrodsburg in the spring of 1783, and eight were for fornication.

Among these indictments, there is one brought by the Grand Jury on November 24, 1789, and reading as follows:

"Lucy Hanks for fornication."

This wasn't Lucy's first offense. The first had been years before, back in Virginia.

That was a long time ago, and the old records are meager: they give only a few bare facts and no setting for the facts. From them and from other sources, however, a probable story can be reconstructed. The essential elements, at any rate, are well established.

The Virginia home of the Hanks family had been on a narrow strip of land bounded on one side by the Rappahannock River, on the other by the Potomac. On this same narrow strip of land dwelt the Washingtons and the Lees, the Carters and the Fauntleroys, and many another snuff-and-silk-breeches family. These aristocrats attended services at Christ Church, and so did the poor and illiterate families of the neighborhood such as the Hankses.

Lucy Hanks was present, as usual, on the second Sunday in November, 1781, when General Washington caused a great craning of necks by bringing General La Fayette to church, as his guest. Every one was eager to see the distinguished Frenchman who, only a month before, had helped Washington capture the army of Lord Cornwallis at Yorktown.

After the last hymn had been sung that morning and the benediction pronounced, the parishioners marched by in single file, shaking hands with the two military heroes.

But La Fayette had a predilection for other things besides military tactics and affairs of state. He took a profound interest in beautiful young ladies; and it was his custom, on being introduced to one that appealed to him, to pay her the compliment of a kiss. On this particular morning he kissed seven girls in front of Christ Church; and in doing so he caused more comment than had the third chapter of the Gospel according to

St. Luke, which had been read so sonorously by the rector. One of the seven fortunate girls that he kissed was Lucy Hanks.

This kiss started a chain of events that did as much to modify the future of the United States as did all the battles La Fayette fought for us. Perhaps more.

There was a bachelor in the congregation that morning—a rich, aristocratic bachelor who for a long time had known vaguely of the Hanks family, an illiterate, poverty-stricken tribe that moved in a world far below his. But this morning—of course it may have been pure imagination—he thought that La Fayette put just a trifle more ardor and enthusiasm into the kiss he gave Lucy Hanks than in those he bestowed upon the other girls.

This planter looked up to the French general, both as a military genius and as a connoisseur of beautiful women. So he fell to dreaming now of Lucy Hanks. And when he stopped to think of it, he knew that some of the world's most celebrated beauties had been bred in circumstances as poor as Lucy's—some in circumstances even more humble. There was Lady Hamilton, for example; and Madame DuBarry, the illegitimate child of a poverty-stricken dressmaker. DuBarry herself was almost illiterate, yet she all but ruled France under Louis XV. They were comforting, these historical precedents; and they helped to dignify the bachelor's desires.

This was Sunday. He turned the matter over in his mind all day Monday; and on Tuesday morning he rode over to the dirt-floor cabin that the Hanks tribe occupied and hired Lucy to be a servant in the farm-house on his plantation.

He already owned a number of slaves, and he didn't need another servant. Nevertheless he hired Lucy, gave her some light tasks about the house, and didn't ask her to associate with the slaves.

It was the custom of many of the wealthy families of Virginia at that time to educate their sons in England. Lucy's employer had attended Oxford, and he had brought back to America a collection of books that he cherished. One day he drifted into the library and found Lucy seated, dust-cloth in hand, poring over the illustrations in a history book.

That was an odd thing for a servant to be doing. But, instead of censuring her, he closed the library door and sat down and read her the captions underneath the pictures, and told her something of what they meant.

She listened with very evident interest; and finally, to his surprise, she confessed that she wanted to learn to read and write.

Just how astonishing that aspiration was in a servant-girl in the year of our Lord 1781, it is difficult now to understand. Virginia at that time did not have any free schools; not half the property-owners of the State could sign their names to a deed, and virtually all of the women made their marks when transferring land.

Yet here was a servant-girl aspiring to read and write. The best people in Virginia would have called it dangerous, if not revolutionary. But the idea appealed to Lucy's employer, and he volunteered to be her tutor. That evening, after supper, he called her into the library and began teaching her the letters of the alphabet. A few evenings later he put his hand over hers as it grasped the quill, and showed her how to form the letters. For a long time after that he taught her, and to his credit let it be recorded that he did a very good job. There is one specimen of her handwriting still in existence, and it shows that she wrote with a bold, self-confident flourish. There are spirit and personality and character in her handwriting; and she not only used the word "approbation," but spelled it correctly. That was no little achievement at a time when the orthography of men like George Washington was not always flawless.

And when the reading and spelling lessons were finished for the evening Lucy and her tutor sat side by side in the library, looking at the dancing flames in the fireplace, and watching the moon rise over the rim of the forest.

She fell in love with him, and trusted him; but she trusted him too far. . . . Then came weeks of anxiety. She couldn't eat. She hardly slept. She worried a haggard look into her face. When she could no longer deny the truth even to herself she told him. For a moment he considered marrying her. But only for a moment. Family. Friends. Social position. Complications. Unpleasant scenes. . . . No. Besides, he was begining to tire of her. So he gave her some money and sent her away.

As the months went by people pointed at Lucy and shunned her.

One Sunday morning she created a sensation by shamelessly bringing her baby to church. The good women of the congregation were indignant, and one stood up in the meeting-house and demanded that "that slut be sent away."

That was enough. Lucy's father did not mean to have his

daughter insulted any longer. So the Hanks tribe loaded their few earthly possessions into a wagon and traveled out over the Wilderness Road, through the Cumberland Gap, and settled at Fort Harrod, Kentucky. No one knew them there: they could lie more effectively about the father of Lucy's child.

But in Fort Harrod Lucy was quite as pretty, quite as attractive to men as she had been back in Virginia. She was sought after, and flattered. She fell in love again. This time it was a little easier to stray. Somebody found it out. Somebody told somebody else. Then it was repeated at Ann McGinty's. And, as we have already recorded, the Grand Jury indicted Lucy for fornication. But the sheriff knew Lucy wasn't the kind of woman to have the law upon; so he stuck the summons in his pocket, and went off deer-hunting and left her alone.

That was in November. In March the court met again. And when it met, a certain woman appeared with further gossip and slander about Lucy and demanded that the hussy be haled into court and made to answer to the charges against her. So another summons was issued; but high-spirited Lucy tore it up and flung it into the face of the man who served it. In May the court would convene again; and Lucy would doubtless have been forced into court at that time, had not a remarkable young man appeared on the scene.

His name was Henry Sparrow. He rode into town, tied his horse in front of her cabin, and went in.

"Lucy," he probably said to her, "I don't give a damn about what these women are saying about you. I love you and want you to be my wife." At any rate, he did ask her to marry him.

However, she was not willing to marry immediately. She was not willing to have the gossips of the town say that Sparrow had been forced into matrimony.

"We'll wait a year, Henry," she insisted. "During that time I want to prove to every one that I can live a decent life. If at the end of that time, you still want me, come; I'll be waiting for you."

Henry Sparrow took out the license at once, April 26, 1790, and nothing more was heard of the summons. Almost a year later they were married.

That set the Ann McGinty crowd to shaking their heads and wagging their tongues: the marriage wouldn't last long, Lucy would be up to her old tricks again. Henry Sparrow heard this talk. Every one heard it. He wanted to shield Lucy. So he suggested that they move farther West and begin life all over again in kindlier surroundings. She refused that customary means of escape. She wasn't bad, she said; and she held her head high as she said it. She wasn't going to run away. She was determined to settle down there in Fort Harrod and fight it out.

And she did. She reared eight children and redeemed her name in the very community where it had once been a signal for coarse jests.

In time two of her sons became preachers; and one of her grandsons, the son of her illegitimate daughter, became President of the United States. His name was Abraham Lincoln.

I have told this story to show Lincoln's more immediate ancestry. He himself set great store by his well-bred Virginia grandfather.

William H. Herndon was Lincoln's law partner for twenty-one years. He probably knew Lincoln better than any other man who ever lived. Fortunately, he wrote a three-volume biography of Lincoln that appeared in 1888. It is one of the most important of the multitude of works on Lincoln. I quote now from pages 3 and 4 of Volume I:

> On the subject of his ancestry and origin I only remember one time when Mr. Lincoln ever referred to it. It was about 1850, when he and I were driving in his one-horse buggy to the court in Menard county, Illinois. The suit we were going to try was one in which we were likely, either directly or collaterally, to touch upon the subject of hereditary traits. During the ride he spoke, for the first time in my hearing, of his mother, dwelling on her characteristics, and mentioning or enumerating what qualities he inherited from her. He said, among other things, that she was the illegitimate daughter of Lucy Hanks and a well-bred Virginia farmer or planter; and he argued that from this last source came his power of analysis, his logic, his mental activity, his ambition, and all the qualities that distinguished him from the other members and descendants of the Hanks family. His theory in discussing the matter of hereditary traits has been, that, for certain reasons, illegitimate children are oftentimes sturdier and brighter than those born in lawful wedlock; and in his case, he believed that his better nature and finer qualities came from this

broad-minded, unknown Virginian. The revelation—painful as it was—called up the recollection of his mother, and, as the buggy jolted over the road, he added ruefully, "God bless my mother; all that I am or ever hope to be I owe to her," and immediately lapsed into silence. Our interchange of ideas ceased, and we rode on for some time without exchanging a word. He was sad and absorbed. Burying himself in thought, and musing no doubt over the disclosure he had just made, he drew round him a barrier which I feared to penetrate. His words and melancholy tone made a deep impression on me. It was an experience I can never forget.

LINCOLN'S MOTHER, Nancy Hanks, was brought up by her aunt and uncle, and probably had no schooling at all. We know she could not write, for she made her mark when signing a deed.

She lived deep in the somber woods and made few friends; and, when she was twenty-two, she married one of the most illiterate and lowly men in all Kentucky—a dull, ignorant day-laborer and deer-hunter. His name was Thomas Lincoln, but the people in the backwoods and canebrake settlements where he lived called him "Linkhorn."

Thomas Lincoln was a rover, a drifter, a ne'er-do-well, floating about from one place to another, taking any kind of job he could get when hunger drove him to it. He worked on roads, cut brush, trapped bear, cleared land, plowed corn, built log cabins; and the old records show that on three different occasions he was employed to guard prisoners, with a shot-gun. In 1805 Hardin County, Kentucky, paid him six cents an hour for catching and whipping recalcitrant slaves.

He had no money sense whatever: he lived for fourteen years on one farm in Indiana, and during that period he was unable to save and pay as much as ten dollars a year on his land. At a time when he was so poor that his wife had to pin her dresses together with wild thorns, he went to a store in Elizabethtown, Kentucky, and bought a pair of silk suspenders for himself—and bought them on credit. Shortly after that, at an auction sale, he paid three dollars for a sword. Probably he wore his silk suspenders and carried his sword even when going barefoot.

Shortly after his marriage he moved to town and tried to make a living as a carpenter. He got a job building a mill, but he did not square his timbers or cut them the right length. So his employer sharply refused to pay him for his bungling efforts, and three lawsuits followed.

Tom Lincoln had come from the woods, and, dull as he was, he soon realized now that he belonged to the woods. He took his wife back to a poor, stony farm on the edge of the forest, and never again did he have the temerity to forsake the soil for the village.

Not far from Elizabethtown there was a vast stretch of treeless land known as "the barrens." For generations the Indians had started fires there and burned away the forests and brush and undergrowth, so that the coarse prairie-grass could grow in the sun, and the buffaloes would come there to wallow and graze.

In December, 1808, Tom Lincoln purchased a farm on "the barrens" for sixty-six and two thirds cents per acre. There was a hunter's hut on it, a crude sort of cabin surrounded with wild crab-apple trees; and half a mile away flowed the South Fork of Nolin Creek, where the dogwood blossomed in the spring. In the summertime, hawks circled lazily in the blue overhead, and the tall grasses surged in the wind like an illimitable sea of green. Few people had had the poor judgment to settle there. So in the wintertime it was one of the most lonely and desolate regions in all Kentucky.

And it was in a hunter's hut on the edge of these lonely barrens, deep in the winter of 1809, that Abraham Lincoln came into the world. He was born on a Sunday morning—born on a bed of poles covered with corn husks. It was storming outside, and the February wind blew the snow through the cracks between the logs and drifted it across the bearskin that covered Nancy Hanks and her baby. She was destined to die nine years later, at the age of thirty-five, worn out by the strain and hardships of pioneer life. She never knew much of happiness. Wherever she lived, she was hounded by gossip about her illegitimate birth. What a pity she could not have looked into the future that morning, and seen the marble temple that a grateful people have now erected on the spot which she then consecrated with her suffering!

The paper money in circulation at that time, in the wilderness, was often of very doubtful value. Much of it was worthless. So hogs, venison hams, whisky, coon-skins, bear-hides, and farm produce were much used as mediums of exchange. Even preachers sometimes took whisky as part pay for their services. In the autumn of 1816, when Abraham was seven years old, old Tom Lincoln bartered his Kentucky farm for about four hundred gallons of corn whisky, and moved his family into the gloom and solitude of the wild and desolate forests of Indiana. Their nearest neighbor was a bear-hunter; and all about them the trees and brush and grape-vines and undergrowth were so thick that a man had to cut and hack his way through it. This was the spot, "Rite in the Brush," as Dennis Hanks described it, where Abraham Lincoln was to spend the next fourteen years of his life.

The first snow of winter was already falling when the family arrived; and Tom Lincoln hastily built what was then known as "a three-faced camp." To-day it would be called a shed. It had no floor, no door, no windows—nothing but three sides and a roof of poles and brush. The fourth side was entirely open to wind and snow and sleet and cold. Nowadays an up-to-date farmer in Indiana wouldn't winter his cattle or hogs in such a crude shelter, but Tom Lincoln felt it was good enough for himself and his family all during the long winter of 1816–17, one of the severest and most violent winters in our history.

Nancy Hanks and her children slept there that winter like dogs, curled up on a heap of leaves and bearskins dumped on the dirt floor in a corner of the shed.

As for food, they had no butter, no milk, no eggs, no fruit, no vegetables, not even potatoes. They lived chiefly on wild game and nuts.

Tom Lincoln tried to raise hogs, but the bears were so hungry that they seized the hogs and ate them alive.

For years, there in Indiana, Abraham Lincoln endured more terrible poverty than did thousands of the slaves whom he would one day liberate.

Dentists were almost unknown in that region, and the nearest doctor was thirty-five miles away; so when Nancy Lincoln had a toothache, probably old Tom Lincoln did what the other pioneers did; he whittled out a hickory peg, set the end of it against the complaining molar, and hit the peg a hard blow with a rock.

From the earliest times in the Middle West the pioneers suffered from a mysterious malady known as the "milk sick." It was fatal to cattle, sheep, and horses, and sometimes carried off entire communities of people. No one knew what caused it, and for a hundred years it baffled the medical profession. It was not until the beginning of the present century that science showed that the poisoning was due to animals eating a plant known as white snakeroot. The poison was transmitted to humans through the milk of cows. White snakeroot thrives in wooded pastures and deeply shaded ravines, and to this day it continues to take its toll of human life. Every year the Department of Agriculture of the State of Illinois posts placards in the county court-houses, warning farmers that if they do not eradicate this plant, they may die.

In the autumn of 1818 this dreadful scourge came to the Buckhorn Valley of Indiana, wiping out many families. Nancy Lincoln helped nurse the wife of Peter Brooner, the bear-hunter, whose cabin was only half a mile away. Mrs. Brooner died, and Nancy herself suddenly felt ill. Her head swam, and sharp pains shot through her abdomen. Vomiting severely, she was carried home to her wretched pallet of leaves and skins. Her hands and feet were cold, but her vitals seemed to be on fire. She kept calling for water. Water. Water. More water.

Tom Lincoln had a profound faith in signs and omens; so, on the second night of her illness, when a dog howled long and piteously outside the cabin, he abandoned all hope and said she was going to die.

Finally Nancy was unable even to raise her head from the pillow, and she could not talk above a whisper. Beckoning Abraham and his sister to her, she tried to speak. They bent over to catch her words: she pleaded with them to be good to each other, to live as she had taught them, and to worship God.

These were her last words, for her throat and entire intestinal tract were already in the first stages of paralysis. She sank into a prolonged coma, and finally died on the seventh day of her illness, October 5, 1818.

Tom Lincoln put two copper pennies on her eyelids, to hold them shut; and then went out into the forest and felled a tree and cut it into rough, uneven boards and fastened these together with wooden pegs; and in this crude coffin he placed the tired, worn body of the sad-faced daughter of Lucy Hanks.

Two years before, he had brought her into this settlement on a sled; and now, again on a sled, he hauled her body to the summit of a thickly wooded hill, a quarter of a mile away, and buried her without service or ceremony.

So perished the mother of Abraham Lincoln. We shall probably never know what she looked like or what manner of woman she was, for she spent most of her short life in the gloomy forests, and made only a faint impression upon the few people who crossed her path.

Shortly after Lincoln's death one of his biographers set out to get some information about the President's mother. She had been dead then for half a century. He interviewed the few people living who had ever seen her, but their memories were as vague as a faded dream. They were unable to agree even as to her physical appearance. One described her as a "heavy built, squatty woman," but another said she had a "spare, delicate form." One man thought she had black eyes, another described them as hazel, another was sure they were bluish green. Dennis Hanks, her cousin, who had lived under the same roof with her for fifteen years, wrote that she had "lite hair." After further reflection, he reversed himself and said her hair was black.

For sixty years after her death there was not so much as a stone to mark her resting-place, so that to-day only the approximate position of her grave is known. She is buried beside her aunt and uncle, who reared her; but it is impossible to say which of the three graves is hers.

A short time before Nancy's death Tom Lincoln had built a new cabin. It had four sides, but no floor, no windows, no door. A dirty bearskin hung over the entrance, and the interior was dark and foul. Tom Lincoln spent most of his time hunting in the woods, leaving his two motherless children to run the place. Sarah did the cooking, while Abraham kept the fire going and carried water from the spring a mile away. Having no knives and forks, they ate with their fingers, and with fingers that were seldom clean, for water was hard to get and they had no soap. Nancy had probably made her own soft lye soap, but the small supply that she left at her death had long since vanished, and the children didn't know how to make more; and Tom Lincoln wouldn't make it. So they lived on in their poverty and dirt.

During the long, cold winter months they made no attempt to wash their bodies; and few, if any, attempts to wash their soiled and ragged garments. Their beds of leaves and skins grew filthy. No sunlight warmed and purified the cabin. The only light they had was from the fireplace or from hog fat. We know from accurate descriptions of other cabins on the frontier what the womanless Lincoln cabin must have been like. It smelled. It was infested with fleas, crawling with vermin.

After a year of this squalor even old Tom Lincoln could stand it no longer; he decided to get a new wife who would clean up.

Thirteen years before he had proposed to a woman in Kentucky named Sarah Bush. She had refused him then and married the jailer of Hardin County, but the jailer had since died and left her with three children and some debts. Tom Lincoln felt that the time was auspicious now for renewing his proposal; so he went to the creek, washed up, scrubbed his grimy hands and face with sand, strapped on his sword, and started back through the deep, dark woods to Kentucky.

When he reached Elizabethtown he bought another pair of silk suspenders, and marched whistling down the street.

That was in 1819. Things were happening, and people were talking of progress. A steamship had crossed the Atlantic Ocean!

WHEN LINCOLN was fifteen he knew his alphabet and could read a little but with difficulty. He could not write at all. That autumn—1824—a wandering backwoods pedagogue drifted into the settlement along Pigeon Creek and started a school. Lincoln and his sister walked four miles through the forests, night and morning, to study under the new teacher, Azel Dorsey. Dorsey kept what was known as a "blab" school; the children studied aloud. In that way the teacher believed he could tell whether or not they were applying themselves. He marched about the room, switch in hand, giving a cut to those who were silent. With such a premium on vociferousness, each pupil strove to out-blab the others. The uproar could often be heard a quarter of a mile away.

While attending this school Lincoln wore a cap of squirrel-skin, and breeches made from the hide of a deer. The breeches failed by a considerable stretch to meet the top of his shoes, leaving several inches of sharp, blue shinbone exposed to the wind and snow.

The school was held in a crude cabin barely high enough for the teacher to stand up in. There were no windows; a log had been left out at each side, and the opening covered with greased paper to let in the light. The floor and seats were made of split logs.

Lincoln's reading lessons were chapters from the Bible; and in his writing exercises he took the chirography of Washington and Jefferson as his models. His handwriting resembled theirs. It was unusually clear and distinct. People commented on it, and the illiterate neighbors walked for miles to have Abraham write their letters.

He was finding a real tang and zest, now, in learning. The hours at school were all too short, he carried his studies home. Paper was scarce and high, so he wrote on a board with a charcoal stick. Sometimes he ciphered on the flat sides of the hewn logs that formed the cabin walls. Whenever a bare surface became covered with figures and writing he shaved them off with a drawing-knife and began anew.

Too poor to buy an arithmetic, he borrowed one and copied it on sheets of paper about the size of an ordinary letter-head. Then he sewed them together with twine, and so had a home-made arithmetic of his own. At the time of his death his step-mother still had portions of this book.

Now he began to exhibit a trait which sharply distinguished him from the rest of the backwoods scholars. He wanted to write out his opinions on various topics; at times he even broke into verse. And he took his verse and prose composition to William Wood, a neighbor, for criticism. He memorized and recited his rhymes, and his essays attracted attention. A lawyer was so impressed with his article on national politics that he sent it away and had it published. A newspaper in Ohio featured an article he wrote on temperance.

But this was later. His first composition here in school was inspired by the cruel sports of his playmates. They used to catch terrapins and put burning coals on their backs. Lincoln pleaded with them to stop it, and ran and kicked off the coals with his bare feet. His first essay was a plea for mercy to animals. Already the boy was showing that deep sympathy for the suffering which was to be so characteristic of the man.

Five years later he attended another school irregularly—"by littles," as he phrased it.

Thus ended all his formal attempts at education, with a total of not more than twelve months of schooling.

When he went to Congress in 1847 and filled out a biographical blank, he came to the question, "What has been your education?" He answered it with one word: "Defective."

After he was nominated for the Presidency he said: "When I came of age, I did not know much. Still, somehow, I could read, write, and cipher to the rule of three; but that was all.

I have not been to school since. The little advance I now have upon this store of education, I have picked up from time to time under the pressure of necessity."

And who had been his teachers? Wandering, benighted pedagogues who had faith in witches and believed that the world was flat. Yet, during these broken and irregular periods, he had developed one of the most valuable assets any man can have, even from a university education: a love of knowledge and a thirst for learning.

The ability to read opened up a new and magic world for him, a world he had never dreamed of before. It changed him. It broadened his horizon and gave him vision; and, for a quarter of a century, reading remained the dominant passion of his life. His stepmother had brought a little library of five volumes with her: the Bible, Æsop's Fables, "Robinson Crusoe," "The Pilgrim's Progress," and "Sinbad the Sailor." The boy pored over these priceless treasures. He kept the Bible and Æsop's Fables within easy reach and read them so often that they profoundly affected his style, his manner of talking, his method of presenting arguments.

But these books weren't enough. He longed for more things to read, but he had no money. So he began to borrow books, newspapers, anything in print. Walking down to the Ohio River, he borrowed a copy of the Revised Laws of Indiana from a lawyer. Then, for the first time, he read the Declaration of Independence and the Constitution of the United States.

He borrowed two or three biographies from a neighboring farmer for whom he had often grubbed stumps and hoed corn. One was the Life of Washington by Parson Weems. It fascinated Lincoln, and he read it at night as long as he could see; and, when he went to sleep, he stuck it in a crack between the logs so that he could begin it again as soon as daylight filtered into the hut. One night a storm blew up, and the book was soaked. The owner refused to take it back, so Lincoln had to cut and shock fodder for three days to pay for it.

But in all his book-borrowing expeditions, he never made a richer find than "Scott's Lessons." This book gave him instruction in public speaking, and introduced him to the renowned speeches of Cicero and Demosthenes and those of Shakespeare's characters.

With "Scott's Lessons" open in his hand, he would walk back and forth under the trees, declaiming Hamlet's instructions to the players, and repeating Antony's oration over the dead body of Cæsar: "Friends, Romans, countrymen, lend me your ears; I come to bury Cæsar, not to praise him."

When he came across a passage that appealed especially to him, he would chalk it down on a board if he had no paper. Finally he made a crude scrap-book. In this he wrote all his favorites, using a buzzard's quill for a pen and pokeberry juice for ink. He carried the scrap-book with him and studied it until he could repeat many long poems and speeches by heart.

When he went out in the field to work his book went with him. While the horses rested at the end of the corn row he sat on the top rail of a fence and studied. At noontime, instead of sitting down and eating with the rest of the family, he took a corn-dodger in one hand and a book in the other and, hoisting his feet higher than his head, lost himself in the lines of print.

When court was in session Lincoln would often walk fifteen miles to the river towns to hear the lawyers argue. Later, when he was out working in the fields with other men, he would now and then drop the grub-hoe or hay-fork, mount a fence, and repeat the speeches he had heard the lawyers make down at Rockport or Boonville. At other times he mimicked the shouting hard-shell Baptist preachers who held forth in the Little Pigeon Creek church on Sundays.

Abe often carried "Quinn's Jests," a joke-book, to the fields; and when he sat astride a log and read parts of it aloud, the woods resounded with the loud guffaws of his audience; but the weeds throve in the corn rows and the wheat yellowed in the fields.

The farmers who were hiring Lincoln complained that he was lazy, "awful lazy." He admitted it. "My father taught me to work," he said, "but he never taught me to love it."

Old Tom Lincoln issued peremptory orders: all this foolishness had to stop. But it didn't stop; Abe kept on telling his jokes and making his speeches. One day—in the presence of others—the old man struck him a blow in the face and knocked him down. The boy wept, but he said nothing. There was already growing up between father and son an estrangement that would last for the rest of their lives. Although Lincoln looked after his father financially in his old age, yet when the old man lay on his death-bed, in 1851, the son did not go to see him, "If we met now," he said, "it is doubtful whether it would not be more painful than pleasant."

In the winter of 1830 the "milk sick" came again, spreading death once more through the Buckhorn Valley of Indiana.

Filled with fear and discouragement, the roving and migratory Tom Lincoln disposed of his hogs and corn, sold his stump-infested farm for eighty dollars, made a cumbersome wagon—the first he had ever owned—loaded his family and furniture into it, gave Abe the whip, yelled at the oxen, and started out for a valley in Illinois which the Indians called the Sangamon, "the land of plenty to eat."

For two weeks the oxen crept slowly forward as the heavy wagon creaked and groaned over the hills and through the deep forests of Indiana and out across the bleak, desolate, uninhabited prairies of Illinois, carpeted then with withered yellow grass that grew six feet tall under the summer sun.

At Vincennes Lincoln saw a printing-press for the first time; he was then twenty-one.

At Decatur the emigrants camped in the court-house square; and, twenty-six years later, Lincoln pointed out the exact spot where the wagon had stood.

"I didn't know then that I had sense enough to be a lawyer," he said.

Herndon tells us:

> Mr. Lincoln once described this journey to me. He said the ground had not yet yielded up the frosts of winter; that during the day the roads would thaw out on the surface and at night freeze over again, thus making travelling, especially with oxen, painfully slow and tiresome. There were, of course, no bridges, and the party were consequently driven to ford the streams, unless by a circuitous route they could avoid them. In the early part of the day the latter were also frozen slightly, and the oxen would break through a square yard of thin ice at every step. Among other things which the party brought with them was a pet dog, which trotted along after the wagon. One day the little fellow fell behind and failed to catch up till after they had crossed the stream. Missing him they looked back, and there, on the opposite bank, he stood, whining and jumping about in great distress. The water was running over the broken edges of the ice, and the poor animal was afraid to cross. It would not pay to turn the oxen and wagon back and ford the stream again in order to recover a dog, and so the majority, in

their anxiety to move forward, decided to go on without him. "But I could not endure the idea of abandoning even a dog," related Lincoln. "Pulling off shoes and socks I waded across the stream and triumphantly returned with the shivering animal under my arm. His frantic leaps of joy and other evidences of a dog's gratitude amply repaid me for all the exposure I had undergone."

While the oxen were pulling the Lincolns across the prairies Congress was debating with deep and ominous emotion the question of whether or not a State had a right to withdraw from the Union; and during that debate Daniel Webster arose in the United States Senate and, in his deep, golden, bell-like voice, delivered a speech which Lincoln afterward regarded "as the grandest specimen of American oratory." It is known as "Webster's Reply to Hayne" and ends with the memorable words which Lincoln later adopted as his own political religion: "Liberty and Union, now and forever, one and inseparable!"

This cyclonic issue of secession was to be settled a third of a century later, not by the mighty Webster, the gifted Clay, or the famous Calhoun, but by an awkward, penniless, obscure driver of oxen who was now heading for Illinois, wearing a coonskin cap and buckskin trousers, and singing with ribald gusto:

> "Hail Columbia, happy land,
> If you ain't drunk, then I'll be damned."

THE LINCOLNS SETTLED near Decatur, Illinois, on a stretch of timber land running along a bluff overlooking the Sangamon River.

Abe helped to fell trees, erect a cabin, cut brush, clear the land, break fifteen acres of sod with a yoke of oxen, plant it to corn, split rails, and fence the property in.

The next year he worked as a hired man in the neighborhood, doing odd jobs for farmers: plowing, pitching hay, mauling rails, butchering hogs.

The first winter Abe Lincoln spent in Illinois was one of the coldest the State had known. Snow drifted fifteen feet deep on the prairies; cattle died, the deer and wild turkey were almost exterminated, and even people were frozen to death.

During this winter Lincoln agreed to split a thousand rails for a pair of trousers made from brown jean cloth dyed with white-walnut bark. He had to travel three miles each day to work. Once, while crossing the Sangamon, his canoe was upset, he was thrown into the icy water, and before he could reach the nearest house, Major Warnick's, his feet froze. For a month he was unable to walk, and so he spent that time lying in front of the fireplace at Major Warnick's telling stories, and reading a volume of the Statutes of Illinois.

Prior to this, Lincoln had courted the major's daughter, but the major frowned on the idea. What? A daughter of his, a Warnick, married to this gawky, uneducated rail-splitter? A man without land, without cash, and without prospects? Never!

True, Lincoln didn't own any land; and that wasn't all—he didn't want to own any. He had spent twenty-two years on farms, and he had had enough of pioneer farming. He hated the grinding toil, the lonely monotony of the life. Longing for distinction, as well as for contact with other social beings, he wanted a job where he could meet people and gather a crowd around him and keep them roaring at his stories.

While living back in Indiana Abe had once helped float a flatboat down the river to New Orleans, and what fun he had had! Novelty. Excitement. Adventure. One night while the boat was tied up to the shore at the plantation of Madame Duchesne, a gang of Negroes, armed with knives and clubs, climbed aboard. They meant to kill the crew, throw their bodies into the river, and float the cargo down to the thieves' headquarters at New Orleans.

Lincoln seized a club, and with his long, powerful arms knocked three of the marauders into the river, then chased the others ashore; but, in the fight, one of the Negroes slashed Lincoln's forehead with a knife and left over his right eye a scar that he carried to his grave.

No, Tom Lincoln could not hold the boy Abe to a pioneer farm.

Having seen New Orleans once, Abe now got himself another river job. For fifty cents a day and a bonus he and his stepbrother and second cousin cut down trees, hewed logs, floated them to a sawmill, built a flatboat eighty feet long, loaded it with bacon, corn, and hogs, and floated it down the Mississippi.

Lincoln did the cooking for the crew, steered the boat, told stories, played seven-up, and sang in a loud voice:

> "The turbaned Turk that scorns the world
> And struts about with his whiskers curled
> For no other man but himself to see."

This trip down the river made a profound and lasting impression upon Lincoln. Herndon says:

> In New Orleans, for the first time Lincoln beheld the true horrors of human slavery. He saw *"negroes in chains—whipped and scourged."* Against this inhumanity his sense of right and justice rebelled, and his mind and con-

science were awakened to a realization of what he had often heard and read. No doubt, as one of his companions has said, "Slavery ran the iron into him then and there." One morning in their rambles over the city the trio passed a slave auction. A vigorous and comely mulatto girl was being sold. She underwent a thorough examination at the hands of the bidders; they pinched her flesh and made her trot up and down the room like a horse, to show how she moved, and in order, as the auctioneer said, that "bidders might satisfy themselves" whether the article they were offering to buy was sound or not. The whole thing was so revolting that Lincoln moved away from the scene with a deep feeling of "unconquerable hate." Bidding his companions follow him he said, *"By God, boys, let's get away from this. If ever I get a chance to hit that thing* [meaning slavery], *I'll hit it hard."*

Lincoln became very popular with Denton Offut, the man who hired him to go to New Orleans. Offut liked his jokes and stories and honesty. He employed the young man to go back to Illinois, fell trees, and build a log-cabin grocery store in New Salem, a tiny village composed of fifteen or twenty cabins perched on a bluff high above the winding Sangamon. Here Lincoln clerked in the store and also ran a grist and sawmill, and here he lived for six years—years that had a tremendous influence on his future.

The village had a wild, pugnacious, hell-raising gang of ruffians called the Clary's Grove Boys, a crowd who boasted that they could drink more whisky, swear more profanely, wrestle better, and hit harder than any other group in all Illinois.

At heart they weren't a bad lot. They were loyal, frank, generous, and sympathetic, but they loved to show off. So when the loud-mouthed Denton Offut came to town and proclaimed the physical prowess of his grocery clerk, Abe Lincoln, the Clary's Grove Boys were delighted. They would show this upstart a thing or two.

But the showing was all the other way, for this young giant won their foot-races and jumping contests; and with his extraordinarily long arms he could throw a maul or toss a cannon-ball farther than any of them. Besides, he could tell the kind of funny stories they could understand; and he kept them laughing for hours at his back-woods tales.

He reached the high-water mark of his career in New Salem, as far as the Clary's Grove Boys were concerned, on the day all the town gathered under the white-oak trees to see him wrestle with their leader, Jack Armstrong. When Lincoln laid Armstrong out, he had arrived, he had achieved the ultimate. From that time on the Clary's Grove Boys gave him their friendship and crowned him with their allegiance. They appointed him judge of their horse-races and referee of their cock-fights. And when Lincoln was out of work and had no home, they took him into their cabins and fed him.

Lincoln found here in New Salem an opportunity he had been seeking for years, an opportunity to conquer his fears and learn to speak in public. Back in Indiana the only chance that he had had at this sort of thing had been in talking to little groups of laborers in the fields. But here in New Salem there was an organized "literary society" that met every Saturday night in the dining-room of the Rutledge tavern. Lincoln joined it with alacrity and took a leading part on its program, telling stories, reading verses that he had written himself, making extemporaneous talks on such subjects as the navigation of the Sangamon River, and debating the various questions of the day.

This activity was priceless. It widened his mental horizon and awakened his ambition. He discovered that he had an unusual ability to influence other men by his speech. That knowledge developed his courage and self-confidence as nothing else had ever done.

In a few months Offut's store failed and Lincoln was out of a job. An election was coming on, the State was seething with politics, and so he proposed to cash in on his ability to speak.

With the aid of Mentor Graham, the local school-teacher, he toiled for weeks over his first address to the public, in which he announced that he was a candidate for the State Legislature. He stated that he favored "internal improvements . . . the navigation of the Sangamon . . . better education . . . justice," and so on.

In closing he said:

"I was born and have ever remained in the most humble walks of life. I have no wealthy or popular relatives or friends to recommend me." And he concluded with this pathetic sentence: "But if the good people in their wisdom shall see fit to keep me in the background, I have been too familiar with disappointments to be very much chagrined."

A few days later a horseman dashed into New Salem with the startling news that the great Sac Indian chief, Black Hawk, was on the war-path with his braves, burning homes, capturing women, massacring settlers, and spreading red terror along Rock River.

In a panic Governor Reynolds was calling for volunteers; and Lincoln, "out of work, penniless, a candidate for office," joined the forces for thirty days, was elected captain, and tried to drill the Clary's Grove Boys, who shouted back at his commands, "Go to the devil."

Herndon says Lincoln always regarded his participation in the Black Hawk War "as a sort of holiday affair and chicken-stealing expedition." It was just about that.

Later, in the course of a speech in Congress, Lincoln declared that he didn't attack any redskins, but that he made "charges upon the wild onions." He said he didn't see any Indians, but that he had "a good many bloody struggles with the mosquitoes."

Returning from the war, "Captain Lincoln" plunged again into his political campaign, going from cabin to cabin, shaking hands, telling stories, agreeing with every one, and making speeches whenever and wherever he could find a crowd.

When the election came he was defeated, although he received all but three of the two hundred and eight votes cast in New Salem.

Two years later he ran again, was elected, and had to borrow money to buy a suit of clothes to wear to the legislature.

He was reëlected in 1836, 1838, and 1840.

There was living in New Salem at that time a ne'er-do-well whose wife had to take in boarders while he fished and played the fiddle and recited poetry. Most of the people in town looked down upon Jack Kelso as a failure. But Lincoln liked him, chummed with him, and was greatly influenced by him. Before he met Kelso, Shakspere and Burns had meant little to Lincoln; they had been merely names, and vague names at that. But now as he sat listening to Jack Kelso reading "Hamlet" and reciting "Macbeth," Lincoln realized for the first time what symphonies could be played with the English language. What a thing of infinite beauty it could be! What a whirlwind of sense and emotion!

Shakspere awed him, but Bobby Burns won his love and sympathy. He felt even a kinship with Burns. Burns had been poor like Lincoln. Burns had been born in a cabin no better than the one that had seen Abe's birth. Burns too had been a plowboy. But a plowboy to whom the plowing up of the nest of a field-mouse was a tiny tragedy, an event worthy of being caught up and immortalized in a poem. Through the poetry of Burns and Shakspere, a whole new world of meaning and feeling and loveliness opened up to Abraham Lincoln.

But to him the most astounding thing of all was this: neither Shakspere nor Burns had gone to college. Neither of them had had much more schooling and education than he.

At times he dared to think that perhaps he too, the unschooled son of illiterate Tom Lincoln, might be fitted for finer things. Perhaps it would not be necessary for him to go on forever selling groceries or working as a blacksmith.

From that time on Burns and Shakspere were his favorite authors. He read more of Shakspere than of all other authors put together, and this reading left its imprint upon his style. Even after he reached the White House, when the burdens and worries of the Civil War were chiseling deep furrows in his face, he devoted much time to Shakspere. Busy as he was, he discussed the plays with Shaksperian authorities, and carried on a correspondence regarding certain passages. The week he was shot, he read "Macbeth" aloud for two hours to a circle of friends.

The influence of Jack Kelso, the shiftless New Salem fisherman, had reached to the White House. . . .

The founder of New Salem and the keeper of the tavern was a Southerner named James Rutledge, and he had a most attractive daughter, Ann. She was only nineteen when Lincoln met her—a beautiful girl with blue eyes and auburn hair. Despite the fact that she was already engaged to the richest merchant in town, Lincoln fell in love with her.

Ann had already promised to become the wife of John McNeil, but it was understood that they were not to be married until she had had two years of college.

Lincoln had not been in New Salem very long when a strange thing happened. McNeil sold his store and said that he was returning to New York State to bring his mother and father and family back to Illinois. But before leaving town he confessed something to Ann Rutledge that almost stunned her. However, she was young and she loved him, and she believed his story.

A few days later, he set out from Salem, waving good-by to Ann and promising to write often.

Lincoln was postmaster of the village then. The mail arrived by stage-coach twice a week, and there was very little of it, for it cost from six and a quarter cents to twenty-five to send a letter, depending on the distance it must travel. Lincoln carried the letters about in his hat. When people met him they would ask if he had any mail for them, and he would pull off his hat and look through his collection to see what he had.

Twice each week Ann Rutledge inquired for a letter. Three months passed before the first one arrived. McNeil explained that he had not written sooner because he had been taken sick with a fever while crossing Ohio, and had been in bed for three weeks—part of the time unconscious.

Three more months passed before the next letter came; and when it arrived it was almost worse than no letter at all. It was cold and vague. He said that his father was very ill, that he was being harassed by his father's creditors, and that he did not know when he would be back.

After that Ann watched the mail for months, hoping for more letters which never came. Had he ever really loved her at all? She had begun now to doubt it.

Lincoln, seeing her distress, volunteered to try to find McNeil.

"No," she said, "he knows where I am, and if he doesn't care enough to write to me I am sure I do not care enough to have you try to find him."

Then she told her father of the extraordinary confession that McNeil had made before he left. He had admitted that he had been living under an assumed name for years. His real name was not McNeil, as every one in New Salem believed, but McNamar.

Why had he practised this deception? His father, he explained, had failed in business, back in New York State, and had become heavily involved in debts. He, being the eldest son, had, without disclosing his destination, come West to make money. He feared that if he used his right name, his family might learn of his whereabouts and follow him, and he would be obliged to support them all. He didn't want to be hampered by any such burden while struggling to make a start. It might delay his progress for years. So he took an assumed name. But now that he had accumulated property he was going to bring his parents to Illinois and let them share his prosperity.

When the story got abroad in the village it created a sensation. People called it a damn lie and branded him as an impostor. The situation looked bad and gossip made the worst of it. He was—well, there was no telling what he was. Perhaps he was already married. Maybe he was hiding from two or three wives. Who knew? Maybe he had robbed a bank. Maybe he had murdered somebody. Maybe he was this. Maybe he was that. He had deserted Ann Rutledge, and she ought to thank God for it.

Such was New Salem's verdict. Lincoln said nothing, but he thought much.

At last the chance for which he had hoped and prayed had come.

THE RUTLEDGE TAVERN was a rough, weather-beaten affair with nothing whatever to distinguish it from a thousand other log cabins along the frontier. A stranger would not have given it a second glance; but Lincoln could not keep his eyes off it now, nor his heart out of it. To him, it filled the earth and towered to the sky, and he never crossed the threshold of it without a quickening of his heart.

Borrowing a copy of Shakspere's plays from Jack Kelso, he stretched himself out on top of the store counter, and, turning over the pages, he read these lines again and again:

> But, soft! what light through yonder window breaks?
> It is the east, and Juliet is the sun.

He closed the book. He could not read. He could not think. He lay there for an hour, dreaming, living over in memory all the lovely things Ann had said the night before. He lived now for only one thing—for the hours that he spent with her.

Quilting parties were popular in those days, and Ann was invariably invited to these affairs, where her slender fingers plied the needle with unusual swiftness and art. Lincoln used to ride with her in the morning to the place where the quilting was to be held, and call for her again in the evening. Once he boldly went into the house—a place where men seldom ventured on such occasions—and sat down beside her. Her heart throbbed, and a flood of color rose to her face. In her excitement she made irregular and uncertain stitches, and the older and more composed women noticed it. They smiled. The owner kept this quilt for years, and after Lincoln became President she proudly displayed it to visitors and pointed out the irregular stitches made by his sweetheart.

On summer evenings Lincoln and Ann strolled together along the banks of the Sangamon, where whippoorwills called in the trees and fireflies wove golden threads through the night.

In the autumn they drifted through the woods when the oaks were flaming with color and hickory-nuts were pattering to the ground. In the winter, after the snow had fallen, they walked through the forest, when—

> Every oak and ash and walnut
> Wore ermine too dear for an earl
> And the poorest twig on the elm tree
> Was ridged inch-deep with pearl.

For both of them, now, life had taken on a sacred tenderness, a new and strangely beautiful meaning. When Lincoln but stood and looked down into Ann's blue eyes her heart sang within her; and at the mere touch of her hands he caught his breath and was amazed to discover that there was so much felicity in all the world. . . .

A short time before this, Lincoln had gone into business with a drunkard, a preacher's son, named Berry. The little village of New Salem was dying, all its stores were gasping for breath. But neither Lincoln nor Berry could see what was happening, so they bought the wrecks of three of those log-cabin groceries, consolidated them, and started an establishment of their own.

One day a mover who was driving out to Iowa halted his covered wagon in front of the Lincoln & Berry store. The roads were soft, his horses were tired, and the mover decided to lighten his load. So he sold Lincoln a barrel of household plunder. Lincoln didn't want the plunder, but he felt sorry for the horses; he paid the mover fifty cents, and without examining the barrel rolled it into the back room of the store.

A fortnight later he emptied the contents of the barrel out on the floor, idly curious to see what he had bought. There, at the bottom of the rubbish, he found a complete edition of Blackstone's Commentaries on Law; and started to read. The farmers were busy in their fields, and customers were few and far between, so he had plenty of time. And the more he read, the more interested he became. Never before had he been so absorbed in a book. He read until he had devoured all four volumes.

Then he made a momentous decision: he would be a lawyer. He would be the kind of man Ann Rutledge would be proud to marry. She approved his plans, and they were to be married as soon as he completed his law studies and established himself in the profession.

After finishing Blackstone he set out across the prairies for Springfield, twenty miles away, to borrow other law-books from an attorney he had met in the Black Hawk War. On his way home he carried an open book in one hand, studying as he walked. When he struck a knotty passage, he shuffled to a standstill, and concentrated on it until he had mastered the sense.

He kept on studying, until he had conquered twenty or thirty pages, kept on until dusk fell and he could no longer see to read. . . . The stars came out, he was hungry, he hastened his pace.

He pored over his books now incessantly, having heart for little else. By day he lay on his back, reading in the shade of an elm that grew beside the store, his bare feet angling up against the trunk of the tree. By night he read in the cooper's shop, kindling a light from the waste material lying about. Frequently he read aloud to himself, now and then closing the book and writing down the sense of what he had just read, revising, rephrasing it until it became clear enough for a child to comprehend.

Wherever Lincoln went now—on his rambles along the river, on his walks through the woods, on his way to labor in the fields—wherever he went, a volume of Chitty or Blackstone was under his arm. Once a farmer, who had hired him to cut firewood, came around the corner of the barn in the middle of the afternoon and found Lincoln sitting barefooted on top of the woodpile, studying law.

Mentor Graham told Lincoln that if he aspired to get ahead in politics and law he must know grammar.

"Where can I borrow one?" Lincoln asked.

Graham said that John Vance, a farmer living six miles out in the country, had a copy of Kirkham's Grammar; and Lincoln arose immediately, put on his hat, and was off after the book.

He astonished Graham with the speed with which he mastered Kirkham's rules. Thirty years later this schoolmaster said he had taught more than five thousand students, but that Lincoln was the "most studious, diligent, straightforward young man in the pursuit of knowledge and literature" he had ever met.

"I have known him," said Mentor Graham, "to study for hours the best way of three to express an idea."

Having mastered Kirkham's Grammar, Lincoln devoured next Gibbon's "Decline and Fall of the Roman Empire," Rollin's "Ancient History," a volume on American military biography, lives of Jefferson, Clay, and Webster, and Tom Paine's "Age of Reason."

Dressed in "blue cotton roundabout coat, stoga shoes, and pale-blue casinet pantaloons which failed to make the connection with either coat or socks, coming about three inches below the former and an inch or two above the latter," this extraordinary young man drifted about New Salem, reading, studying, dreaming, telling stories, and making "a host of friends wherever he went."

The late Albert J. Beveridge, the outstanding Lincoln scholar of his time, says in his monumental biography:

"Not only did his wit, kindliness and knowledge attract the people, but his strange clothes and uncouth awkwardness advertised him, the shortness of his trousers causing particular remark and amusement. Soon the name of 'Abe Lincoln' became a household word."

Finally the grocery firm of Lincoln & Berry failed. This was to be expected, for, with Lincoln absorbed in his books and Berry half groggy with whisky, the end was inevitable. Without a dollar left to pay for his meals and lodging now, Lincoln had to do any kind of manual labor he could find: he cut brush, pitched hay, built fences, shucked corn, labored in a sawmill, and worked for a while as a blacksmith.

Then, with the aid of Mentor Graham, he plunged into the intricacies of trigonometry and logarithms, prepared himself to be a surveyor, bought a horse and compass on credit, cut a grape-vine to be used as a chain, and started out surveying town lots for thirty-seven and a half cents apiece.

In the meantime the Rutledge tavern also had failed, and Lincoln's sweetheart had had to go to work as a servant in a farmer's kitchen. Lincoln soon got a job plowing corn on the same farm. In the evening he stood in the kitchen wiping the dishes which Ann washed. He was filled with a vast happiness at the very thought of being near her. Never again was he to experience such rapture and such content. Shortly before his death he confessed to a friend that he had been happier as a barefoot farm laborer back in Illinois than he had ever been in the White House.

But the ecstasy of the lovers was as short as it was intense. In August, 1835, Ann fell ill. At first there was no pain, nothing but great fatigue and weariness. She tried to carry on her work as usual, but one morning she was unable to get out of bed. That day the fever came, and her brother rode over to New Salem for Dr. Allen. He pronounced it typhoid. Her body seemed to be burning, but her feet were so cold that they had to be warmed with hot stones. She kept begging vainly for water. Medical science now knows that she should have been packed in ice and given all the water she could drink, but Dr. Allen didn't know that.

Dreadful weeks dragged by. Finally Ann was so exhausted that she could no longer raise even her hands from the sheets. Dr. Allen ordered absolute rest, visitors were forbidden, and that night when Lincoln came even he was not permitted to see her. But the next day and the following day she kept murmuring his name and calling for him so pitifully that he was sent for. When he arrived, he went to her bedside immediately, the door was closed, and they were left alone. This was the last hour of the lovers together.

The next day Ann lost consciousness and remained unconscious until her death.

The weeks that followed were the most terrible period of Lincoln's life. He couldn't sleep. He wouldn't eat. He repeatedly said that he didn't want to live, and he threatened to kill himself. His friends became alarmed, took his pocket-knife away, and watched to keep him from throwing himself into the river. He avoided people, and when he met them he didn't speak, didn't even seem to see them, but appeared to be staring into another world, hardly conscious of the existence of this.

Day after day he walked five miles to the Concord Cemetery, where Ann was buried. Sometimes he sat there so long that his friends grew anxious, and went and brought him home. When the storms came, he wept, saying that he couldn't bear to think of the rain beating down upon her grave.

Once he was found stumbling along the Sangamon, mumbling incoherent sentences. People feared he was losing his mind.

So Dr. Allen was sent for. Realizing what was wrong, he said Lincoln must be given some kind of work, some activity to occupy his mind.

A mile to the north of town lived one of Lincoln's closest friends, Bowling Greene. He took Lincoln to his home, and assumed complete charge of him. It was a quiet, secluded spot. Behind the house oak-covered bluffs rose and rolled back to the west. In front the flat bottom-lands stretched away to the Sangamon River, framed in trees. Nancy Greene kept Lincoln busy cutting wood, digging potatoes, picking apples, milking the cows, holding the yarn for her as she spun.

The weeks grew into months, and the months into years, but Lincoln continued to grieve. In 1837, two years after Ann's death, he said to a fellow-member of the State Legislature:

"Although I seem to others to enjoy life rapturously at times, yet when I am alone I am so depressed that I am afraid to trust myself to carry a pocket-knife."

From the day of Ann's death he was a changed individual. The melancholy that then settled upon him lifted at times for short intervals; but it grew steadily worse, until he became the saddest man in all Illinois.

Herndon, later his law partner, said:

"If Lincoln ever had a happy day in twenty years, I never knew of it. . . . Melancholy dripped from him as he walked."

From this time to the end of his life, Lincoln had a fondness, almost an obsession, for poems dealing with sorrow and death. He would often sit for hours without saying a word, lost in reverie, the very picture of dejection, and then would suddenly break forth with these lines from "The Last Leaf":

The mossy marbles rest
On the lips that he has prest
    In their bloom;
And the names he loved to hear
Have been carved for many a year
    On the tomb.

Shortly after Ann's death, he memorized a poem "Mortality" and beginning, "Oh, why should the spirit of mortal be proud?"

It became his favorite. He often repeated it to himself when he thought no one else was listening; repeated it to people in the country hotels of Illinois; repeated it in public addresses; repeated it to guests in the White House; wrote copies of it for his friends; and said:

"I would give all I am worth, and go in debt, to be able to write like that."

He loved the last two stanzas best:

Yea! hope and despondency, pleasure and pain,
Are mingled together in sunshine and rain;
And the smile and the tear and the song and the dirge
Still follow each other, like surge upon surge.

'Tis the wink of an eye, 'tis the draught of a breath,
From the blossom of health to the paleness of death,
From the gilded saloon to the bier and the shroud,—
Oh, why should the spirit of mortal be proud?

The old Concord Cemetery, where Ann Rutledge was buried, is a peaceful acre in the midst of a quiet farm, surrounded on three sides by wheat-fields and on the fourth by a blue-grass pasture where cattle feed and sheep graze. The cemetery itself is overgrown now with brush and vines, and is seldom visited by man. In the springtime the quails make their nests in it and the silence of the place is broken only by the bleating of sheep and the call of the bob-white.

For more than half a century the body of Ann Rutledge lay there in peace. But in 1890 a local undertaker started a new cemetery in Petersburg, four miles away. Petersburg already had a beautiful and commodious burying-ground known as the Rose Hill Cemetery; so selling lots in the new one was slow and difficult. Consequently, the greedy undertaker, in an unholy moment, conceived the gruesome scheme of violating the grave of Lincoln's sweetheart, bringing her dust to his cemetery, and using its presence there as an argument to boost sales.

So "on or about the fifteenth of May, 1890"—to quote the exact words of his shocking confession—he opened her grave. And what did he find? We know, for there is a quiet old lady still living in Petersburg who told the story to the author of this volume, and made an affidavit to its veracity. She is the daughter of McGrady Rutledge, who was a first cousin of Ann Rutledge. McGrady Rutledge often worked with Lincoln in the fields, helped him as a surveyor, ate with him and shared his bed with him, and probably knew more about Lincoln's love for Ann than any other third person has ever known.

On a quiet summer evening this old lady sat in a rocking-chair on her porch and told the author: "I have often heard Pa say that after Ann's death Mr. Lincoln would walk five miles out to Ann's grave and stay there so long that Pa would get worried and fear something would happen to him, and go and bring him home. . . . Yes, Pa was with the undertaker when Ann's grave was opened, and I have often heard him tell that the only trace they could find of Ann's body was four pearl buttons from her dress."

So the undertaker scooped up the four pearl buttons, and some dirt and interred them in his new Oakland Cemetery at Petersburg—and then advertised that Ann Rutledge was buried there.

And now, in the summer months, thousands of pilgrims motor there to dream over what purports to be her grave; I have seen them stand with bowed heads and shed tears above the four pearl buttons. Over those four buttons there stands a beautiful granite monument bearing this verse from Edgar Lee Masters' "Spoon River Anthology":

> Out of me unworthy and unknown
> The vibrations of deathless music:
> "With malice toward none, with charity for all."
> Out of me the forgiveness of millions toward millions,
> And the beneficent face of a nation
> Shining with justice and truth.
> I am Ann Rutledge who sleep beneath these weeds,
> Beloved in life of Abraham Lincoln,
> Wedded to him, not through union,
> But through separation.
> Bloom forever, O Republic,
> From the dust of my bosom!

But Ann's sacred dust remains in the old Concord Cemetery. The rapacious undertaker could not carry it away—she and her memories are still there. Where the bob-white calls and the wild rose blows, there is the spot that Abraham Lincoln hallowed with his tears, there is the spot where he said his heart lay buried, there would Ann Rutledge wish to be.

★ ★ ★

6

★ ★ ★

IN MARCH, 1837, two years after Ann's death, Lincoln turned his back on New Salem and rode into Springfield on a borrowed horse, to begin what he called his "experiment as a lawyer."

He carried in his saddle-bag all his earthly possessions. The only things he owned were several law-books and some extra shirts and some underwear. He also carried an old blue sock stuffed with six-and-a-quarter-cent and twelve-and-a-half-cent pieces—money that he had collected for postage before the post-office "winked out" back in New Salem. During this first year in Springfield, Lincoln needed cash often, and he needed it badly. He could have spent this money and paid the Government out of his own pocket, but he would have felt that that was dishonest. So when the post-office auditor finally came around for a settlement, Lincoln turned over to him not only the exact amount, but the exact coins he had taken in as post-master during the preceding year or two.

The morning that Lincoln rode into Springfield, he not only had no cash reserves of his own; but, to make matters worse, he was eleven hundred dollars in debt. He and Berry had lost that amount in their ill-fated grocery venture back in New Salem. Then Berry had drunk himself to death and left Lincoln to shoulder the obligations alone.

To be sure, Lincoln didn't have to pay; he could have pleaded divided responsibility and the failure of the business and have found a legal loophole of escape.

But that wasn't Lincoln's way. Instead, he went to his creditors and promised to pay them every dollar with interest, if they would only give him time. They all agreed, except one, Peter Van Bergen. He brought suit immediately, obtained a judgment, and had Lincoln's horse and surveying instruments sold at public auction. The others waited, however, and Lincoln scraped and saved and denied himself for fourteen years in order to keep faith with them. Even as late as 1848, when he was a member of Congress, he sent part of his salary home to pay off the last remnant of this old grocery debt.

The morning that Lincoln arrived in Springfield, he tied his horse in front of Joshua F. Speed's general store at the northwest corner of the public square; and here is the remainder of the story told in Speed's own words:

> He had ridden into town on a borrowed horse, and engaged from the only cabinet-maker in the village a single bedstead. He came into my store, set his saddle-bags on the counter, and enquired what the furniture for a single bedstead would cost. I took slate and pencil, made a calculation, and found the sum for furniture complete would amount to seventeen dollars in all. Said he: "It is probably cheap enough; but I want to say that, cheap as it is, I have not the money to pay. But if you will credit me until Christmas and my experiment here as a lawyer is a success, I will pay you then. If I fail in that I will probably never pay you at all." The tone of his voice was so melancholy that I felt for him. I looked up at him and I thought then, as I think now, that I never saw so gloomy and melancholy a face in my life. I said to him, "So small a debt seems to affect you so deeply, I think I can suggest a plan by which you will be able to attain your end without incurring any debt. I have a very large room and a very large double bed in it, which you are perfectly welcome to share with me if you choose." "Where is your room?" he asked. "Upstairs," said I, pointing to the stairs leading from the store to my room. Without saying a word he took his saddle-bags on his arm, went upstairs, set them down on the floor, came down again, and with a face beaming with pleasure and smiles, exclaimed, "Well, Speed, I'm moved."

And so, for the next five and a half years, Lincoln slept in the bed with Speed, over the store, without paying any rent at all.

Another friend, William Butler, took Lincoln into his home and not only boarded him for five years, but bought many of his clothes for him.

Lincoln probably paid Butler a little something when, as, and if he could; but there was no specific charge. The whole thing was a haphazard arrangement between friends.

And Lincoln thanked God that it was, for if it hadn't been for the help of Butler and Speed, he could never have made a go of the law.

He went into partnership with another attorney, named Stuart. Stuart devoted most of his time to politics, and saddled the office routine on Lincoln. But there wasn't much routine to saddle, and there wasn't much of an office. The furnishings consisted of "a small, dirty bed, a buffalo robe, a chair, a bench" and a sort of bookcase containing a few legal volumes.

The office records show that during the first six months the firm took in only five fees: one was for two dollars and a half, two were for five dollars each, one was a ten-dollar fee, and they had to take an overcoat as part payment in another case.

Lincoln became so discouraged that he stopped one day at Page Eaton's carpenter shop in Springfield and confessed that he had a notion to abandon law and go to work as a carpenter. A few years before that, while studying law back in New Salem, Lincoln had seriously thought of giving up his books and becoming a blacksmith.

That first year in Springfield was a lonely one for Lincoln. About the only people he met were the men who forgathered of an evening, in the back of Speed's store, to argue politics and kill time. Lincoln wouldn't go to church on Sundays, because, as he said, he wouldn't know how to act in fine churches like those in Springfield.

Only one woman spoke to him during that first year, and he wrote to a friend that she wouldn't have spoken "if she could have avoided it."

But in 1839 a woman came to town who not only spoke to him, but courted him and determined to marry him. Her name was Mary Todd.

Somebody asked Lincoln once why the Todds spelled their name as they did, and he replied that he reckoned that one "d" was good enough for God, but that the Todds had to have two.

The Todds boasted of a genealogical chart extending back to the sixth century. Mary Todd's grandfathers and great-grandfathers and great-uncles had been generals and governors, and one had been Secretary of the Navy. She, herself, had been educated in a snobbish French school in Lexington, Kentucky, conducted by Madame Victorie Charlotte Le Clere Mentelle and her husband—two French aristocrats who had fled from Paris during the Revolution in order to save their necks from the guillotine. They had drilled Mary to speak French with a Parisian accent, and had taught her to dance the cotillion and the Circassian Circle as the silken courtiers had danced them at Versailles.

Mary was possessed of a high and haughty manner, an exalted opinion of her own superiority, and an abiding conviction that she would one day marry a man who would become President of the United States. Incredible as it seems, she not only believed that, but she openly boasted of it. It sounded silly, and people laughed and said things; but nothing could shake her conviction and nothing could stop her boasting.

Her own sister, speaking of Mary, said she "loved glitter, show, pomp and power," and was "the most ambitious woman I ever knew."

Unfortunately, Mary had a temper that was frequently out of control; so one day in 1839, she quarreled with her stepmother, slammed the front door, and walked out of her father's home in a rage and came to live with her married sister in Springfield.

If she was determined to marry a future President, she had certainly chosen the right place, for there wasn't another spot in all the world where her prospects would have been brighter than there in Springfield, Illinois. At that time it was a dirty little frontier village, sprawling out over the treeless prairie, with no pavements, no lights, no sidewalks, no sewers. Cattle roamed about the town at will, hogs wallowed in the mud-holes of the principal streets, and piles of rotton manure filled the air with a stench. The total population of the town was only fifteen hundred; but two young men who were destined to be candidates for the Presidency in 1860 lived there in Springfield in 1839—Stephen A. Douglas, candidate for the Northern wing of the Democratic party, and Abraham Lincoln for the Republicans.

Both of them met Mary Todd, both courted her at the same time, both held her in their arms, and she once stated that both of them had proposed.

When asked which suitor she intended to marry, Mary always answered, according to her sister's report, "Him who has the best prospects of being President."

And that was tantamount to saying Douglas, for, just then, Douglas's political prospects seemed a hundred times brighter than Lincoln's. Although Douglas was only twenty-six, he had already been nicknamed "the Little Giant," and he was already Secretary of the State, while Lincoln was only a struggling lawyer living in an attic over Speed's store and hardly able to pay a board bill.

Douglas was destined to become one of the mightiest political forces in the United States years and years before Abe Lincoln was even heard of outside his own State. In fact, two years before Lincoln became President, about the only thing that the average American knew about him was that he had once debated with the brilliant and powerful Stephen A. Douglas.

Mary's relatives all thought she cared more for Douglas than she did for Lincoln, and she probably did. Douglas was far more of a ladies' man; he had more personal charm, better prospects, better manners, and better social standing.

Besides, he had a deep golden voice, a wavy black pompadour, he waltzed superbly, and he paid Mary Todd lovely little compliments.

He was her beau-ideal of a man; and she looked in her mirror, whispering to herself, "Mary Todd Douglas." It sounded beautiful, and she dreamed dreams and saw herself waltzing with him in the White House. . . .

While Douglas was courting her he had a fight one day, right in the public square in Springfield, with a newspaper editor—the husband of one of Mary's dearest friends.

Probably she told him what she thought of that.

And probably she told him also what she thought of his getting drunk at a public banquet, climbing on top of a table and waltzing back and forth, shouting, singing, and kicking wineglasses and roast turkey, whisky bottles and gravy dishes onto the floor.

And if he took another girl to a dance while he was paying her attention, she made a disagreeable scene.

The courtship came to nothing. Senator Beveridge says:

> Although it was afterwards given out that Douglas had proposed to Mary and was refused because of his bad "morals," that statement was obviously protective propaganda usual in such cases; for the shrewd, alert and, even then, worldly-wise Douglas never asked Miss Todd to marry him.

Immeasurably disappointed, she tried to arouse Douglas's jealousy by giving her ardent attention to one of his bitter political opponents, Abraham Lincoln. But that didn't bring back Douglas, and she laid her plans to capture Lincoln.

Mrs. Edwards, Mary Todd's sister, afterward described the courtship in this fashion:

> I have often happened in the room where they were sitting, and Mary invariably led the conversation. Mr. Lincoln would sit at her side and listen. He scarcely said a word, but gazed on her as if irresistibly drawn toward her by some superior and unseen power. He was charmed with her wit, and fascinated by her quick sagacity. But he could not maintain himself in a continued conversation with a lady reared as Mary was.

In July of that year the great gathering of Whigs which had been talked of for months swarmed down upon Springfield and overwhelmed the town. They came from hundreds of miles around, with banners waving and bands playing. The Chicago delegation dragged half-way across the State a government yawl rigged as a two-masted ship. Music was playing on the ship, girls dancing, cannon belching into the air.

The Democrats had spoken of the Whig candidate, William Henry Harrison, as an old woman who lived in a log cabin and drank hard cider. So the Whigs mounted a log cabin on wheels and drew it through the streets of Springfield, behind thirty yoke of oxen. A hickory tree swayed beside the cabin; coons were playing in the tree; a barrel of hard cider was on tap by the door.

At night, under the light of flaming torches, Lincoln made a political speech.

At one meeting his party, the Whigs, had been accused of being aristocratic and wearing fine clothes while pleading for the votes of the plain people, Lincoln replied:

"I came to Illinois as a poor, strange, friendless, uneducated boy, and started working on a flatboat for eight dollars a month, and I had only one pair of breeches to my back, and they were buckskin. When buckskin gets wet and dried by the sun, it shrinks; and my breeches kept shrinking until they left several inches of my legs bare between the lower part of my breeches and the top of my socks. And while I was growing taller, the breeches were getting wet and becoming shorter and tighter until they left a blue streak around my legs that can be seen to this day. Now, if you call that being a fancily dressed aristocrat, I must plead guilty to the charge."

The audience whistled and shouted and shrieked its approval.

When Lincoln and Mary reached the Edwards house, she told him how proud she was of him, that he was a great speaker, and that some day he would be President.

He looked down at her, standing beside him in the moonlight, and her manner told him everything. Reaching over, he took her in his arms and kissed her tenderly. . . .

The wedding-day was set for the first of January, 1841.

That was only six months away, but many a storm was to brew and blow before then.

* * *

7

* * *

MARY TODD and Abraham Lincoln hadn't been engaged very long before she wanted to make him over. She didn't like the way he dressed. She often contrasted him with her father. Almost every morning for a dozen years she had seen Robert Todd walking down the streets of Lexington, carrying a gold-headed cane, clad in a blue broadcloth coat, and wearing white linen trousers strapped under his boots. But Lincoln in hot weather didn't wear a coat at all; and what was worse, sometimes he didn't wear even a collar. Usually he had only one gallus holding up his trousers, and when a button came off he whittled a peg and pinned things together with that.

Such crudeness irritated Mary Todd, and she told him so. But, unfortunately, she didn't use any tact or diplomacy or sweetness in her telling.

Though at Madame Victorie Charlotte Le Clere Mentelle's school back in Lexington she had been taught to dance the cotillion, she had been taught nothing about the fine art of handling people. So she took the surest way, the quickest way to annihilate a man's love: she nagged. She made Lincoln so uncomfortable that he wanted to avoid her. Instead of coming to see her two or three nights a week now, as he had formerly done, he sometimes let ten days drift by without calling; and she wrote him complaining letters, censuring him for his neglect.

Presently Matilda Edwards came to town. Matilda was a tall, stately, charming blonde, a cousin of Ninian W. Edwards, Mary

Todd's brother-in-law. She too took up her residence in the spacious Edwards mansion. And when Lincoln called to see Mary, Matilda contrived to be very much in evidence. She couldn't speak French with a Parisian accent or dance the Circassian Circle, but she knew how to handle men, and Lincoln grew very fond of her. When she swept into the room, Lincoln was so interested in watching her that he sometimes ceased to listen to what Mary Todd was saying. That made Mary indignant. Once he took Mary to a ball; but he didn't care for dancing, so he let her dance with other men while he sat in a corner talking to Matilda.

Mary accused him of being in love with Matilda, and he didn't deny it; she broke down and wept, and demanded that he cease even looking at Matilda.

What had once been a promising love-affair had now degenerated into a thing of strife and dissension and fault-finding.

Lincoln now saw that he and Mary were opposites in every way: in training, in background, in temperament, in tastes, in mental outlook. They irritated each other constantly, and Lincoln realized that their engagement ought to be broken, that their marriage would be disastrous.

Mary's sister and brother-in-law both arrived at a similar conclusion. They urged Mary to abandon all thought of marrying Lincoln, warning her over and over that they were strikingly unfit for each other, and that they could never be happy.

But Mary refused to listen.

Lincoln, after weeks of trying to screw up his courage to tell her the painful truth, came into Speed's store one night, walked back to the fireplace, drew a letter out of his pocket, and asked Speed to read it. Speed relates:

> The letter was addressed to Mary Todd, and in it he made a plain statement of his feelings, telling her that he had thought the matter over calmly and with great deliberation, and now felt that he did not love her sufficiently to warrant her in marrying him. This letter he desired me to deliver. Upon my declining to do so he threatened to intrust it to some other person's hand. I reminded him that the moment he placed the letter in Miss Todd's hand, she would have the advantage over him. "Words are forgotten," I said, "misunderstood, unnoticed in a private conversation, but once put your words in writing and they

stand a living and eternal monument against you." Thereupon I threw the unfortunate letter in the fire.

So we shall never know precisely what Lincoln said to her; but "we can form a good idea of what he wrote to Mary Todd," says Senator Beveridge "by again reading his final letter to Miss Owens."

The story of Lincoln's affair with Miss Owens can be told briefly. It had occurred four years earlier. She was a sister of Mrs. Bennett Abell, whom Lincoln knew in New Salem. In the autumn of 1836 Mrs. Abell returned to Kentucky to visit her family, saying that she would bring her sister back to Illinois with her if Lincoln would agree to marry her.

Lincoln had seen the sister three years before, and he said all right; and presto! the sister appeared. She had a beautiful face, refinement, education, and wealth; but Lincoln didn't want to marry her. He thought "she was a trifle too willing." Besides, she was a year older than he, and short and very corpulent—"a fair match for Falstaff," as Lincoln put it.

"I was not at all pleased with her," said Lincoln, "but what could I do?"

Mrs. Abell "was very anxious," to have Lincoln stick to his promise.

But he wasn't. He admits he was "continually repenting the rashness" which had led him to make it, and dreaded the thought of marrying her as "an Irishman does the halter."

So he wrote to Miss Owens, frankly and tactfully telling her how he felt and trying to get out of the engagement.

Here is one of his letters. It was written in Springfield on May 7, 1837, and I believe it gives us a very good idea of what he wrote to Mary Todd.

Friend Mary:

I have commenced two letters to send you before this, both of which displeased me before I got half done, and so I tore them up. The first I thought wasn't serious enough, and the second was on the other extreme. I shall send this, turn out as it may.

This thing of living in Springfield is rather a dull business after all—at least it is so to me. I am quite as lonesome here as [I] ever was anywhere in my life. I have been spoken to by but one woman since I've been here, and should not have been by her if she could have avoided it.

I've never been to church yet, and probably shall not be soon. I stay away because I am conscious I should not know how to behave myself. I am often thinking of what we said of your coming to live at Springfield. I am afraid you would not be satisfied. There is a great deal of flourishing about in carriages here, which it would be your doom to see without sharing in it. You would have to be poor without the means of hiding your poverty. Do you believe you could bear that patiently? Whatever woman may cast her lot with mine, should anyone ever do so, it is my intention to do all in my power to make her happy and contented, and there is nothing I can imagine that would make me more unhappy than to fail in the effort. I know I should be much happier with you than the way I am, provided I saw no signs of discontent in you.

What you have said to me may have been in jest or I may have misunderstood it. If so, then let it be forgotten; if otherwise I much wish you would think seriously before you decide. For my part I have already decided. What I have said I will most positively abide by, provided you wish it. My opinion is you had better not do it. You have not been accustomed to hardship, and it may be more severe than you imagine. I know you are capable of thinking correctly on any subject; and if you deliberate maturely upon this before you decide, then I am willing to abide your decision.

You must write me a good long letter after you get this. You have nothing else to do, and though it might not seem interesting to you after you have written it, it would be a good deal of company in this busy wilderness. Tell your sister I don't want to hear any more about selling out and moving. That gives me the hypo whenever I think of it.

Yours, etc.

LINCOLN.

So much for Lincoln's affair with Mary Owens. To return to his affair with Mary Todd: Speed tossed into the fire the letter which Lincoln had written to Miss Todd, and, turning to his friend and room-mate, said:

"Now, if you have the courage of manhood, go see Mary yourself; tell her, if you do not love her, the facts, and that you will not marry her. Be careful not to say too much, and then leave at your earliest opportunity."

"Thus admonished," Speed relates, "he buttoned his coat, and with a rather determined look started out to perform the serious duty for which I had just given him explicit directions."

Herndon says:

> That night Speed did not go upstairs to bed with us, but under pretense of wanting to read, remained in the store below. He was waiting for Lincoln's return. Ten o'clock passed, and still the interview with Miss Todd had not ended. At length, shortly after eleven, he came stalking in. Speed was satisfied, from the length of Lincoln's stay, that his directions had not been followed.
>
> "Well, old fellow, did you do as I told you and as you promised?" were Speed's first words.
>
> "Yes, I did," responded Lincoln, thoughtfully, "and when I told Mary I did not love her, she burst into tears and almost springing from her chair and wringing her hands as if in agony, said something about the deceiver being himself deceived." Then he stopped.
>
> "What else did you say?" inquired Speed, drawing the facts from him.
>
> "To tell you the truth, Speed, it was too much for me. I found the tears trickling down my own cheeks. I caught her in my arms and kissed her."
>
> "And that's how you broke the engagement," sneered Speed. "You not only acted the fool, but your conduct was tantamount to a renewal of the engagement, and in decency you cannot back down now."
>
> "Well," drawled Lincoln, "if I am in again, so be it. It's done, and I shall abide by it."

Weeks rolled on, and the marriage date drew near. Seamstresses were at work upon Mary Todd's trousseau. The Edwards mansion was freshly painted, the living-rooms were redecorated, the rugs renovated, and the furniture polished and shifted.

But, in the meantime, a dreadful thing was happening to Abraham Lincoln. One is at a loss to know how to describe it. Profound mental depression is not like grief of the normal type; it is a dangerous illness affecting both mind and body.

Lincoln was sinking day by day, now, into just such a state.

His mind came very near being unbalanced; and it is doubtful whether he ever fully recovered from the effects of these awful weeks of unspeakable torture. Although he had definitely agreed to the marriage, his whole soul rebelled against it. Without realizing it, he was seeking a way of escape. He sat for hours in the room above the store, with no desire to go to his office or to attend the meetings of the legislature of which he was a member. Sometimes he arose at three o'clock in the morning, went down below, lighted a fire in the fireplace, and sat staring at it until daybreak. He ate less, and began to lose weight. He was irritable, avoided people, and would talk to no one.

He had begun now to recoil with horror from his approaching marriage. His mind seemed to be whirling through a dark abyss, and he feared that he was losing his reason. He wrote a long letter to Dr. Daniel Drake of Cincinnati, the most eminent physician in the West, the head of the medical department of the College of Cincinnati, describing his case and asking the physician to recommend a course of treatment. But Dr. Drake replied that it would be impossible for him to do so without a personal examination.

The marriage was set for January 1, 1841. The day dawned bright and clear, and the aristocracy of Springfield flourished about in sleighs, making their New Year's calls. Out of nostrils of horses issued breaths of steam, and the tinkle of tiny bells filled the air.

At the Edwards mansion the bustle and hurry of final preparation went on apace. Delivery boys hastened to the back door with this article and that that had been ordered at the last minute. A special chef had been hired for the occasion. The dinner was to be cooked, not in an old iron oven on the hearth, but in a new invention that had just been installed—a cooking stove.

The early evening of New Year's Day descended on the town, candles glowed softly, holly wreaths hung in the windows. The Edwards house was hushed with excitement, vibrant with expectation.

At six-thirty happy guests began to arrive. At six forty-five came the minister, the ritual of the Church under his arm. The rooms were banked with plants, colorful with flowers. Huge fires crackled and blazed on the hearths. The place resounded with pleasant and friendly chatter.

The clock struck seven. . . . Seven-thirty. Lincoln had not arrived. . . . He was late.

Minutes passed. . . . Slowly, inexorably, the grandfather's clock in the hallway ticked off a quarter of an hour. Half an hour. . . . Still there was no bridegroom. Going to the front door, Mrs. Edwards stared nervously down the driveway. What was wrong? Could he . . . ? No! Unthinkable! Impossible!

The family withdrew. . . . Whisperings. . . . A hurried consultation.

In the next room, Mary Todd, bedecked with bridal veil, attired in silken gown, waited . . . waited . . . nervously toying with the flowers in her hair. She walked to the window constantly. She peered down the street. She couldn't keep her eyes off the clock. The palms of her hands grew wet, perspiration gathered on her brow. Another awful hour passed. He had promised . . . Surely . . .

At nine-thirty, one by one, the guests withdrew, softly, wonderingly, and with embarrassment.

When the last one had disappeared the bride-to-be tore her veil from her head, snatched the flowers from her hair, rushed sobbing up the stairway, and flung herself on the bed. She was rent with grief. Oh, God! what would people say? She would be laughed at. Pitied. Disgraced. Ashamed to walk the streets. Great waves of bitterness, of violence, swept over her. One moment, she longed to have Lincoln there to take her in his arms. The next, she longed to kill him for the hurt, for the humiliation, he had heaped upon her.

Where was Lincoln? Had he met with foul play? Had there been an accident? Had he run away? Had he committed suicide? No one knew.

At midnight men came with lanterns, and searching parties set out. Some explored his favorite haunts in town, others searched the roads leading out into the country.

THE SEARCH continued all through the night, and shortly after daybreak Lincoln was found sitting in his office, talking incoherently. His friends feared he was losing his mind. Mary Todd's relatives declared that he was already insane. That was the way they explained his failure to show up at the wedding.

Dr. Henry was called immediately. Lincoln threatened to commit suicide, so the doctor ordered Speed and Butler to watch over him constantly. His knife was taken from him now and kept from him just as it had been after the death of Ann Rutledge.

Dr. Henry, wanting to keep his mind occupied, urged Lincoln to attend the sessions of the State Legislature. As the floor leader for the Whigs, he ought to have been there constantly. But the records show that he was present but four times in three weeks—and even then only for an hour or two. On January 19 John J. Hardin announced his illness to the House.

Three weeks after he had fled from his wedding Lincoln wrote to his law partner the saddest letter of his life:

> I am now the most miserable man living. If what I feel were equally distributed to the whole human family, there would not be one cheerful face on earth. Whether I shall ever be any better, I cannot tell. I awfully forbode that I shall not. To remain as I am is impossible. I must die or be better, it seems to me.

As the late Dr. William E. Barton says in his well-known biography of Lincoln, this letter "can mean nothing else than that Abraham Lincoln was mentally distraught . . . that he had grave fears for his own sanity."

He thought constantly of death, now, and longed for it and wrote a poem on suicide and had it published in the "Sangamo Journal."

Speed feared that he was going to die; so Lincoln was taken to the home of Speed's mother, near Louisville. Here he was given a Bible and assigned a quiet bedroom looking out over a brook meandering through meadows to the forest a mile away. Each morning a slave brought Lincoln his coffee in bed.

Mrs. Edwards, Mary's sister, says that Mary, "to set herself right and to free Mr. Lincoln's mind, wrote a letter to Mr. Lincoln, stating that she would release him from his engagement." But in releasing him, according to Mr. Edwards, "she left Lincoln the privilege of renewing it if he wished."

But that was the last thing in the world that he wished. He never wanted to see her again. Even a year after Lincoln had fled from his wedding, his good friend James Matheny "thought Lincoln would commit suicide."

For almost two years after the "fatal first of January," 1841, Lincoln ignored Mary Todd completely, hoping that she would forget him, praying that she would interest herself in some other man. But she did not, for her pride was at stake, her precious self-respect. She was determined to prove to herself and to those who had scorned and pitied her that she *could* and *would marry Abraham Lincoln.*

And he was *equally determined not to marry her.*

In fact, he was so determined that he proposed within a year to another girl. He was thirty-two at the time, the girl he proposed to was half that age. She was Sarah Rickard, the little sister of Mrs. Butler, at whose house Lincoln had been boarding for four years.

Lincoln pleaded his case with her, arguing that since his name was Abraham and hers Sarah it was evident that they were meant for one another.

But she refused him, because, as she later confessed in writing to a friend:

> I was young, only sixteen years old and I had not thought much about matrimony. . . . I allway liked him as

> a friend but you Know his peculiar manner and his General deportment would not be likely to fascinate a Young Girl just entering into the society world. . . . He seemed allmost like an older Brother being as it were one of my sister's family.

Lincoln frequently wrote editorials for the local Whig paper, "The Springfield Journal"; and the editor, Simeon Francis, was one of his closest friends. Francis's wife, unfortunately, had never learned the fine art of minding her own business. Childless, over forty, she was the self-appointed match-maker of Springfield.

Early in October, 1842, she wrote Lincoln, asking him to call at her home the following afternoon. That was a strange request, and he went, wondering what it could mean. When he arrived, he was ushered into the parlor; and there, to his astonishment, he saw Mary Todd sitting before him.

What Lincoln and Mary Todd said, and how they said it, and what they did, that is not recorded. But of course the poor, tender-hearted fellow hadn't a chance to escape. If she cried—and of course she did—he probably delivered himself into her hands at once, and abjectly apologized for having gotten out of her hands.

They met often after that, but always secretly and behind closed doors in the Francis home.

At first Mary didn't let even her sister know that Lincoln was seeing her again.

Finally, when her sister did find out, she asked Mary "why she was so secretive."

And Mary replied "evasively that after all that had occurred, it was best to keep the courtship from all eyes and ears. Men and women of the world were uncertain and slippery, Mary continued, and if misfortune befell the engagement, all knowledge of it would be hidden from the world."

In other words, to put it bluntly, having learned a little lesson, she resolved to keep even the courtship secret, this time, until she was positive that Lincoln would marry her.

What technique did Miss Todd now employ?

James Matheny declared that Lincoln often told him "that he was driven into the marriage, and that Miss Todd told him he was in honor bound to marry her."

Herndon ought to have known if anybody did, and he said:

> To me it has always seemed plain that Mr. Lincoln married Mary Todd to save his honor, and in doing that he sacrificed his domestic peace. He had searched himself subjectively, introspectively, thoroughly: he knew he did not love her, but he had promised to marry her. The hideous thought came up like a nightmare. . . . At last he stood face to face with the great conflict between honor and domestic peace. He chose the former, and with it years of self-torture, sacrificial pangs, and the loss forever of a happy home.

Before he was willing to proceed, he wrote Speed, who had gone back to Kentucky, asking him if he had found happiness in his marriage.

"Please answer quickly," Lincoln urged, "as I am impatient to know."

Speed replied that he was far happier than he had ever expected to be.

So the next afternoon, Friday, November 4, 1842, Lincoln, reluctantly and with an aching heart, asked Mary Todd to be his wife.

She wanted to have the ceremony performed that very night. He hesitated, surprised, and a little frightened at the celerity with which events were moving. Knowing she was superstitious, he pointed out that the day was Friday. But, remembering what had happened before, she feared nothing now so much as delay. She was unwilling to wait even twenty-four hours. Besides, it was her birthday, her twenty-fourth birthday, so they hurried to Chatterton's jewelry store, bought a wedding-ring, and had these words engraved inside it: "Love is eternal."

Late that afternoon Lincoln asked James Matheny to be his best man, saying, "Jim, I shall have to marry that girl."

While Lincoln was putting on his best clothes that evening at Butler's house, and blacking his boots, Butler's little boy rushed in and asked him where he was going.

Lincoln replied: "To hell, I suppose."

In despair, Mary Todd had given away the trousseau that she had had made for the first wedding date, so that now she had to be married in a simple white muslin dress.

All arrangements were carried through with nervous haste.

Mrs. Edwards says she had only two hours' notice of the marriage and that the frosting on the wedding-cake which she hurriedly baked for the occasion was too warm to cut well when it was served.

As the Rev. Charles Dresser, clad in his clerical vestments, read the impressive Episcopal service, Lincoln seemed far from cheerful and happy. His best man testified that he "looked and acted as if he were going to the slaughter."

The only comment that Lincoln ever made in writing about his marriage was a postscript to a business letter that he wrote to Samuel Marshall about a week after the event. This letter is now in the possession of the Chicago Historical Society.

"Nothing new here," writes Lincoln, "except my marriage which to me is a matter of profound wonder."

★

PART TWO

★

★ ★ ★

9

★ ★ ★

While I was writing this book, out in New Salem, Illinois, my good friend Henry Pond, a local attorney, said to me a number of times:

"You ought to go and see Uncle Jimmy Miles, for one of his uncles, Herndon, was Lincoln's law partner, and one of his aunts ran a boarding-house where Mr. and Mrs. Lincoln lived for a while."

That sounded like an interesting lead; so Mr. Pond and I climbed into his car one Sunday afternoon in July, and drove out to the Miles farm near New Salem—a farm where Lincoln used to stop and swap stories for a drink of cider while walking to Springfield to borrow law-books.

When we arrived, Uncle Jimmy dragged a trio of rocking-chairs out into the shade of a huge maple tree in the front yard; and there, while young turkeys and little ducks ran noisily through the grass about us, we talked for hours; and Uncle Jimmy related an illuminating and pathetic incident about Lincoln that has never been put into print heretofore. The story is this:

Mr. Miles's Aunt Catherine married a physician named Jacob M. Early. About a year after Lincoln arrived in Springfield—during the night of March 11, 1838, to be exact—an unknown man on horseback rode up to Dr. Early's house, knocked, called the physician to the door, emptied both barrels of a shot-gun into his body, then leaped upon a horse and dashed away.

Small as Springfield was at the time, no one was ever charged with the murder, and the killing remains a mystery to this day.

Dr. Early left a very small estate; so his widow was obliged to take in boarders to support herself; and, shortly after their marriage, Mr. and Mrs. Abraham Lincoln came to Mrs. Early's home to live.

Uncle Jimmy Miles told me that he had often heard his aunt, Dr. Early's widow, relate the following incident: One morning Mr. and Mrs. Lincoln were having breakfast when Lincoln did something that aroused the fiery temper of his wife. What, no one remembers now. But Mrs. Lincoln, in a rage, dashed a cup of hot coffee into her husband's face. And she did it in front of the other boarders.

Saying nothing, Lincoln sat there in humiliation and silence while Mrs. Early came with a wet towel and wiped off his face and clothes. That incident was probably typical of the married life of the Lincolns for the next quarter of a century.

Springfield had eleven attorneys, and they couldn't all make a living there; so they used to ride horseback from one county-seat to another, following Judge David Davis while he was holding court in the various places throughout the Eighth Judicial District. The other attorneys always managed to get back to Springfield each Saturday and spend the week-end with their families.

But Lincoln didn't. He dreaded to go home, and for three months in the spring, and again for three months in the autumn, he remained out on the circuit and never went near Springfield.

He kept this up year after year. Living conditions in the country hotels were often wretched; but wretched as they were, he preferred them to his own home and Mrs. Lincoln's constant nagging and wild outbursts of temper. "She vexed and harassed the soul out of him"—that was what the neighbors said; and the neighbors knew, for they saw her, and they couldn't help hearing her.

Mrs. Lincoln's "loud shrill voice," says Senator Beveridge, "could be heard across the street, and her incessant outbursts of wrath were audible to all who lived near the house. Frequently her anger was displayed by other means than words, and accounts of her violence are numerous and unimpeachable."

"She led her husband a wild and merry dance," says Herndon.

And Herndon felt he knew why "she unchained the bitterness of a disappointed and outraged nature."

It was her desire for vengeance. "He had crushed her proud womanly spirit," suggests Herndon, and "she felt degraded in the eyes of the world: Love fled at the approach of revenge."

She was always complaining, always criticizing her husband; nothing about him was ever right: He was stoopshouldered, he walked awkwardly and lifted his feet straight up and down like an Indian. She complained that there was no spring to his step, no grace to his movements; and she mimicked his gait and nagged at him to walk with his toes pointed down, as she had been taught at Madame Mentelle's.

She didn't like the way his huge ears stood out at right angles from his head. She even told him that his nose wasn't straight, that his lower lip stuck out, that he looked consumptive, that his feet and hands were too large, his head too small.

His shocking indifference to his personal appearance grated on her sensitive nature, and made her woefully unhappy. "Mrs. Lincoln," says Herndon, "was not a wildcat without cause." Sometimes her husband walked down the street with one trouser leg stuffed inside his boot-top and the other dangling on the outside. His boots were seldom blackened or greased. His collar often needed changing, his coat frequently needed brushing.

James Gourly, who lived next door to the Lincolns for years, wrote: "Mr. Lincoln used to come to our house, his feet encased in a pair of loose slippers, and with an old faded pair of trousers fastened with one suspender"—or "gallis" as Lincoln himself called it.

In warm weather he made extended trips "wearing a dirty linen duster for a coat, on the back of which the perspiration had splotched wide stains that resembled a map of the continent."

A young lawyer who once saw Lincoln in a country hotel, getting ready for bed, and clad "in a home made yellow flannel night shirt" that reached "halfway between his knees and his ankles," exclaimed, "He was the ungodliest figure I ever saw."

He never owned a razor in his life, and he didn't visit a barber as frequently as Mrs. Lincoln thought he should.

He neglected to groom his coarse, bushy hair, that stood out all over his head like horsehair. That irritated Mary Todd beyond words, and when she combed it, it was soon mussed again, by his bank-book, letters, and legal papers, which he carried in the top of his hat.

One day he was having his picture taken in Chicago, and the

photographer urged him to "slick up" a bit. He replied that "a portrait of a slicked-up Lincoln wouldn't be recognized down in Springfield."

His table manners were large and free. He didn't hold his knife right, and he didn't even lay it on his plate right. He had no skill whatever in the art of eating fish with a fork and a crust of bread. Sometimes he tilted the meat platter and raked or slid a pork chop off onto his plate. Mrs. Lincoln raised "merry war" with him because he persisted in using his own knife for the butter; and once when he put chicken bones on the side dish on which his lettuce had been served, she almost fainted.

She complained and scolded because he didn't stand up when ladies came into the room; because he didn't jump around to take their wraps, and didn't see callers to the door when they left.

He loved to read lying down. As soon as he came home from the office, he took off his coat and shoes and collar and dropped his one "gallis" from his shoulder, turned a chair upside down in the hallway, padded its sloping back with a pillow, propped his head and shoulders against it, and stretched out on the floor.

In that position he would lie and read for hours—usually the newspapers. Sometimes he read what he considered a very humorous story about an earthquake, from a book entitled "Flush Times in Alabama." Often, very often, he read poetry. And whatever he read, he read aloud. He had gotten the habit from the "blab" schools back in Indiana. He also felt that by reading aloud he could impress a thing on his sense of hearing as well as his sense of sight, and so remember it longer.

Sometimes he would lie on the floor and close his eyes and quote Shakspere or Byron or Poe; for example:

"For the moon never beams without bringing me dreams
Of the beautiful Annabel Lee,
And the stars never rise, but I feel the bright eyes
Of the beautiful Annabel Lee."

A lady—a relative—who lived with the Lincolns two years says that one evening Lincoln was lying down in the hall, reading, when company came. Without waiting for the servant to answer the door, he got up in his shirtsleeves, ushered the callers into the parlor, and said he would "trot the women folks out."

Mrs. Lincoln from an adjoining room witnessed the ladies' entrance, and overheard her husband's jocose expression. Her indignation was so instantaneous she made the situation exceedingly interesting for him, and he was glad to retreat from the mansion. He did not return until very late at night, and then slipped quietly in at a rear door.

Mrs. Lincoln was violently jealous, and she had little use for Joshua Speed. He had been her husband's intimate friend, and she suspected that he might have influenced Lincoln to run away from his wedding. Before his marriage, Lincoln had been in the habit of ending his letters to Speed with "Love to Fanny." But, after the marriage, Mrs. Lincoln demanded that that greeting be tempered down to "Regards to Mrs. Speed."

Lincoln never forgot a favor. That was one of his outstanding characteristics; so, as a little gesture of appreciation, he had promised that the first boy would be named Joshua Speed Lincoln. But when Mary Todd heard it she burst out in a storm. It was *her* child, and *she* was going to name it! And, what was more, the name was *not* going to be Joshua Speed! It was going to be Robert Todd, after her own father . . . and so on and so on.

It is hardly necessary to add that the boy *was* named Robert Todd. He was the only one of the four Lincoln children to reach maturity. Eddie died in 1850 at Springfield—age 4. Willie died in the White House—age 12. Tad died in Chicago in 1871—age 18. Robert Todd Lincoln died in Manchester, Vermont, July 26, 1926—age 83.

Mrs. Lincoln complained because the yard was without flowers, shrubs, or color. So Lincoln set out a few roses, but he took no interest in them and they soon perished of neglect. She urged him to plant a garden, and one spring he did, but the weeds overran it.

Though he was not much given to physical exertion, he did feed and curry "Old Buck"; he also "fed and milked his own cow and sawed his own wood." And he continued to do this, even after he was elected President, until he left Springfield.

However, John Hanks, Lincoln's second cousin, once remarked that "Abe was not good at any kind of work except dreamin'." And Mary Lincoln agreed with him.

Lincoln was absent-minded, often sank into curious spells of abstraction, and appeared to be entirely oblivious of the earth and everything that was on it. On Sundays, he would put one of his babies into a little wagon and haul the child up and down the rough sidewalk in front of his house. Sometimes the little chap happened to roll overboard. But Lincoln pulled steadily ahead, his eyes fixed on the ground, unconscious of the loud lamentations behind him. He never knew what had happened until Mrs. Lincoln thrust her head out at the door and yelled at him in a shrill, angry voice.

Sometimes he came into the house after a day at the office and looked at her and apparently didn't see her and didn't even speak. He was seldom interested in food; after she had prepared a meal, she frequently had hard work to get him into the dining-room. She called, but he seemed not to hear. He would sit down at the table and stare off dreamily into space, and forget to eat until she reminded him of it.

After dinner he sometimes stared into the fireplace for half an hour at a time, saying nothing. The boys literally crawled all over him and pulled his hair and talked to him, but he seemed unconscious of their existence. Then suddenly he would come to and tell a joke or recite one of his favorite verses:

"Oh, why should the spirit of mortal be proud?
Like a swift-fleeting meteor, a fast-flying cloud,
A flash of the lightning, a break of the wave,
He passes from life to his rest in the grave."

Mrs. Lincoln criticized him for never correcting the children. But he so adored them that "he was blind and deaf to their faults." "He never neglected to praise them for any of their good acts," said Mrs. Lincoln, "and declared: 'It is my pleasure that my children are free and happy, and unrestrained by parental tyranny. Love is the chain whereby to bind a child to its parents.' "

The liberties he allowed his children at times appear extraordinary. For example, once when he was playing chess with a judge of the Supreme Court, Robert came and told his father it was time to go to dinner. Lincoln replied, "Yes, yes." But, being very fond of the game, he quite forgot that he had been called, and played on.

Again the boy appeared, with another urgent message from Mrs. Lincoln. Again Lincoln promised to come, again he forgot.

A third time Robert arrived with a summons, a third time Lincoln promised, and a third time he played on. Then, suddenly, the boy drew back and violently kicked the chess-board higher than the players' heads, scattering the chessmen in every direction.

"Well, Judge," Lincoln said with a smile, "I reckon we'll have to finish this game some other time."

Lincoln apparently never even thought of correcting his son.

The Lincoln boys used to hide behind a hedge in the evening and stick a lath through the fence. As there were no street lights, passers-by would run into the lath and their hats would be knocked off. Once, in the darkness, the boys knocked off their father's hat by mistake. He didn't censure them, but merely told them that they ought to be careful, for they might make somebody mad.

Lincoln did not belong to any church, and avoided religious discussions even with his best friends. However, he once told Herndon that his religious code was like that of an old man named Glenn, in Indiana, whom he had heard speak at a church meeting, and who said: "When I do good, I feel good, when I do bad I feel bad, and that's my religion."

On Sunday mornings, as the children grew older, he usually took them out for a stroll, but once he left them at home and went to the First Presbyterian Church with Mrs. Lincoln. Half an hour later Tad came into the house and, missing his father, ran down the street and dashed into the church during the sermon. His hair was awry, his shoes unbuttoned, his stockings sagging down, and his face and hands were grimy with the black soil of Illinois. Mrs. Lincoln, herself elegantly attired, was shocked and embarrassed; but Lincoln calmly stretched out one of his long arms and lovingly drew Tad to him and held the boy's head close against his breast.

Sometimes on Sunday morning, Lincoln took the boys downtown to his office. There they were permitted to run wild. "They soon gutted the shelves of books," says Herndon, "rifled the drawers and riddled boxes, battered the point of my gold pen . . . threw the pencils into the spittoon, turned over the inkstands on the papers, scattered letters over the office and danced on them."

And Lincoln "never reproved them or gave them a fatherly frown. He was the most indulgent parent I have ever known," Herndon concludes.

Mrs. Lincoln seldom went to the office; but when she did, she was shocked. She had reason to be: the place had no order, no system, things were piled about everywhere. Lincoln tied up one bundle of papers and labeled it thus: "When you can't find it anywhere else, look in here."

As speed said, Lincoln's habits were "regularly irregular."

On one wall loomed a huge black stain, marking the place where one law student had hurled an inkstand at another one's head—and missed.

The office was seldom swept and almost never scrubbed. Some garden seeds that were lying on top of the bookcase had started to sprout and grow there, in the dust and dirt.

★ ★ ★

10

★ ★ ★

IN MOST RESPECTS, there wasn't a more economical housewife in all Springfield than Mary Lincoln. She was extravagant chiefly in matters having to do with showing off. She bought a carriage when the Lincolns could ill afford it and paid a neighbor's boy twenty-five cents an afternoon for driving her about town to make social calls. The place was a mere village, and she could have walked or hired a vehicle. But no, that would have been beneath her. And no matter how poor they were, she could always find money for clothes costing more than she could afford.

In 1844, the Lincolns paid fifteen hundred dollars for the home of the Rev. Charles Dresser who, two years before, had performed their marriage ceremony. The house had a living-room, kitchen, parlor, bedrooms; and, in the back yard, there was a woodpile, an outhouse, and a barn where Lincoln kept his cow and Old Buck.

At first the place seemed to Mary Lincoln an earthly paradise; and it was, in comparison with the bleak, bare rooms of the boarding-house she had just left. Besides, she had the new-found joy and pride of ownership. But its perfections soon began to fade, and she was forever finding fault with the home. Her sister lived in a huge two-story house, and this one was only a story and a half high. She once told Lincoln that no man who ever amounted to much lived in a story-and-a-half house.

Usually, when she asked him for anything, he never inquired

whether it was necessary. "You know what you want," he would say, "so go and get it." But in this instance, he rebelled: the family was small, and the house was entirely adequate. Besides, he was a poor man: he had only five hundred dollars when they were married, and he had not added much to it since. He knew that they couldn't afford to enlarge the house; and she knew it also; but she kept on urging and complaining. Finally, in order to quiet her, he had a contractor estimate the cost, and Lincoln told him to make it high. He did, and Lincoln showed her the figures. She gasped, and he imagined that settled the matter.

But he was too hopeful, for the next time he went away on the circuit she called in another carpenter, got a lower estimate, and ordered the work done at once.

When Lincoln returned to Springfield and walked down Eighth Street, he hardly recognized his own house. Meeting a friend, he inquired with mock seriousness, "Stranger, can you tell me where Mr. Lincoln lives?"

His income from the law was not large; and he often had, as he put it, "hard scratching" to meet his bills. And now he had come home to find a large and unnecessary carpenter bill added to his burdens.

It saddened him, and he said so.

Mrs. Lincoln answered him in the only way that she knew how to react to a criticism—with an attack. She told him testily that he had no money sense, that he didn't know how to manage, that he didn't charge enough for his services.

That was one of her favorite grievances, and many people would have backed her stand on that. The other attorneys were constantly irritated and annoyed by Lincoln's trifling charges, declaring that he was impoverishing the whole bar.

As late as 1853, when Lincoln was forty-four years old and only eight years away from the White House, he handled four cases in the McLean Circuit Court for a total charge of thirty dollars.

Many of his clients, he said, were as poor as he, and he didn't have the heart to charge them much.

Once a man sent him twenty-five dollars; and Lincoln returned ten, saying he had been too liberal.

In another instance, he prevented a swindler from getting hold of ten thousand dollars' worth of property owned by a demented girl. Lincoln won the case in fifteen minutes. An hour later, his associate, Ward Lamon, came to divide their fee of two hundred and fifty dollars. Lincoln rebuked him sternly. Lamon protested that the fee had been settled in advance, that the girl's brother was entirely satisfied to pay it.

"That may be," Lincoln retorted, "but I am not satisfied. That money comes out of the pocket of a poor, demented girl; and I would rather starve than swindle her in this manner. You return half this money at least, or I'll not take a cent of it as my share."

In another instance, a pension agent had charged the widow of a Revolutionary soldier half the four hundred dollars to which her pension amounted, for getting her claim allowed. The old woman was bent with age, and in poverty. Lincoln had her sue the pension agent, won the case for her, and charged her nothing. Besides, he paid her hotel bill and gave her money to buy a ticket home.

One day the Widow Armstrong came to Lincoln in great trouble. Her son Duff was charged with having murdered a man in a drunken brawl, and she pleaded with Abe to come and save the boy. Lincoln had known the Armstrongs back in New Salem. In fact, he had rocked Duff to sleep when he was a baby in the cradle. The Armstrongs had been a wild, rough lot; but Lincoln liked them. Jack Armstrong, Duff's father, had been the leader of the Clary's Grove Boys, and the renowned athlete whom Lincoln vanquished in a wrestling-match that has gone down in history.

Old Jack was dead now. Lincoln gladly went before the jury and made one of the most moving and appealing addresses of his career, and saved the boy from the gallows.

All the widowed mother had in the world was forty acres of land, which she offered to turn over to Lincoln.

"Aunt Hannah," he said, "you took me in years ago when I was poor and homeless, and you fed me and mended my clothes, and I shan't charge you a cent now."

Sometimes he urged his clients to settle out of court, and charged them nothing whatever for his advice. In one instance, he refused to take a judgment against a man, saying, "I am really sorry for him—poor and a cripple as he is."

Such kindness and consideration, beautiful though it was, didn't bring in cash; so Mary Lincoln scolded and fretted. Her husband wasn't getting on in the world, while other lawyers were growing wealthy with their fees and investments. Judge

David Davis, for example, and Logan. Yes, and Stephen A. Douglas. By investing in Chicago real estate, Douglas had amassed a fortune and even become a philanthropist, giving Chicago University ten acres of valuable land upon which to erect its buildings. Besides, he was now one of the most famous political leaders in the nation.

How often Mary Lincoln thought of him, and how keenly she wished she had married him! As Mrs. Douglas she would be a social leader in Washington, wear Paris clothes, enjoy trips to Europe, dine with queens, and some day live in the White House. So she probably pictured herself in vain day-dreams.

What was her future as Lincoln's wife? He would go on like this to the end: riding the circuit for six months out of the year, leaving her alone at home, lavishing no love on her, and giving her no attention. . . . How different, how poignantly different, the realities of life were from the romantic visions she had once dreamed at Madame Mentelle's in the long ago!

IN MOST RESPECTS, as has been said, Mrs. Lincoln was economical, and took pride in the fact. She purchased supplies carefully and the table was set sparingly, very sparingly; there were just barely enough scraps left to feed the cats. The Lincolns had no dog.

She bought bottle after bottle of perfume, broke the seals, sampled them, and returned them, contending that they were inferior, that they had been misrepresented. She did this so often that the local druggist refused to honor her orders for more. His account-book may still be seen in Springfield with the penciled notations: "Perfume returned by Mrs. Lincoln."

She frequently had trouble with the tradespeople. For example, she felt that Myers, the iceman, was cheating her with short weights; so she turned on him and berated him in such a shrill, loud voice that neighbors half a block away ran to their doors to look and listen.

This was the second time she had made this accusation, and he swore that he would see her sizzling in hell before he would sell her another piece of ice.

He meant it, and he stopped his deliveries. That was awkward. She had to have ice, and he was the only man in town who supplied it; so, for once in her life, Mary Lincoln humbled herself. But she didn't do it personally: she paid a neighbor a quarter to go downtown and salve over the wound and coax Myers to resume his deliveries.

One of Lincoln's friends started a little newspaper called "The Springfield Republican." He canvassed the town, and Lincoln subscribed for it. When the first copy was delivered at the door, Mary Todd was enraged. What! Another worthless paper? More money thrown away when she was trying so hard to save every penny! She lectured and scolded; and, in order to pacify her, Lincoln said that he had not ordered the paper to be delivered. That was literally true. He had merely said he would pay for a subscription. He hadn't specifically said he wanted it delivered. A lawyer's finesse!

That evening, unknown to her husband, Mary Todd wrote a fiery letter, telling the editor what she thought of his paper, and demanding that it be discontinued.

She was so insulting that the editor answered her publicly in a column of the paper, and then wrote Lincoln, demanding an explanation. Lincoln was so distressed by the publicity that he was positively ill. In humiliation, he wrote the editor, saying it was all a mistake, trying to explain as best he could.

Once Lincoln wanted to invite his stepmother to spend Christmas at his home, but Mary Todd objected. She despised the old folks, and held Tom Lincoln and the Hanks tribe in profound contempt. She was ashamed of them, and Lincoln feared that even if they came to the house she wouldn't admit them. For twenty-three years his stepmother lived seventy miles away from Springfield, and he went to visit her, but she never saw the inside of his home.

The only relative of his that ever visited him after his marriage was a distant cousin, Harriet Hanks, a sensible girl with a pleasing disposition. Lincoln was very fond of her and invited her to live at his home while she attended school in Springfield. Mrs. Lincoln not only made a servant of her but tried to turn her into a veritable household drudge. Lincoln rebelled at this, refused to countenance such rank injustice, and the whole thing resulted in a distressing scene.

She had incessant trouble with her "hired girls." One or two explosions of her fiery wrath, and they packed up and left, an unending stream of them. They despised her and warned their friends; so the Lincoln home was soon on the maids' black-list.

She fumed and fussed and wrote letters about the "wild Irish" she had to employ. But all Irish became "wild" when they tried to work for her. She openly boasted that if she outlived her husband, she would spend the rest of her days in a

Southern State. The people with whom she had been brought up, back in Lexington, did not put up with any impudence from their servants. If a Negro did not mind, he was sent forthwith to the whipping-post in the public square, to be flogged. One of the Todds' neighbors flogged six of his Negroes until they died.

"Long Jake" was a well-known character in Springfield at that time. He had a span of mules and an old dilapidated wagon, and he ran what he vaingloriously described as an "express service." His niece, unfortunately, went to work for Mrs. Lincoln. A few days later, the servant and mistress quarreled; the girl threw off her apron, packed her trunk, and walked out of the house, slamming the door behind her.

That afternoon, Long Jake drove his mules down to the corner of Eighth and Jackson streets and told Mrs. Lincoln that he had come for his niece's baggage. Mrs. Lincoln flew into a rage, abused him and his niece in bitter language, and threatened to strike him if he entered her house. Indignant, he rushed down to Lincoln's office and demanded that the poor man make his wife apologize.

Lincoln listened to his story, and then said sadly:

"I regret to hear this, but let me ask you in all candor, can't you endure for a few moments what I have had as my daily portion for the last fifteen years?"

The interview ended in Long Jake's extending his sympathy to Lincoln and apologizing for having troubled him.

Once Mrs. Lincoln kept a maid for more than two years, and the neighbors marveled; they could not understand it. The explanation was very simple: Lincoln had made a secret bargain with this one. When she first came, he took her aside and told her very frankly what she would have to endure; that he was sorry, but it couldn't be helped. The girl must ignore it. Lincoln promised her an extra dollar a week, himself, if she would do so.

The outbursts went on as usual; but with her secret moral and monetary backing, Maria persisted. After Mrs. Lincoln had given her a tongue-lashing, Lincoln would watch his chance and steal out into the kitchen while the maid was alone and pat her on the shoulder, admonishing her:

"That's right. Keep up your courage, Maria. Stay with her. Stay with her."

This servant afterward married, and her husband fought

under Grant. When Lee surrendered, Maria hurried to Washington to obtain her husband's immediate release, for she and her children were in want. Lincoln was glad to see her, and sat down and talked to her about old times. He wanted to invite her to stay for dinner, but Mary Todd wouldn't hear of it. He gave her a basket of fruit and money to buy clothes, and told her to call again the next day and he would provide her with a pass through the lines. But she didn't call, for that night he was assassinated.

And so Mrs. Lincoln stormed on through the years, leaving in her wake a train of heartaches and hatred. At times she behaved as if insane.

There was something a trifle queer about the Todd family; and since Mary's parents were cousins, perhaps this queer streak had been accentuated by inbreeding. Some people—among others, her own physician—feared she was suffering from an incipient mental disease.

Lincoln bore it all with Christ-like patience, and seldom censured her. But his friends weren't so docile.

Herndon denounced her as a "wildcat" and a "she wolf."

Turner King, one of Lincoln's warmest admirers, described her as "a hellion, a she devil," and declared that he had seen her drive Lincoln out of the house time after time.

John Hay, as secretary to the President in Washington, called her a short, ugly name that it is best not to print.

The pastor of the Methodist Church in Springfield lived near the Lincoln house. He and Lincoln were friends; and his wife testified that the Lincolns "were very unhappy in their domestic life, and that *Mrs. Lincoln was seen frequently to drive him from the house with a broomstick.*"

James Gourley, who lived next door for sixteen years, declared that Mrs. Lincoln "had the devil in her," that she had hallucinations and carried on like a crazy woman, weeping and wailing until she could be heard all over the neighborhood, demanding that some one guard the premises, swearing that some rough character was going to attack her.

Her outbursts of wrath grew more frequent, more fiery, with the passing of time. Lincoln's friends felt deeply sorry for him. He had no home life, and he never invited even his most intimate companions to dine with him—not even men like Herndon and Judge Davis. He was afraid of what might happen. He himself avoided Mary as much as possible, spending his evenings spinning yarns with the other attorneys down at the law library or telling stories to a crowd of men in Diller's drugstore.

Sometimes he was seen wandering alone, late at night, through unfrequented streets, his head on his chest, gloomy and funereal. Sometimes he said, "I hate to go home." A friend, knowing what was wrong, would take him to his house for the night.

No one knew more than Herndon about the tragic home life of the Lincolns; and this is what Herndon had to say on pages 430-434 of the third volume of his Lincoln biography:

> Mr. Lincoln never had a confidant, and therefore never unbosomed himself to others. He never spoke of his trials to me or, so far as I knew, to any of his friends. It was a great burden to carry, but he bore it sadly enough and without a murmur. I could always realize when he was in distress, without being told. He was not exactly an early riser, that is, he never usually appeared at the office till about nine o'clock in the morning. I usually preceded him an hour. Sometimes, however, he would come down as early as seven o'clock—in fact, on one occasion I remember he came down before daylight. If, on arriving at the office, I found him in, I knew instantly that a breeze had sprung up over the domestic sea, and that the waters were troubled. He would either be lying on the lounge looking skyward, or doubled up in a chair with his feet resting on the sill of a back window. He would not look up on my entering, and only answered my "Good morning" with a grunt. I at once busied myself with pen and paper, or ran through the leaves of some book; but the evidence of his melancholy and distress was so plain, and his silence so significant, that I would grow restless myself, and finding some excuse to go to the court-house or elsewhere, would leave the room.
>
> The door of the office opening into a narrow hallway was half glass, with a curtain on it working on brass rings strung on wire. As I passed out on these occasions I would draw the curtain across the glass, and before I reached the bottom of the stairs I could hear the key turn in the lock, and Lincoln was alone in his gloom. An hour in the clerk's office at the court-house, an hour longer in a neighboring store having passed, I would return. By that time either a

client had dropped in and Lincoln was propounding the law, or else the cloud of despondency had passed away, and he was busy in the recital of an Indiana story to whistle off the recollections of the morning's gloom. Noon having arrived I would depart homeward for my dinner. Returning within an hour, I would find him still in the office,—although his home stood but a few squares away,—lunching on a slice of cheese and a handful of crackers which, in my absence, he had brought up from a store below. Separating for the day at five or six o'clock in the evening, I would still leave him behind, either sitting on a box at the foot of the stairway, entertaining a few loungers, or killing time in the same way on the court-house steps. A light in the office after dark attested his presence there till late along in the night, when, after all the world had gone to sleep, the tall form of the man destined to be the nation's President could have seen strolling along in the shadows of trees and buildings, and quietly slipping in through the door of a modest frame house, which it pleased the world, in a conventional way, to call his home.

Some persons may insist that this picture is too highly colored. If so, I can only answer, they do not know the facts.

Once Mrs. Lincoln attacked her husband so savagely, and kept it up so long, that even he—"with malice toward none; with charity for all"—even he lost his self-control, and seizing her by the arm, he forced her across the kitchen and pushed her toward the door, saying: "You're ruining my life. You're making a hell of this home. Now, damn you, you get out of it."

12

IF LINCOLN had married Ann Rutledge, in all probability he would have been happy, but he would not have been President. He was slow in thought and movement, and she was not the type that would have driven him to achieve political distinction. But Mary Todd, obsessed with an undying determination to live in the White House, was no sooner married to Lincoln than she had him out running for the Whig nomination for Congress.

The battle was a fierce one; and, incredible as it seems, his political enemies accused him of being an infidel because he belonged to no church, and denounced him as a tool of wealth and aristocracy because he had affiliated himself through marriage with the haughty Todd and Edwards families. Ridiculous as the charges were, Lincoln realized that they might hurt him politically. So he answered his critics: "Only one of my relatives has ever visited me since I came to Springfield, and that one, before he got out of town, was accused of stealing a jew's-harp. Now, if that is being a member of a proud, aristocratic family, then I am guilty of the offense."

When the election came, Lincoln was defeated. It was the first political setback of his career.

Two years later he ran again and won. Mary Lincoln was ecstatic; believing that his political triumphs had just begun, she ordered a new evening gown and polished up her French verbs. As soon as her husband reached the capital, she addressed her letters to "The Honorable A. Lincoln." But he put a stop to that at once.

She wanted to live in Washington, too, she longed to bask in the social prestige that she was sure awaited her. But when she came East to join him, she found things vastly different from what she had anticipated. Lincoln was so poor that he had had to borrow money from Stephen A. Douglas to pay his expenses until he got his first salary check from the Government; so Mr. and Mrs. Lincoln stopped at Mrs. Spriggs's boarding-house in Duff Green's Row. The street in front of Mrs. Spriggs's establishment was unpaved, the sidewalk was made of ashes and gravel, the rooms were bleak, and there was no plumbing. In her back yard Mrs. Spriggs had an outhouse, a goose-pen, and a garden; and, as the neighbors' hogs were constantly breaking in to eat her vegetables, her little boy had to run out at intervals with a club to drive the animals away.

The city of Washington did not trouble in those days to collect the garbage; so Mrs. Spriggs dumped her refuse in the back alley, and depended upon the cows, pigs, and geese that wandered about the streets at will, to come and devour it.

Mrs. Lincoln found the door to the exclusive society of Washington shut tightly against her. She was ignored, and left alone to sit in her bleak boarding-house bedroom, with her spoiled children and a headache—listening to Mrs. Spriggs's boy, shouting to drive the hogs out of the cabbage-patch.

Disappointing as that was, it was nothing in comparison with the political disaster that lurked around the corner. When Lincoln entered Congress, the country had been waging a war against Mexico for twenty months—a shameful war of aggression, deliberately provoked by the slave power in Congress in order that the nation might acquire more territory where slavery would flourish and from which pro-slavery senators would be elected.

America accomplished two things in that war. Texas had once belonged to Mexico and then seceded. We forced Mexico to renounce all of her claims to Texas; and, in addition, we deliberately robbed Mexico of half of all the territory she owned and carved it up into the States of New Mexico, Arizona, Nevada, and California.

Grant said it was one of the wickedest wars in all history, and that he could never forgive himself for having fought in it. A great many of the American soldiers rebelled and went over to the enemy; one famous battalion in Santa Anna's army was composed entirely of American deserters.

Lincoln stood up in Congress and did what many other

Whigs had already done: he attacked the President for having started "a war of rapine and murder, a war of robbery and dishonor," and declared that the God of heaven had "forgotten to defend the weak and innocent, and permitted the strong band of murderers and demons from hell to kill men, women, and children and lay waste and pillage the land of the just."

The capital paid no attention whatever to this speech, for Lincoln was unknown. But back in Springfield, it raised a hurricane. Illinois had sent six thousand men to fight, as they believed, for the holy cause of liberty; and now their representative was standing up in Congress and calling their soldiers demons from hell, and accusing them of murder. In a rage, excited partizans held public meetings and denounced Lincoln as "base" . . . "dastardly" . . . "infamous" . . . "a reasonable guerilla" . . . "a second Benedict Arnold."

At one meeting resolutions were adopted declaring that never until then had they "known disgrace so black." . . . "Such black odium and infamy heaped upon the living brave and illustrious dead can but excite the indignation of every true Illinoisan."

The hatred was so bitter that it smoldered for more than a decade; and when Lincoln was running for the Presidency thirteen years later these denunciations were again hurled at his head.

"I have committed political suicide," Lincoln confessed to his law partner.

He dreaded to go back home now and face his resentful constituents; so he tried to secure a position that would keep him in Washington, and maneuvered to secure an appointment as Commissioner of the Land Office, but he failed.

Then he tried to have himself named Governor of the Territory of Oregon, with the hope that he might be one of the first senators when it came into the Union, but he failed in that too.

So he returned to Springfield and his dirty law office. Once more he hitched up Old Buck to his ramshackle buggy, and again he started driving over the circuit of the Eighth Judicial District—one of the most dejected men in all Illinois.

He was determined now to forget all about politics, and devote himself to his profession. He realized that he had no method in his work, that he lacked mental discipline; and so, to train himself to reason more closely and to demonstrate a proposition, he bought a geometry and carried it with him as he rode the circuit.

Herndon records in his biography:

> At the little country inns, we usually occupied the same bed. In most cases the beds were too short for Lincoln, and his feet would hang over the footboard, thus exposing a limited expanse of shin bone. Placing a candle on a chair at the head of the bed, he would read and study for hours. I have known him to study in this position until two o'clock in the morning. Meanwhile, I and others who chanced to occupy the same room would be safely and soundly asleep. On the circuit in this way he studied Euclid until he could with ease demonstrate all the propositions in the six books.

After he had mastered geometry, he studied algebra, then astronomy, then he prepared a lecture on the origin and growth of languages. But no other study interested him as did Shakspere. The literary tastes that Jack Kelso had nurtured in New Salem still persisted.

The most striking characteristic of Abraham Lincoln, from this time on to the end of his life, was a sadness so profound, a melancholy so deep that mere words can hardly convey its depths.

When Jesse Weik was helping Herndon prepare his immortal biography, he felt that surely the reports of Lincoln's sadness must be exaggerated. So he went and discussed this point at length with the men who had been associated with Lincoln for years—men such as Stuart, Whitney, Matheny, Swett, and Judge Davis.

Then Weik was firmly convinced "that men who never saw Lincoln could scarcely realize his tendency to melancholy," and Herndon, agreeing with him, went farther, making the statement from which I have already quoted: "If Lincoln ever had a happy day in twenty years, I never knew of it. A perpetual look of sadness was his most prominent feature. Melancholy dripped from him as he walked."

When he was riding the circuit he would frequently sleep in the same room with two or three other attorneys. They would be awakened early in the morning by the sound of his voice and find him sitting on the edge of the bed, mumbling incoherently to himself. Getting up, he would start a fire and sit for hours, staring into the blaze. Frequently, on such occasions, he would recite "Oh, why should the spirit of mortal be proud?"

Sometimes as he walked down the street, he was so deep in

despair that he took no notice of those who met him and spoke to him. Occasionally he shook hands with people without knowing what he was doing.

Jonathan Birch, who all but worshiped Lincoln's memory, says:

> When attending court at Bloomington, Lincoln would keep his hearers in the court room, office or on the street convulsed with laughter at one hour and the next hour be so deeply submerged in speculation that no one dared arouse him. . . . He would sit in a chair tilted against the wall, his feet on the lower rung, legs drawn up and knees level with his chin, hat tipped forward, hands clasped about knees, eyes infinitely sad, the very picture of dejection and gloom. Thus absorbed I have seen him sit for hours at a time, defying the interruption of even his closest friends.

Senator Beveridge, after studying Lincoln's career perhaps more exhaustively than any one else has ever done, came to the conclusion that "the dominant quality in Lincoln's life from 1849 to the end was a sadness so profound that the depths of it cannot be sounded or estimated by normal minds."

Yet Lincoln's inexhaustible humor, his amazing capacity for telling stories, were as striking and inseparable a part of his personality as his sadness.

At times Judge Davis even stopped court to listen to his boisterous humor.

"Crowds thronged about him, crowds of two hundred and three hundred," says Herndon, holding their sides and laughing the hours away.

One eye-witness declares that when Lincoln reached the "nub" of a good story, men "whooped" and rolled off their chairs.

Those who knew Lincoln intimately agreed that "his abysmal sadness" was caused by two things: his crushing political disappointments and his tragic marriage.

And so the poignant years of apparently permanent political oblivion dragged by—six of them—and then suddenly an event occurred that altered the whole course of Lincoln's life, and started him toward the White House.

The instigator and moving spirit behind this event was Mary Lincoln's old sweetheart, Stephen A. Douglas.

IN 1854, a tremendous thing happened to Lincoln. It came about as a result of the repeal of the Missouri Compromise. The Missouri Compromise, in brief, was this: In 1819, Missouri had wanted to come into the Union as a slave State. The North had opposed its doing so and the situation became serious. Finally, the ablest public men of that day arranged what is now known as the Missouri Compromise. The South got what it wanted: the admission of Missouri as a slave State. The North got what it wanted: thereafter slavery was never to be permitted in the West anywhere north of the southern boundary of Missouri.

People thought that would stop the quarreling about slavery, and it did—for a while. But now, a third of a century later, Stephen A. Douglas secured the repeal of the Compromise, and made it possible for a new area lying west of the Mississippi and equal in size to the original thirteen States, to be blighted with the curse of slavery. He fought long and hard in Congress for the repeal. The struggle lasted for months. Once during the bitter debates in the House of Representatives, members leaped on top of their desks, knives flashed, and guns were drawn. But finally, after an impassioned plea by Douglas, lasting from midnight until almost dawn, the Senate passed his bill on March 4, 1854. It was a tremendous event. Messengers ran through the streets of the slumbering city of Washington, shouting the news. Cannon in the Navy Yard boomed to salute the dawn of a new era—a new era that was to be drenched in blood.

Why did Douglas do it? No one seems to know. Historians in skullcaps are still arguing about it. Of this much, however, we are certain: Douglas hoped to be elected President in 1856. He knew this repeal would help him in the South.

But what of the North?

"By God, I know it will raise a hell of a storm there," he declared.

He was right. It did. It raised a regular tornado that blew both the great parties into bits, and eventually whirled the nation into civil war.

Meetings of protest and indignation flared up spontaneously in hundreds of cities and villages and hamlets. Stephen Arnold Douglas was denounced as the "traitor Arnold." People said that he had been named after Benedict Arnold. He was branded as a modern Judas, and presented with thirty pieces of silver. He was given a rope and told to hang himself.

The churches leaped into the fight with a holy frenzy. Three thousand and fifty clergymen in New England wrote a protest "in the name of Almighty God and in His presence," and laid it before the Senate. Fiery and indignant editorials fed the flames of public indignation. In Chicago even the Democratic papers turned upon Douglas with vindictive fierceness.

Congress adjourned in August, and Douglas started home. Amazed at the sights that met his eyes, he declared afterward that he could have traveled all the way from Boston to Illinois by the light of burning effigies of himself hanging by the neck.

Daring and defiant, he announced that he was going to speak in Chicago. The hatred against him there, in his own home town, amounted to nothing less than fanaticism. The press assailed him, and wrathful ministers demanded that he never again be permitted to "pollute the pure air of Illinois with his perfidious breath." Men rushed to the hardware stores, and, by sundown, there wasn't another revolver left for sale in all the city. His enemies swore that he should never live to defend his infamous deeds.

The moment Douglas entered the city, boats in the harbor lowered their flags to half-mast; and bells in a score of churches tolled, mourning the death of Liberty.

The night that he spoke was one of the hottest Chicago had ever known. Perspiration rolled down the faces of men as they sat idling in their chairs. Women fainted as they struggled to get out to the shore of the lake where they could sleep on the cool sands. Horses fell in their harness and lay dying in the streets.

But notwithstanding the heat, thousands of excited men, guns in their pockets, flocked to hear Douglas. No hall in Chicago could hold the throng. They packed a public square, and hundreds stood on balconies and sat astride the roofs of near-by houses.

The very first sentence that Douglas uttered was greeted with groans and hisses. He continued to talk—or, at least, he continued to try—and the audience yelled and booed and sang insulting songs and called him names that are unprintable.

His excited partizans wanted to start a fight. Douglas begged them to be quiet. He would tame the mob. He kept on trying, but he kept on failing. When he denounced the "Chicago Tribune," the great gathering cheered the paper. When he threatened to stand there all night unless they let him speak, eight thousand voices sang: "We won't go home until morning. We won't go home until morning."

It was a Saturday night. Finally, after four hours of futility and insult, Douglas took out his watch and shouted at the howling, bellowing, milling mob: "It is now Sunday morning, I'll go to church. And you can go to hell."

Exhausted, he gave up and left the speaker's stand. The Little Giant had met humiliation and defeat for the first time in his life.

The next morning the papers told all about it; and down in Springfield, a proud, plump brunette, trembling on the brink of middle age, read it with peculiar satisfaction. Fifteen years before, she had dreamed of being Mrs. Douglas. For years she had watched him mount on wings until he had become the most popular and powerful leader in the nation, while her husband had gone down in humiliating defeat; and, deep in her heart, she resented it.

But now, thank God, the haughty Douglas was doomed. He had split his own party in his own State. And just before the election. This was Lincoln's chance. And Mary Lincoln knew it—his chance to win back the public favor that he had lost in 1848, his chance to reinstate himself politically, his chance to be elected to the United States Senate. True, Douglas still had four more years to serve. But his colleague was coming up for reëlection in a few months.

And who was his colleague? A swaggering, pugnacious Irishman named Shields. Mary Lincoln had an old score to settle with Shields, too. Back in 1842, largely because of insulting letters that she herself had written, Shields had challenged Lincoln to a duel; and the two of them, armed with cavalry swords and accompanied by their seconds, had met on a sand-bar in the Mississippi River, prepared to kill each other. But, at the last moment, friends interceded and prevented bloodshed. Since that time, Shields had gone up in politics, but Lincoln had gone down.

But now Lincoln had struck bottom, and had started to rebound. The repeal of the Missouri Compromise had, as he said, "aroused" him. He could no longer remain quiet. He was determined to strike with all the vigor and conviction of his soul.

So he began preparing his speech, working for weeks in the State library, consulting histories, mastering facts, classifying, clarifying, studying all the hot debates that had been thundered back and forth across the Senate chamber during the stormy passage of this bill.

On October 3 the State Fair opened at Springfield. Thousands of farmers poured into town; men bringing their prize hogs and horses, their cattle and corn; women fetching their jellies and jam, their pies and preserves. But these displays were all but forgotten in the excitement of another attraction. For weeks it had been advertised that Douglas was to speak the opening day of the fair, and political leaders from all parts of the State had thronged there to hear him.

That afternoon he spoke for more than three hours, going over his record, explaining, defending, attacking. He hotly denied that he was trying either "to legislate slavery into a territory or to exclude it therefrom." Let the people in a territory do whatever they pleased about slavery.

"Surely," he shouted, "if the people of Kansas and Nebraska are able to govern themselves, surely they are able to govern a few miserable Negroes."

Lincoln sat near the front, listening to every word, weighing every argument. When Douglas finished, Lincoln declared: "I'll hang his hide on the fence to-morrow."

The next morning handbills were scattered all over town and the fair-grounds, announcing that Lincoln would reply to Douglas. The public interest was intense, and before two o'clock every seat was occupied in the hall where the speaking was to take place. Presently Douglas appeared and sat on the platform. As usual, he was immaculately attired and faultlessly groomed.

Mary Lincoln was already in the audience. Before leaving the house that morning she had vigorously brushed Lincoln's coat, had laid out a fresh collar and carefully ironed his best tie. She was anxious to have him appear to advantage. But the day was hot, and Lincoln knew the air in the hall would be oppressive. So he strode onto the platform without a coat, without a vest, without a collar, without a tie. His long, brown, skinny neck rose out of the shirt that hung loosely on his gaunt frame. His hair was disordered, his boots rusty and unkempt. One single knitted "gallis" held up his short, ill-fitting trousers.

At the first sight of him, Mary Lincoln flushed with anger and embarrassment. She could have wept in her disappointment and despair.

No one dreamed of it at the time, but we know now that this homely man, whose wife was ashamed of him, was starting out that hot October afternoon on a career that was to give him a place among the immortals.

That afternoon, he made the first great speech of his life. If all the addresses that he had made previously were collected and placed in one book, and those that he made from that afternoon on were placed in another volume, you could hardly believe that the same man was the author of them all. It was a new Lincoln speaking that day—a Lincoln stirred to the depths by a mighty wrong, a Lincoln pleading for an oppressed race, a Lincoln touched and moved and lifted up by moral grandeur.

He reviewed the history of slavery, and gave five fiery reasons for hating it.

But with lofty tolerance, he declared: "I have no prejudice against the Southern people. They are just what we would be in their situation. If slavery did not now exist among them, they would not introduce it. If it did now exist among us, we should not instantly give it up.

"When Southern people tell us they are no more responsible for the origin of slavery than we are, I acknowledge the fact. When it is said that the institution exists, and that it is very difficult to get rid of it in any satisfactory way, I can understand and appreciate the saying. I surely will not blame them for not doing what I should not know how to do myself. If all earthly power were given me, I should not know what to do with the existing institution."

For more than three hours, with the perspiration rolling down his face, he continued to answer Douglas, revealing the senator's sophistry, showing the utter falseness of his position.

It was a profound speech, and it made a profound impression. Douglas winced and writhed under it. Time after time he rose to his feet and interrupted Lincoln.

The election wasn't far off. Progressive young Democrats were already bolting the ticket and attacking Douglas, and when the voters of Illinois cast their ballots, the Douglas Democrats were overwhelmed.

Senators were chosen in those days by the State legislatures; and the Illinois Legislature met in Springfield on February 8, 1855, for that purpose. Mrs. Lincoln had bought a new dress and hat for the occasion and her brother-in-law, Ninian W. Edwards, had with sanguine anticipation arranged for a reception to be given that night in Senator Lincoln's honor.

On the first ballot, Lincoln led all the other candidates, and came within six votes of victory. But he steadily lost after that; and on the tenth ballot he was definitely defeated, and Lyman W. Trumbull was elected.

Lyman Trumbull had married Julia Jayne, a young woman who had been bridesmaid at Mary Lincoln's wedding and probably had been the most intimate friend that Mrs. Lincoln ever had. Mary and Julia sat side by side in the balcony of the Hall of Representatives that afternoon, watching the senatorial election, and when the victory of Julia's husband was announced, Mrs. Lincoln turned in a temper and walked out of the building. Her anger was so fierce, and her jealousy was so galling, that from that day on, to the end of her life, she never again spoke to Julia Trumbull.

Saddened and depressed, Lincoln returned to his dingy law office with the ink-stain on the wall and the garden seeds sprouting in the dust on top of the bookcase.

A week later he hitched up Old Buck and once more started driving over the unsettled prairies, from one country courthouse to another. But his heart was no longer in the law. He talked now of little else but politics and slavery. He said that the thought of millions of people held in bondage continually made him miserable. His periods of melancholy returned now more frequently than ever; and they were more prolonged and more profound.

One night he was sharing a bed with another lawyer in a country tavern. His companion awoke at dawn and found Lincoln sitting in his nightshirt on the edge of the bed, brooding, dejected, mumbling to himself, lost in unseeing abstraction. When at last he spoke, the first words were:

"I tell you this nation cannot endure permanently half slave and half free."

Shortly after this a colored woman in Springfield came to Lincoln with a pitiful story. Her son had gone to St. Louis and taken a job on a Mississippi steamboat. When he arrived in New Orleans he was thrown into jail. He had been born free, but he had no papers to prove it. So he was kept in prison until his boat left. Now he was going to be sold as a slave to pay the prison expenses.

Lincoln took the case to the Governor of Illinois. The governor replied that he had no right or power to interfere. In response to a letter, the Governor of Louisiana replied that he couldn't do anything, either. So Lincoln went back to see the Governor of Illinois a second time, urging him to act, but the governor shook his head.

Lincoln rose from his chair, exclaiming with unusual emphasis: "By God, Governor, you may not have the legal power to secure the release of this poor boy, but I intend to make the ground in this country too hot for the foot of a slave-owner."

The next year Lincoln was forty-six, and he confided to his friend Whitney that he "kinder needed" glasses; so he stopped at a jewelry store and bought his first pair—for thirty-seven and a half cents.

★ ★ ★

14

★ ★ ★

WE HAVE NOW COME to the summer of 1858, and we are about to watch Abraham Lincoln making the first great fight of his life. We shall see him emerge from his provincial obscurity and engage in one of the most famous political battles in United States history.

He is forty-nine now—and where has he arrived after all his years of struggle?

In business, he has been a failure.

In marriage, he has found stark, bleak unhappiness.

In law, he is fairly successful, with an income of three thousand a year; but in politics and the cherished desires of his heart, he has met with frustration and defeat.

"With me," he confessed, "the race of ambition has been a failure, a flat failure."

But from now on events move with a strange and dizzying swiftness. In seven more years he will be dead. But in those seven years he will have achieved a fame and luster that will endure to the remotest generations.

His antagonist in the contest we are to watch is Stephen A. Douglas. Douglas is now a national idol. In fact, he is world-renowned.

In the four years that had elapsed since the repeal of the Missouri Compromise, Douglas had made one of the most amazing recoveries in history. He had redeemed himself by a dramatic and spectacular political battle. It came about in this way:

Kansas knocked at the door of the Union, asking to be admitted as a slave State. But should she be so admitted? Douglas said "no," because the legislature that had framed her constitution was not a real legislature. Its members had been elected by chicanery and shot-guns. Half the settlers in Kansas—men who had a right to vote—were never registered, and so couldn't vote. But five thousand pro-slavery Democrats who lived in western Missouri and had not the shadow of a legal right to cast ballots in Kansas went to a United States arsenal, armed themselves, and, on election day, marched over into Kansas with flags flying and bands playing—and voted for slavery. The whole thing was a farce, a travesty on justice.

And what did the free-State men do? They prepared for action. They cleaned up their shot-guns, oiled their rifles, and began banging away at signs on trees and knot-holes in barn doors, to improve their marksmanship. They were soon marching and drilling and drinking. They dug trenches, threw up breastworks, and turned hotels into forts. If they couldn't win justice with ballots, they would win it with bullets!

In almost every town and village throughout the North, professional orators harangued the citizenry, passed hats, and collected money to buy arms for Kansas. Henry Ward Beecher, pounding his pulpit in Brooklyn, cried that guns would do more for the salvation of Kansas than Bibles. From that time on, Sharp's rifles were known as "Beecher's Bibles." They were shipped from the East in boxes and barrels labeled as "Bibles," as "Crockery," as "Revised Statutes."

After five free-State settlers had been murdered, an old sheep-raiser, a religious fanatic who cultivated grapes and made wine on the side, rose up on the plains of Kansas and said: "I have no choice. It has been decreed by Almighty God that I should make an example of these pro-slavery men."

His name was John Brown, and he lived at Osawatomie.

One night in May he opened the Bible, read the Psalms of David to his family, and they knelt in prayer. Then after the singing of a few hymns, he and his four sons and a son-in-law mounted their horses and rode across the prairie to a pro-slavery man's cabin, dragged the man and his two boys out of bed, chopped off their arms, and split their heads open with an ax. It rained before morning, and the water washed some of the brains out of the dead men's skulls.

From that time on, both sides slew and stabbed and shot.

The term "Bleeding Kansas" was written on the pages of history.

Now, Stephen A. Douglas knew that a constitution framed by a bogus legislature in the midst of all that fraud and treachery was not worth the blotting-paper that it took to dry it.

So Douglas demanded that the people of Kansas be permitted to vote at an honest and peaceful election on the question of whether Kansas should be admitted as a slave or a free State.

His demand was altogether right and proper. But the President of the United States, James Buchanan, and the haughty pro-slavery politicians in Washington wouldn't tolerate such an arrangement.

So Buchanan and Douglas quarreled.

The President threatened to send Douglas to the political shambles, and Douglas retaliated: "By God, sir, I made James Buchanan; and by God, sir, I'll unmake him."

As Douglas said that, he not only made a threat, but he made history. In that instant, slavery had reached the apex of its political power and arrogance. From that moment on, its power declined with a swift and dramatic abruptness.

The battle that followed was the beginning of the end, for in that fight Douglas split his own party wide open and prepared the way for Democratic disaster in 1860, and so made the election of Lincoln not only possible but inevitable.

Douglas had staked his own political future on what he believed, and on what almost every one in the North believed, was an unselfish fight for a magnificent principle. And Illinois loved him for it. He had now come back to his home State, the most admired and idolized man in the nation.

The same Chicago that had hooted and lowered the flags to half-mast and tolled the church bells as he entered the city in 1854—that same Chicago now despatched a special train with brass bands and reception committees to escort him home. As he entered the city, one hundred and fifty cannon in Dearborn Park roared a welcome, hundreds of men fought to shake his hand, and thousands of women tossed flowers at his feet. People named their first-born in his honor; and it is probably no exaggeration to say that some of his frenzied followers would actually have died for him on the scaffold. Forty years after his death men still boasted that they were "Douglas Democrats."

A few months after Douglas made his triumphal entry into

Chicago the people of Illinois were scheduled to elect a United States Senator. Naturally the Democrats nominated Douglas. And whom did the Republicans put up to run against him? An obscure man named Lincoln.

During the campaign that followed, Lincoln and Douglas met in a series of fiery debates, and these debates made Lincoln famous. They fought over a question charged with emotional dynamite, public excitement rose to fever heat. Throngs such as had never been known before in the history of the United States rushed to hear them. No halls were large enough to accommodate them; so the meetings were held in the afternoon in groves or out on the prairies. Reporters followed them, newspapers played up the sensational contests, and the speakers soon had a nation for their audience.

Two years later, Lincoln was in the White House.

These debates had advertised him, they had paved the way.

For months before the contest began Lincoln had been preparing; as thoughts and ideas and phrases formed in his mind, he wrote them down on stray scraps of paper—on the backs of envelopes, on the margins of newspapers, on pieces of paper sacks. These he stored in his tall silk hat and carried about wherever he went. Finally he copied them on sheets of paper, speaking each sentence aloud as he wrote it, constantly revising, recasting, improving.

After completing the final draft of his first speech, he invited a few intimate friends to meet him one night in the library of the State House. There, behind locked doors, he read his speech, pausing at the end of each paragraph, asking for comments, inviting criticisms. This address contained the prophetic words that have since become famous:

"A house divided against itself cannot stand."

"I believe this government cannot endure permanently half slave and half free.

"I do not expect the Union to be dissolved—I do not expect the house to fall—but I do expect it will cease to be divided.

"It will become all one thing or all the other."

As he read that, his friends were astonished and alarmed. It was too radical, they said; it was "a damn fool utterance," it would drive voters away.

Finally Lincoln rose slowly and told the group of the intense thought that he had given the subject, and ended the conference by declaring that the statement "A house divided against itself cannot stand" was the truth of all human experience.

"It has been true," said Lincoln, "for six thousand years. And I want some universally known figure, expressed in a simple language, that will arouse men to the peril of the times. The time has come when this truth should be uttered, and I am determined neither to change nor modify my assertion. I am willing, if necessary, to perish with it. If it is decreed that I should go down because of this speech, then let me go down linked to the truth. Let me die in the advocacy of what is just and right."

The first of the great debates was held on the twenty-first day of August in the little farming town of Ottawa, seventy-five miles out of Chicago. Crowds began arriving the night before. Soon the hotels, private houses, and livery-stables were filled to capacity; and for a mile up and down the valley camp-fires blazed on bluffs and bottom-lands as if the town were surrounded by an invading army.

Before daybreak the tide set in again; and the sun rose that morning over the Illinois prairies to look down on country roads filled with buggies and wagons, with pedestrians, and with men and women on horseback. The day was hot, the weather had been dry for weeks. Huge clouds of dust arose and drifted over the corn-fields and meadows.

At noon a special train of seventeen cars arrived from Chicago; seats were packed, aisles jammed, and eager passengers rode on the roofs.

Every town within forty miles had brought its band. Drums rolled, horns tooted, there was the tramp, tramp of parading militia. Quack doctors gave free snake-shows and sold their pain-killers. Jugglers and contortionists performed in front of saloons. Beggars and scarlet women plied their trades. Firecrackers exploded, cannon boomed, horses shied and ran away.

In some towns, the renowned Douglas was driven through the streets in a fine carriage drawn by six white horses. A mighty hurrah arose. The cheering was continuous.

Lincoln's supporters, to show their contempt for this display and elegance, drove their candidate through the street on a decrepit old hay-rack drawn by a team of white mules. Behind him came another hay-rack filled with thirty-two girls. Each girl bore the name of a State, and above them rose a huge motto:

Westward the star of empire takes its way.
The girls link on to Lincoln as their mothers linked to Clay.

The speakers, committees, and reporters wedged and squeezed their way through the dense crowd for half an hour before they could reach the platform.

It was protected from the broiling sun by a lumber awning. A score of men climbed on the awning; it gave way under their weight; boards tumbled down on the Douglas committee.

In almost every way the two speakers differed sharply.

Douglas was five feet four. Lincoln was six feet four.

The big man had a thin tenor voice. The little man had a rich baritone.

Douglas was graceful and suave. Lincoln was ungainly and awkward.

Douglas had the personal charm of a popular idol. Lincoln's sallow wrinkled face was filled with melancholy, and he was entirely lacking in physical magnetism.

Douglas was dressed like a rich Southern planter, in ruffled shirt, dark-blue coat, white trousers, and a white broad-brimmed hat. Lincoln's appearance was uncouth, grotesque: the sleeves of his rusty black coat were too short, his baggy trousers were too short, his high stovepipe hat was weather-beaten and dingy.

Douglas had no flair for humor whatever, but Lincoln was one of the greatest story-tellers that ever lived.

Douglas repeated himself wherever he went. But Lincoln pondered over his subject ceaselessly, until he said he found it easier to make a new speech each day than to repeat an old one.

Douglas was vain, and craved pomp and fanfare. He traveled on a special train draped in flags. On the rear of the train was a brass cannon mounted on a box-car. As he approached a town, his cannon fired time after time, to proclaim to the natives that a mighty man was at their gates.

But Lincoln, detesting what he called "fizzlegigs and fireworks," traveled in day-coaches and freight-trains and carried a battered old carpet-bag, and a green cotton umbrella with the handle gone and a string tied around the middle to keep it from flapping open.

Douglas was an opportunist. He had no "fixed political morals," as Lincoln said. To win—that was his goal. But Lincoln was fighting for a great principle, and it mattered to him very little who won now, if only justice and mercy triumphed in the end.

"Ambition has been ascribed to me," he said. "God knows how sincerely I prayed from the first that this field of ambition might not be opened. I claim no insensibility to political honors; but to-day, could the Missouri Compromise be restored, and the whole slavery question replaced on the old ground of 'toleration' by necessity where it exists, with unyielding hostility to the spread of it, on principle, I would, in consideration, gladly agree that Judge Douglas should never be out, and I never in, an office, so long as we both or either, live.

"It makes little difference, very little difference, whether Judge Douglas or myself is elected to the United States Senate; but the great issue which we have submitted to you to-day is far above and beyond any personal interests or the political fortunes of any man. And that issue will live, and breathe, and burn, when the poor, feeble, stammering tongues of Judge Douglas and myself are silent in the grave."

During these debates Douglas maintained that any State, anywhere, at any time, had a right to have slavery if the majority of its citizens voted for it. And he didn't care whether they voted it up or down. His celebrated slogan was this: "Let each State mind its own business and let its neighbors alone."

Lincoln took directly the opposite stand.

"Judge Douglas's thinking slavery is right," he explained, "and my thinking it wrong, is the precise fact upon which depends the whole controversy.

"He contends that whatever community wants slaves has a right to have them. So they have, if it is not a wrong. But if it is a wrong, he cannot say people have a right to do wrong.

"He cares as little whether a State shall be slave or free as whether his neighbor shall plant his farm with tobacco or stock it with horned cattle. But the great mass of mankind differ with Judge Douglas: they consider slavery a great moral wrong."

Douglas went up and down the State, crying out time after time that Lincoln favored giving Negroes social equality.

"No," retorted Lincoln, "all I ask for the Negro is that, if you do not like him, you let him alone. If God gave him but little, let him enjoy that little. He is not my equal in many respects, but in his right to enjoy 'life, liberty, and the pursuit of happiness,' in his right to put into his mouth the bread that his hands have earned, he is my equal and the equal of Judge Douglas and the equal of every living man."

In debate after debate Douglas accused Lincoln of wanting the whites to "hug and marry the blacks."

And time after time, Lincoln was forced to deny it: "I object to the alternative which says that because I do not want a Negro woman for a slave, I must want her for a wife. I have lived until my fiftieth year, and have never had a Negro woman either for a slave or a wife. There are enough white men to marry all the white women; and enough Negro men to marry all the Negro women; and, for God's sake, let them be so married."

Douglas tried to dodge and befog the issues. His arguments, Lincoln said, had got down to the point where they were as thin as "soup made by boiling the shadow of a pigeon that had starved to death." He was using "specious and fantastic arrangements of words, by which a man can prove a horse-chestnut to be a chestnut horse."

"I can't help feeling foolish," continued Lincoln, "in answering arguments that are no arguments at all."

Douglas said things that weren't true. He knew that they were falsehoods, and so did Lincoln.

"If a man," responded Lincoln, "will stand up and assert, and repeat and reassert, that two and two do not make four, I know nothing that will stop him. I cannot work an argument into the consistency of a mental gag and actually close his mouth with it. I don't like to call Judge Douglas a liar, but when I come square up to him, I don't know what else to call him."

And so the fight raged on, week after week. Day after day Lincoln continued his attacks. Others leaped into the fray. Lyman Trumbull called Douglas a liar, and declared that he had been guilty of "the most damnable effrontery that ever man put on." Frederick Douglas, the famous Negro orator, came to Illinois and joined in the assault. The Buchanan Democrats waxed vicious and ferocious in their denunciation of Douglas. Carl Schurz, the fiery German-American reformer, indicted him before the foreign voters. The Republican press in screaming head-lines branded him as "a forger." With his own party divided, and himself hounded and harassed on every side, Douglas was fighting against tremendous odds. In desperation, he wired his friend Usher F. Linder: "The hell-hounds are on my track. For God's sake, Linder, come and help me fight them."

The operator sold a copy of the telegram to the Republicans, and it was head-lined in a score of papers.

Douglas's enemies screamed with delight, and from that day

on as long as he lived, the recipient of the telegram was called "For God's Sake Linder."

On election night, Lincoln remained in the telegraph office, reading the returns. When he saw that he had lost, he started home. It was dark and rainy and gloomy. The path leading to his house had been worn pig-backed and was slippery. Suddenly, one foot shot from under and hit the other. Quickly he recovered his balance. "It's a slip," he said, "and not a fall."

Shortly after that he read an editorial about himself in an Illinois paper. It said:

> Hon. Abe Lincoln is undoubtedly the most unfortunate politician that has ever attempted to rise in Illinois. In everything he undertakes, politically, he seems doomed to failure. He has been prostrated often enough in his political schemes to have crushed the life out of any ordinary man.

The vast crowds that had rushed to hear him debate with Douglas encouraged Lincoln to believe that he might make a little money now by giving lectures; so he prepared to talk on "Discoveries and Inventions," rented a hall in Bloomington, stationed a young lady at the door to sell tickets—and not one solitary person came to hear him. Not one!

So once more he returned to his dingy office with the ink-stain on the wall and the garden seeds sprouting on top of the bookcase.

It was high time he was getting back, for he had been away from his law practice for six months, earning nothing. Now he was out of funds entirely; he didn't have enough cash on hand even to pay his butcher's and grocer's bills.

So again he hitched up Old Buck to his ramshackle buggy, and again he started driving over the prairie circuit.

It was November, and a cold snap was coming. Across the gray sky above him wild geese flew southward, honking loudly; a rabbit darted across the road; off in the woods somewhere a wolf howled. But the somber man in the buggy neither saw nor heard what was going on about him. Hour after hour, he rode on, his chin on his breast, lost in speculation, submerged in despair.

★ ★ ★

15

★ ★ ★

When the newly formed Republican party met in Chicago in the spring of 1860 to nominate a Presidential candidate, few people dreamed that Abraham Lincoln had a chance. A short time before that, he himself had written to a newspaper editor: "I must in all candor say I do not think myself fit for the presidency."

It was generally accepted in 1860 that the nomination honors were going to the handsome William H. Seward of New York. There could hardly be any question about that, for straw ballots were taken on the trains carrying the delegates to Chicago, and they gave Seward twice as many votes as all the other candidates combined. On many of the trains there was not a single ballot cast for Abraham Lincoln. It is possible that some of the delegates did not even know that such a man existed.

The convention met on Seward's fifty-ninth birthday. How fitting! He was positive that he would receive the nomination as a birthday present. He was so confident of it that he said good-by to his colleagues in the United States Senate and invited his intimate friends to attend a great feast of celebration at his home in Auburn, New York; and a cannon was rented, hauled into his front yard, loaded, and cocked up in the air, ready to boom the joyous news to the town.

If the convention had started balloting on Thursday night, that cannon would have been fired, and the story of a nation would have been changed; but the voting could not begin until the printer delivered the papers necessary for keeping the tally. And the printer, on his way to the convention, probably stopped for a glass of beer. At any rate, he was late, and consequently there was nothing for the convention to do that Thursday evening but sit and wait for him.

Mosquitoes were bad in the hall, the place was hot and stuffy, and the delegates hungry and thirsty; so some one stood up and moved that the convention adjourn until ten o'clock the next morning. A motion to adjourn is always in order; it takes precedence over all other motions and it is nearly always popular. This one carried with a rush of enthusiasm.

Seventeen hours elapsed before the convention assembled again. That is not a long time, but it was long enough for Seward's career to be wrecked, and Lincoln's made.

The person largely responsible for the wrecking was Horace Greeley, a grotesque-looking man with a head as round as a cantaloupe; with thin, silky hair as light as an albino's; and with a string necktie that usually worked itself out of place until the bow was approximately under his left ear.

Greeley was not even advocating the nomination of Lincoln, but he was determined with all the bitterness of his soul to even up an old score with William H. Seward and Seward's manager, Thurlow Weed.

The trouble was this: For fourteen years, Greeley had fought side by side with these men; he had helped make Seward Governor of New York and then United States Senator; and he had aided Weed tremendously in his battle to become and remain political boss of the State.

And what had Greeley gotten out of all this struggle and combat? Very little but neglect. He had wanted to be made State printer, and Weed had taken that place for himself. He had longed to be appointed postmaster of New York City, and Weed did not offer to recommend him. He had aspired to be governor, or even lieutenant-governor, and Weed not only said "no," but said it in a way that hurt and rankled.

Finally, when he could stand no more, Greeley sat down and wrote a long, stinging letter to Seward. It would fill seven pages of this book, and every paragraph of it was seared with bitterness.

That fiery message had been written on Saturday night, November 11, 1854. . . . And this was 1860. Greeley had waited six long years for an opportunity to get his revenge, but at last it had arrived, and he made the most of it. He didn't go to bed at all, that fateful Thursday night while the Republican nominating convention was having a recess in Chicago; but from sundown until long after dawn, he hurried from delegation to delegation, reasoning, arguing, pleading. His paper, the "New York Tribune," was read all over the North; and it influenced public opinion as no other paper had ever done. He was a famous man, voices were hushed whenever he appeared, and the delegates listened to him with respect.

He hurled all kinds of arguments against Seward. He pointed out that Seward had repeatedly denounced the Masonic order; that in 1830 he had been elected to the State Senate on the anti-Mason ticket, and, as a consequence had aroused bitter, widespread, and undying resentment.

Later, when he was Governor of New York, Seward had favored the destruction of the common-school fund and the establishment of separate schools for foreigners and Catholics, and thus had stirred up another hornet's nest of fiery hatred.

Greeley pointed out that the men who had made up the once powerful Know Nothing party were violently opposed to Seward and would vote for a hound dog in preference to him.

And that wasn't all. Greeley pointed out that this "arch agitator" had been too radical, that his "bloody program" and talk of a higher law than the Constitution had frightened the border States, and that they would turn against him.

"I will bring you the men who are candidates for governor in these States," Greeley promised, "and they will confirm what I say."

He did, and the excitement was intense.

With clenched fists and blazing eyes, the gubernatorial candidates in Pennsylvania and Indiana declared that Seward's nomination meant inevitable defeat in their States, inevitable disaster.

And the Republicans felt that, to win, they must carry those States.

So, suddenly, the flood-tide that had been running toward Seward began to recede. And Lincoln's friends rushed about from delegation to delegation, trying to persuade those who were opposed to Seward to concentrate on Lincoln. Douglas was sure to be nominated by the Democrats, they said, and no man in the country was better equipped to fight Douglas than Lincoln. To him, it was an old job; he was used to it. Besides, Lincoln was born a Kentuckian, and he could win votes in the doubtful border States. Furthermore, he was the kind of candidate the Northwest wanted—a man who had fought his way up from splitting rails and breaking sod, a man who understood the common people.

When arguments like these didn't succeed, they used others. They won Indiana's delegates by promising Caleb B. Smith a place in the Cabinet, and they won Pennsylvania's fifty-six votes with the assurance that Simeon Cameron would sit at Lincoln's right hand.

On Friday morning the balloting began. Forty thousand people had poured into Chicago, eager for excitement. Ten thousand wedged into the convention hall, and thirty thousand packed the streets outside. The seething mob reached for blocks.

Seward led on the first ballot. On the second, Pennsylvania cast her fifty-two votes for Lincoln, and the break began. On the third, it was all but a stampede.

Inside the hall, ten thousand people, half crazed with excitement, leaped upon the seats, shouting, yelling, smashing their hats on one another's heads. A cannon boomed on the roof—and thirty thousand people in the streets raised a shout.

Men hugged one another and danced about wildly, weeping and laughing and shrieking.

One hundred guns at the Tremont House belched and barked their volleys of fire; a thousand bells joined in the clamor; while whistles on railway engines, on steamboats, on factories, were opened and tied open for the day.

For twenty-hour hours the excitement raged.

"No such uproar," declared the "Chicago Tribune," "has been heard on earth since the walls of Jericho fell down."

In the midst of all this rejoicing, Horace Greeley saw Thurlow Weed, the erstwhile "maker of Presidents," shedding bitter tears. At last, Greeley had his sweet revenge.

In the meantime what was happening down in Springfield? Lincoln had gone to his law office as usual that morning and tried to work on a case. Too restless to concentrate, he soon tossed the legal papers aside and went out and pitched ball for a while back of a store, then played a game or two of billiards, and finally went to the "Springfield Journal" to hear the news. The telegraph office occupied the room above. He was sitting in a big arm-chair, discussing the second ballot, when suddenly the operator burst down the stairway, crying: "Mr. Lincoln, you are nominated! You are nominated!"

Lincoln's lower lip trembled slightly, his face flushed. For a few seconds he stopped breathing.

It was the most dramatic moment of his life.

After nineteen years of desolating defeats, he had been suddenly whirled to the dizzy heights of victory.

Men rushed up and down the streets shouting the news. The mayor ordered the firing of a hundred guns.

Scores of old friends flocked about Lincoln, half laughing, half crying, shaking his hands, tossing their hats into the air, yelling in mad excitement.

"Excuse me, boys," he pleaded; "there is a little woman down on Eighth Street who will want to hear this."

And away he dashed, his coat-tails sailing behind him.

The streets of Springfield were rosy all that night with the light of bonfires fed by tar-barrels and rail fences, and the saloons never closed their doors.

It wasn't long before half of the nation was singing:

"Old Abe Lincoln came out of the wilderness,
Out of the wilderness, out of the wilderness;
Old Abe Lincoln came out of the wilderness,
Down in Illinois."

★ ★ ★

16

★ ★ ★

STEPHEN A. DOUGLAS did more than any one else to elevate Lincoln to the White House, for Douglas split the Democratic party and put three candidates in the field against Lincoln instead of one.

With the opposition hopelessly divided, Lincoln realized, early in the contest, that he would be victorious; but, nevertheless, he feared that he would not be able to carry his own precinct or his home town. A committee made a house-to-house canvass in advance, to find out how the people in Springfield were going to ballot. When Lincoln saw the result of this canvass, he was astonished: all except three of the twenty-three ministers and theological students in town were against him, and so were many of their stanchest followers. Lincoln commented bitterly: "They pretend to believe in the Bible and be God-fearing Christians; yet by their ballots they are demonstrating that they don't care whether slavery is voted up or down. But I know God cares and humanity cares, and if they don't, surely they have not read their Bibles aright."

It is surprising to discover that all of Lincoln's relatives on his father's side, and all except one on his mother's side, voted against him. Why? Because they were Democrats.

Lincoln was elected by a minority of the votes of the nation. His opponents had approximately three votes to his two. It was a sectional triumph, for of his two million votes only twenty-four thousand came from the South. A change of only one vote in twenty would have given the Northwest to Douglas and thrown the election into the House of Representatives, where the South would have won.

In nine Southern States no one cast a Republican ballot. Think of it. In all Alabama, Arkansas, Florida, Georgia, Louisiana, Mississippi, North Carolina, Tennessee, and Texas not one man voted for Abraham Lincoln. This was ominous.

To appreciate what happened immediately after Lincoln's election, we must review the story of a movement that had raged over the North like a hurricane. For thirty years a fanatical group, obsessed by a holy zeal for the destruction of slavery, had been preparing the country for war. During all that time an unbroken stream of vitriolic pamphlets and bitter books had flowed from their presses; and paid lecturers had visited every city, town, and hamlet in the North, exhibiting the tattered, filthy garments worn by slaves, displaying their chains and manacles, holding up bloodstained whips and spiked collars and other instruments of torture. Escaped slaves themselves were pressed into service and toured the country, giving inflammatory accounts of brutalities they had seen and atrocities they had endured.

In 1839 the American Anti-Slavery Society issued a booklet entitled "American Slavery As It Is—The Testimony of 1,000 Witnesses." In this pamphlet, eye-witnesses related specific instances of cruelties they had observed: slaves had had their hands plunged into boiling water, they had been branded with red-hot irons, their teeth had been knocked out, they had been stabbed with knives, their flesh had been torn by bloodhounds, they had been whipped until they died, had been burned at the stake. Shrieking mothers had had their children torn from them forever and sold in the slave-pen and on the auction-block. Women were whipped because they did not bear more children, and strong white men with big bones and large muscles were offered twenty-five dollars for cohabiting with black women, since light-colored children sold for more money, especially if they were girls.

The favorite and most flaming indictment of the Abolitionist was miscegenation. Southern men were accused of cherishing negro slavery because of their love of "unbridled licentiousness."

"The South," cried Wendell Phillips, "is one great brothel where half a million women are flogged to prostitution."

Tales of sensuality so revolting that they could not be reprinted now, were broadcast in Abolition pamphlets then. Slave-owners were accused of violating their own mulatto daughters and selling them to be the mistresses of other men.

Stephen S. Foster declared that the Methodist Church in the South had fifty thousand black female members who were forced with whips to lead immoral lives, and he declared that the sole reason why Methodist preachers of that region favored slavery was because they wanted concubines for themselves.

Lincoln himself, during his debates with Douglas, declared that in 1850 there were 405,751 mulattoes in the United States, and that nearly all had sprung from black slaves and white masters.

Because the Constitution protected the rights of slave-owners, the Abolitionists cursed it as "a covenant with death and an agreement with hell."

As a climax to all Abolition literature, the wife of a poverty-stricken professor of theology sat down at her dining-room table and wrote a book which she called "Uncle Tom's Cabin." Sobbing as she wrote, she told her story in a storm of feeling. Finally she said God was writing the story. It dramatized and made real the tragedies of slavery as nothing else had ever done. It stirred the emotions of millions of readers and achieved a greater sale and exerted a more profound influence than any other novel that has ever been written.

When Lincoln was introduced to Harriet Beecher Stowe, the author, he called her the little woman that started the big war.

And what was the result of this well-meant but fanatical campaign of overstatement waged by the Abolitionists of the North? Did it convince the Southerners that they were wrong? Far from it. The effect was such as might have been expected. The hatred stirred up by the Abolitionists did what hatred always does: it bread hatred in return. It made the South wish to part company with its insolent, meddlesome critics. Truth seldom flourishes in an atmosphere of politics or of emotion, and on both sides of the Mason and Dixon's Line tragic error had grown to its bloody blossom time.

When the "black Republicans" elected Lincoln in 1860, the Southerners were firmly convinced that slavery was doomed, and that they had to choose at once between abolition and secession. So why not secede? Didn't they have a right to?

That question had been hotly debated back and forth for half a century, and various States at one time or another had threatened to leave the Union. For example: during the War of 1812 the New England States talked very seriously of forming a separate nation; and the Connecticut Legislature passed a resolution declaring that "the state of Connecticut is a free, sovereign and independent state."

Even Lincoln himself had once believed in the right of secession. He had said during a speech in Congress: "Any people anywhere, being inclined and having the power, have the right to rise up and shake off the existing government, and form a new one that suits them better. That is a most valuable, a most sacred right—a right which we hope and believe is to liberate the world.

"Nor is the right confined to cases in which the whole people of an existing government may choose to exercise it. Any portion of such people that can, may revolutionize and make their own of so much of the territory as they inhabit."

He had said that in 1848. This, however, was 1860, and he no longer believed it. But the South did. Six weeks after Lincoln's election South Carolina passed an Ordinance of Secession. Charleston celebrated the new "Declaration of Independence" with martial music and bonfires and fireworks and dancing in the streets. Six other States followed in rapid succession; and two days before Lincoln left Springfield for Washington, Jefferson Davis was elected President of a new nation, founded upon what was called "the great truth . . . that slavery is the negro's natural and normal condition."

The outgoing administration of Buchanan, honeycombed with disloyalty, did nothing whatever to prevent all this; so Lincoln was obliged to sit helplessly in Springfield for three months, and watch the Union dissolving and the republic tottering on the verge of ruin. He saw the Confederacy buying guns and building forts and drilling soldiers; and he realized that he would have to lead a people through a civil war—bitter and bloody.

He was so distressed that he couldn't sleep at night. He lost forty pounds in weight, from worry.

Lincoln, who was superstitious, believed that coming events cast their shadow through dreams and omens. The day after his election in 1860 he went home in the afternoon and threw himself down on a haircloth sofa. Opposite him was a bureau with a swinging mirror; and, as he looked into the mirror, he saw himself reflected with one body but with two faces—one very pale. He was startled, and he got up, but the illusion vanished. He lay down again, and there was the ghost, plainer than before. The thing worried and haunted him; and he told Mrs. Lincoln about it. She was sure it was a sign that he would be elected to a second term of office, but that the death pallor of one face meant he would not live through the second term.

Lincoln himself soon came to believe very strongly that he was going to Washington to die. He received scores of letters with sketches of gibbets and stilettoes; and almost every mail brought him threats of death.

After the election, Lincoln said to a friend:

"I am worrying to know what to do with my house. I don't want to sell myself out of a home, but if I rent it, it will be pretty well used up by the time I get back."

But finally he found a man who he thought would take care of the place and keep it in repair; so Lincoln rented it to him for ninety dollars a year; and then inserted this notice in the "Springfield Journal":

> The furniture consisting of Parlor and Chamber Sets, Carpets, Sofas, Chairs, Wardrobes, Bureaus, Bedsteads, Stoves, China, Queensware, Glass, etc., at the residence on the corner of Eighth and Jackson Street is offered at private sale without reserve. For particulars apply at the premises at once.

The neighbors came and looked things over. One wanted a few chairs and a cook-stove, another asked the price of a bed.

"Take whatever you want," Lincoln probably replied, "and pay me what you think it is worth."

They paid him little enough.

Mr. L. L. Tilton, superintendent of the Great Western Railway, bought most of the furniture; and later took it with him to Chicago, where it was destroyed in the great fire of 1871.

A few pieces remained in Springfield; and years afterward a bookseller purchased as much of it as possible and took it to Washington and installed it in the rooming-house where Lincoln died. That house stands almost directly across the street from Ford's Theater, and is now the property of the United States Government—a national shrine and museum.

The second-hand chairs that Lincoln's neighbors could have bought for a dollar and a half apiece, are to-day worth more than their weight in gold and platinum. Everything that Lincoln touched intimately has now taken on value and glory. The black walnut rocking-chair in which he sat when Booth shot him, sold in 1929 for two thousand five hundred dollars. And a letter that he wrote appointing Major-General Hooker Commander-in-Chief of the Army of the Potomac recently sold at public auction for ten thousand dollars, while a collection of four hundred and eighty-five telegrams that he sent during the war, now owned by Brown University, are valued at a quarter of a million dollars. An unsigned manuscript of one of his unimportant talks was recently purchased for eighteen thousand dollars, and a copy of the Gettysburg address in Lincoln's handwriting brought hundreds of thousands.

The people of Springfield in 1861 little realized what caliber of man Lincoln was, and what he was destined to become.

For years the future great President had been walking down their streets almost every morning with a market-basket over his arm, a shawl about his neck, going to the grocery store and butcher's shop and carrying home his provisions. For years he had been going out each evening to a pasture on the edge of town and cutting out his cow from the rest of the herd and driving her home and milking her, grooming his horse, cleaning the stable, and cutting the firewood and carrying it in for the kitchen stove.

Three weeks before he left for Washington, Lincoln began the preparation of his first inaugural address. Wanting solitude and seclusion, he locked himself in an upstairs room over a general store and set to work. He owned very few books himself; but his law partner had something of a library, and Lincoln asked Herndon to bring him a copy of the Constitution, Andrew Jackson's Proclamation against Nullification, Henry Clay's great speech of 1850, and Webster's Reply to Hayne. And so amidst a lot of plunder in dingy, dusty surroundings, Lincoln wrote the famous speech ending with this beautiful plea to the Southern States:

> I am loath to close. We are not enemies but friends. We must not be enemies. Though passion may have strained, it must not break our bonds of affection. The mystic chords of memory, stretching from every battlefield and patriot's grave to every living heart and hearthstone all over this

broad land, will swell the chorus of the Union when again touched, as surely they will be, by the better angel of our nature.

Before leaving Illinois he traveled seventy miles to Charleston, in that State, to say farewell to his stepmother. He called her "Mamma," as he had always done; and she clung to him, saying between her sobs: "I didn't want you to run for President, Abe, and I didn't want to see you elected. My heart tells me that something will happen to you, and that I'll never see you again till we meet in heaven."

During those last days in Springfield, he thought often of the past and New Salem and Ann Rutledge, dreaming once again the dreams that had proved to be far beyond all earthly realities. A few days before he left for Washington he talked at length about Ann, to a New Salem pioneer who had come to Springfield to reminisce and say farewell. "I loved her deeply," Lincoln confessed, "and I think of her now very, very often."

The night before he left Springfield forever Lincoln visited his dingy law office for the last time and settled a few business details. Herndon tells us:

> After these things were all disposed of, he crossed to the opposite side of the room and threw himself down on the old office sofa, which, after many years of service, had been moved against the wall for support. He lay for some moments, his face toward the ceiling, without either of us speaking. Presently he inquired, "Billy, how long have we been together?"
>
> "Over sixteen years," I answered.
>
> "We've never had a cross word during all that time, have we?" to which I returned a vehement, "No, indeed we have not."
>
> He then recalled some incidents of his early practice and took great pleasure in delineating the ludicrous features of many a lawsuit on the circuit. . . . He gathered a bundle of books and papers he wished to take with him and started to go; but before leaving he made the strange request that the sign-board which swung on its rusty hinges at the foot of the stairway should remain. "Let it hang there undisturbed," he said, with a significant lowering of his voice. "Give our clients to understand that the election of a President makes no change in the firm of Lincoln and Herndon.

If I live I'm coming back some time, and then we'll go right on practising law as if nothing had ever happened."

He lingered for a moment as if to take a last look at the old quarters, and then passed through the door into the narrow hallway. I accompanied him downstairs. On the way he spoke of the unpleasant features surrounding the Presidential office. "I am sick of office-holding already," he complained, "and I shudder when I think of the tasks that are still ahead."

Lincoln probably was worth about ten thousand dollars at the time; but he was so short of cash then that he had to borrow money from his friends to pay for his trip to Washington.

The Lincolns spent their last week in Springfield at the Chenery House. The night before they left, their trunks and boxes were brought down to the hotel lobby and Lincoln himself roped them. Then he asked the clerk for some of the hotel cards, turned them over, and wrote on the back: "A. Lincoln, Executive Mansion, Washington, D.C.," and tacked them on his baggage.

The next morning, at half-past seven, the dilapidated old bus backed up to the hotel, and Lincoln and his family got in and jolted away to the Wabash station, where a special train was waiting to take them to Washington.

It was dark and rainy, but the station platform was crowded with a thousand or fifteen hundred of his old neighbors. They formed a line and slowly filed by Lincoln, shaking his great bony hand. Finally the ringing of the engine bell warned him that it was time to go aboard. He entered his private car by the front steps and a minute later appeared on the rear platform.

He had not intended to make a speech. He had told the newspaper reporters that it would not be necessary for them to be at the station, as he would have nothing to say. However, as he looked for the last time into the faces of his old neighbors, he felt he must say something. The words he uttered that morning in the falling rain are not to be compared with those he spoke at Gettysburg, or placed beside the sublime spiritual masterpiece that he pronounced on the occasion of his second inauguration. But this farewell speech is as beautiful as one of the Psalms of David, and it contains perhaps more of personal emotion and pathos than any other of Lincoln's addresses.

There were only two times in his life that Lincoln wept when trying to speak. This morning was one of them:

"My friends: No one, not in my situation, can appreciate my feeling of sadness at this parting. To this place, and the kindness of these people, I owe everything. Here I have lived a quarter of a century, and have passed from a young to an old man. Here my children have been born, and one is buried. I now leave, not knowing when or whether ever I may return, with a task before me greater than that which rested upon Washington. Without the assistance of that Divine Being who ever attended him, I cannot succeed. With that assistance, I cannot fail. Trusting in Him, who can go with me, and remain with you, and be everywhere for good, let us confidently hope that all will yet be well. To His care commending you as I hope in your prayers you will commend me, I bid you an affectionate farewell."

WHILE LINCOLN was en route to Washington for his inauguration, both the United States Secret Service and private detectives discovered what they believed was a plot to assassinate him as he passed through Baltimore.

In alarm Lincoln's friends pleaded with him to abandon the schedule that had been announced, and urged him to slip into Washington incognito by night.

That sounded cowardly, and Lincoln knew it would raise a storm of scoffs and sneers. He was decidedly against it. But finally, after hours of pleading, he bowed to the wishes of his trusted advisers, and prepared to make the rest of the trip secretly.

As soon as Mrs. Lincoln heard about the altered arrangements she insisted that she would go with him, and when she was told most emphatically that she must come on a later train she lost her temper and protested so loudly that she all but gave the plan away.

It had been announced that Lincoln would speak in Harrisburg, Pennsylvania, on February 22, spend the night there, and then leave the next morning for Baltimore and Washington.

He made his speech in Harrisburg according to schedule; but, instead of spending the night there, he slipped out of the back door of the hotel that evening at six and, disguised in an old threadbare overcoat and a soft wool hat such as he had never worn before, he was driven to an unlighted railway coach, and a few minutes later an engine was whirling him away to Philadelphia, and the telegraph wires in Harrisburg were cut at once so that the information would not be relayed to the would-be assassins.

At Philadelphia, his party had to wait for an hour to change trains and stations. In order to prevent recognition during that time, Lincoln and Allan Pinkerton, the famous detective, drove about the streets of the city in a darkened cab.

At 10:55, leaning on Pinkerton's arm and stooping so as not to draw attention to his height, Lincoln entered the station by a side door. He carried his head bent forward and had his old traveling shawl drawn close so that it almost covered his face. In that guise, he crossed the waiting-room and made his way to the rear section of the last sleeping-car on the train, which one of Pinkerton's aides, a woman, had had cut off from the rest of the car by a heavy curtain and reserved for her "invalid brother."

Lincoln had received scores of threatening letters, declaring that he would never live to enter the White House, and General Winfield Scott, Commander-in-Chief of the Army, feared that Lincoln would be shot during the inaugural address—and so did thousands of others.

Many people in Washington were afraid to attend the ceremony.

So old General Scott had sixty soldiers stationed under the platform at the east portico of the Capitol from which Lincoln read his inaugural address; and he had soldiers standing on guard in the Capitol behind the President, and soldiers encircling the audience in front of him. And after the ceremony, the new President stepped into a carriage and rode back through Pennsylvania Avenue under the protection of buildings covered with sharpshooters in green coats, and between rows of infantrymen with bristling bayonets.

When he finally reached the White House without a bullet in his heart, many people were surprised.

Others were disappointed.

For several years prior to 1861 the nation had been struggling under a financial depression. Suffering had been so intense that the Government had been compelled to send troops to New York City to prevent hungry mobs from breaking into the sub-Treasury.

Thousands of gaunt, desperate men were still looking for work when Lincoln was inaugurated; and they knew that the Republicans, coming into power for the first time, would dismiss all Democratic office-holders, even down to the ten-dollar-a-week clerks.

Scores of applicants were scrambling for every job; and Lincoln had not been in the White House two hours when he was overwhelmed by them. They rushed through the halls; jammed the corridors; took entire possession of the East Room; and invaded even the private parlors.

Beggars came, importuning him for the price of a lunch. One man wanted Lincoln to give him an old pair of pants.

A widow came, seeking an appointment for a man who had promised to marry her provided she could get him an office that would support a family.

Hundreds came merely to get his autograph. An Irishwoman who kept a boarding-house rushed to the White House to implore Lincoln to help her collect a board bill from a government clerk.

As soon as an office-holder became seriously ill, dozens of applicants flocked to Lincoln, asking for the appointment "in case he should die."

Every one was armed with testimonials, but of course Lincoln couldn't read a tenth of them. One day when two applicants for the same post-office thrust huge bundles of letters into his hands he simplified matters by tossing both packages unopened onto the scales, and appointed the man who had the heavier one.

Scores came to see Lincoln again and again, demanding jobs and abusing him savagely because he refused. Many were loafers without a shred of merit. One woman came asking for an appointment for her husband, admitting he was too drunk to come himself.

Their sordid selfishness, their voracious greed, appalled Lincoln. They intercepted him on his way to lunch. They rushed up to his carriage as he drove through the streets, presenting their credentials, begging for jobs. Even after Lincoln had been President for a year and the nation had been at war for ten months, the milling mob still hounded him.

"Will they never cease?" he exclaimed.

The mad onslaught of office-seekers had killed Zachary Taylor before he had been President a year and a half. The worry of it killed "Tippecanoe" Harrison in four weeks. But Lincoln had to endure the office-seekers and run a war at the same time. Finally, however, even his iron constitution all but broke under the strain. Stricken with an attack of smallpox, he said:

"Tell all the office-seekers to come at once, for now I have something I can give to all of them."

Lincoln hadn't been in the White House twenty-four hours when he was confronted with a grave and momentous problem. The garrison holding Fort Sumter, in the harbor at Charleston, South Carolina, was almost out of food. The President had to decide whether to provision the fort or surrender it to the Confederates.

His army and navy advisers said: "Don't try to send food. If you do, it will mean war."

Six of the seven members of his Cabinet said the same thing. But Lincoln knew that he couldn't evacuate Sumter without virtually recognizing secession and encouraging it, and dissolving the Union.

In his inaugural address he had declared that he had the most solemn oath "registered in heaven" to "preserve, protect, and defend" the Union. He intended to keep his oath.

So he gave the orders, and away sailed the U.S.S. *Powhatan*, carrying bacon and beans and bread for Fort Sumter. But no guns, no men, no ammunition.

When Jefferson Davis heard the news he telegraphed General Beauregard to attack Fort Sumter if he thought it necessary.

Major Anderson, in command of the fortress, sent word to General Beauregard that, if he would wait only four days, the garrison would be compelled to evacuate through starvation, for they were already living on nothing but salt pork.

Why didn't Beauregard wait?

Perhaps it was because a few of his advisers felt that "unless blood were sprinkled in the faces of the people," some of the seceding States might return to the Union.

Shooting a few Yankees would arouse enthusiasm and cement the Confederacy.

So Beauregard issued his tragic orders; and, at half-past four on the morning of April 12, a shell screamed through the air and fell hissing into the sea near the walls of the fort.

For thirty-four hours, the bombardment continued.

The Confederates turned the affair into a social event. Brave young men, gay in their new uniforms, fired their cannon to the applause of fashionable society women promenading the wharves and the Battery.

On Sunday afternoon the Union soldiers surrendered the fort and four barrels of salt pork; and, with the Stars and Stripes flying, and the band playing "Yankee Doodle," they sailed away, bound for New York.

For a week Charleston abandoned itself to joy. A *Te Deum* was sung with great pomp in the cathedral; and crowds paraded the streets, drinking and singing and carousing in tap rooms and taverns.

Judged by the loss of life, the bombardment of Sumter was nothing. Neither side lost a man. But judged by the train of events which it set in motion, few battles have been more momentous. It was the beginning of the bloodiest war the world had ever known up to that time.

★

PART THREE

★

★ ★ ★

18

★ ★ ★

LINCOLN ISSUED A CALL for seventy-five thousand men, and threw the country into a frenzy of patriotic fervor. Mass-meetings were held in thousands of halls and public squares, bands played, flags waved, orators harangued, fireworks were set off; and men, leaving the plow and the pencil, flocked to the flag.

In ten weeks, a hundred and ninety thousand recruits were drilling and marching and singing:

> "John Brown's body lies a-mouldering in the grave,
> But his soul goes marching on."

But who was to lead these troops to victory? There was one recognized military genius in the army then—and only one. His name was Robert E. Lee. He was a Southerner; but, nevertheless, Lincoln offered him the command of the Union Army. If Lee had accepted, the whole history of the war would have been vastly different. For a time he did think seriously of accepting: thought about it, read his Bible, and got down on his knees and prayed about it, and paced the floor of his bedchamber all night, trying honestly to come to a righteous decision.

He agreed with Lincoln on many things. He hated slavery as Lincoln hated it; Lee had freed his own negroes long ago. He loved the Union almost as Lincoln loved it; he believed that it was "perpetual," that secession was "revolution," that "no greater calamity" could befall the nation.

But—and this was the trouble—he was a Virginian, a proud Virginian, a Virginian who put State above Nation. For two hundred years his forebears had been mighty factors in the destiny, first of the Colony, and then of the State. His father, the famous "Light Horse Harry" Lee, had helped Washington chase the redcoats of King George; after that, he had been Governor of Virginia; and he had taught his son, Robert E., to love the State more than the Union.

So when Virginia cast her lot with the South, Lee quietly announced: "I cannot lead a hostile army against my relatives, my children and my home. I go to share the miseries of my people."

That decision probably lengthened the Civil War by two or three years.

To whom could Lincoln now turn for help and guidance? General Winfield Scott was then in command of the army. Scott was an old man. He had won a notable victory at Lundy's Lane in the War of 1812. And this was 1861. Forty-nine years later. He was weary, now, in body and mind. His youthful initiative and courage had long since perished.

Besides, he was suffering from a spinal affliction. "For more than three years," he wrote, "I have been unable to mount a horse or walk more than a few paces at a time, and that with much pain."

In addition, he now had "other and new infirmities—dropsy and vertigo."

Such was the man to whom Lincoln had to look to lead the nation to victory: a broken old soldier who ought to have been in the hospital, with a nurse and a water mattress.

Lincoln had called in April for seventy-five thousand men to serve for three months. Their enlistments would expire in July; so, in the last part of June, a great hue and cry arose for action! Action! Action!

Day after day Horace Greeley kept "The Nation's War Cry" standing in bold type at the head of the "Tribune's" editorial columns: "Forward to Richmond!"

Business was bad. The banks were afraid to extend credit. Even the Government had to pay twelve per cent for borrowed money. People were disturbed. "Now, look here," they said, "there is no use fooling any longer. Let's strike one sharp blow, capture Lee's army, and have this nasty mess over and done with once and for all."

That sounded attractive, and every one agreed.

Every one except the military authorities: they knew the army wasn't ready. But the President, bowing to public clamor, finally ordered an advance.

So, on a hot, brilliant July day, McDowell, with his "Grand Army," thirty thousand strong, marched away to attack the Confederates at Bull Run, a creek in Virginia. No American general then living had ever before commanded so large a body of men.

What an army it was! Raw. Half trained. Several of the regiments had arrived within the last ten days, and had no idea of discipline.

"With all my personal effort," said Sherman, who commanded a brigade, "I could not prevent the men from straggling for water, blackberries, and anything on the way that they fancied."

The Zouaves and Turcos in those days were regarded as mighty warriors; so many soldiers aspired to dress like them and act like them. Consequently, thousands of the troops marched away to Bull Run, that day, with their heads in scarlet turbans, their legs in red baggy breeches. They looked more like a comic-opera troupe than men marching to death.

Several silk-hatted Congressmen drove out to watch the battle, taking with them their wives and pet dogs, and baskets of sandwiches and bottles of Bordeaux.

Finally, at ten o'clock on a broiling day in late July, the first real battle of the Civil War began.

What happened?

As soon as some of the inexperienced troops saw cannonballs crashing through the trees, heard men shrieking, and saw them pitching forward on the ground with blood running out of their mouths—as soon as they saw this, the Pennsylvania regiment and the New York Battery happened to recall that their ninety-day term of enlistment had expired; and they insisted on being mustered out of service. Then and there! Quick! And, as McDowell reports, they "moved to the rear to the sound of the enemy's cannon."

The rest of the troops fought surprisingly well until about half-past four in the afternoon. Then suddenly the Confederates, throwing twenty-three hundred fresh men into the assault, took the field by storm.

From mouth to mouth ran the report, "Johnston's army has come."

A panic ensued.

Twenty-five thousand soldiers, refusing to obey orders, broke from the field in mad confusion. McDowell and scores of officers made frantic efforts to stem the rout, but it was useless.

Quickly the Confederate artillery shelled the road, already jammed with fleeing soldiers and commissariat wagons and ambulances and the carriages of silk-hatted, sightseeing Congressmen. Women screamed and fainted. Men shouted and cursed and trampled on one another, A wagon was upset on a bridge. The highway was clogged. Plunging and kicking horses were cut from wagons and ambulances and artillery pieces; and frightened men in red turbans and yellow trousers leaped upon them and dashed away, the traces trailing in the dust, the harness dragging at their heels.

They imagined that the Confederate cavalry was in close pursuit. The cry of "the cavalry! the cavalry!" convulsed them with fear.

The grand debacle had now become a terror-stricken mob.

Nothing like it had ever before been witnessed on any American battle-field.

Maddened men threw away their guns, coats, caps, belts, bayonets, and fled as if driven by some unknown fury. Some sank on the road in utter exhaustion and were crushed beneath the oncoming horses and wagons.

The day was Sunday, and the distant roar of the cannon twenty miles away reached Lincoln's ears as he sat in church. At the close of the services, he rushed to the War Department, to read the telegrams that had already begun to pour in from different parts of the field. Fragmentary and incomplete as they were, Lincoln was eager to discuss them with General Scott; so he hurried to the old general's quarters, and found him taking a nap.

General Scott awoke, yawned, rubbed his eyes; but he was so infirm he couldn't get up without help. "He had some sort of harness with a pulley arrangement attached to the ceiling of the room; and, grasping the strap, he pulled his vast bulk into an upright position and swung his feet off the lounge upon the floor."

"I don't know," he said, "how many men are in the field, where they are, how they are armed, how they are equipped, or what they are capable of doing. Nobody comes to tell me, and I am in ignorance about it."

And he was the head of all the Union armies!

The old general looked at a few telegrams that were coming in from the battle-field, told Lincoln there was nothing to worry about, complained of his aching back, and went to sleep again.

At midnight the broken army, in a riot of disorder, began to stagger across the Long Bridge and pour over the Potomac into Washington.

Tables were quickly set up on the sidewalks, wagon-loads of bread suddenly appeared from somewhere, and society women stood over wash-boilers of steaming soup and coffee, dispensing food.

McDowell, utterly exhausted, had fallen asleep under a tree while writing a despatch, his pencil still in his hand, a sentence half finished. His soldiers were too weary now to care for anything, so they threw themselves on the sidewalks and slept, inert as dead men, in the steadily falling rain—some still clutching their muskets as they slept.

Lincoln sat that night until long after dawn, listening to the stories of the newspaper correspondents and silk-hatted civilians who had witnessed the debacle.

Many public men were thrown into a panic. Horace Greeley wanted to end the war at once, on any terms. He was positive the South could never be conquered.

London bankers were so certain that the Union would be destroyed that their agent in Washington rushed to the Treasury Department on Sunday afternoon, demanding that the United States Government give security immediately for forty thousand dollars that was owing them.

He was told to come back on Monday, that the United States Government would probably still be doing business at the old stand then.

Failure and defeat were not new experiences to Lincoln. He had known them all his life; they did not crush him; his faith in the ultimate triumph of his cause remained firm, his confidence unshaken. He went among the disheartened soldiers, shaking hands with them, and saying over and over: "God bless you. God bless you." He cheered them, sat down and ate beans with them, revived their drooping spirits, and talked of brighter to-morrows.

It was to be a long war. He saw that now. So he asked Congress for a levy of four hundred thousand men. Congress raised him a hundred thousand, and authorized half a million to serve for three years.

But who could lead them? Old Scott, unable to walk, unable to get out of bed without a harness and pulley, and snoring the afternoon away during a battle? Absolutely not. He was slated for the discard.

And there now gallops into the limelight one of the most charming and disappointing generals that ever sat in a saddle.

Lincoln's troubles were not over. They were just beginning.

★ ★ ★

19

★ ★ ★

DURING THE first few weeks of the war a handsome young general named McClellan marched into West Virginia with twenty cannon and a portable printing-press, and whipped a few Confederates. His battles didn't amount to much—mere skirmishes. That was all. But they were the first victories of the North, so they seemed important. McClellan saw to that; he dashed off scores of dramatic and bombastic despatches on his portable press, proclaiming his achievements to the nation.

A few years later his absurd antics would have been laughed at; but the war was new then, people were confused and eager for some kind of leader to appear; so they took this boastful young officer at his own valuation. Congress offered him a resolution of thanks, people called him "the Young Napoleon," and after the defeat at Bull Run Lincoln brought him to Washington and made him commander of the Army of the Potomac.

He was a born leader of men. His troops would burst into applause when they saw him galloping toward them on his white charger. Besides, he was a hard and conscientious worker; he took the army that had been crushed at Bull Run, drilled it, renewed its self-confidence, and built up its morale. No one could excel him at that sort of thing; and by the time October came he had one of the largest and best-trained armies that had ever been seen in the Western world. His troops were not only trained to fight; they were eager for the fray.

Every one was crying for action—every one but McClellan.

Lincoln repeatedly urged him to strike a blow. But he wouldn't do it. He held parades and talked a lot about what he was going to do; but that was all it amounted to—talk.

He delayed, he procrastinated, he gave all manner of excuses. But go forward he would not.

Once he said he couldn't advance because the army was resting. Lincoln asked him what it had done to make it tired.

Another time—after the Battle of Antietam—an amazing thing happened. McClellan had far more men than Lee. Lee had been defeated; and had McClellan pursued him, he might have captured his army and ended the war. Lincoln kept urging him for weeks to follow Lee—urging by letter, by telegram, and by special messenger. Finally McClellan said he couldn't move because his horses were fatigued and had sore tongues!

It you ever visit New Salem, you will see a depression about a rod down the hillside from Offut's grocery where Lincoln worked as a clerk. The Clary's Grove Boys used to have their cock-fights there, and Lincoln acted as referee. For weeks Bab McNab had been boasting of a young rooster that could whip anything in Sangamon County. But when this fowl was finally put into the pit, he turned tail and refused to fight. Bab, in disgust, grabbed him and tossed him high into the air. The rooster alighted on a pile of firewood near by, then strutted and ruffled up his feathers and crowed defiantly.

"Yes, damn you!" said McNab. "You're great on dress-parade, but you are not worth a cuss in a fight."

Lincoln said that McClellan reminded him of Bab McNab's rooster.

Once, during the Peninsular Campaign, General Magruder with five thousand men held up McClellan with a hundred thousand. McClellan, afraid to attack, threw up breastworks and kept nagging Lincoln for more men, more men, more men.

"If by magic," said Lincoln, "I could reinforce McClellan with a hundred thousand men, he would go into ecstasy, thank me, and tell me he would go to Richmond to-morrow; but when to-morrow came, he would telegraph that he had certain information that the enemy had four hundred thousand men and that he could not advance without reinforcements."

"If McClellan had a million men," said Stanton, Secretary of War, "he would swear that the enemy had two million, and then sit down in the mud and yell for three million."

"The Young Napoleon" had bounded into fame with one

leap, and it had gone to his head like champagne. His egotism was boundless. He described Lincoln and his Cabinet as "hounds" . . . "wretches" . . . "some of the greatest geese I have ever seen."

He was positively insulting to Lincoln; and when the President came to see him, McClellan kept him waiting for half an hour in the anteroom.

Once the general got home at eleven o'clock at night and his servant informed him that Lincoln had been waiting there for hours to see him. McClellan passed the door of the room where the President sat, ignored him, went on upstairs, and sent down word that he had gone to bed.

The newspapers played up incidents like these, and they became the gossip and scandal of Washington. With tears rolling down her cheeks, Mrs. Lincoln implored the President to remove "that awful wind-bag," as she called him.

"Mother," he replied, "I know he doesn't do right, but I mustn't consider my feelings at a time like this. I am willing to hold McClellan's hat, if he will only bring us victories."

The summer drifted into autumn; autumn passed into winter; spring was almost at hand; and still McClellan did nothing but drill men and have dress-parades, and talk.

The nation was aroused, and Lincoln was being condemned and criticized on all sides for McClellan's inaction.

"Your delay is ruining us," cried Lincoln, as he issued an official order for an advance.

McClellan had to move now or resign. So he rushed to Harper's Ferry, ordering his troops to follow immediately. He planned to invade Virginia from that point, after bridging the Potomac with boats which were to be brought through the Chesapeake and Ohio Canal. But, at the last moment, the whole project had to be abandoned because the boats were six inches too wide to float through the canal locks.

When McClellan told Lincoln of this fiasco and said that the pontoons were not ready, the patient, long-suffering President lost his temper at last; and, lapsing into the phraseology of the hay-fields of Pigeon Creek Valley, Indiana, he demanded, *"Why, in the hell, ain't they ready?"*

The nation was asking the same question in about the same tone.

At last, in April, "the Young Napoleon" made a grand speech

to his soldiers, as the older Napoleon used to do, and then started off with one hundred and twenty thousand men singing "The Girl I Left Behind Me."

The war had been going on for a year. McClellan boasted that he was going to clean up the whole thing now, at once, and let the boys get home in time to plant a little late corn and millet.

Incredible as it seems, Lincoln and Stanton were so optimistic that they wired the governors of the various States to accept no more volunteers, to close the recruiting-places, and to sell the public property belonging to these organizations.

One of the military maxims of Frederick the Great was: "Know the man you are fighting." Lee and Stonewall Jackson appreciated full well the kind of a weak-kneed Napoleon they had to deal with—a timid, cautious, whining Napoleon who was never on the battle-field, because he couldn't endure the sight of blood.

So Lee let him spend three months crawling up to Richmond. McClellan got so close that his men could hear the clocks in the church towers striking the hour.

Then the inspired Lee crashed upon him in a series of terrific onslaughts, and, in seven days, forced him back to the shelter of his gunboats and killed fifteen thousand of his men.

Thus the "en grande affair," as McClellan called it, ended in one of the bloodiest failures of the war.

But, as usual, McClellan blamed it all on "those traitors in Washington." The old story: they hadn't sent him enough men. Their "cowardice and folly" made his "blood boil." He hated Lincoln and the Cabinet, now, more than he despised the Confederates. He denounced their actions as "the most infamous thing history has ever recorded."

McClellan had more troops than his enemies—usually far more. He was never able to use at one time all that he then possessed. But he kept on demanding more. More. He asked for an additional ten thousand, then for fifty thousand, finally for a hundred thousand. They were not to be had. He knew it, and Lincoln knew that he knew it. Lincoln told him his demands were "simply absurd."

McClellan's telegrams to Stanton and the President were fiery and insulting. They sounded like the ravings of a madman. They accused Lincoln and Stanton of doing their best to destroy his army. They made charges so grave that the telegraph operator refused to deliver them.

The nation was appalled, Wall Street was seized with panic, the country was submerged in gloom.

Lincoln grew thin and haggard. "I am as nearly inconsolable," he said, "as one can be and live."

McClellan's father-in-law and chief of staff, P. B. Marcy, said there was nothing to do now but capitulate.

When Lincoln heard this, he flushed with anger, sent for Marcy, and said:

"General, I understand you have used the word 'capitulate.' That is a word not to be used in connection with our army."

★ ★ ★

20

★ ★ ★

LINCOLN HAD LEARNED, back in New Salem, that it was easy to rent a building and stock it with groceries; but to make it pay required qualities which neither he nor his drunken partner possessed.

He was destined to discover, through years of heartbreak and bloodshed, that it was easy to get a half million soldiers who were willing to die, and a hundred million dollars to equip them with rifles and bullets and blankets; but to win victories required a kind of leadership which it was almost impossible to find.

"How much in military matters," exclaimed Lincoln, "depends on one master mind!"

So, time and again, he went down on his knees, asking the Almighty to send him a Robert E. Lee or a Joseph E. Johnston or a Stonewall Jackson.

"Jackson," he said, "is a brave, honest, Presbyterian soldier. If we only had such a man to lead the armies of the North, the country would not be appalled with so many disasters."

But where in all the Union forces was another Stonewall Jackson to be found? Nobody knew. Edmund Clarence Stedman published a famous poem every verse of which ended with the plea, "Abraham Lincoln, give us a Man."

It was more than the refrain of a poem. It was the cry of a bleeding and distraught nation.

The President wept as he read it.

For two years he tried to find the leader for whom the

nation was crying. He would give the army to one general who would lead it to futile slaughter, and set ten or thirty or forty thousand widows and orphans weeping and wailing throughout the land. Then this discredited commander would be relieved; and another, equally inept, would try his hand and get ten thousand more slaughtered; and Lincoln, clad in dressing-gown and carpet-slippers, would pace the floor all night as the reports came in, crying over and over:

"My God! What will the country say? My God! What will the country say?"

Then another general would assume command, and the futile slaughter would go on.

Some military critics now hold that McClellan, with all his astounding faults and amazing incapacity, was probably the best commander the Army of the Potomac ever had. So imagine, if you can, what the others must have been!

After McClellan's failure, Lincoln tried John Pope. Pope had done splendid work out in Missouri, had captured an island in the Mississippi and several thousand men.

He was like McClellan in two ways: he was handsome, and he was boastful. He declared that his headquarters was "in the saddle"; and he issued so many bombastic announcements that he was soon called "Proclamation Pope."

"I have come to you from the West, where we have always seen the backs of our enemies." With that blunt, tactless sentence, he opened his first address to the army. He then proceeded to rebuke the troops for their inaction in the East, and insinuated that they were infernal cowards; and ended by boasting of the military miracles he would perform.

This proclamation made the new commander about as popular as a diamond-backed rattlesnake in dog-days: officers and men alike detested him.

McClellan's hatred for him was intense. Pope had come to take his place. Nobody realized that better than did McClellan—he was already writing for a position in New York—and he was consumed with jealousy, was bitter with envy and resentment.

Pope led the army into Virginia; a great battle was imminent; he needed every man he could get; so Lincoln showered McClellan with telegrams, ordering him to rush his men to Pope's aid with all possible celerity.

But did McClellan obey? He did not. He argued, he delayed,

he protested, he telegraphed excuses, he recalled corps that he had sent ahead, and he "exhausted all the resources of a diabolical ingenuity in order to keep Pope from receiving reinforcements." "Let Mr. Pope," said he, contemptuously, "get out of his own scrape."

Even after he heard the roar of the Confederate artillery, he still managed to keep thirty thousand of his troops from going to the aid of his obnoxious rival.

So Lee overwhelmed Pope's army on the old battle-field of Bull Run. The slaughter was terrible. The Federal soldiers again fled in a panic.

It was the story of the first Bull Run over again: once more a bloody and beaten mob poured into Washington.

Lee pursued them with his victorious troops. And even Lincoln believed the capital was lost. Gunboats were ordered up the river, and all the clerks in Washington—civilian and government alike—were called to arms to defend the city.

Stanton, Secretary of War, in a wild panic, telegraphed the governors of half a dozen States, imploring them to send all their militia and volunteer forces by special trains.

Saloons were closed, church bells tolled; men fell on their knees, beseeching Almighty God to save the city.

The old people and the women and children fled in terror. The streets resounded with the hoofs of hurrying horses, with the rattle of carriages dashing away to Maryland.

Stanton, preparing to transfer the Government to New York, ordered the arsenal stripped and all its supplies shipped North.

Chase, Secretary of the Treasury, ordered the nation's silver and gold transferred in feverish haste to the sub-Treasury in Wall Street.

Lincoln, weary and discouraged, exclaimed with a mingled groan and sigh:

"What shall I do? . . . What shall I do? . . . The bottom is out of the tub, the bottom is out of the tub."

People believed that McClellan, in order to get revenge, had longed to see "Mr. Pope" defeated and his army crushed.

Even Lincoln had already called him to the White House and told him that people were accusing him of being a traitor, of wanting to see Washington captured and the South triumphant.

Stanton stormed about in a rage, his face fiery with indignation and hatred. Those who saw him said that if McClellan had walked into the war-office then, Stanton would have rushed at him and knocked him down.

Chase was even more bitter. He didn't want to hit McClellan. He said the man ought to be shot.

And the pious Chase wasn't speaking figuratively. Neither was he exaggerating. He literally wanted McClellan blindfolded, backed up against a stone wall, and a dozen bullets sent crashing through his heart.

But Lincoln, with his understanding nature and Christ-like spirit, condemned no one. True, Pope had failed, but hadn't he done his best? Lincoln, himself, had met defeat too often to blame any one else for failure.

So he sent Pope out to the Northwest to subdue an uprising of Sioux Indians, and gave the army back to McClellan. Why? Because, Lincoln said: "There is no man in the army who can lick these troops of ours into shape half as well as he. . . . If he can't fight, himself, he excels in making others ready to fight." The President knew that he would be condemned for restoring "little Mac" to command. And he was—bitterly. Even by his Cabinet. Stanton and Chase actually declared that they would rather have Washington captured by Lee than to see the traitorous and contemptible McClellan given command of the army again.

Lincoln was so hurt at their violent opposition that he said he would resign if the Cabinet wished it.

A few months later, after the Battle of Antietam, McClellan absolutely refused to obey Lincoln's orders to follow Lee and attack him, so the army was taken away from him again; and his military career was ended forever.

The Army of the Potomac must have another leader. But who was he? Where was he? No one knew.

In desperation, Lincoln offered the command to Burnside. He wasn't fit for it, and he knew it. He refused it twice; and, when it was forced upon him, he wept. Then he took the army and made a rash attack on Lee's fortifications at Fredericksburg, and lost thirteen thousand men. Men uselessly butchered, for there wasn't the faintest hope of success.

Officers as well as privates began to desert in large numbers.

So Burnside, in turn, was relieved, and the army given to another braggart, "Fighting Joe" Hooker.

"May God have mercy on Lee," he vaunted, "for I shall not."

He led what he called "the finest army on the planet" against Lee. He had twice as many men as the Confederates, but Lee hurled him back across the river at Chancellorsville and destroyed seventeen thousand of his troops.

It was one of the most disastrous defeats of the war.

It occurred in May, 1863; and the President's secretary records that he heard the tramp of Lincoln's feet during all the terrible hours of sleepless nights as he paced up and down his room, crying, "Lost! Lost! All is lost!" Finally, however, he went down to Fredericksburg to cheer up "Fighting Joe" and encourage the army.

Lincoln was denounced bitterly for all this futile slaughter; and gloom and discouragement settled over the nation.

And quickly on top of these military sorrows, came a domestic tragedy. Lincoln was inordinately fond of his two little sons, Tad and Willie. He often stole away, on a summer evening, to play "town ball" with them, his coat-tails flying out behind him as he ran from base to base. Sometimes, he would shoot marbles with them all the way from the White House to the war-office. At night he loved to get down on the floor and roll and romp with them. On bright, warm days he would sometimes go out back of the White House and play with the boys and their two goats.

Tad and Willie kept the White House in an uproar, organizing minstrel shows, putting the servants through military drill, running in and out among the office-seekers. If they took a fancy to a certain applicant, they would see that he got in to see "Old Abe" immediately. If they couldn't get him in the front way, they knew of back entrances.

With as little respect for ceremony and precedent as their father had, they dashed in and interrupted a Cabinet meeting once to inform the President that the cat in the basement had just had kittens.

On another occasion the stern Salmon P. Chase was irritated and disgusted because Tad climbed all over his father and finally perched on his shoulder and sat astride of his neck while Chase was discussing the grave financial situation that confronted the country.

Some one gave Willie a pony. He insisted on riding it in all kinds of winter weather; so he got wet and chilled and came down with a severe cold. Soon it had become a serious fever. Night after night Lincoln sat for hours by his bedside; and when the little fellow passed away, his father, choking with sobs, cried:

"My poor boy! My poor boy! He was too good for this earth. God has called him home. It is hard, hard to have him die."

Mrs. Keckley, who was in the room at the time, says:

> He buried his head in his hands, and his tall frame was convulsed with emotion. . . . The pale face of her dead boy threw Mrs. Lincoln into convulsions. She was so completely overwhelmed with sorrow she did not attend the funeral.

After Willie's death Mrs. Lincoln could not bear to look upon his picture. Mrs. Keckley tells us:

> She could not bear the sight of anything he loved, not even a flower. Costly bouquets were presented to her, but she turned from them with a shudder, and either placed them in a room where she could not see them, or threw them out of the window. She gave away all of Willie's toys . . . and, after his death, she never again crossed the threshold of the Guests' Room in which he died or the Green Room in which he was embalmed.

In a frenzy of grief Mrs. Lincoln called in a so-called spiritualist who masqueraded under the title of "Lord Colchester." This unmitigated impostor was exposed later and ordered out of town under a threat of imprisonment. But Mrs. Lincoln, in her distress, received "Lord Colchester" in the White House; and there, in a darkened room, she was persuaded that the scratching on the wainscoting, the tapping on the wall, and the rapping of the table, were loving messages from her lost boy.

She wept as she received them.

Lincoln, prostrate with grief, sank into a listless despair. He could hardly discharge his public duties. Letters, telegrams lay on his desk unanswered. His physician feared that he might never rally, that he might succumb entirely to his desolation.

The President would sometimes sit and read aloud for hours, with only his secretary or his aide for an audience. Generally it was Shakspere he read. One day he was reading "King John" to his aide, and when he came to the passage in which Constance bewails her lost boy, Lincoln closed the book, and repeated these words from memory:

> And, father cardinal, I have heard you say
> That we shall see and know our friends in heaven:
> If that be true, I shall see my boy again.

"Colonel, did you ever dream of a lost friend," the President asked, "and feel that you were holding sweet communion with him, and yet have a sad consciousness that it was not a reality? I often dream of my boy Willie like that." And dropping his head on the table, Lincoln sobbed aloud.

WHEN LINCOLN turned to his Cabinet, he found there the same quarrels and jealousy that existed in the army.

Seward, Secretary of State, regarded himself as the "Premier," snubbed the rest of the Cabinet, meddled in their affairs, and aroused deep resentment.

Chase, Secretary of the Treasury, despised Seward; detested General McClellan; hated Stanton, Secretary of War; and loathed Blair, the Postmaster-General.

Blair, in turn, went around "kicking over beehives," as Lincoln put it, and boasting that when he "went in for a fight" he "went in for a funeral." He denounced Seward as "an unprincipled liar," and refused to have any dealings with him whatever; and as for Stanton and Chase, he wouldn't condescend even to speak to those scoundrels—not even at a Cabinet meeting.

Blair went in for so many fights that finally he went in for his own funeral—as far as politics were concerned. The hatred that he aroused was so fiery and widespread that Lincoln had to ask him to resign.

There was hatred everywhere in the Cabinet.

The Vice-President, Hannibal Hamlin, wouldn't speak to Gideon Welles, Secretary of the Navy; and Welles, topped with an elaborate wig and decorated with a vast growth of white whiskers, kept a diary, and from almost every page of it, he "hurls the shafts of his ridicule and contempt" at well-nigh all his colleagues.

Welles especially detested Grant, Seward, and Stanton.

And as for the violent, insolent Stanton, he was the most prodigious hater of all. He despised Chase, Welles, Blair, Mrs. Lincoln, and apparently almost every one else in creation.

"He cared nothing for the feeling of others," wrote Grant, "and it gave him more pleasure to refuse a request than to grant it."

Sherman's hatred for the man was so fierce that he humiliated Stanton on a reviewing-stand before a vast audience, and rejoiced about it ten years later as he wrote his Memoirs.

"As I approached Mr. Stanton," says Sherman, "he offered me his hand, but I declined it publicly, and the fact was universally noticed."

Few men who ever lived have been more savagely detested than Stanton.

Almost every man in the Cabinet considered himself superior to Lincoln.

After all, who was this crude, awkward, story-telling Westerner they were supposed to serve under?

A political accident, a "dark horse" that had got in by chance and crowded them out.

Bates, the Attorney-General, had entertained high hopes of being nominated for President, himself, in 1860; and he wrote in his diary that the Republicans made a "fatal blunder" in nominating Lincoln, a man who "lacks will and purpose," and "has not the power to command."

Chase, too, had hoped to be nominated instead of Lincoln; and, to the end of his life, he regarded Lincoln with "a sort of benevolent contempt."

Seward also was bitter and resentful. "Disappointment? You speak to me of disappointment," he once exclaimed to a friend as he paced the floor, "to me who was justly entitled to the Republican nomination for the Presidency and who had to stand aside and see it given to a little Illinois lawyer!

"You speak to me of disappointment!"

Seward knew that if it hadn't been for Horace Greeley, he himself would have been President. He knew how to run things, he had had twenty years of experience in handling the vast affairs of state.

But what had Lincoln ever run? Nothing except a log-cabin

grocery store in New Salem, and he had "run that in the ground."

Oh, yes, and he had had a post-office once, which he carried around in his hat.

That was the extent of the executive experience of this "prairie politician."

And now here he sat, blundering and confused, in the White House, letting things drift, doing nothing, while the country was on a greased chute headed straight for disaster.

Seward believed—and thousands of others believed—that he had been made Secretary of State in order to rule the nation, that Lincoln was to be a mere figurehead. People called Seward the Prime Minister. He liked it. He believed that the salvation of the United States rested with him and him alone.

"I will try," he said when accepting his appointment, "to save freedom and my country."

Before Lincoln had been in office five weeks Seward sent him a memorandum that was presumptuous. Amazing. It was more than that. It was positively insulting. Never before in the history of the nation had a Cabinet member sent such an impudent, arrogant document to a President.

"We are at the end of a month's administration," Seward began, "and yet without a policy either domestic or foreign." Then with a calm assumption of superior wisdom, he proceeded to criticize this ex-grocery, store keeper from New Salem and inform him how the Government ought to be run.

He ended by brazenly suggesting that from now on Lincoln ought to sit in the background where he belonged, and let the suave Seward assume control and prevent the country from going to hell.

One of Seward's suggestions was so wild and erratic as to stun Lincoln. Seward didn't like the way France and Spain had been carrying on lately in Mexico. So he proposed to call them to account. Yes, and Great Britain and Russia, too. And if "satisfactory explanations are not received"—what do you suppose he intended to do?

Declare war. Yes. One war wasn't enough for this statesman. He was going to have a nice little assortment of wars going full blast at the same time.

He did prepare an arrogant note which he proposed sending to England—a note bristling with warnings, threats, and insults.

If Lincoln hadn't deleted the worst passages and toned the others down, it might have caused war.

Seward took a pinch of snuff and declared that he would love to see a European power interfere in favor of South Carolina, for then the North would "pitch into that power," and all the Southern States would help fight the foreign foe.

And it very nearly became necessary to fight England. A Northern gunboat held up a British mail-steamer on the high seas, took off two Confederate commissioners destined for England and France, and lodged them behind prison bars in Boston.

England began preparing for war, shipped thousands of troops across the Atlantic, landed them in Canada, and was ready to attack the North.

Although Lincoln admitted it was "the bitterest pill he had ever swallowed," nevertheless he had to surrender the Confederate commissioners and apologize.

Lincoln was utterly astounded by some of Seward's wild ideas. From the outset Lincoln had keenly realized that he, himself, was inexperienced in handling the vast and cruel responsibilities that confronted him. He needed help—and wisdom, and guidance. He had appointed Seward hoping to get just that. And see what had happened!

All Washington was talking about Seward's running the administration. It touched Mrs. Lincoln's pride, and aroused her boiling wrath. With fire in her eye, she urged her humble husband to assert himself.

"I may not rule myself," Lincoln assured her, "but certainly Seward shall not. The only ruler I have is my conscience and my God and these men will have to learn that yet."

The time came when all of them did.

Salmon P. Chase was the Chesterfield of the Cabinet: strikingly handsome, six feet two inches tall, looking the part of a man born to rule, cultured, a classical scholar, master of three languages, and father of one of the most charming and popular hostesses in Washington society. Frankly, he was shocked to see a man in the White House who didn't know how to order a dinner.

Chase was pious, very pious: he attended church three times on Sunday, quoted the Psalms in his bathtub, and put the motto "In God We Trust" on our national coins. Reading his

Bible and a book of sermons every night before retiring, he was utterly unable to comprehend a President who took to bed with him a volume of Artemus Ward or Petroleum Nasby.

Lincoln's flair for humor, at almost all times and under nearly all circumstances, irritated and annoyed Chase.

One day an old crony of Lincoln's from Illinois called at the White House. The doorkeeper, looking him over with a critical eye, announced that the President couldn't be seen, that a Cabinet meeting was in session.

"That don't make no difference," the caller protested. "You just tell Abe that Orlando Kellogg is here and wants to tell him the story of the stuttering justice. He'll see me."

Lincoln ordered him shown in at once, and greeted him with a fervent handshake. Turning to the Cabinet, the President said:

"Gentlemen: This is my old friend, Orlando Kellogg, and he wants to tell us the story of the stuttering justice. It is a very good story, so let's lay all business aside now."

So grave statesmen and the affairs of the nation waited while Orlando told his yarn and Lincoln had his loud guffaw.

Chase was disgusted. He feared for the future of the nation. He complained that Lincoln "was making a joke out of the war," that he was hurrying the country on to "the abyss of bankruptcy and ruin."

Chase was as jealous as a member of a high-school sorority. He had expected to be made Secretary of State. Why hadn't he? Why had he been snubbed? Why had the post of honor gone to the haughty Seward? Why had he been made a mere Secretary of the Treasury? He was bitter and resentful.

He had to play third fiddle now. Yes, but he would show them; 1864 was coming. There would be another election then, and he was determined to occupy the White House himself after that. He thought of little else now. He threw his whole heart and soul into what Lincoln called "Chase's mad hunt for the Presidency."

To Lincoln's face, he pretended to be his friend. But the moment he was out of sight and out of hearing, Chase was the President's ceaseless, bitter, and sneaking foe. Lincoln was frequently compelled to make decisions that offended influential people. When he did, Chase hurried to the disgruntled victim, sympathized with him, assured him that he was right, whipped up his resentment toward Lincoln, and persuaded him that if

Salmon P. Chase had been running things he would have been treated fairly.

"Chase is like the blue-bottle fly," said Lincoln; "he lays his eggs in every rotten place he can find."

For months Lincoln knew all of this; but with a magnanimous disregard of his own rights, he said:

"Chase is a very able man, but on the subject of the Presidency, I think he is a little insane. He has not behaved very well lately, and people say to me, 'Now is the time to crush him out.' Well, I'm not in favor of crushing anybody out. If there is anything that a man can do and do it well, I say, let him do it. So I am determined, so long as he does his duty as head of the Treasury Department, to shut my eyes to his attack of the White House fever."

But the situation grew steadily worse. When things didn't go Chase's way, he sent in his resignation. He did this five times, and Lincoln went to him and praised him and persuaded him to resume his duties. But finally even the long-suffering Lincoln had enough of it. There had now developed such ill feeling between them that it was unpleasant for them to meet each other. So the next time, the President took Chase at his word and accepted his resignation.

Chase was amazed. His bluff had been called.

The Senate Committee on Finance hurried to the White House in a body. They protested. Chase's going would be a misfortune, a calamity. Lincoln listened, and let them talk themselves out. He then related his painful experiences with Chase; said that Chase always wanted to rule, and resented his (Lincoln's) authority.

"He is either determined to annoy me," said Lincoln, "or that I shall pat him on the shoulder and coax him to stay. I don't think I ought to do it. I will take him at his word. His usefulness as a Cabinet officer is at an end. I will no longer continue the association. I am willing, if necessary, to resign the office of President. I would rather go back to a farm in Illinois and earn my bread with a plow and an ox than to endure any longer the state I have been in."

But what was Lincoln's estimate of the man who had humiliated and insulted him? "Of all the great men I have ever known, Chase is equal to about one and a half of the best of them."

Despite all the ill feeling that had been stirred up, Lincoln then performed one of the most beautiful and magnanimous acts of his career. He conferred upon Chase one of the highest honors a President of the United States can bestow: he made him Chief Justice of the United States Supreme Court.

Chase, however, was a docile kitten in comparison with the stormy Stanton. Short, heavy-set, with the build of a bull, Stanton had something of that animal's fierceness and ferocity.

All his life he had been rash and erratic. His father, a physician, hung a human skeleton in the barn where the boy played, hoping that he too would become a doctor. The young Stanton lectured to his playmates about the skeleton, Moses, hell fire, and the flood; and then went off to Columbus, Ohio, and became a clerk in a book-store. He boarded in a private family, and one morning shortly after he left the house, the daughter of the family fell ill with cholera, and was dead and in her grave when Stanton came home for supper that night.

He refused to believe it.

Fearing that she had been buried alive, he hurried to the cemetery, found a spade, and worked furiously for hours, digging up her body.

Years later, driven to despair by the death of his own daughter, Lucy, he had her body exhumed after she had been buried thirteen months, and kept her corpse in his bedroom for more than a year.

When Mrs. Stanton died, he put her nightcap and nightgown beside him in bed each night and wept over them.

He was a strange man. Some people said that he was half crazy.

Lincoln and Stanton had first met during the trial of a patent case in which they, together with George Harding of Philadelphia, had been retained as counsel for the defendant. Lincoln had studied the case minutely, had prepared with extraordinary care and industry, and wanted to speak. But Stanton and Harding were ashamed of him; they brushed him aside with contempt, humiliated him, and refused to let him say a word at the trial.

Lincoln gave them a copy of his speech, but they were sure it was "trash" and didn't bother to look at it.

They wouldn't walk with Lincoln to and from the courthouse; they wouldn't invite him to their rooms; they wouldn't even sit at a table and eat with him. They treated him as a social outcast.

Stanton said—and Lincoln heard him say it:

"I will not associate with such a damned, gawky, long-armed ape as that. If I can't have a man who is a gentleman in appearance with me in the case, I will abandon it."

"I have never before been so brutally treated as by that man Stanton," Lincoln said. He returned home, mortified, sunk once more in terrible melancholy.

When Lincoln became President, Stanton's contempt and disgust for him deepened and increased. He called him "a painful imbecile," declared that he was utterly incapable of running the Government, and that he ought to be ousted by a military dictator. Stanton repeatedly remarked that Du Chaillu was a fool to run off to Africa, looking for a gorilla, when the original gorilla was, at that moment, sitting in the White House scratching himself.

In his letters to Buchanan, Stanton abused the President in language so violent that it can't be put into print.

After Lincoln had been in office ten months, a national scandal reverberated throughout the land. The Government was being robbed! Millions lost! Profiteers! Dishonest war contracts! And so on.

In addition to that, Lincoln and Simon Cameron, Secretary of War, differed sharply on the question of arming slaves.

Lincoln asked Cameron to resign. He must have a new man to run the War Department. Lincoln knew that the future of the nation might depend upon his choice. He also knew precisely the man he needed. So Lincoln said to a friend:

"I have made up my mind to sit down on all my pride—it may be a portion of my self-respect—and appoint Stanton Secretary of War."

That proved to be one of the wisest appointments Lincoln ever made.

Stanton stood at his desk in the war-office, a regular tornado in trousers, surrounded by clerks trembling like Eastern slaves before their pasha. Working day and night, refusing to go home, eating and sleeping in the war-office, he was filled with wrath and indignation by the loafing, swaggering, incompetent officers that infested the army.

And he fired them right and left and backward and forward.

Cursing and swearing, he insulted meddlesome Congressmen. He waged a fierce and relentless war on dishonest contractors; ignored and violated the Constitution; arrested even generals, clapped them into prison and kept them there for months without trial. He lectured McClellan as if he were drilling a regiment, declared that he must fight. He swore that "the champagne and oysters on the Potomac must stop"; seized all the railroads; commandeered all the telegraph lines, made Lincoln send and receive his telegrams through the war-office; assumed command of all the armies, and wouldn't let even an order from Grant pass through the adjutant-general's office without his approval.

For years Stanton had been racked with head pains, had suffered from asthma and indigestion.

However, he was driven like a dynamo by one absorbing passion: to hack and stab and shoot until the South came back into the Union.

Lincoln could endure anything to achieve that goal.

One day a Congressman persuaded the President to give him an order transferring certain regiments. Rushing to the war-office with the order, he put it on Stanton's desk; and Stanton said very sharply that he would do no such thing.

"But," the politician protested, "you forget I have an order here from the President."

"If the President gave you such an order," Stanton retorted, "he is a damned fool."

The Congressman rushed back to Lincoln, expecting to see him rise up in wrath and dismiss the Secretary of War.

But Lincoln listened to the story, and said with a twinkle in his eye: "If Stanton said I was a damned fool, then I must be, for he is nearly always right. I'll just step over and see him myself."

He did, and Stanton convinced him that his order was wrong and Lincoln withdrew it.

Realizing that Stanton bitterly resented interference, Lincoln usually let him have his way.

"I cannot add to Mr. Stanton's troubles," he said. "His position is the most difficult in the world. Thousands in the army blame him because they are not promoted, and other thousands blame him because they are not appointed. The pressure upon him is immeasurable and unending. He is the rock on the beach of our national ocean against which the breakers dash and roar, dash and roar without ceasing. He fights back the angry waters and prevents them from undermining and overwhelming the land. I do not see how he survives, why he is not crushed and torn to pieces. Without him, I should be destroyed."

Occasionally, however, the President "put his foot down," as he called it; and then—look out. If "Old Mars" said then that he wouldn't do a thing, Lincoln would reply very quietly: "I reckon, Mr. Secretary, you'll *have* to do it."

And done it was.

On one occasion he wrote an order saying: "Without an *if* or an *and* or *but,* let Colonel Elliott W. Rice be made Brigadier-General in the United States army—Abraham Lincoln."

On another occasion he wrote Stanton to appoint a certain man "regardless of whether he knows the color of Julius Cæsar's hair or not."

In the end Stanton and Seward and most of those who began by reviling and scorning Abraham Lincoln learned to revere him.

When Lincoln lay dying in a rooming-house across the street from Ford's Theater, the iron Stanton, who had once denounced him as "a painful imbecile," said, "There lies the most perfect ruler of men the world has ever seen."

John Hay, one of Lincoln's secretaries, has graphically described Lincoln's manner of working in the White House:

> He was extremely unmethodical. It was a four years' struggle on Nicolay's part and mine to get him to adopt some systematic rules. He would break through every regulation as fast as it was made. Anything that kept the people themselves away from him, he disapproved, although they nearly annoyed the life out of him by unreasonable complaints and requests.
>
> He wrote very few letters, and did not read one in fifty that he received. At first we tried to bring them to his notice, but at last he gave the whole thing over to me, and signed, without reading them, the letters I wrote in his name.
>
> He wrote perhaps half a dozen a week himself—not more.
>
> When the President had any rather delicate matter to manage at a distance from Washington, he rarely wrote but sent Nicolay or me.
>
> He went to bed ordinarily from ten to eleven o'clock . . .

and rose early. When he lived in the country at the Soldiers' Home, he would be up and dressed, eat his breakfast (which was extremely frugal, an egg, a piece of toast, coffee, etc.) and ride into Washington all before eight o'clock. In the winter, at the White House, he was not quite so early. He did not sleep well, but spent a good while in bed. . . .

At noon he took a biscuit, a glass of milk in winter, some fruit or grapes in summer. . . . He was abstemious—ate less than any man I know.

He drank nothing but water, not from principle, but because he did not like wine or spirits. . . .

Sometimes he would run away to a lecture or concert or theater for the sake of a little rest. . . .

He read very little. He scarcely ever looked into a newspaper unless I called his attention to an article on some special subject. He frequently said, "I know more about it than any of them." It is absurd to call him a modest man. No great man was ever modest.

ASK the average American citizen to-day why the Civil War was fought; and the chances are that he will reply, "To free the slaves."

Was it?

Let's see. Here is a sentence taken from Lincoln's first inaugural address: "I have no purpose, directly or indirectly, to interfere with the institution of slavery in the States where it now exists. I believe I have no lawful right to do so, and I have no inclination to do so."

The fact is that the cannon had been booming and the wounded groaning for almost eighteen months before Lincoln issued the Emancipation Proclamation. During all that time the radicals and the Abolitionists had urged him to act at once, storming at him through the press and denouncing him from the public platform.

Once a delegation of Chicago ministers appeared at the White House with what they declared was a direct command from Almighty God to free the slaves immediately. Lincoln told them that he imagined that if the Almighty had any advice to offer He would come direct to headquarters with it, instead of sending it around via Chicago.

Finally Horace Greeley, irritated by Lincoln's procrastination and inaction, attacked the President in an article entitled, "The Prayer of Twenty Millions." Two columns bristling with bitter complaints.

Lincoln's answer to Greeley is one of the classics of the war —clear, terse, and vigorous. He closed his reply with these memorable words:

> My paramount object in this struggle is to save the Union, and is not either to save or destroy slavery. If I could save the Union without freeing any slave, I would do it; and if I could save it by freeing all the slaves, I would do it; and if I could save it by freeing some and leaving others alone, I would also do that. What I do about slavery and the colored race, I do because I believe it helps to save the Union; and what I forbear, I forbear because I do not believe it would help to save the Union. I shall do less whenever I shall believe what I am doing hurts the cause, and I shall do more whenever I shall believe doing more will help the cause. I shall try to correct errors when shown to be errors, and I shall adopt new views so fast as they shall appear to be true views.
>
> I have here stated my purpose according to my view of official duty; and I intend no modification of my oft-expressed personal wish that all men everywhere could be free.

Lincoln believed that if he saved the Union and kept slavery from spreading, slavery would, in due time, die a natural death. But if the Union were destroyed, it might persist for centuries.

Four slave States had remained with the North, and Lincoln realized that if he issued his Emancipation Proclamation too early in the conflict he would drive them into the Confederacy, strengthen the South, and perhaps destroy the Union forever. There was a saying at the time that "Lincoln would like to have God Almighty on his side; but he must have Kentucky."

So he bided his time, and moved cautiously.

He himself had married into a slave-owning, border-State family. Part of the money that his wife received upon the settlement of her father's estate had come from the sale of slaves. And the only really intimate friend that he ever had—Joshua Speed—was a member of a slave-owning family. Lincoln sympathized with the Southern point of view. Besides, he had the attorney's traditional respect for the Constitution and for law and property. He wanted to work no hardships on any one.

He believed that the North was as much to blame for the existence of slavery in the United States as was the South; and that in getting rid of it, both sections should bear the burden equally. So he finally worked out a plan that was very near to his heart. According to this, the slave-owners in the loyal border States were to receive four hundred dollars for each of their negroes. The slaves were to be emancipated gradually, very gradually. The process was not to be entirely completed until January 1, 1900. Calling the representatives of the border States to the White House, he pleaded with them to accept his proposal.

"The change it contemplates," Lincoln argued, "would come gently as the dews of heaven, not rending or wrecking anything. Will you not embrace it? So much good has not been done, by one effort, in all past time, as, in the providence of God, it is now your high privilege to do. May the vast future not have to lament you have neglected it."

But they did neglect it, and rejected the whole scheme. Lincoln was immeasurably disappointed.

"I must save this Government, if possible," he said; "and it may as well be understood, once for all, that I shall not surrender this game, leaving any available card unplayed. . . . I believe that freeing the slaves and arming the blacks has now become an indispensable military necessity. I have been driven to the alternative of either doing that or surrendering the Union."

He had to act at once, for both France and England were on the verge of recognizing the Confederacy. Why? The reasons were very simple.

Take France's case first. Napoleon III had married Marie Eugénie de Montijo, Comtesse de Teba, reputed to be the most beautiful woman in the world, and he wanted to show off a bit. He longed to cover himself with glory, as his renowned uncle, Napoleon Bonaparte, had done. So when he saw the States slashing and shooting at one another, and knew they were much too occupied to bother about enforcing the Monroe Doctrine, he ordered an army to Mexico, shot a few thousand natives, conquered the country, called Mexico a French empire, and put the Archduke Maximilian on the throne.

Napoleon believed, and not without reason, that if the Confederates won they would favor his new empire; but that if the Federals won, the United States would immediately take steps to put the French out of Mexico. It was Napoleon's wish, therefore, that the South would make good its secession, and he wanted to help it as much as he conveniently could.

At the outset of the war, the Northern navy closed all Southern ports, guarded 189 harbors and patrolled 9,614 miles of coast line, sounds, bayous, and rivers.

It was the most gigantic blockade the world had ever seen.

The Confederates were desperate. They couldn't sell their cotton; neither could they buy guns, ammunition, shoes, medical supplies, or food. They boiled chestnuts and cotton-seed to make a substitute for coffee, and brewed a decoction of blackberry leaves and sassafras root to take the place of tea. Newspapers were printed on wall-paper. The earthen floors of smokehouses, saturated with the drippings of bacon, were dug up and boiled to get salt. Church bells were melted and cast into cannon. Street-car rails in Richmond were torn up to be made into gunboat armor.

The Confederates couldn't repair their railroads or buy new equipment, so transportation was almost at a standstill; corn that could be purchased for two dollars a bushel in Georgia, brought fifteen dollars in Richmond. People in Virginia were going hungry.

Something had to be done at once. So the South offered to give Napoleon III twelve million dollars' worth of cotton if he would recognize the Confederacy and use the French fleet to lift the blockade. Besides, they promised to overwhelm him with orders that would start smoke rolling out of every factory chimney in France night and day.

Napoleon therefore urged Russia and England to join him in recognizing the Confederacy. The aristocracy that ruled England adjusted their monocles, poured a few drinks of Johnny Walker, and listened eagerly to Napoleon's overtures. The United States was getting too rich and powerful to please them. They wanted to see the nation divided, the Union broken. Besides, they needed the South's cotton. Scores of England's factories had closed, and a million people were not only idle but destitute and reduced to actual pauperism. Children were crying for food; hundreds of people were dying of starvation. Public subscriptions to buy food for British workmen were taken up in the remotest corners of the earth: even in far-off India and poverty-stricken China.

There was one way, and only one way, that England could get cotton, and that was to join Napoleon III in recognizing the Confederacy and lifting the blockade.

If that were done, what would happen in America? The South

would get guns, powder, credit, food, railroad equipment, and a tremendous lift in confidence and morale.

And what would the North get? Two new and powerful enemies. The situation, bad enough now, would be hopeless then.

Nobody knew this better than Abraham Lincoln. "We have about played our last card," he confessed in 1862. "We must either change our tactics now or lose the game."

As England saw it, all the colonies had originally seceded from her. Now the Southern colonies had, in turn, seceded from the Northern ones; and the North was fighting to coerce and subdue them. What difference did it make to a lord in London or a prince in Paris whether Tennessee and Texas were ruled from Washington or Richmond? None. To them, the fighting was meaningless and fraught with no high purpose.

"No war ever raging in my time," wrote Carlyle, "was to me more profoundly foolish looking."

Lincoln saw that Europe's attitude toward the war must be changed, and he knew how to do it. A million people in Europe had read "Uncle Tom's Cabin"—had read it and wept and learned to abhor the heartaches and injustice of slavery. So Abraham Lincoln knew that if he issued his Proclamation of Emancipation, Europeans would see the war in a different light. It would no longer be a bloody quarrel over the preservation of a Union that meant nothing to them. Instead, it would be exalted into a holy crusade to destroy slavery. European governments would then not dare to recognize the South. Public opinion wouldn't tolerate the aiding of a people supposed to be fighting to perpetuate human bondage.

Finally, therefore, in July, 1862, Lincoln determined to issue his proclamation; but McClellan and Pope had recently led the army to humiliating defeats. Seward told the President that the time was not auspicious, that he ought to wait and launch the proclamation on the crest of a wave of victory.

That sounded sensible. So Lincoln waited; and two months later the victory came. Then Lincoln called his Cabinet together to discuss the issuing of the most famous document in American history since the Declaration of Independence.

It was a momentous occasion—and a grave one. But did Lincoln act gravely and solemnly? He did not. Whenever he came across a good story, he liked to share it. He used to take one of Artemus Ward's books to bed with him; and when he read something humorous, he would get up, and, clad in nothing but his night-shirt, he would make his way through the halls of the White House to the office of his secretaries, and read it to them.

The day before the Cabinet meeting which was to discuss the issuing of the Emancipation Proclamation, Lincoln had gotten hold of Ward's latest volume. There was a story in it that he thought very funny. So he read it to the Cabinet now, before they got down to business. It was entitled, "High-handed Outrage in Utiky."

After Lincoln had had his laugh, he put the book aside and began solemnly: "When the rebel army was at Frederick, I determined, as soon as it should be driven out of Maryland, to issue a proclamation of emancipation. I said nothing to any one, but I made the promise to myself and—to my Maker. The rebel army is now driven out, and I am going to fulfil that promise. I have called you together to hear what I have written down. I do not wish your advice upon the main matter, for that I have determined for myself. What I have written is that which my reflections have determined me to say. But if there is anything in the expressions I use, or in any minor matter, which any of you thinks had best be changed, I shall be glad to receive the suggestions."

Seward suggested one slight change in wording; then, a few minutes later, he proposed another.

Lincoln asked him why he hadn't made both suggestions at the same time. And then Lincoln interrupted the consideration of the Emancipation Proclamation to tell a story. He said a hired man back in Indiana told the farmer who had employed him that one steer in his best yoke of oxen had died. Having waited a while, the hired man said, "The other ox in that team is dead, too."

"Then why didn't you tell me at once," asked the farmer, "that both of them were dead?"

"Well," answered the hired man, "I didn't want to hurt you by telling you too much at the same time."

Lincoln presented the proclamation to his Cabinet in September, 1862; but it was not to take effect until the first day of January, 1863. So when Congress met the following December, Lincoln appealed to that body for support. In making his plea he uttered one of the most magnificent sentences he ever penned —a sentence of unconscious poetry.

Speaking of the Union, he said:

> "We shall nobly save or meanly lose
> The last, best hope of earth."

On New Year's Day, 1863, Lincoln spent hours shaking hands with the visitors that thronged the White House. In the middle of that afternoon, he retired to his office, dipped his pen in the ink, and prepared to sign his proclamation of freedom. Hesitating, he turned to Seward and said: "If slavery isn't wrong, nothing is wrong, and I have never felt more certain in my life that I was doing right. But I have been receiving calls and shaking hands since nine o'clock this morning, and my arm is stiff and numb. Now this signature is one that will be closely examined, and if they find my hand trembled, they will say, 'He had some compunctions.' "

He rested his arm a moment, then slowly signed the document, and gave freedom to three and a half million slaves.

The proclamation did not meet with popular approval then. "The only effect of it," wrote Orville H. Browning, one of Lincoln's closest friends and strongest supporters, "was to unite and exasperate the South and divide and distract us in the North."

A mutiny broke out in the army. Men who had enlisted to save the Union swore that they wouldn't stand up and be shot down to free niggers and make them their social equals. Thousands of soldiers deserted, and recruiting fell off everywhere.

The plain people upon whom Lincoln had depended for support failed him utterly. The autumn elections went overwhelmingly against him. Even his home state of Illinois repudiated the Republican party.

And quickly, on top of the defeat at the polls, came one of the most disastrous reverses of the war—Burnside's foolhardy attack on Lee at Fredericksburg and the loss of thirteen thousand men. A stupid and futile butchery. This sort of thing had been going on for eighteen months now. Was it never going to stop? The nation was appalled. People were driven to despair. The President was violently denounced everywhere. He had failed. His general had failed. His policies had failed. People wouldn't put up with this any longer. Even the Republican members of the Senate revolted; and, wanting to force Lincoln out of the White House, they called upon him, demanding that he change his policies and dismiss his entire Cabinet.

This was a humiliating blow. Lincoln confessed that it distressed him more than any other one event of his political life.

"They want to get rid of me," he said, "and I am half disposed to gratify them."

Horace Greeley now sharply regretted the fact that he had forced the Republicans to nominate Lincoln in 1860.

"It was a mistake," he confessed, "the biggest mistake of my life."

Greeley and a number of other prominent Republicans organized a movement having these objects in view: to force Lincoln to resign, to put Hamlin, the Vice-President, in the White House, and then to compel Hamlin to give Rosecrans command of all the Union armies.

"We are now on the brink of destruction," Lincoln confessed. "It appears to me that even the Almighty is against us. I can see hardly a ray of hope."

★ ★ ★

23

★ ★ ★

IN THE spring of 1863, Lee, flushed with a phenomenal series of brilliant victories, determined to take the offensive and invade the North. He planned to seize the rich manufacturing centers of Pennsylvania, secure food, medicine, and new clothes for his ragged troops, possibly capture Washington, and compel France and Great Britain to recognize the Confederacy.

A bold, reckless move! True, but the Southern troops were boasting that one Confederate could whip three Yankees, and they believed it; so when their officers told them they could eat beef twice a day when they reached Pennsylvania, they were eager to be off at once.

Before he quit Richmond, Lee received disquieting news from home. A terrible thing had happened! One of his daughters had actually been caught reading a novel. The great general was distressed; so he wrote, pleading with her to devote her leisure to such innocuous classics as Plato and Homer, and Plutarch's Lives. After finishing the letter, Lee read his Bible and knelt in prayer, as was his custom; then he blew out the candle and turned in for the night. . . .

Presently he was off with seventy-five thousand men. His hungry army plunged across the Potomac, throwing the country into a panic. Farmers rushed out of the Cumberland Valley, driving their horses and cattle before them; and negroes, their eyes white with fear, fled in terror, lest they be dragged back to slavery.

Lee's artillery was already thundering before Harrisburg, when he learned that, back in the rear, the Union Army was threatening to break his lines of communication. So he whirled around as an angry ox would to gore a dog snapping at his heels; and, quite by chance, the ox and the dog met at a sleepy little Pennsylvania village with a theological seminary, a place called Gettysburg, and fought there the most famous battle in the history of our country.

During the first two days of the fighting the Union Army lost twenty thousand men; and, on the third day, Lee hoped finally to smash the enemy by a terrific assault of fresh troops under the command of General George Pickett.

These were new tactics for Lee. Up to this time, he had fought with his men behind breastworks or concealed in the woods. Now he planned to make a desperate attack out in the open.

The very contemplation of it staggered Lee's most brilliant assistant, General Longstreet.

"Great God!" Longstreet exclaimed. "Look, General Lee, at the insurmountable difficulties between our line and that of the Yankees—the steep hills, the tiers of artillery, the fences. And then we shall have to fight our infantry against their battery. Look at the ground we shall have to charge over, nearly a mile of it there in the open, under the line of their canister and shrapnel. It is my opinion that no fifteen thousand men ever arrayed for battle could take that position."

But Lee was adamant. "There were never such men in an army before," he replied. "They will go anywhere and do anything if properly led."

So Lee held to his decision, and made the bloodiest blunder of his career.

The Confederates had already massed one hundred and fifty cannon along Seminary Ridge. If you visit Gettysburg, you can see them there to-day, placed precisely as they were on that fateful July afternoon when they laid down a barrage such as, up to that time, had never before been heard on earth.

Longstreet in this instance had keener judgment than Lee. He believed that the charge could result in nothing but pointless butchery; so he bowed his head and wept and declined to issue the order. Consequently, another officer had to give the command for him; and, in obedience to that command, General

George Pickett led his Southern troops in the most dramatic and disastrous charge that ever occurred in the Western world.

Strangely enough, this general who led the assault on the Union lines was an old friend of Lincoln's. In fact, Lincoln had made it possible for him to go to West Point. He was a picturesque character, this man Pickett. He wore his hair so long that his auburn locks almost touched his shoulders; and, like Napoleon in his Italian campaigns, he wrote ardent love-letters almost daily on the battle-field. His devoted troops cheered him that afternoon as he rode off jauntily toward the Union lines, with his cap set at a rakish angle over his right ear. They cheered and they followed him, man touching man, rank pressing rank, with banners flying and bayonets gleaming in the sun. It was picturesque. Daring. Magnificent. A murmur of admiration ran through the Union lines as they beheld it.

Pickett's troops swept forward at an easy trot, through an orchard and corn-field, across a meadow, and over a ravine. All the time, the enemy's cannon were tearing ghastly holes in their ranks. But on they pressed, grim, irresistible.

Suddenly the Union infantry rose from behind the stone wall on Cemetery Ridge where they had been hiding, and fired volley after volley into Pickett's defenseless troops. The crest of the hill was a sheet of flame, a slaughter-house, a blazing volcano. In a few minutes, all of Pickett's brigade commanders, except one, were down, and four fifths of his five thousand men had fallen.

A thousand fell where Kemper led;
A thousand died where Garnett bled;
In blinding flame and strangling smoke
The remnant through the batteries broke,
And crossed the line with Armistead.

Armistead, leading the troops in the final plunge, ran forward, vaulted over the stone wall, and, waving his cap on the top of his sword, shouted:

"Give 'em the steel, boys!"

They did. They leaped over the wall, bayoneted their enemies, smashed skulls with clubbed muskets, and planted the battle-flags of the South on Cemetery Ridge.

The banners waved there, however, only for a moment. But that moment, brief as it was, recorded the high-water mark of the Confederacy.

Pickett's charge—brilliant, heroic—was nevertheless the beginning of the end. Lee had failed. He could not penetrate the North. And he knew it.

The South was doomed.

As the remnant of Pickett's bleeding men struggled back from their fatal charge, Lee, entirely alone, rode out to encourage them, and greeted them with a self-condemnation that was little short of sublime.

"All this has been my fault," he confessed. "It is I who have lost this fight."

During the night of July 4 Lee began to retreat. Heavy rains were falling, and by the time he reached the Potomac the water was so high that he couldn't cross.

There Lee was, caught in a trap, an impassable river in front of him, a victorious enemy behind him. Meade, it seemed, had him at his mercy. Lincoln was delighted; he was sure the Federal troops would swoop down upon Lee's flank and rear now, rout and capture his men, and bring the war to an abrupt and triumphant close. And if Grant had been there, that is probably what would have happened.

But the vain and scholarly Meade was not the bulldog Grant. Every day for an entire week Lincoln repeatedly urged and commanded Meade to attack, but he was too cautious, too timid. He did not want to fight; he hesitated, he telegraphed excuses, he called a council of war in direct violation of orders—and did nothing, while the waters receded and Lee escaped.

Lincoln was furious.

"What does this mean?" he cried. "Great God! What does this mean? We had them within our grasp, and had only to stretch forth our hands and they were ours; yet nothing that I could say or do could make the army move. Under the circumstances, almost any general could have defeated Lee. If I had gone up there, I could have whipped him, myself."

In bitter disappointment, Lincoln sat down and wrote Meade a letter, in which he said:

> My dear General, I do not believe you appreciate the magnitude of the misfortune involved in Lee's escape. He was within our easy grasp, and to have closed upon him would, in connection with our other late successes, have ended the war. As it is, the war will be prolonged indefi-

> nitely. If you could not safely attack Lee last Monday, how can you possibly do so south of the river, when you can take with you very few more than two-thirds of the force you then had in hand? It would be unreasonable to expect and I do not expect that you can now effect much. Your golden opportunity is gone, and I am distressed immeasurably because of it.

Lincoln read this letter, and then stared out the window with unseeing eyes, and did a bit of thinking: "If I had been in Meade's place," he probably mused to himself, "and had had Meade's temperament and the advice of his timid officers, and if I had been awake as many nights as he had, and had seen as much blood, I might have let Lee escape, too."

The letter was never sent. Meade never saw it. It was found among Lincoln's papers after his death.

The Battle of Gettysburg was fought during the first week of July; six thousand dead and twenty-seven thousand wounded were left on the field. Churches, schools, and barns were turned into hospitals; groans of the suffering filled the air. Scores were dying every hour, corpses were decaying rapidly in the intense heat. The burial parties had to work fast. There was little time to dig graves; so, in many instances, a little dirt was scooped over a body where it lay. After a week of hard rains, many of the dead were half exposed. The Union soldiers were gathered from their temporary graves, and buried in one place. The following autumn the Cemetery Commission decided to dedicate the ground, and invited Edward Everett, the most famous orator in the United States, to deliver the address.

Formal invitations to attend the exercises were sent to the President, to the Cabinet, to General Meade, to all members of both houses of Congress, to various distinguished citizens, and to the members of the diplomatic corps. Very few of these people accepted; many didn't acknowledge the invitation.

The committee had not the least idea that the President would come. In fact, they had not even troubled to write him a personal invitation. He got merely a printed one. They imagined that his secretaries might drop it in the waste-basket without even showing it to Lincoln.

So when he wrote saying he would be present, the committee was astonished. And a bit embarrassed. What should they do?

Ask him to speak? Some argued that he was too busy for that, that he couldn't possibly find time to prepare. Others frankly asked, "Well, even if he had the time, has he the ability?" They doubted it.

Oh, yes, he could make a stump speech in Illinois; but speaking at the dedication of a cemetery? No. That was different. That was not Lincoln's style. However, since he was coming anyway, they had to do something. So they finally wrote him, saying that after Mr. Everett had delivered his oration, they would like to have him make "a few appropriate remarks." That was the way they phrased it—"a few appropriate remarks."

The invitation just barely missed being an insult. But the President accepted it. Why? There is an interesting story behind that. The previous autumn Lincoln had visited the battle-field of Antietam; and, one afternoon while he and an old friend from Illinois, Ward Lamon, were out driving, the President turned to Lamon and asked him to sing what Lincoln called his "sad little song." It was one of Lincoln's favorites.

"Many a time, on the Illinois circuit and often at the White House when Lincoln and I were alone," says Lamon, "I have seen him in tears while I was rendering that homely melody."

It went like this:

I've wandered to the village, Tom; I've sat beneath the tree
Upon the schoolhouse play-ground, that sheltered you and me;
But none were left to greet me, Tom, and few were left to know
Who played with us upon the green, some twenty years ago.

Near by the spring, upon the elm you know I cut your name,—
Your sweetheart's just beneath it, Tom; and you did mine the same.
Some heartless wretch has peeled the bark—'twas dying sure but slow,
Just as she died whose name you cut, some twenty years ago.

My lids have long been dry, Tom, but tears came to my eyes;
I thought of her I loved so well, those early broken ties:
I visited the old churchyard, and took some flowers to strow
Upon the graves of those we loved, some twenty years ago.

As Lamon sang it now, probably Lincoln fell to dreaming of the only woman he had ever loved, Ann Rutledge, and he thought of her lying back there in her neglected grave on the Illinois prairie; and the rush of these poignant memories filled his eyes with tears. So Lamon, to break the spell of Lincoln's melancholy, struck up a humorous negro melody.

That was all there was to the incident. It was perfectly harmless, and very pathetic. But Lincoln's political enemies distorted it and lied about it and tried to make it a national disgrace. They made it appear like a gross indecency. The New York "World" repeated some version of the scandal every day for almost three months. Lincoln was accused of cracking jokes and singing funny songs on the battle-field where "heavy details of men were engaged in burying the dead."

The truth is that he had cracked no jokes at all, that he had sung no songs, that he had been miles away from the battle-field when the incident occurred, that the dead had all been buried before that, and rain had fallen upon their graves. Such were the facts. But his enemies didn't want facts. They were lusting for blood. A bitter cry of savage denunciation swept over the land.

Lincoln was deeply hurt. He was so distressed that he could not bear to read these attacks, yet he didn't feel that he ought to answer them, for that would merely dignify them. So he suffered in silence, and when the invitation came to speak at the dedication of the Gettysburg cemetery, he welcomed it. It was just the opportunity he desired to silence his enemies and pay his humble tribute to the honored dead.

The invitation came late, and he had only a crowded fortnight in which to prepare his speech. He thought it over during his spare moments—while dressing, while being shaved, while eating his lunch, while walking back and forth between Stanton's office and the White House. He mused upon it while stretched out on a leather couch in the war-office, waiting for the late telegraphic reports. He wrote a rough draft of it on a piece of pale-blue foolscap paper, and carried it about in the top of his hat. The Sunday before it was delivered he said: "I have written it over two or three times, but it is not finished. I shall have to give it another lick before I am satisfied."

He arrived in Gettysburg the night before the dedication. The little town was filled to overflowing. Its usual population of thirteen hundred had been swelled to almost thirty thousand. The weather was fine; the night was clear; a bright full moon rode high through the sky. Only a fraction of the crowd could find beds; thousands paraded up and down the village until dawn. The sidewalks soon became clogged, impassable; so hundreds, locked arm in arm, marched in the middle of the dirt streets, singing, "John Brown's body lies a-mouldering in the grave."

Lincoln devoted all that evening to giving his speech "another lick." At eleven o'clock he went to an adjoining house, where Secretary Seward was staying, and read the speech aloud to him, asking for his criticisms. The next morning, after breakfast, Lincoln continued working over it until a rap at the door reminded him that it was time for him to take his place in the procession headed for the cemetery.

As the procession started, he sat erect at first; but presently his body slouched forward in the saddle; his head fell on his chest, and his long arms hung limp at his sides. . . . He was lost in thought, going over his little speech, giving it "another lick." . . .

Edward Everett, the selected orator of the occasion, made two mistakes at Gettysburg. Both bad—and both uncalled for. First, he arrived an hour late; and, secondly, he spoke for two hours.

Lincoln had read Everett's oration and when he saw that the speaker was nearing his close, he knew his time was coming, and he honestly felt that he wasn't adequately prepared; so he grew nervous, twisted in his chair, drew his manuscript from the pocket of his Prince Albert coat, put on his old-fashioned glasses, and quickly refreshed his memory.

Presently he stepped forward, manuscript in hand, and delivered his little address in two minutes.

Did his audience realize, that soft November afternoon, that they were listening to the greatest speech that had ever fallen from human lips up to that time? No, most of his hearers were merely curious: they had never seen nor heard a President of the United States, they strained their necks to look at Lincoln, and were surprised to discover that such a tall man had such a high, thin voice, and that he spoke with a Southern accent. They had forgotten that he was born a Kentuckian and that he had retained the intonation of his native State; and about the time they felt he was getting through with his introduction and ready to launch into his speech—he sat down.

What! Had he forgotten? Or was it really all he had to say? People were too surprised and disappointed to applaud.

Many a spring, back in Indiana, Lincoln had tried to break ground with a rusty plow; but the soil had stuck to its moldboard, and made a mess. It wouldn't "scour." That was the term people used. Throughout his life, when Lincoln wanted to indicate that a thing had failed, he frequently resorted to the phraseology of the corn-field. Turning now to Ward Lamon, Lincoln said:

"That speech is a flat failure, Lamon. It won't scour. The people are disappointed."

He was right. Every one was disappointed, including Edward Everett and Secretary Seward, who were sitting on the platform with the President. They both believed he had failed woefully; and both felt sorry for him.

Lincoln was so distressed that he worried himself into a severe headache; and on the way back to Washington, he had to lie down in the drawing-room of the train and have his head bathed with cold water.

Lincoln went to his grave believing that he had failed utterly at Gettysburg. And he had, as far as the immediate effect of his speech was concerned.

With characteristic modesty, he sincerely felt that the world would "little note nor long remember" what he said there, but that it would never forget what the brave men who died had done there. How surprised he would be if he should come back to life now and realize that the speech of his that most people remember is the one that didn't "scour" at Gettysburg! How amazed he would be to discover that the ten immortal sentences he spoke there will probably be cherished as one of the literary glories and treasures of earth centuries hence, long after the Civil War is all but forgotten.

Lincoln's Gettysburg address is more than a speech. It is the divine expression of a rare soul exalted and made great by suffering. It is an unconscious prose poem, and has all the majestic beauty and profound roll of epic lines:

Four score and seven years ago
Our fathers brought forth upon this continent,
A new nation, conceived in Liberty,
And dedicated to the proposition
That all men are created equal.

Now we are engaged in a great civil war,
Testing whether that nation, or any nation
So conceived and so dedicated,
Can long endure. We are met

On a great battle-field of that war.
We have come to dedicate a portion of
That field as a final resting-place
For those who here gave their lives
That that nation might live.
It is altogether fitting and proper
That we should do this.

But, in a larger sense,
We can not dedicate—we can not consecrate—
We can not hallow this ground. The brave men,
Living and dead, who struggled here
Have consecrated it far above our poor power
To add or detract. The world will little note,
Nor long remember what we say here,
But it can never forget what they did here.
It is for us the living, rather, to be dedicated here
To the unfinished work which they who fought here
Have thus far so nobly advanced.
It is rather for us to be here dedicated
To the great task remaining before us—
That from these honored dead we take
Increased devotion to that cause for which
They gave the last full measure of devotion—
That we here highly resolve that these dead
Shall not have died in vain—that this nation,
Under God, shall have a new birth of freedom—
And that government of the people,
By the people, for the people,
Shall not perish from the earth.

WHEN the war began, in 1861, a shabby and disappointed man was sitting on a packing-case in a leather store in Galena, Illinois, smoking a clay pipe. His job, so far as he had one, was that of bookkeeper and buyer of hogs and hides from farmers.

His two younger brothers who owned the store didn't want him around at any price, but for months he had tramped the streets of St. Louis, looking in vain for some kind of position, until his wife and four children were destitute. Finally, in despair, he had borrowed a few dollars for a railway ticket and gone to see his father in Kentucky, begging for assistance. The old man had considerable cash, but, being loath to part with any of it, he sat down and wrote his two younger sons in Galena, instructing them to give their elder brother a job.

So they put him on the pay-roll at once, more as a matter of family politics and family charity than anything else.

Two dollars a day—that was his wage—and it was probably more than he was worth, for he had no more business ability than a jack-rabbit; he was lazy and slovenly, he loved corn-whisky, and he was eternally in debt. He was always borrowing small sums of money; so when his friends saw him coming, they used to look the other way and cross the street to avoid meeting him.

Everything he had undertaken in life, so far, had ended in failure and frustration.

So far.

But no more.

For good news and astounding good fortune were just around the corner.

In a little while he was to go flaring and flaming like a shooting star across the firmament of fame.

He couldn't command the respect of his home town now; but in three years he would command the most formidable army the world had ever seen.

In four years he would conquer Lee, end the war, and write his name in blazing letters of fire on the pages of history.

In eight years he would be in the White House.

After that he would make a triumphal tour of the world, with the high and mighty of all lands heaping honors, medals, flowers, and after-dinner oratory upon him—whom people back in Galena had crossed the street to avoid.

It is an astonishing tale.

Everything about it is strange. Even the attitude of his mother was abnormal. She never seemed to care much for him. She refused to visit him when he was President, and she didn't trouble even to name him when he was born. Her relatives attended to that, in a sort of lottery. When he was six weeks old, they wrote their favorite names on strips torn from a paper sack, mixed them in a hat, and drew one out. His grandmother Simpson had been reading Homer, and she wrote on her slip: "Hiram Ulysses." It was drawn, and so, by chance, that was the name he bore at home for seventeen years.

But he was bashful and slow-witted, so the village wits called him "Useless" Grant.

At West Point he had still another name. The politician who made out the papers giving him an appointment to the Military Academy imagined that his middle name must be Simpson, his mother's maiden name, so he went as "U. S. Grant." When the cadets learned this, they laughed and tossed their hats in the air, and shouted, "Boys, we've got Uncle Sam with us!" To the end of his life those who had been his classmates there called him Sam Grant.

He didn't mind. He made few friends, and he didn't care what people called him, and he didn't care how he looked. He wouldn't keep his coat buttoned or his gun clean or his shoes shined, and he was often late for roll-call. And, instead of mastering the military principles used by Napoleon and Frederick the Great, he spent much of his time at West Point poring over novels such as "Ivanhoe" and "The Last of the Mohicans."

The incredible fact is that he never read a book on military strategy in his life.

After he had won the war the people of Boston raised money to buy him a library, appointing a committee to find out what books he already possessed. To its amazement, the committee learned that Grant didn't own a single military treatise of any description.

He disliked West Point and the army and everything connected with it; and, after he had become world-famous, he said to Bismarck while reviewing Germany's troops:

"I haven't much interest in military affairs. The truth is, I am more of a farmer than a soldier. Although I have been in two wars, I never entered the army without regret, and never left it without pleasure."

Grant admitted that his besetting sin was laziness, and that he never liked to study. Even after he graduated from West Point he spelled *knocked* without the initial *k* and *safety* without an *e;* yet he was fairly good at figures, and hoped to be a professor of mathematics. But no position was available, so he spent eleven years with the regular army. He had to have something to eat, and that seemed the easiest way to get it.

In 1853 he was stationed at Fort Humboldt in California. In a near-by village there was a curious character named Ryan. Ryan ran a store, operated a sawmill, and did surveying during the week. On Sunday he preached. Whisky was cheap in those days, and Pastor Ryan kept an open barrel of it in the back of his store. A tin cup was hanging on the barrel, so you could go and help yourself whenever you had the urge. Grant had it often. He was lonely and wanted to forget the army life that he despised; as a result he got drunk so many times that he had virtually to be dismissed from the army.

He didn't have a dollar, and he didn't have a job; so he drifted back east to Missouri and spent the next four years plowing corn and slopping hogs on an eighty-acre farm belonging to his father-in-law. In the wintertime he cut cord-wood, hauled it to St. Louis, and sold it to the city people. But every year he got farther and farther behind, had to borrow more and more.

Finally he quit the farm, moved to St. Louis, and sought employment there. He tried to sell real estate, was a total failure at that, and then drifted about the town for weeks, looking for a job—any kind of job. At last he was in such desperate circumstances that he tried to hire out his wife's negroes, in order to get money to pay the grocer's bill.

Here is one of the most surprising facts about the Civil War: Lee believed that slavery was wrong, and had freed his own negroes long before the conflict came; but Grant's wife owned slaves at the very time that her husband was leading the armies of the North to destroy slavery.

When the war began, Grant was sick of his work in the Galena leather store and wanted to get back into the army.

That ought to have been easy for a West Point graduate, when the army had hundreds of thousands of raw recruits to whip into shape. But it wasn't. Galena raised a company of volunteers, and Grant drilled them because he was the only man in town who knew anything at all about drilling, but when they marched away to war with bouquets in their gun-barrels Grant stood on the sidewalk watching them. They had chosen another man as captain.

Then Grant wrote to the War Department, telling of his experience and asking to be appointed colonel of a regiment. His letter was never answered. It was found in the files of the War Department while he was President.

Finally he got a position in the adjutant's office in Springfield, doing clerical work that a fifteen-year-old girl could have done. He worked all day with his hat on, smoking constantly and copying orders on an old broken-down table with three legs, which had been shoved into a corner for support.

Then a wholly unexpected thing happened, an event that set his feet on the road to fame. The 21st Regiment of Illinois Volunteers had degenerated into an armed mob. They ignored orders, cursed their officers, and chased old Colonel Goode out of camp, vowing that if he showed up again they would nail his hide on a sour-apple tree.

Governor Yates was worried.

He didn't think much of Grant, but after all the man had been graduated from West Point, so the governor took a chance. And on a sunny June day in 1861 Grant walked out to the Springfield fair-grounds to take over the command of a regiment that no one else could rule.

A stick that he carried, and a red bandana tied around his waist—these were his only visible signs of authority.

He didn't have a horse or a uniform, or the money to buy either. There were holes in the top of his sweat-stained hat, and his elbows stuck out of his old coat.

His men began making fun of him at once. One chap started sparring at him behind his back, and another fellow rushed up behind the pugilist and shoved him so hard that he stumbled forward and hit Grant between the shoulders.

Grant stopped all their foolishness immediately. If a man disobeyed orders he was tied to a post and left there all day. If he cursed a gag was put into his mouth. If the regiment was late at roll-call—as they all were on one occasion—they got nothing to eat for twenty-four hours. The ex-hide-buyer from Galena tamed their tempestuous spirits and led them away to do battle down in Missouri.

Shortly after that another piece of amazing good fortune came his way. In those days the War Department was making brigadier-generals by the dozens. Northwestern Illinois had sent Elihu B. Washburne to Congress. Washburne, fired with political ambitions, was desperately eager to show the folks back home that he was on the job, so he went to the War Department and demanded that one brigadier-general come from his district. All right. But who? That was easy: there was only one West Point graduate among Washburne's constituents.

So a few days later Grant picked up a St. Louis newspaper, and read the surprising news that he was a brigadier-general.

He was assigned headquarters at Cairo, Illinois, and immediately began to do things. He loaded his soldiers on boats, steamed up the Ohio, occupied Paducah, a strategic point in Kentucky, and proposed marching down into Tennessee to attack Fort Donelson, which commanded the Cumberland River. Military experts like Halleck said: "Nonsense! You are talking foolishly, Grant. It can't be done. It would be suicide to attempt it."

Grant went ahead and tried it, and captured the fort and fifteen thousand prisoners in one afternoon.

While Grant was attacking, the Confederate general sent him a note, begging for a truce, to arrange terms of capitulation, but Grant replied rather tartly:

"My only terms are unconditional and immediate surrender. I propose to move immediately upon your works."

Simon Buckner, the Confederate general to whom this curt message was addressed, had known Sam Grant at West Point and had lent him money to pay his board bill when he was fired from the army. In view of that loan, Buckner felt that Grant ought to have been a trifle more gracious in his phraseology. But Buckner forgave him and surrendered and spent the afternoon smoking and reminiscing with Grant about old times.

The fall of Fort Donelson had far-reaching consequences: it saved Kentucky for the North, enabled the Union troops to advance two hundred miles without opposition, drove the Confederates out of a large part of Tennessee, cut off their supplies, caused the fall of Nashville and of Fort Columbus, the Gibraltar of the Mississippi, spread profound depression throughout the South, and set church bells ringing and bonfires blazing from Maine to the Mississippi.

It was a stupendous victory, and created a tremendous impression even in Europe. It was really one of the turning-points of the war.

From that time on, U. S. Grant was known as "Unconditional Surrender" Grant, and "I propose to move on your works immediately" became the battle-cry of the North.

Here, at last, was the great leader for which the country had been waiting. Congress made him a major-general; he was appointed commander of the Military Department of Western Tennessee, and quickly became the idol of the nation. One newspaper mentioned that he liked to smoke during a battle, and, presto! over ten thousand boxes of cigars were showered upon him.

But in less than three weeks after all this Grant was actually in tears of rage and mortification because of unfair treatment by a jealous superior officer.

His immediate superior in the West was Halleck, a colossal and unmitigated ass. Admiral Foote called Halleck "a military imbecile," and Gideon Welles, Lincoln's Secretary of the Navy, who knew Halleck intimately, sums him up thus:

"Halleck originates nothing, anticipates nothing, suggests nothing, plans nothing, decides nothing, is good for nothing and does nothing except scold, smoke and scratch his elbows."

But Halleck thought very well of himself. He had been an assistant professor at West Point, had written books on military strategy, international law, and mining, had been director of a silver-mine, president of a railway, a successful attorney, had mastered French and translated a tome on Napoleon. In his own opinion, he was the distinguished scholar, *Henry Wager Halleck.*

And who was Grant? A nobody, a drunken and discredited army captain. When Grant came to see him, before attacking Fort Donelson, Halleck was rude, and dismissed his military suggestions with irritation and contempt. Now Grant had won a great victory and had the nation at his feet, while Halleck was still scratching his elbows in St. Louis, unnoticed and ignored. And it galled Halleck.

To make matters worse, he felt that this erstwhile hide-buyer was insulting him. He telegraphed Grant day after day, and Grant brazenly ignored his orders. At least, so Halleck imagined. But he was wrong. Grant had sent report upon report; but, after the fall of Donelson, a break in telegraphic communications had made it impossible for his telegrams to get through. However, Halleck didn't know this, and he was indignant. Victory and public adulation had gone to Grant's head, had they? Well, he would teach this young upstart a lesson. So he wired McClellan repeatedly, denouncing Grant. Grant was this, Grant was that—insolent, drunk, idle, ignoring orders, incompetent. "I'm tired and worn out with this neglect and inefficiency."

McClellan, too, was envious of Grant's popularity; so he sent Halleck what, in the light of history, is the most amazing telegram of the Civil War: "Do not hesitate to arrest him [Grant] at once if the good of the service requires it, and place C. F. Smith in command."

Halleck immediately took Grant's army away from him, virtually placed him under arrest, and then leaned back in his chair and scratched his elbows with savage satisfaction.

The war was almost a year old now, and the only general who had won a considerable victory for the North stood stripped of all power and in public disgrace.

Later Grant was restored to command. Then he blundered woefully at the Battle of Shiloh; if Johnston, the Confederate general, had not bled to death during the fighting, Grant's entire army might have been surrounded and captured. Shiloh was, at that time, the greatest battle that had ever been fought on this continent, and Grant's losses were staggering—thirteen thousand men. He had acted stupidly; he had been taken by surprise. He deserved criticism, and it came roaring down upon him. He was falsely accused of being intoxicated at Shiloh, and millions believed it. A tidal wave of popular indignation swept over the country, and the public clamored for his removal. But Lincoln said:

"I can't spare this man. He fights."

When people told him Grant drank too much whisky, he inquired: "What brand? I want to send a few barrels to some of my other generals."

The following January Grant assumed command of the expedition against Vicksburg. The campaign against this natural fortress, perched on a high bluff two hundred feet above the Mississippi, was long and heartbreaking. The place was heavily fortified, and the gunboats on the river couldn't elevate their cannon high enough to touch it. Grant's problem was to get his army close enough to attack it.

He went back to the heart of Mississippi and tried to march on it from the east. That failed.

Then he cut away the levees of the river, put his army on boats, and tried to float through the swamps and get at the place from the north. That failed.

Then he dug a canal and tried to change the course of the Mississippi. That failed.

It was a trying winter. Rain fell almost continuously, the river flooded the whole valley, and Grant's troops floundered through miles of swamps, ooze, bayous, tangled forests, and trailing vines. Men stood up to their waists in mud, they ate in the mud, they slept in the mud. Malarial fever broke out, and measles and smallpox. Sanitation was well-nigh impossible, and the death-rate was appalling.

The Vicksburg campaign was a failure—that was the cry that went up everywhere. A stupid failure, a tragic failure, a criminal failure.

Grant's own generals—Sherman, McPherson, Logan, Wilson—regarded his plans as absurd, and believed they would end in black ruin. The press throughout the country was vitriolic, and the nation was demanding Grant's removal.

"He has hardly a friend left except myself," Lincoln said.

Despite all opposition, Lincoln clung to Grant; and he had his faith richly rewarded, for, on July 4, the same day that the timid Meade let Lee escape at Gettysburg, Grant rode into Vicksburg on a horse taken from the plantation of Jefferson Davis, and won a greater victory than any American general had achieved since the days of Washington.

After eight months of desolating failure, Grant had captured forty thousand prisoners at Vicksburg, placed the entire Mississippi River in the hands of the North, and split the Confederacy.

The news set the nation aflame with enthusiasm.

Congress passed a special act in order that Grant could be made lieutenant-general—an honor that no man had worn since the death of Washington—and Lincoln, calling him to the White House, made a short address appointing him commander of all the armies of the Union.

Forewarned that he would have to reply with a speech of acceptance, Grant drew out of his pocket a little wrinkled piece of paper containing only three sentences. As he began to read, the paper shook, his face flushed, his knees trembled, and his voice failed. Breaking down completely, he clutched the shaking paper with both hands, shifted his position, took a deep breath, and began all over again.

The hog-and-hide buyer from Galena found it easier to face bullets than to deliver a speech of eighty-four words before an audience of eleven men.

Mrs. Lincoln, eager to make a social event out of Grant's presence in Washington, had already arranged a dinner and a party in the general's honor. But Grant begged to be excused, saying he must hasten back to the front.

"But we can't excuse you," the President insisted. "Mrs. Lincoln's dinner without you would be 'Hamlet' without Hamlet."

"A dinner to me," replied Grant, "means a million dollars a day loss to the country. Besides, I've had about enough of this show business, anyway."

Lincoln loved a man who would talk like that—one who, like himself, despised "fizzlegigs and fireworks," and one who would "take responsibility and act."

Lincoln's hopes rose and towered now. He was sure that, with Grant in command, all would soon be well.

But he was wrong. Within four months the country was plunged into blacker gloom and deeper despair than ever, and once more Lincoln was pacing the floor throughout the night, haggard and worn and desperate.

25

In May 1864, the triumphant Grant plunged across the Rapidan River with 122,000 men. He was going to destroy's Lee's army forthwith and end the war at once.

Lee met him in the "wilderness" of North Virginia. The place was well named. It was a jungle of rolling hills and swampy swales smothered with a dense second growth of pine and oaks and matted with underbrush so thick that a cottontail could hardly crawl through it. And in those gloomy and tangled woods, Grant fought a grim and bloody campaign. The slaughter was appalling. The jungle itself caught on fire and hundreds of the wounded were consumed by the flames.

At the end of the second day even the stolid Grant was so shaken that he retired to his tent and wept.

But after every battle, no matter what the results, he gave the same order: "Advance! Advance!"

At the end of the sixth bloody day he sent the famous telegram: "I propose to fight it out on this line if it takes all summer."

Well, it did take all summer. Moreover, it took all autumn, and all winter, and a part of the next spring.

Grant had twice as many men in the field now as the enemy had, and back of him, in the North, lay a vast reservoir of manpower upon which he could draw, while the South had almost exhausted its recruits and supplies.

"The rebels," said Grant, "have already robbed the cradle and the grave."

Grant held that the quick way and the only way to end the war was to keep on killing Lee's men until Lee surrendered.

What if two Northern soldiers were shot for every one the South lost? Grant could make up the wastage, but Lee couldn't. So Grant kept on blasting and shooting and slaying.

In six weeks he lost 54,926 men—as many as Lee had in his entire army.

In one hour at Cold Harbor he lost seven thousand—a thousand more than had been killed on both sides in three days during the Battle of Gettysburg.

And what advantage was achieved by this ghastly loss?

We shall let Grant himself answer the question: "None whatever." That was his estimate.

The attack at Cold Harbor was the most tragic blunder of his career.

Such slaughter was more than human nerves and human bodies could endure. It broke the morale of the troops; the rank and file of the army were on the verge of mutiny, and the officers themselves were ready to rebel.

"For thirty-six days now," said one of Grant's corps commanders, "there has been one unbroken funeral procession past me."

Lincoln, broken-hearted though he was, realized that there was nothing to do but keep on. He telegraphed Grant to "hold on with a bull dog grip and chew and choke." Then he issued a call for half a million more men, to serve from one to three years.

The call staggered the country. The nation was plunged into an abyss of despair.

"Everything now is darkness and doubt and discouragement," one of Lincoln's secretaries recorded in his diary.

On July 2 Congress adopted a resolution that sounded like the lamentations of one of the Hebrew prophets of the Old Testament. It requested the citizens to "confess and repent of their manifold sins, implore the compassion and forgiveness of the Almighty, and beseech him as the Supreme Ruler of the world not to destroy us as a people."

Lincoln was being cursed now almost as violently in the North as in the South. He was denounced as a usurper, a traitor, a tyrant, a fiend, a monster, "a bloody butcher shouting war to the knife and knife to the hilt, and crying for more victims for his slaughter pens."

Some of his most bitter enemies declared that he ought to be killed. And one evening as he was riding out to his summer headquarters at the Soldiers' Home, a would-be assassin fired at him and put a bullet through his tall silk hat.

A few weeks later the proprietor of a hotel in Meadville, Pennsylvania, found this inscription scratched on a windowpane: "Abe Lincoln Departed this Life August 13, 1864, by the effect of poison." The room had been occupied the night before by a popular actor named Booth—John Wilkes Booth.

The preceding June the Republicans had nominated Lincoln for a second term. But they felt now that they had made a mistake, a woeful mistake. Some of the most prominent men in the party urged Lincoln to withdraw. Others demanded it. They wanted to call another convention, admit that Lincoln was a failure, cancel his nomination, and place another candidate at the head of the ticket.

Even Lincoln's close friend Orville Browning recorded in his diary in July, 1864, that the "nation's great need is a competent leader at the head of affairs."

Lincoln himself now believed that his case was hopeless. He abandoned all thought of being elected for a second term. He had failed. His generals had failed. His war policy had failed. The people had lost faith in his leadership, and he feared that the Union itself would be destroyed.

"Even the heavens," he exclaimed, "are hung in black."

Finally a large group of radicals, disgusted with Lincoln, called another convention, nominated the picturesque General John C. Frémont as their candidate, and split the Republican party.

The situation was grave; and there is hardly a doubt that if Frémont hadn't withdrawn from the race later, General McClellan, the Democratic candidate, would have triumphed over his divided opponents and the history of the nation would have been changed.

Even with Frémont out of the race, Lincoln received only 200,000 more votes than McClellan.

Notwithstanding the vitriolic condemnation poured upon him, Lincoln went calmly on, doing his best and answering no one.

"I desire," he said, "to so conduct the affairs of this administration that if, at the end, when I come to lay down the reins of power, I have lost every other friend on earth, I shall at least have one friend left, and that friend shall be deep down inside of me. . . . I am not bound to win, but I am bound to be true. I am not bound to succeed, but I am bound to live up to the light I have."

Weary and despondent, he often stretched himself out on a sofa, picked up a small Bible, and turned to Job for comfort: "Gird up now thy loins like a man; for I will demand of thee, and answer thou me."

In the summer of 1864, Lincoln was a changed man, changed in mind and body from the physical giant who had come off the prairies of Illinois three years before. Year by year his laughter had grown less frequent; the furrows in his face had deepened; his shoulders had stooped; his cheeks were sunken; he suffered from chronic indigestion; his legs were always cold; he could hardly sleep; he wore habitually an expression of anguish. He said to a friend: "I feel as though I shall never be glad again."

When Augustus Saint-Gaudens saw a life-mask of Lincoln that had been made in the spring of 1865, the famous sculptor thought that it was a death-mask, insisted that it must be, for already the marks of death were upon his face.

Carpenter, the artist who lived at the White House for months while he was painting the scene of the Emancipation Proclamation, wrote:

> During the first week of the battle of the Wilderness, the President scarcely slept at all. Passing through the main hall of the domestic apartment on one of those days, I met him, clad in a long morning wrapper, pacing back and forth, his hands behind him, great black rings under his eyes, his head bent forward upon his breast—the picture of sorrow and care and anxiety. . . . There were whole days when I could scarcely look into his furrowed face without weeping.

Callers found him collapsed in his chair, so exhausted that he did not look up or speak when they first addressed him.

"I sometimes fancy," he declared, "that every one of the throng that comes to see me daily darts at me with thumb and finger and picks out his piece of my vitality and carries it away."

He told Mrs. Stowe, the author of "Uncle Tom's Cabin," that he would never live to see peace.

"This war is killing me," he said.

His friends, alarmed at the change in his appearance, urged him to take a vacation.

"Two or three weeks would do me no good," he replied. "I cannot fly from my thoughts. I hardly know how to rest. What is tired lies within me and can't be got at."

"The cry of the widow and the orphan," said his secretary, "was always in Lincoln's ear."

Mothers and sweethearts and wives, weeping and pleading, rushed to him daily to obtain pardons for men who had been condemned to be shot. No matter how worn he was, how exhausted, Lincoln always heard their stories, and generally granted their requests, for he never could bear to see a woman cry, especially if she had a baby in her arms.

"When I am gone," he moaned, "I hope it can be said of me that I plucked a thistle and planted a flower wherever I thought a flower would grow."

The generals scolded and Stanton stormed: Lincoln's leniency was destroying the discipline of the army, he must keep his hands off. But the truth is he hated the brutal methods of brigadier generals, and the despotism of the regular army. On the other hand, he loved the volunteers on whom he had to depend for winning the war—men who, like himself, had come from the forest and farm.

Was one of them condemned to be shot for cowardice? Lincoln would pardon him, saying, "I have never been sure but what I might drop my gun and run, myself, if I were in battle."

Had a volunteer become homesick and run away? "Well, I don't see that shooting will do him any good."

Had a tired and exhausted Vermont farm boy been sentenced to death for falling asleep on sentinel duty? "I might have done the same thing, myself," Lincoln would say.

A mere list of his pardons would fill many pages.

He once wired to General Meade, "I am unwilling for any boy under eighteen to be shot." And there were more than a million boys under that age in the Union armies. In fact, there were a fifth of a million under sixteen, and a hundred thousand under fifteen.

Sometimes the President worked a bit of humor into his most serious messages; as, for example, when he wired Colonel Mulligan, "If you haven't shot Barney D. yet, don't."

The anguish of bereaved mothers touched Lincoln very deeply. On November 21, 1864, he wrote the most beautiful and famous letter of his life. Oxford University has a copy of this letter hanging on its wall, "as a model of pure and exquisite diction which has never been excelled."

Although written as prose, it is really unconscious and resonant poetry:

Executive Mansion,
Washington, Nov. 21, 1864.

To Mrs. Bixby, Boston, Mass.
Dear Madame:
I have been shown in the files of the War Department
A statement of the Adjutant General of Massachusetts
That you are the mother of five sons
Who have died gloriously on the field of battle. I feel
How weak and fruitless must be any words of mine
Which would attempt to beguile you from the grief
Of a loss so overwhelming. But I cannot refrain
From tendering to you the consolation that may be found
In the thanks of the Republic they died to save.
I pray that our Heavenly Father may assuage
The anguish of your bereavement, and leave you only
The cherished memory of the loved and lost,
And the solemn pride that must be yours to have laid
So costly a sacrifice upon the altar of freedom.
Yours very sincerely and respectfully,
A. LINCOLN.

One day Noah Brooks gave Lincoln a volume of Oliver Wendell Holmes's verses. Opening the book, Lincoln began reading the poem "Lexington" aloud, but when he came to the stanza beginning:

Green be the grass where her martyrs are lying!
Shroudless and tombless they sunk to their rest,

his voice quavered, he choked, and handing the volume back to Brooks, he whispered: "You read it. I can't."

Months afterward he recited the entire poem to friends in the White House, without missing a word.

On April 5, 1864, Lincoln received a letter from a brokenhearted girl in Washington County, Pennsylvania. "After long hesitation through dread and fear," she began, "I have at last concluded to inform you of my troubles." The man to whom she had been engaged for some years had joined the army, had later been permitted to go home to vote, and they had, as she put it, "very foolishly indulged too freely in matrimonial affairs." And now "the results of our indulgences are going to bring upon us both an unlawful family providing you do not take mercy upon us and grant him a leave of absence in order to ratify past events. . . . I hope and pray to God that you will not cast me aside in scorn and dismay."

Reading the letter, Lincoln was deeply touched. He stared out the window with unseeing eyes in which there were doubtlessly tears. . . .

Picking up his pen, Lincoln wrote the following words to Stanton across the bottom of the girl's letter: "Send him to her by all means."

The terrible summer of 1864 dragged to an end, and the autumn brought good news: Sherman had taken Atlanta and was marching through Georgia. Admiral Farragut, after a dramatic naval battle, had captured Mobile Bay and tightened the blockade in the Gulf of Mexico. Sheridan had won brilliant and spectacular victories in the Shenandoah Valley. And Lee was now afraid to come out in the open; so Grant was laying siege to Petersburg and Richmond. . . .

The Confederacy had almost reached the end.

Lincoln's generals were winning now, his policy had been vindicated, and the spirits of the North rose as on wings; so, in November, he was elected for a second term. But instead of taking it as a personal triumph, he remarked laconically that evidently the people had not thought it wise "to swap horses while crossing a stream."

After four years of fighting, there was no hatred in Lincoln's heart for the people of the South. Time and again he said: " 'Judge not that ye be not judged.' They are just what we would be in their position."

So in February, 1865, while the Confederacy was already crumbling to dust, and Lee's surrender was only two months away, Lincoln proposed that the Federal Government pay the Southern States four hundred million dollars for their slaves; but every member of his Cabinet was unfriendly to the idea and he dropped it.

The following month, on the occasion of his second inauguration, Lincoln delivered a speech that the late Earl Curzon, Chancellor of Oxford University, declared to be "the purest gold of human eloquence, nay of eloquence almost divine."

Stepping forward and kissing a Bible open at the fifth chapter of Isaiah, he began an address that sounded like the speech of some great character in drama.

"It was like a sacred poem," wrote Carl Schurz. "No ruler had ever spoken words like these to his people. America had never before had a president who had found such words in the depths of his heart."

The closing words of this speech are, in the estimation of the writer, the most noble and beautiful utterances ever delivered by the lips of mortal man. He never reads them without thinking somehow of an organ playing in the subdued light of a great cathedral.

> Fondly do we hope—fervently do we pray—that this mighty scourge of war may speedily pass away. Yet, if God wills that it continue until all the wealth piled by the bondman's two hundred and fifty years of unrequited toil shall be sunk, and until every drop of blood drawn with the lash shall be paid by another drawn with the sword, as was said three thousand years ago, so still it must be said, "The judgments of the Lord are true and righteous altogether."
>
> With malice toward none; with charity for all; with firmness in the right, as God gives us to see the right, let us strive on to finish the work we are in; to bind up the nation's wounds; to care for him who shall have borne the battle, and for his widow, and his orphan—to do all which may achieve and cherish a just and lasting peace among ourselves, and with all nations.

Two months later, to a day, this speech was read at Lincoln's funeral services in Springfield.

★ ★ ★

26

★ ★ ★

IN THE LATTER PART of March, 1865, something very significant happened in Richmond, Virginia. Mrs. Jefferson Davis, wife of the President of the Confederacy, disposed of her carriage horses, placed her personal effects on sale at a dry-goods store, packed up the remainder of her belongings, and headed farther south. . . . Something was about to happen.

Grant had been besieging the Confederate capital now for nine months. Lee's troops were ragged and hungry. Money was scarce, and they were rarely paid; and when they were, it was with the paper script of the Confederacy, which was almost worthless now. It took three dollars of it to buy a cup of coffee, five dollars to buy a stick of firewood, and a thousand dollars was demanded for a barrel of flour.

Secession was a lost cause. And so was slavery. Lee knew it. And his men knew it. A hundred thousand of them had already deserted. Whole regiments were packing up now and walking out together. Those that remained were turning to religion for solace and hope. Prayer-meetings were being held in almost every tent; men were shouting and weeping and seeing visions, and entire regiments were kneeling before going into battle.

But notwithstanding all this piety, Richmond was tottering to its fall.

On Sunday, April 2, Lee's army set fire to the cotton and tobacco warehouses in the town, burned the arsenal, destroyed the half-finished ships at the wharves, and fled from the city at night while towering flames were roaring up into the darkness.

They were no sooner out of town than Grant was in hot pursuit with seventy-two thousand men, banging away at the Confederates from both sides and the rear, while Sheridan's cavalry was heading them off in front, tearing up railway lines, and capturing supply-trains.

Sheridan telegraphed to headquarters, "I think if this thing is pushed, Lee will surrender."

Lincoln wired back, "Let the thing be pushed."

It was; and, after a running fight of eighty miles, Grant finally hemmed the Southern troops in on all sides. They were trapped, and Lee realized that further bloodshed would be futile.

In the meantime Grant, half blind with a violent sick headache, had fallen behind his army and halted at a farmhouse on Saturday evening.

"I spent the night," he records in his Memoirs, "in bathing my feet in hot water and mustard, and putting mustard plasters on my wrists and the back part of my neck, hoping to be cured by morning."

The next morning, he was cured instantaneously. And the thing that did it was not a mustard plaster, but a horseman galloping down the road with a letter from Lee, saying he wanted to surrender.

"When the officer [bearing the message] reached me," Grant wrote, "I was still suffering with the sick-headache, but the instant I saw the contents of the note, I was cured."

The two generals met that afternoon in a small bare parlor of a brick dwelling to arrange terms. Grant as usual was slouchily dressed: his shoes were grimy, he had no sword, and he wore the same uniform that every private in the army wore—except that his had three silver stars on the shoulder to show who he was.

What a contrast he made to the aristocratic Lee, wearing beaded gauntlets and a sword studded with jewels! Lee looked like some royal conqueror who had just stepped out of a steel engraving, while Grant looked more like a Missouri farmer who had come to town to sell a load of hogs and a few hides. For once Grant felt ashamed of his frowzy appearance, and he apologized to Lee for not being better dressed for the occasion.

Twenty years before, Grant and Lee had both been officers

in the regular army while the United States was waging a war against Mexico. So they fell to reminiscing now about the days of long ago, about the winter the "regulars" spent on the border of Mexico, about the poker games that used to last all night, about their amateur production of "Othello" when Grant played the sweetly feminine rôle of Desdemona.

"Our conversation grew so pleasant," Grant records, "that I almost forgot the object of our meeting."

Finally, Lee brought the conversation around to the terms of surrender; but Grant replied to that very briefly, and then his mind went rambling on again, back across two decades, to Corpus Christi and the winter in 1845 when the wolves howled on the prairies . . . and the sunlight danced on the waves . . . and wild horses could be bought for three dollars apiece.

Grant might have gone on like that all afternoon if Lee had not interrupted and reminded him, for the second time, that he had come there to surrender his army.

So Grant asked for pen and ink, and scrawled out the terms. There were to be no humiliating ceremonies of capitulation such as Washington had exacted from the British at Yorktown in 1781, with the helpless enemy parading without guns, between long lines of their exultant conquerors. And there was to be no vengeance. For four bloody years the radicals of the North had been demanding that Lee and the other West Point officers who had turned traitor to their flag be hanged for treason. But the terms that Grant wrote out had no sting. Lee's officers were permitted to keep their arms, and his men were to be paroled and sent home; and every soldier who claimed a horse or a mule could crawl on it and ride it back to his farm or cotton-patch and start tilling the soil once more.

Why were the terms of surrender so generous and gentle? Because Abraham Lincoln himself had dictated the terms.

And so the war that had killed half a million men came to a close in a tiny Virginia village called Appomattox Court House. The surrender took place on a peaceful spring afternoon when the scent of lilacs filled the air. It was Palm Sunday.

On that very afternoon Lincoln was sailing back to Washington on the good ship *River Queen.* He spent several hours reading Shakspere aloud to his friends. Presently he came to this passage in "Macbeth":

Duncan is in his grave;
After life's fitful fever he sleeps well;
Treason has done his worst: nor steel, nor poison,
Malice domestic, foreign levy, nothing,
Can touch him further.

These lines made a profound impression on Lincoln. He read them once, then paused, gazing with unseeing eyes through the port-hole of the ship.

Presently he read them aloud again.

Five days later Lincoln himself was dead.

★ ★ ★

27

★ ★ ★

WE MUST retrace our steps now, for I want to tell you of an amazing thing that happened shortly before the fall of Richmond—an incident that gives one a vivid picture of the domestic miseries that Lincoln endured in silence for almost a quarter of a century.

It happened near Grant's headquarters. The general had invited Mr. and Mrs. Lincoln to spend a week with him near the front.

They were glad to come, for the President was almost exhausted. He hadn't had a vacation since he entered the White House, and he was eager to get away from the throng of office-seekers who were harassing him once more at the opening of his second term.

So he and Mrs. Lincoln boarded the *River Queen* and sailed away down the Potomac, through the lower reaches of Chesapeake Bay, past old Point Comfort, and up the James River to City Point. There, high on a bluff, two hundred feet above the water, sat the ex-hide-buyer from Galena, smoking and whittling.

A few days later the President's party was joined by a distinguished group of people from Washington, including M. Geoffroi, the French minister. Naturally the visitors were eager to see the battle lines of the Army of the Potomac, twelve miles away; so the next day they set out upon the excursion—the men on horseback, Mrs. Lincoln and Mrs. Grant following in a half-open carriage.

General Adam Badeau, Grant's military secretary and aide-de-camp and one of the closest friends General Grant ever had, was detailed to escort the ladies that day. He sat on the front seat of the carriage, facing them and with his back to the horses. He was an eye-witness to all that occurred, and I am quoting now from pages 356-362 of his book entitled "Grant in Peace":

> In the course of conversation, I chanced to mention that all the wives of officers at the army front had been ordered to the rear—a sure sign that active operations were in contemplation. I said not a lady had been allowed to remain, except Mrs. Griffin, the wife of General Charles Griffin, who had obtained a special permit from the President.
>
> At this Mrs. Lincoln was up in arms. "What do you mean by that, sir?" she exclaimed. "Do you mean to say that she saw the President alone? Do you know that I never allow the President to see any woman alone?"
>
> She was absolutely jealous of poor, ugly Abraham Lincoln.
>
> I tried to pacify her and to palliate my remark, but she was fairly boiling over with rage. "That's a very equivocal smile, sir," she exclaimed: "Let me out of this carriage at once. I will ask the President if he saw that woman alone."
>
> Mrs. Griffin, afterward the Countess Esterhazy, was one of the best known and most elegant women in Washington, a Carroll, and a personal acquaintance of Mrs. Grant, who strove to mollify the excited spouse, but all in vain. Mrs. Lincoln again bade me stop the driver, and when I hesitated to obey, she thrust her arms past me to the front of the carriage and held the driver fast. But Mrs. Grant finally prevailed upon her to wait till the whole party alighted. . . .
>
> At night, when we were back in camp, Mrs. Grant talked over the matter with me, and said the whole affair was so distressing and mortifying that neither of us must ever mention it; at least, I was to be absolutely silent, and she would disclose it only to the General. But the next day I was released from my pledge, for "worse remained behind."
>
> The same party went in the morning to visit the Army of the James on the north side of the river, commanded

by General Ord. The arrangements were somewhat similar to those of the day before. We went up the river in a steamer, and then the men again took horses and Mrs. Lincoln and Mrs. Grant proceeded in an ambulance. I was detailed as before to act as escort, but I asked for a companion in the duty; for after my experience, I did not wish to be the only officer in the carriage. So Colonel Horace Porter was ordered to join the party. Mrs. Ord accompanied her husband; as she was the wife of the commander of an army she was not subject to the order for return; though before that day was over she wished herself in Washington or anywhere else away from the army, I am sure. She was mounted, and as the ambulance was full, she remained on her horse and rode for a while by the side of the President, and thus preceded Mrs. Lincoln.

As soon as Mrs. Lincoln discovered this her rage was beyond all bounds. "What does the woman mean," she exclaimed, "by riding by the side of the President? and ahead of me? Does she suppose that he wants her by the side of him?"

She was in a frenzy of excitement, and language and action both became more extravagant every moment.

Mrs. Grant again endeavored to pacify her, but then Mrs. Lincoln got angry with Mrs. Grant; and all that Porter and I could do was to see that nothing worse than words occurred. We feared she might jump out of the vehicle and shout to the cavalcade.

Once she said to Mrs. Grant in her transports: "I suppose you think you'll get to the White House yourself, don't you?" Mrs. Grant was very calm and dignified, and merely replied that she was quite satisfied with her present position; it was far greater than she had ever expected to attain. But Mrs. Lincoln exclaimed; "Oh! you had better take it if you can get it. 'Tis very nice." Then she reverted to Mrs. Ord, while Mrs. Grant defended her friend at the risk of arousing greater vehemence.

When there was a halt, Major Seward, a nephew of the Secretary of State, and an officer of General Ord's staff, rode up, and tried to say something jocular. "The President's horse is very gallant, Mrs. Lincoln," he remarked; "he insists on riding by the side of Mrs. Ord."

This of course added fuel to the flame.

"What do you mean by that, sir?" she cried.

Seward discovered that he had made a huge mistake, and his horse at once developed a peculiarity that compelled him to ride behind, to get out of the way of the storm.

Finally the party arrived at its destination and Mrs. Ord came up to the ambulance. Then Mrs. Lincoln positively insulted her, called her vile names in the presence of a crowd of officers, and asked what she meant by following up the President. The poor woman burst into tears and inquired what she had done, but Mrs. Lincoln refused to be appeased, and stormed till she was tired. Mrs. Grant still tried to stand by her friend, and everybody was shocked and horrified. But all things come to an end, and after a while we returned to City Point.

That night the President and Mrs. Lincoln entertained General and Mrs. Grant and the General's staff at dinner on the steamer, and before us all Mrs. Lincoln berated General Ord to the President, and urged that he should be removed. He was unfit for his place, she said, to say nothing of his wife. General Grant sat next and defended his officer bravely. Of course General Ord was not removed.

During all this visit similar scenes were occurring. Mrs. Lincoln repeatedly attacked her husband in the presence of officers because of Mrs. Griffin and Mrs. Ord, and I never suffered greater humiliation and pain on account of one not a near personal friend than when I saw the Head of the State, the man who carried all the cares of the nation at such a crisis—subjected to this inexpressible public mortification. He bore it as Christ might have done; with an expression of pain and sadness that cut one to the heart, but with supreme calmness and dignity. He called her "mother," with his old-time plainness; he pleaded with eyes and tones, and endeavored to explain or palliate the offenses of others, till she turned on him like a tigress; and then he walked away, hiding that noble, ugly face that we might not catch the full expression of its misery.

General Sherman was a witness of some of these episodes and mentioned them in his memoirs many years ago.

Captain Barnes, of the navy, was a witness and a sufferer too. Barnes had accompanied Mrs. Ord on her unfortunate ride and refused afterward to say that the lady was to blame. Mrs. Lincoln never forgave him. A day or two afterward he went to speak to the President on some official matter when Mrs. Lincoln and several others were present. The President's wife said something to him unusually offensive that all the company could hear. Lincoln was silent, but after a moment he went up to the young officer, and taking him by the arm led him into his own cabin, to show him a map or a paper, he said. He made no remark, Barnes told me, upon what had occurred. He could not rebuke his wife; but he showed his regret, and his regard for the officer, with a touch of what seemed to me the most exquisite breeding imaginable.

Shortly before these occurrences Mrs. Stanton had visited City Point, and I chanced to ask her some question about the President's wife.

"I do not visit Mrs. Lincoln," was the reply.

But I thought I must have been mistaken; the wife of the Secretary of War must visit the wife of the President; and I renewed my inquiry.

"Understand me, sir?" she repeated; "I do not go to the White House; I do not visit Mrs. Lincoln." I was not at all intimate with Mrs. Stanton and this remark was so extraordinary that I never forgot it; but I understood it afterward.

Mrs. Lincoln continued her conduct toward Mrs Grant, who strove to placate her and then Mrs. Lincoln became more outrageous still. She once rebuked Mrs. Grant for sitting in her presence. "How dare you be seated," she said, "until I invite you?"

Elizabeth Keckley, who accompanied Mrs. Lincoln on this trip to Grant's headquarters, tells of a dinner party that "Mrs. President" gave aboard the *River Queen.*

One of the guests was a young officer attached to the Sanitary Commission. He was seated near Mrs. Lincoln, and, by way of pleasantry, remarked: "Mrs. Lincoln, you should have seen the President the other day, on his triumphal entry into Richmond. He was the cynosure of all eyes. The ladies kissed their hands to him, and greeted him with the waving of handkerchiefs. He is quite a hero when surrounded by pretty young ladies."

The young officer suddenly paused with a look of embarrassment.

Mrs. Lincoln turned to him with flashing eyes, with the remark that his familiarity was offensive to her.

Quite a scene followed, and I do not think that the Captain who incurred Mrs. Lincoln's displeasure will ever forget that memorable evening.

"I never in my life saw a more peculiarly constituted woman," says Mrs. Keckley. "Search the world over and you will not find her counterpart."

"Ask the first American you meet, 'What kind of a woman was Lincoln's wife?'" says Honoré Willsie Morrow in her book "Mary Todd Lincoln," "and the chances are ninety nine to one hundred that he'll reply that she was a shrew, a curse to her husband, a vulgar fool, insane."

The great tragedy of Lincoln's life was not his assassination, but his marriage.

When Booth fired, Lincoln did not know what had hit him, but for twenty-three years he had reaped almost daily what Herndon described as "the bitter harvest of conjugal infelicity."

"Amid storms of party hate and rebellious strife," says General Badeau, "amid agonies . . . like those of the Cross . . . the hyssop of domestic misery was pressed to Lincoln's lips, and he too said: 'Father, forgive: they know not what they do.'"

One of Lincoln's warmest friends during his life as President was Orville H. Browning, Senator from Illinois. These two men had known each other for a quarter of a century, and Browning was frequently a dinner guest in the White House and sometimes spent the night there. He kept a detailed diary, but one can only wonder what he recorded in it about Mrs. Lincoln, for authors have not been permitted to read the manuscript without pledging their honor not to divulge anything derogatory to her character. This manuscript was recently sold for publication with the provision that all shocking statements regarding Mrs. Lincoln should be deleted before it was put into print.

At public receptions in the White House it had always been customary for the President to choose some lady other than his wife to lead the promenade with him.

But custom or no custom, tradition or no tradition, Mrs.

Lincoln wouldn't tolerate it. What? Another woman ahead of her? And on the President's arm? Never!

So she had her way, and Washington society hooted.

She not only refused to let the President walk with another woman, but she eyed him jealously and criticized him severely for even talking to one.

Before going to a public reception Lincoln would come to his jealous wife, asking whom he might talk to. She would mention woman after woman, saying she detested this one and hated that one.

"But Mother," he would remonstrate, "I must talk with somebody. I can't stand around like a simpleton and say nothing. If you will not tell me who I may talk with, please tell me who I may *not* talk with."

She determined to have her own way, cost what it might, and, on one occasion, she threatened to throw herself down in the mud in front of every one unless Lincoln promoted a certain officer.

At another time she dashed into his office during an important interview, pouring out a torrent of words. Without replying to her, Lincoln calmly arose, picked her up, carried her out of the room, set her down, returned, locked the door, and went on with his business as if he had never been interrupted.

She consulted a spiritualist, who told her that all of Lincoln's Cabinet were his enemies.

That didn't surprise her. She had no love for any of them.

She despised Seward, calling him "a hypocrite," "an abolition sneak," saying that he couldn't be trusted, and warning Lincoln to have nothing to do with him.

"Her hostility to Chase," says Mrs. Keckley, "was bitter."

And one of the reasons was this: Chase had a daughter, Kate, who was married to a wealthy man and was one of the most beautiful and charming women in Washington society. Kate would attend the White House receptions; and, to Mrs. Lincoln's immense disgust, she would draw all the men about her and run away with the show.

Mrs. Keckley says that "Mrs. Lincoln, who was jealous of the popularity of others, had no desire to build up the social position of Chase's daughter through political favor to her father."

With heat and temper, she repeatedly urged Lincoln to dismiss Chase from the Cabinet.

She loathed Stanton, and when he criticized her, she "would return the compliment by sending him books and clippings describing him as an irascible and disagreeable personality."

To all these bitter condemnations, Lincoln would say:

"Mother, you are mistaken; your prejudices are so violent you do not stop to reason. If I listened to you, I should soon be without a cabinet."

She disliked Andrew Johnson intensely; she hated McClellan; she despised Grant, calling him "an obstinate fool and a butcher," declaring that she could handle an army better than he could, and frequently vowing that if he were ever made President, she would leave the country and never come back to it as long as he was in the White House.

"Well, Mother," Lincoln would say, "supposing that we give you command of the army. No doubt you would do much better than any general that has been tried."

After Lee surrendered, Mr. and Mrs. Grant came to Washington. The town was a blaze of light: crowds were making merry with songs and bonfires and revelry; so Mrs. Lincoln wrote the general, inviting him to drive about the streets with her and the President "to see the illumination."

But she did not invite Mrs. Grant.

A few nights later, however, she arranged a theater party and invited Mr. and Mrs. Grant and Mr. and Mrs. Stanton to sit in the President's box.

As soon as Mrs. Stanton received the invitation, she hurried over to Mrs. Grant, to inquire if she were going.

"Unless you accept the invitation," said Mrs. Stanton, "I shall refuse. I will not sit in the box with Mrs. Lincoln unless you are there too."

Mrs. Grant was afraid to accept.

She knew that if the general entered the box, the audience would be sure to greet the "hero of Appomattox" with a salvo of applause.

And then what would Mrs. Lincoln do? There was no telling. She might create another disgraceful and mortifying scene.

Mrs. Grant refused the invitation, and so did Mrs. Stanton; and by refusing, they may have saved the lives of their husbands, for that night Booth crept into the President's box and shot Lincoln; and if Stanton and Grant had been there, he might have tried to kill them also.

★ ★ ★

28

★ ★ ★

In 1863 a group of Virginia slave barons formed and financed a secret society the object of which was the assassination of Abraham Lincoln; and in December, 1864, an advertisement appeared in a newspaper published in Selma, Alabama, begging for public subscriptions for a fund to be used for the same purpose, while other Southern journals offered cash rewards for his death.

But the man who finally shot Lincoln was actuated neither by patriotic desires nor commercial motives. John Wilkes Booth did it to win fame.

What manner of man was Booth? He was an actor, and nature had endowed him with an extraordinary amount of charm and personal magnetism. Lincoln's own secretaries described him as "handsome as Endymion on Latmos, the pet of his little world." Francis Wilson, in his biography of Booth, declares that "he was one of the world's successful lovers. . . . Women halted in the streets and instinctively turned to admire him as he passed."

By the time he was twenty-three, Booth had achieved the status of a matinée idol; and, naturally, his most famous rôle was Romeo. Wherever he played, amorous maidens deluged him with saccharine notes. While he was playing in Boston huge crowds of women thronged the streets in front of the Tremont House, eager to catch but one glimpse of their hero as he passed. One night a jealous actress, Henrietta Irving, knifed him in a hotel room, and then tried to commit suicide; and the morning after Booth shot Lincoln, another of his sweethearts, Ella Turner, an inmate of a Washington "parlor house," was so distressed to learn that her lover had turned murderer and fled the city, that she clasped his picture to her heart, took chloroform, and lay down to die.

But did this flood of female adulation bring happiness to Booth? Very little, for his triumphs were confined almost wholly to the less discriminating audiences of the hinterland, while there was gnawing at his heart a passionate ambition to win the plaudits of the metropolitan centers.

But New York critics thought poorly of him, and in Philadelphia he was hooted off the stage.

This was galling, for other members of the Booth family were famous on the stage. For well-nigh a third of a century, his father, Junius Brutus Booth, had been a theatrical star of the first magnitude. His Shakesperian interpretations were the talk of the nation. No one else in the history of the American stage had ever won such extraordinary popularity. And the old man Booth had reared his favorite son, John Wilkes, to believe that he was to be the greatest of the Booths.

But the truth is that John Wilkes Booth possessed very little talent, and he didn't make the most of the trifling amount he did have. He was good-looking and spoiled and lazy, and he refused to bore himself with study. Instead, he spent his youthful days on horseback, dashing through the woods of the Maryland farm, spouting heroic speeches to the trees and squirrels, and jabbing the air with an old army lance that had been used in the Mexican War.

Old Junius Brutus Booth never permitted meat to be served at the family table, and he taught his sons that it was wrong to kill any living thing—even a rattlesnake. But John Wilkes evidently was not seriously restrained by his father's philosophy. He liked to shoot and destroy. Sometimes he banged away with his gun at the cats and hound dogs belonging to the slaves, and once he killed a sow owned by a neighbor.

Later he became an oyster pirate in Chesapeake Bay, then an actor. Now, at twenty-six, he was a favorite of gushing high-school girls, but, in his own eyes, he was a failure. And besides, he was bitterly jealous, for he saw his elder brother, Edwin, achieving the very renown that he himself so passionately desired.

He brooded over this a long time, and finally decided to make himself forever famous in one night.

This was his first plan: He would follow Lincoln to the theater some night; and, while one of his confederates turned off the gas-lights, Booth would dash into the President's box, rope and tie him, toss him onto the stage below, hustle him through a back exit, pitch him into a carriage, and scurry away like mad in the darkness.

By hard driving, he could reach the sleepy old town of Port Tobacco before dawn. Then he would row across the broad Potomac, and gallop on south through Virginia until he had lodged the Commander-in-Chief of the Union Army safely behind the Confederate bayonets in Richmond.

And then what?

Well, then the South could dictate terms and bring the war to an end at once.

And the credit for this brilliant achievement would go to whom? To the dazzling genius John Wilkes Booth. He would become twice as famous, a hundred times as famous as his brother Edwin. He would be crowned in history with the aura of a William Tell. Such were his dreams.

He was making twenty thousand dollars a year then in the theater, but he gave it all up. Money meant little to him now, for he was playing for something far more important than material possessions. So he used his savings to finance a band of Confederates that he fished out of the backwash of Southern sympathizers floating around Baltimore and Washington. Booth promised each one of them that he should be rich and famous.

And what a motley crew they were! There was Spangler, a drunken stage-hand and crab-fisherman; Atzerodt, an ignorant house-painter and blockade-runner with stringy hair and whiskers, a rough, fierce fellow; Arnold, a lazy farm-hand and a deserter from the Confederate Army; O'Laughlin, a livery-stable worker, smelling of horses and whisky; Surratt, a swaggering nincompoop of a clerk; Powell, a gigantic penniless brute, the wild-eyed, half-mad son of a Baptist preacher; Herold, a silly, giggling loafer, lounging about stables, talking horses and women, and living on the dimes and quarters given him by his widowed mother and his seven sisters.

With this supporting cast of tenth-raters, Booth was preparing to play the great rôle of his career. He spared neither time nor money in planning the minutest details. He purchased a pair of handcuffs, arranged for relays of fast horses at the proper places, bought three boats, and had them waiting in Port Tobacco Creek, equipped with oars and rowers ready to man them at a moment's notice.

Finally, in January, 1865, he believed that the great moment had come. Lincoln was to attend Ford's Theater on the eighteenth of that month, to see Edwin Forrest play "Jack Cade." So the rumor ran about town. And Booth heard it. So he was on hand that night with his ropes and hopes—and what happened? Nothing. Lincoln didn't appear.

Two months later it was reported that Lincoln was going to drive out of the city on a certain afternoon to attend a theatrical performance in a near-by soldiers' encampment. So Booth and his accomplices, mounted on horses and armed with bowie-knives and revolvers, hid in a stretch of woods that the President would have to pass. But when the White House carriage rolled by, Lincoln was not in it.

Thwarted again, Booth stormed about, cursing, pulling at his raven-black mustache, and striking his boots with his riding-whip. He had had enough of this. He was not going to be frustrated any longer. If he couldn't capture Lincoln, by God, he could kill him.

A few weeks later Lee surrendered and ended the war, and Booth saw then that there was no longer any point in kidnapping the President; so he determined to shoot Lincoln at once.

Booth did not have to wait long. The following Friday he had a hair-cut, and then went to Ford's Theater to get his mail. There he learned that a box had been reserved for the President for that night's performance.

"What!" Booth exclaimed. "Is that old scoundrel going to be here to-night?"

Stage-hands were already making ready for a gala performance, draping the left-hand box with flags against a background of lace, decorating it with a picture of Washington, removing the partition, doubling the space, lining it with crimson paper and putting in an unusually large walnut rocking-chair to accommodate the President's long legs.

Booth bribed a stage-hand to place the chair in the precise position that he desired; he wanted it in the angle of the box nearest the audience, so that no one would see him enter. Through the inner door, immediately behind the rocker, he bored a small peep-hole; then dug a notch in the plastering behind the door leading from the dress-circle to the boxes, so that he could bar that entrance with a wooden plank. After that Booth went to his hotel and wrote a long letter to the editor of the "National Intelligencer," justifying the plotted assassination in the name of patriotism, and declaring that posterity would honor him. He signed it and gave it to an actor, instructing him to have it published the next day.

Then he went to a livery-stable, hired a small bay mare that he boasted could run "like a cat," and rounded up his assistants and put them on horses; gave Atzerodt a gun, and told him to shoot the Vice-President; and handed a pistol and knife to Powell, ordering him to murder Seward.

It was Good Friday, ordinarily one of the worst nights of the year for the theater, but the town was thronged with officers and enlisted men eager to see the Commander-in-Chief of the Army, and the city was still jubilant, celebrating the end of the war. Triumphal arches still spanned Pennsylvania Avenue, and the streets were gay with dancing torch-light processions, shouting with high elation to the President as he drove by that night to the theater. When he arrived at Ford's the house was packed to capacity and hundreds were being turned away.

The President's party entered during the middle of the first act, at precisely twenty minutes to nine. The players paused and bowed. The brilliantly attired audience roared its welcome. The orchestra crashed into "Hail to the Chief." Lincoln bowed his acknowledgment, parted his coat-tails, and sat down in a walnut rocking-chair upholstered in red.

On Mrs. Lincoln's right sat her guests: Major Rathbone of the Provost-Marshal General's office and his fiancée, Miss Clara H. Harris, the daughter of Senator Ira Harris of New York, blue-bloods high enough in Washington society to meet the fastidious requirements of their Kentucky hostess.

Laura Keene was giving her final performance of the celebrated comedy "Our American Cousin." It was a gay and joyous occasion; and sparkling laughter rippled back and forth across the audience.

Lincoln had taken a long drive in the afternoon, with his wife: she remarked afterward that he had been happier that day than she had seen him in years. Why shouldn't he be? Peace. Victory. Union. Freedom. He had talked to Mary that afternoon about what they would do when they left the White House at the close of his second term. First, they would take a long rest in either Europe or California; and when they returned, he might open a law office in Chicago, or drift back to Springfield and spend his remaining years riding over the prairie circuit that he loved so well. Some old friends that he had known in Illinois had called at the White House, that same afternoon, and he had been so elated telling jokes that Mrs. Lincoln could hardly get him to dinner.

The night before, he had had a strange dream. He had told the members of his Cabinet about it that morning: "I seemed to be in a singular and indescribable vessel," he said, "that was moving with great rapidity toward a dark and indefinite shore. I have had this extraordinary dream before great events, before victories. I had it preceding Antietam, Stone River, Gettysburg, Vicksburg."

He believed that this dream was a good omen, that it foretold good news, that something beautiful was going to happen.

At ten minutes past ten Booth, inflamed with whisky, and dressed in dark riding-breeches, boots, and spurs, entered the theater for the last time in his life—and noted the position of the President. With a black slouch hat in his hand, he mounted the stairs leading to the dress-circle, and edged his way down an aisle choked with chairs, until he came to the corridor leading to the boxes.

Halted by one of the President's guards, Booth handed him his personal card with confidence and bravado, saying that the President wished to see him; and, without waiting for permission, pushed in and closed the corridor door behind him, wedging it shut with a wooden upright from a music-stand.

Peeping through the gimlet-hole that he had bored in the door behind the President, he gaged the distance, and quietly swung the door open. Shoving the muzzle of his high-calibered derringer close to his victim's head, he pulled the trigger and quickly leaped to the stage below.

Lincoln's head fell forward and then sidewise as he slumped in his chair.

He uttered no sound whatever.

For an instant the audience thought that the pistol-shot and the leap to the stage were a part of the play. No one, not even the actors themselves, suspected that the President had been harmed.

Then a woman's shriek pierced the theater and all eyes turned to the draped box. Major Rathbone, blood gushing from one arm, shouted: "Stop that man! Stop him! He has killed the President!"

A moment of silence. A wisp of smoke floating out of the Presidential box. Then the suspense broke. Terror and mad excitement seized the audience. They burst through the seats, wrenching the chairs from the floor, broke over railings, and, trying to clamber upon the stage, tore one another down and trampled upon the old and feeble. Bones were broken in the crush, women screamed and fainted, and shrieks of agony mingled with fierce yells of "Hang him!" . . . "Shoot him!" . . . "Burn the theater!"

Some one shouted that the playhouse itself was to be bombed. The fury of the panic doubled and trebled. A company of frantic soldiers dashed into the theater at double-quick, and charged the audience with muskets and fixed bayonets, shouting: "Get out of here! Damn you, get out!"

Physicians from the audience examined the President's wound; and, knowing it to be fatal, refused to have the dying man jolted over the cobblestones back to the White House. So four soldiers lifted him up—two at his shoulders and two at his feet—and carried his long, sagging body out of the theater and into the street, where blood dripping from his wound reddened the pavement. Men knelt to stain their handkerchiefs with it—handkerchiefs which they would treasure a lifetime, and, dying, bequeath as priceless legacies to their children.

With flashing sabers and rearing horses, the cavalry cleared a space; and loving hands bore the stricken President across the street to a cheap lodging-house owned by a tailor, stretched his long frame diagonally across a sagging bed far too short for him, and pulled the bed over to a dismal gas-jet that flickered yellow light.

It was a hall room nine by seventeen feet in size, with a cheap reproduction of Rosa Bonheur's painting of "The Horse Fair" hanging above the bed.

The news of the tragedy swept over Washington like a tornado; and, racing in its wake, came the impact of another disaster: at the same hour of the attack on Lincoln, Secretary Seward had been stabbed in bed and was not expected to live. Out of these black facts, fearsome rumors shot through the night like chain-lightning: Vice-President Johnson had been slain.

Stanton had been assassinated. Grant shot. So ran the wild tales.

People were sure now that Lee's surrender had been a ruse, that the Confederates had treacherously crept into Washington and were trying to wipe out the Government with one blow, that the Southern legions had sprung to arms again, that the war, bloodier than ever, was starting once more.

Mysterious messengers dashed through the residence districts, striking the pavement two short staccato raps, thrice repeated—the danger-call of a secret society, the Union League. Awakened by the summons, members grasped their rifles and rushed wildly into the street.

Mobs with torches and ropes boiled through the town, howling: "Burn the theater!" . . . "Hang the traitor!" . . . "Kill the rebels!"

It was one of the maddest nights this nation has ever known!

The telegraph flashed the news, setting the nation on fire. Southern sympathizers and copperheads were ridden on rails and tarred and feathered; the skulls of some were crushed with paving-stones. Photograph galleries in Baltimore were stormed and wrecked because they were believed to contain pictures of Booth; and a Maryland editor was shot because he had published some scurrilous abuse of Lincoln.

With the President dying; with Johnson, the Vice-President, sprawled on his bed stone-drunk and his hair matted with mud; with Seward, Secretary of State, stabbed to the verge of death, the reins of power were grasped immediately by Edward M. Stanton, the gruff, erratic, and tempestuous Secretary of War.

Believing that all high officers of the Government were marked for slaughter, Stanton, in wild excitement, dashed off order after order, writing them on the top of his silk hat as he sat by the bedside of his dying chief. He commanded guards to protect his house and the residences of his colleagues; he confiscated Ford's Theater and arrested every one connected with it; he declared Washington to be in a state of siege; he called out the entire military and police force of the District of Columbia, all the soldiers in the surrounding camps, barracks, and fortifications, the Secret Service men of the United States, the spies attached to the Bureau of Military Justice; he threw pickets around the entire city, fifty feet apart; he set a watch at every ferry, and ordered tugs, steamers, and gunboats to patrol the Potomac.

Stanton wired the chief of police in New York to rush him

his best detectives, telegraphed orders to watch the Canadian border, and commanded the President of the Baltimore and Ohio Railway to intercept General Grant in Philadelphia and bring him back to Washington at once, running a pilot locomotive ahead of his train.

He poured a brigade of infantry into lower Maryland, and sent a thousand cavalrymen galloping after the assassin, saying over and over: "He will try to get South. Guard the Potomac from the city down."

The bullet that Booth fired pierced Lincoln's head below the left ear, plowed diagonally through the brain, and lodged within half an inch of the right eye. A man of lesser vitality would have been cut down instantly; but for nine hours Lincoln lived, groaning heavily.

Mrs. Lincoln was kept in an adjoining room; but every hour she would insist on being brought to his bedside, weeping and shrieking, "O my God, have I given my husband to die?"

Once as she was caressing his face and pressing her wet cheek against his, he suddenly began groaning and breathing louder than ever. Screaming, the distraught wife sprang back and fell to the floor in a faint.

Stanton, hearing the commotion, rushed into the room, shouting, "Take that woman away, and don't let her in here again."

Shortly after seven o'clock the groaning ceased and Lincoln's breathing became quiet. "A look of unspeakable peace," wrote one of his secretaries who was there, "came over his worn features."

Sometimes recognition and understanding flash back into the secret chambers of consciousness immediately before dissolution.

In those last peaceful moments broken fragments of happy memories may have floated brightly through the deep hidden caverns of his mind—vanished visions of the long ago: a log fire blazing at night in front of the open shed in the Buckhorn Valley of Indiana; the roar of the Sangamon plunging over the mill-dam at New Salem; Ann Rutledge singing at the spinning-wheel; Old Buck nickering for his corn; Orlando Kellogg telling the story of the stuttering justice; and the law office at Springfield with the ink-stain on the wall and garden seeds sprouting on top of the bookcase. . . .

Throughout the long hours of the death-struggle Dr. Leale,

an army surgeon, sat by the President's bedside holding his hand. At twenty-two minutes past seven the doctor folded Lincoln's pulseless arms, put half-dollars on his eyelids to hold them shut, and tied up his jaw with a pocket handkerchief. A clergyman offered a prayer. Cold rain pattered down on the roof. General Barnes drew a sheet over the face of the dead President; and Stanton, weeping and pulling down the window-shades to shut out the light of the dawn, uttered the only memorable sentence of that night: "Now he belongs to the ages."

The next day little Tad asked a caller at the White House if his father was in heaven.

"I have no doubt of it," came the reply.

"Then I am glad he has gone," said Tad, "for he was never happy after he came here. This was not a good place for him."

★

PART FOUR

★

★ ★ ★

29

★ ★ ★

THE FUNERAL TRAIN bearing Lincoln's body back to Illinois crawled through vast crowds of mourning people. The train itself was smothered in crêpe; and the engine, like a hearse-horse, was covered with a huge black blanket trimmed with silver stars.

As it steamed northward faces began to appear beside the track—faces that rapidly multiplied in numbers and increased in sadness.

For miles before the train reached the Philadelphia station it ran between solid walls of humanity, and when it rolled into the city thousands of people were milling and jamming through the streets. Mourners stood in lines three miles long, stretching away from Independence Hall. They edged forward, inch by inch, for ten hours in order to look down at last upon Lincoln's face for but one second. On Saturday at midnight the doors were closed, but the mourners, refusing to be dispersed, kept their places all night long and by three o'clock Sunday morning the crowds were greater than ever and boys were selling their places in line for ten dollars.

Soldiers and mounted police fought to keep traffic lanes open, while hundreds of women fainted, and veterans who had fought at Gettysburg collapsed as they struggled to keep order.

For twenty-four hours before the funeral services were scheduled to take place in New York excursion trains running day and night poured into that city the greatest crowds it had ever known—crowds that filled the hotels and overflowed into private homes and backwashed across the parks and onto steamboat piers.

The next day sixteen white horses, ridden by Negroes, pulled the hearse up Broadway, while women, frantic with grief, tossed flowers in its path. Behind came the tramp, tramp, tramp of marching feet—a hundred and sixty thousand mourners with swaying banners bearing quotations like these: "Ah, the pity of it, Iago—the pity of it!" . . . "Be still, and know that I am God."

Half a million spectators fought and trampled upon one another in an effort to view the long procession. Second-story windows facing Broadway were rented for forty dollars each, and window-panes were removed in order that the openings might accommodate as many heads as possible.

Choirs robed in white sang hymns on street corners, marching bands wailed their dirges, and at intervals of sixty seconds the roar of a hundred cannon reverberated over the town.

As the crowds sobbed by the bier in City Hall, New York, many spoke to the dead man, some tried to touch his face; and, while the guard was not looking, one woman bent over and kissed the corpse.

When the casket was closed in New York, at noon on Tuesday, thousands who had been unable to view the remains hurried to the trains and sped westward to other points where the funeral car was scheduled to stop. From now on until it reached Springfield the funeral train was seldom out of the sound of tolling bells and booming guns. By day it ran under arches of evergreens and flowers and past hillsides covered with children waving flags; by night its passing was illumined by countless torches and flaming bonfires stretching half-way across the continent.

The country was in a frenzy of excitement. No such funeral had ever before been witnessed, in all history. Weak minds here and there snapped under the strain. A young man in New York slashed his throat with a razor, crying, "I am going to join Abraham Lincoln."

Forty-eight hours after the assassination a committee from Springfield had hurried to Washington, pleading with Mrs. Lincoln to have her husband buried in his home town. At first, she was sharply opposed to the suggestion. She had hardly a friend left in Springfield, and she knew it. True, she had three sisters living there, but she thoroughly disliked two of them and despised the third one, and she felt nothing but contempt for the rest of the gossiping little village.

"My God, Elizabeth!" she said to her colored dressmaker, "I can never go back to Springfield."

So she planned to have Lincoln interred in Chicago or placed under the dome of the National Capitol, in the tomb originally constructed for George Washington.

However, after seven days of pleading, she consented to have the body taken back to Springfield. The town raised a public fund, bought a beautiful tract of land consisting of four city blocks—now occupied by the State Capitol—and set men digging day and night.

Finally, on the morning of May 4, the funeral train was in town, the tomb was ready, and thousands of Lincoln's old friends had forgathered for the services, when Mrs. Lincoln, in a sudden rage of erratic temper, countermanded all plans and haughtily decreed that the body must be interred, not where the tomb had been built, but in the Oak Ridge Cemetery, two miles out in the woods.

There were to be no *ifs* or *ands* or *buts* about it. If she did not have her way, she threatened to use "violent" means to carry the remains back to Washington. Why? For a very unlovely reason: the tomb that had been erected in the middle of Springfield stood on what was known as the "Mather block," and Mrs. Lincoln despised the Mather family. Years before, one of the Mathers had, in some way, aroused her fiery wrath; and now, even in the hushed presence of death, she still cherished her bitter resentment, and would not consent to let Lincoln's body lie for one single night on ground that had been contaminated by the Mathers.

For a quarter of a century this woman had lived under the same roof with a husband who had had "malice toward none," and "charity for all." But like the Bourbon kings of France, she had learned nothing, she had forgotten nothing.

Springfield had to bow to the widow's mandate; and so at eleven o'clock the remains were taken out to a public vault in Oak Ridge Cemetery. Fighting Joe Hooker rode ahead of the hearse; and behind it was led Old Buck, covered with a red, white, and blue blanket on which were embroidered the words, "Old Abe's Horse."

By the time Old Buck got back to his stable, there was not a shred of the blanket left; souvenir-hunters had stripped him bare. And, like buzzards, they swooped down upon the empty hearse, snatching at the draperies and fighting over it until soldiers charged them with bayonets.

For five weeks after the assassination Mrs. Lincoln lay weeping in the White House, refusing to leave her chamber night or day.

Elizabeth Keckley, who was at her bedside during all this time, wrote:

> I shall never forget the scene. The wails of a broken heart, the unearthly shrieks, the terrible convulsions, the wild, tempestuous outbursts of grief from the soul. I bathed Mrs. Lincoln's head with cold water, and soothed the terrible tornado as best I could.
>
> Tad's grief at his father's death was as great as the grief of his mother, but her terrible outbursts awed the boy into silence. . . .
>
> Often at night, when Tad would hear her sobbing, he would get up, and come to her bed in his white sleeping-clothes: "Don't cry, Mamma; I can't sleep if you cry! Papa was good, and he has gone to Heaven. He is happy there. He is with God and brother Willie. Don't cry, Mamma, or I will cry too."

★ ★ ★

30

★ ★ ★

THE INSTANT that Booth fired at Lincoln, Major Rathbone, who was sitting in the box with the President, leaped up and grabbed the assassin. But he couldn't hold him, for Booth slashed at him desperately with a bowie-knife, cutting deep gashes in the major's arm. Tearing himself from Major Rathbone's grasp, Booth sprang over the railing of the box and leaped to the stage floor, twelve feet below. But, as he jumped, he caught his spur in the folds of the flag that draped the President's box, fell awkwardly, and broke the small bone in his left leg.

A spasm of pain shot through him. He did not wince or hesitate. He was acting now the supreme rôle of his career: this was the scene that was to make his name immortal.

Quickly recovering himself, he brandished his dagger, shouted the motto of Virginia, *Sic semper tyrannis*—"Thus ever to tyrants"—plunged across the stage, knifed a musician who accidentally got in his way, floored an actress, darted out at the back door, jumped upon his waiting horse, raised the butt of his revolver and knocked down the boy, "Peanut John," who was holding the animal, and spurred madly down the street, the steel shoes from his little horse striking fire from the cobblestones in the night.

For two miles he raced on through the city, passing the Capitol grounds. As the moon rose above the tree-tops he galloped on to the Anacostia bridge. There Sergeant Cobb, the Union sentry, dashed out with rifle and bayonet, demanding:

"Who are you? And why are you out so late? Don't you know it is against the rules to let any one pass after nine o'clock?"

Booth, strange to relate, confessed his real name, saying that he lived in Charles County, and, being in town on business, he had waited for the moon to come up and light him home.

That sounded plausible enough; and, anyway, the war was over, so why make a fuss? Sergeant Cobb lowered his rifle and let the rider pass.

A few minutes later Davy Herold, one of Booth's confederates, hurried across the Anacostia bridge with a similar explanation, joined Booth at their rendezvous, and the two of them raced on through the shadows of lower Maryland, dreaming of the wild acclaim that was sure to be theirs in Dixie.

At midnight they halted in front of a friendly tavern in Surrattville; watered their panting horses; called for the field-glasses, guns, and ammunition that had been left there that afternoon by Mrs. Surratt; drank a dollar's worth of whisky; then, boasting that they had shot Lincoln, spurred on into the darkness.

Originally they had planned to ride from here straight for the Potomac, expecting to reach the river early the next morning and row across at once to Virginia. That sounded easy, and they might have done it and never have been captured at all, except for one thing. They could not foresee Booth's broken leg.

But, despite the pain, Booth galloped on that night with Spartan fortitude—galloped on, although the broken, jagged bone was, as he recorded in his diary, "tearing the flesh at every jump" of his horse. Finally when he could endure the punishment no longer, he and Herold swung their horses off to the left, and shortly before daybreak on Saturday morning reined up in front of the house of a country physician named Mudd—Dr. Samuel A. Mudd—who lived twenty miles southeast of Washington.

Booth was so weak and he was suffering so intensely that he couldn't dismount alone. He had to be lifted out of his saddle and carried groaning to an unstairs bedroom. There were no telegraph lines or railways in this isolated region; so none of the natives had yet learned of the assassination. Hence, the doctor suspected nothing. How had Booth come to break his leg? That was simple as Booth explained it—his horse had fallen on him. Dr. Mudd did for Booth what he would have done for any other suffering man; he cut away the boot from the left leg, set the fractured bone, tied it up with pasteboard splints made from a hat-box, fashioned a rude crutch for the cripple, and gave him a shoe to travel with.

Booth slept all that day at Dr. Mudd's house, but as twilight drew on he edged out of the bed painfully. Refusing to eat anything, he shaved off his handsome mustache, threw a long gray shawl around his shoulders so that the end of it would cover the telltale initials tattooed upon his right hand, disguised himself with a set of false whiskers, and paid the doctor twenty-five dollars in greenbacks. Then once more he and Herold mounted their horses and headed for the river of their hopes.

But directly across their path lay the great Zekiah Swamp, a huge bog matted with brush and dogwood, oozy with mud and slimy with stagnant pools—the home of lizards and snakes. In the darkness the two riders missed their way and for hours wandered about, lost.

Late in the night they were rescued by a negro, Oswald Swann. The pain in Booth's leg was so excruciating now that he couldn't sit astride his horse; so he gave Swann seven dollars to haul him the rest of the night in his wagon, and as dawn was breaking on Easter Sunday the driver halted his white mules before "Rich Hill," the home of a wealthy, well-known Confederate, Captain Cox.

Thus ended the first lap of Booth's futile race for life.

Booth told Captain Cox who he was and what he had done; and, to prove his identity, he showed his initials tattooed in India ink on his hand.

He implored Captain Cox, in the name of his mother, not to betray him, pleading that he was sick and crippled and suffering, and declaring that he had done what he thought was best for the South.

Booth was in such a condition now that he couldn't travel any farther, either on horseback or by wagon; so Captain Cox hid the two fugitives in a thicket of pines near his house. The place was more than a thicket, it was a veritable jungle densely undergrown with laurel and holly; and there, for the next six days and five nights, the fugitives waited for Booth's wounded leg to improve enough to permit them to continue their flight.

Captain Cox had a foster-brother, Thomas A. Jones. Jones was a slave-owner, and for years he had been an active agent of the Confederate Government, ferrying fugitives and contraband mail across the Potomac. Captain Cox urged Jones to look after Herold and Booth; so every morning he brought them food in a basket. Knowing that each wood-path was being searched and that spies were everywhere, he called his hogs as he carried the basket and pretended to be feeding his live stock.

Booth, hungry as he was for food, was hungrier still for information. He kept begging Jones to tell him the news, to let him know how the nation was applauding his act.

Jones brought him newspapers, and Booth devoured them eagerly, searching in vain, however, for the burst of acclaim he had coveted so passionately. He found in them only disillusion and heartbreak.

For more than thirty hours he had been racing toward Virginia, braving the tortures of the flesh. But, violent as they had been, they were easy to endure compared with the mental anguish that he suffered now. The fury of the North—that was nothing, he had expected that. But when the Virginia papers showed that the South—*his South*—had turned upon him, condemning and disowning him, he was frantic with disappointment and despair. He, who had dreamed of being honored as a second Brutus and glorified as a modern William Tell, now found himself denounced as a coward, a fool, a hireling, a cutthroat.

These attacks stung him like the sting of an adder. They were bitter as death.

But did he blame himself? No. Far from it. He blamed everybody else—everybody except himself and God. He had been merely an instrument in the hands of the Almighty. That was his defense. He had been divinely appointed to shoot Abraham Lincoln, and his only mistake had been in serving a people "too degenerate" to appreciate him. That was the phrase he set down in his diary—"too degenerate."

"If the world knew my heart," he wrote, "that one blow would have made me great, though I did not desire greatness. . . . I have too great a soul to die like a criminal."

Lying there, shivering under a horse-blanket, on the damp ground near Zekiah Swamp, he poured out his aching heart in tragic bombast:

> Wet, cold and starving, with every man's hand against me, I am here in despair, and why? For doing what Brutus was honored for—for what made Tell a hero. I have stricken down a greater tyrant than they ever knew, and I am looked upon as a common cut-throat; yet my action was purer than either of theirs. . . . I hoped for no gain.

. . . I think I have done well, I do not repent the blow I struck.

As Booth lay there writing, three thousand detectives and ten thousand cavalrymen were scouring every nook and corner of southern Maryland, searching houses, exploring caves, ransacking buildings, and fine-tooth-combing even the slimy bogs of Zekiah Swamp, determined to hunt Booth down and bring him in, dead or alive, and claim the various rewards—approximating a hundred thousand dollars, offered for his capture. Sometimes he could hear the cavalry who were hunting him, galloping by on a public road only two hundred yards away.

At times he could hear their horses neighing and whinnying and calling to one another. Suppose his and Herold's horses should answer them. That would probably mean capture. So that night Herold led their horses down into Zekiah Swamp and shot them.

Two days later buzzards appeared! Specks in the sky at first, they winged closer and closer, finally wheeling and soaring and soaring and wheeling directly above the dead animals. Booth was frightened. The buzzards might attract the attention of the pursuers, who would almost certainly recognize the body of his bay mare.

Besides, he had decided that he must somehow get to another doctor.

So the next night, Friday, April 21—one week after the assassination—he was lifted from the ground and put astride a horse belonging to Thomas A. Jones, and once more he and Herold set out for the Potomac.

The night was ideal for their purposes: dense with a misty fog, and so dark that the men literally had to feel for one another in the inky blackness.

Jones, faithful dog that he was, piloted them from their hiding-place to the river, stealing through open fields, over a public highway, and across a farm. Realizing that soldiers and Secret Service men were swarming everywhere, Jones would steal ahead fifty yards at a time, stop, listen, and give a low whistle. Then Booth and Herold would advance to him.

In that way, slowly, startled by the slightest noise, they traveled for hours, reaching at last the steep and crooked path that led from the bluff down to the river. A stiff wind had been blowing that day; and, through the darkness, they could hear the mournful sound of the water pounding on the sand below.

For almost a week the Union soldiers had been riding up and down the Potomac, destroying every boat on the Maryland shore. But Jones had outwitted them: he had had his colored man, Henry Rowland, using the boat to fish for shad every day, and had had it hidden in Dent's meadow every night.

So when the fugitives reached the water's edge this evening everything was in readiness. Booth whispered his thanks to Jones, paid him seventeen dollars for his boat and a bottle of whisky, climbed in, and headed for a spot on the Virginia shore five miles away.

All through the foggy, ink-black night Herold pulled at the oars while Booth sat in the stern, trying to navigate with compass and candle.

But they hadn't gone far when they struck a flood-tide which is very strong at this point, owing to the narrowness of the channel. It swept them up the river for miles, and they lost their bearings in the fog. After dodging the Federal gunboats that were patrolling the Potomac, they found themselves, at dawn, ten miles up the river, but not one foot nearer to the Virginia shore than they had been the night before.

So they hid all that day in the swamps of Nanjemoy Cove; and the next night, wet and hungry, they pulled across the river; and Booth exclaimed: "I am safe at last, thank God, in glorious old Virginia."

Hurrying to the home of Dr. Richard Stewart, who was an agent for the Confederate Government and the richest man in King George County, Virginia, Booth expected to be welcomed as the saviour of the South. But the doctor had already been arrested several times for aiding the Confederacy, and, now that the war was over, he wasn't going to risk his neck by helping the man who had killed Lincoln. He was too shrewd for that. So he wouldn't let Booth even enter his house. He did give the fugitives a little food, grudgingly, but he made them eat it in the barn, and then sent them to sleep that night with a family of negroes.

And even the negroes didn't want Booth. He had to frighten them into letting him stay with them.

And this in Virginia!

In Virginia, mind you, where he had confidently expected the very hills to reverberate with the lusty cheers that would greet the mere mention of his name.

The end was drawing near now. It came three days later. Booth had not gotten far. He had ferried across the Rappahannock at Port Royal, in the company of three Confederate cavalrymen returning from the war, had ridden one of their horses three miles farther South, and, with their help, had then palmed himself off on a farmer, saying that his name was Boyd and that he had been wounded in Lee's army near Richmond.

And so for the next two days, Booth stayed at the Garrett farm-house, sunning himself on the lawn, suffering from his wound, consulting an old map, studying a route to the Rio Grande, and making notes of the road to Mexico.

The first evening he was there, while he sat at the supper table, Garrett's young daughter began babbling about the news of the assassination, which she had just heard through a neighbor. She talked on and on, wondering who had done it and how much the assassin had been paid for it.

"In my opinion," Booth suddenly remarked, "he wasn't paid a cent, but did it for the sake of notoriety."

The next afternoon, April 25, Booth and Herold were stretched out under the locust trees in the Garrett yard, when suddenly Major Ruggles, one of the Confederate cavalrymen who had helped them across the Rappahannock, dashed up and shouted: "The Yanks are crossing the river. Take care of yourself."

They scurried away to the woods, but when darkness fell they stole back to the house.

To Garrett, that looked suspicious. He wanted to get rid of his mysterious "guests" at once. Was it because he suspected that they might have shot Lincoln? No, he never even thought of that. He imagined they were horse-thieves. When they said at the supper table that they wanted to buy two horses, his suspicions grew, and when bedtime came, and the fugitives, thinking of their safety, refused to go upstairs and insisted on sleeping under the porch or in the barn—then all doubt was removed.

Garrett was positive now that they were horse-thieves. So he put them in an old tobacco warehouse that was being used then for storing hay and furniture—put them in and locked them in with a padlock. And finally, as a double precaution, the old farmer sent his two sons, William and Henry, tiptoeing out in the darkness with blankets, to spend the night in an adjoining corn-crib, where they could watch and see that no horses were whisked away during the night.

The Garrett family went to bed, that memorable evening, half expecting a little excitement.

And they got it before morning.

For two days and nights, a troop of Union soldiers had been hot on the trail of Booth and Herold, picking up clue after clue, talking to an old negro who had seen them crossing the Potomac, and finding Rollins, the colored ferryman who had poled them across the Rappahannock in a scow. This ferryman told them that the Confederate soldier who had given Booth a lift on his horse as they rode away from the river was Captain Willie Jett, and that the captain had a sweetheart who lived in Bowling Green, twelve miles away. Perhaps he had gone there.

That sounded likely enough, so the troopers climbed quickly into their saddles and spurred on in the moonlight toward Bowling Green. Arriving there at midnight, they thundered into the house, found Captain Jett, jerked him out of his bed, thrust a revolver against his ribs, and demanded:

"Where is Booth? Damn your soul, where did you hide him? Tell us or we'll blow your heart out."

Jett saddled his pony, and led the Northern men back to the Garrett farm.

The night was black, the moon having gone down, and there were no stars. For nine miles the dust rose in choking clouds under the galloping feet of the horses. Soldiers rode one on each side of Jett, with the reins of his horse tied to their saddles, so that he couldn't escape in the dark.

At half-past three in the morning the troopers arrived in front of the worn old whitewashed Garrett house.

Quickly, quietly, they surrounded the house and trained their guns on every door and window. Their leader banged on the porch with his pistol butt, demanding admittance.

Presently Richard Garrett, candle in hand, unbolted the door, while the dogs barked furiously, and the wind whipped the tail of his night-shirt against his trembling legs.

Quickly Lieutenant Baker grabbed him by the throat, thrusting a pistol to his head and demanding that he hand over Booth.

The old man, tongue-tied with terror, swore that the strangers were not in the house, that they had gone to the woods.

That was a lie, and it sounded like it; so the troopers jerked him out of the doorway, dangled a rope in his face, and threatened to string him up at once to a locust tree in the yard.

At that instant one of the Garrett boys who had been sleeping in the corn-crib ran up to the house and told the truth. With a rush the troopers encircled the tobacco barn.

There was a lot of talk before the shooting started. For fifteen or twenty minutes the Northern officers argued with Booth, urging him to surrender. He shouted back that he was a cripple, and asked them to "give a lame man a show," offering to come out and fight the entire squad one by one, if they would withdraw a hundred yards.

Herold lost his courage and wanted to surrender. Booth was disgusted.

"You damned coward," he shouted, "get out of here. I don't want you to stay."

And out Herold went, his arms in front of him, ready to be handcuffed, while he pleaded for mercy, declaring from time to time that he liked Mr. Lincoln's jokes, and swearing that he had had no part in the asassination.

Colonel Conger tied him to a tree and threatened to gag him unless he ceased his silly whimpering.

But Booth would not surrender. He felt that he was acting for posterity. He shouted to his pursuers that the word "surrender" was not in his vocabulary, and he warned them to prepare a stretcher for him as they put "one more stain on the glorious old banner."

Colonel Conger resolved to smoke him out, and ordered one of the Garrett boys to pile dry brush against the barn. Booth saw the boy doing it, and cursed him and threatened to put a bullet through him if he didn't stop. He did stop, but Colonel Conger slipped around to a corner of the barn in the rear, pulled a wisp of hay through a crack, and lighted it with a match.

The barn had originally been built for tobacco, with spacings four inches wide left to let in the air. Through these spacings the troopers saw Booth pick up a table to fight the mounting fire—an actor in the limelight for the last time, a tragedian playing the closing scene of his farewell performance.

Strict orders had been given to take Booth alive. The Government didn't want him shot. It wanted to have a big trial and then hang him.

And possibly he might have been taken alive had it not been for a half-cracked sergeant—"Boston" Corbett, a religious fanatic.

Every one had been warned repeatedly not to shoot without

orders. Corbett afterward declared that he had had orders—orders direct from God Almighty.

Through the wide cracks of the burning barn, "Boston" saw Booth throw away his crutch, drop his carbine, raise his revolver, and spring for the door.

"Boston" was positive that he would shoot his way out and make a last, desperate dash for liberty, firing as he ran.

So, to prevent any futile bloodshed, Corbett stepped forward, rested his pistol across his arm, took aim through a crack, prayed for Booth's soul, and pulled the trigger.

At the crack of the pistol Booth shouted, leaped a foot in the air, plunged forward, and fell face down on the hay, mortally wounded.

The roaring flames were moving rapidly now across the dry hay. Lieutenant Baker, eager to get the dying wretch out of the place before he was roasted, rushed into the flaming building and leaped upon him, wrenching his revolver from his clenched fist and pinioning his arms to his side for fear that he might merely be feigning death.

Quickly Booth was carried to the porch of the farmhouse, and a soldier mounted a horse and spurred down the dusty road three miles to Port Royal for a physician.

Mrs. Garrett had a sister, Miss Halloway, who was boarding with her and teaching school. When Miss Halloway realized that the dying man there under the honeysuckle vine on the porch was the romantic actor and great lover, John Wilkes Booth, she said he must be cared for tenderly, and she had a mattress hauled out for him to lie upon; and then she brought out her own pillow, put it under his head, and, taking his head upon her lap, offered him wine. But his throat seemed paralyzed, and he couldn't swallow. Then she dipped her handkerchief in water and moistened his lips and tongue time after time, and massaged his temples and forehead.

The dying man struggled on for two and a half hours, suffering intensely; begging to be turned on his face, his side, his back; coughing and urging Colonel Conger to press his hands down hard upon his throat; and crying out in his agony: "Kill me! Kill me!"

Pleading to have a last message sent to his mother, he whispered haltingly:

"Tell her . . . I did . . . what I thought . . . was best . . . and that I died . . . for my country."

As the end drew near, he asked to have his hands raised so he could look at them; but they were totally paralyzed, and he muttered:

"Useless! Useless!"

They were his last words.

He died just as the sun was rising above the tops of the venerable locust trees in the Garrett yard. His "jaw drew spasmodically and obliquely downward, his eyeballs rolled toward his feet and began to swell . . . and with a sort of gurgle, and sudden check, he stretched his feet and threw back his head." It was the end.

It was seven o'clock. He had died within twenty-two minutes of the time of day Lincoln had died; and "Boston" Corbett's bullet had struck Booth in the back of the head, about an inch below the spot where he himself had wounded Lincoln.

The doctor cut off a curl of Booth's hair, and gave it to Miss Halloway. She kept the lock of hair and the bloody pillow-slip on which his head had lain—kept them and cherished them until, finally, in later years, poverty overtook her and she was obliged to trade half of the stained pillow-slip for a barrel of flour.

★ ★ ★

31

★ ★ ★

BOOTH HAD hardly ceased breathing before the detectives were kneeling to search him. They found a pipe, a bowie-knife, two revolvers, a diary, a compass greasy with candle drippings, a draft on a Canadian bank for about three hundred dollars, a diamond pin, a nail file, and the photographs of five beautiful women who had adored him. Four were actresses: Effie Germon, Alice Grey, Helen Western, and "Pretty Fay Brown." The fifth was a Washington society woman, whose name has been withheld out of respect for her descendants.

Then Colonel Doherty jerked a saddle-blanket off a horse, borrowed a needle from Mrs. Garrett, sewed the corpse up in the blanket, and gave an old Negro, Ned Freeman, two dollars to haul the body to the Potomac, where a ship was waiting.

On page 505 of his book entitled the "History of the United States Secret Service" Lieutenant La Fayette C. Baker tells the story of that trip to the river:

> When the wagon started, Booth's wound, now scarcely dribbling, began to run anew. Blood fell through the crack of the wagon, and fell dripping upon the axle, and spotting the road with terrible wafers. It stained the planks and soaked the blankets . . . and all the way blood dribbled from the corpse in a slow, incessant, sanguine exudation.

In the midst of all this an unexpected thing happened. Ned Freeman's old wagon, according to Baker, was "a very shaky and absurd" contraption "which rattled like approaching dissolution." It not only "rattled like approaching dissolution," but under the strain and speed of the trip, the rickety old wagon actually began to dissolve there on the roadway. A king-bolt snapped, the wagon pulled apart, the front wheels tore away from the hind ones, the front end of the box fell to the ground with a thud, and Booth's body lurched "forward as if in a last effort to escape."

Lieutenant Baker abandoned the rickety old death-car, commandeered another wagon from a neighboring farmer, pitched Booth's body into that, hurried on to the river, and stowed the corpse aboard a government tug, the *John S. Ide,* which chugged away with it to Washington.

At dawn the next morning the news spread through the city: Booth had been shot. His body was lying that very minute on the gunboat *Montauk,* riding at anchor in the Potomac.

The capital was thrilled, and thousands hurried down to the river, staring in grim fascination at the death-ship.

In the middle of the afternoon Colonel Baker, chief of the Secret Service, rushed to Stanton with the news that he had caught a group of civilians on board the *Montauk,* in direct violation of orders, and that one of them, a woman, had cut off a lock of Booth's hair.

Stanton was alarmed. "Every one of Booth's hairs," he cried, "will be cherished as a relic by the rebels."

He feared that they might become far more than mere relics. Stanton firmly believed that the assassination of Lincoln was part of a sinister plot conceived and directed by Jefferson Davis and the leaders of the Confederacy. And he feared that they might capture Booth's body and use it in a crusade to fire the Southern slaveholders to spring to their rifles once more and begin the war all over again.

He decreed that Booth must be buried with all possible haste, and buried secretly; he must be hidden away and blotted out of existence, with no trinket, no shred of his garments, no lock of his hair, nothing left for the Confederates to use in a crusade.

Stanton issued his orders; and that evening, as the sun sank behind a fiery bank of clouds, two men—Colonel Baker and his cousin, Lieutenant Baker—stepped into a skiff, pulled over to the *Montauk,* boarded her, and did three things in plain sight of the gaping throng on the shore:

First, they lowered Booth's body, now incased in a pine gun-box, over the side of the ship and down into the skiff; next, they lowered a huge ball and heavy chain; then they climbed in themselves, shoved off, and drifted downstream.

The curious crowd on the shore did precisely what the detectives had expected them to do: they raced along the bank, shoving, splashing, talking excitedly, determined to watch the funeral ship and see where the body was sunk.

For two miles they kept even with the drifting detectives. Then darkness crept up the river, clouds blotted out the moon and the stars, and even the sharpest eyes could no longer make out the tiny skiff in midstream.

By the time the detectives reached Geeseborough Point, one of the loneliest spots on the Potomac, Colonel Baker was sure that they were completely hidden from view; so he headed the skiff into the great swamp that begins there—a malodorous spot, rank with rushes and slough weeds, a burial-ground where the army cast its condemned horses and dead mules.

Here, in this eerie morass, the two detectives waited for hours, listening to find out if they had been followed; but the only sounds they could hear were the cry of bullfrogs and the ripple of the water among the sedges.

Midnight came; and, with breathless quiet and the utmost caution, the two men rowed stealthily back up-stream, fearing to whisper, and dreading even the lisping of the oars and the lapping of the water at the gunwales.

They finally reached the walls of the old penitentiary, rowed to a spot where a hole had been chopped in the solid masonry near the water's edge to let them in. Giving the countersign to the officer who challenged them, they handed over a white pine casket with the name "John Wilkes Booth" printed on the lid; and, half an hour later, it was buried in a shallow hole in the southwest corner of a large room in the government arsenal where ammunition was stored. The top of the grave was carefully smoothed over, so that it looked like the rest of the dirt floor.

By sunrise the next morning excited men with grappling-hooks were dragging the Potomac, and raking and prodding among the carcasses of dead mules in the great swamp behind Geeseborough Point.

All over the nation millions were asking what had been done with Booth's body. Only eight men knew the answer—eight loyal men who were sworn never to disclose the secret.

In the midst of all this mystery, wild rumors sprang into existence and newspapers broadcast them over the land. Booth's head and heart had been deposited in the Army Medical Museum at Washington—so said the "Boston Advertiser." Other papers stated that the corpse had been buried at sea. Still others declared it had been burned; and a weekly magazine published an "eye-witness" sketch, showing it being sunk in the Potomac at midnight.

Out of the welter of contradiction and confusion another rumor arose: the soldiers had shot the wrong man, and Booth had escaped.

Probably this rumor arose because Booth dead looked so different from Booth alive. One of the men Stanton ordered to go aboard the gunboat *Montauk* on April 27, 1865, and identify the body, was Dr. John Frederick May, an eminent physician of Washington. Dr. May said that when the tarpaulin that covered the remains was removed—

> to my great astonishment, there was revealed a body in whose lineaments there was to me no resemblance to the man I had known in life. My surprise was so great that I at once said to General Barnes: "There is no resemblance in that corpse to Booth, nor can I believe it to be that of him." . . . It being afterwards, by my request, placed in a sitting position, standing and looking down upon it, I was finally enabled to imperfectly recognize the features of Booth. But never in a human being had a greater change taken place, from the man whom I had seen in the vigor of life and health, than in that of the haggard corpse which was before me, with its yellow and discolored skin, its unkempt and matted hair, and its whole facial expression sunken and sharpened by the exposure and starvation it had undergone.

Other men who saw the corpse did not recognize Booth even "imperfectly," and they told their doubts about the city. And the rumor traveled fast.

Matters were not helped by the secrecy with which the Government guarded the body, the speed and mystery of its burial, and Stanton's refusal to give out any information or to deny ugly tales.

The "Constitutional Union," a paper published in the capital, said the entire performance was a hoax. Other papers joined in the cry. "We know Booth escaped," echoed the "Richmond Examiner." The "Louisville Journal" openly contended that there had been something rotten in the whole show, and that "Baker and his associates had wilfully conspired to swindle the United States Treasury."

The battle raged bitterly; and, as usual in such cases, witnesses sprang up by the hundreds, declaring that they had met Booth and talked to him long after the shooting affray at the Garrett barn. He had been seen here, there, and everywhere: fleeing to Canada, dashing into Mexico, traveling on ships bound for South America, hurrying to Europe, preaching in Virginia, hiding on an island in the Orient.

And so was born the most popular and persistent and mysterious myth in American history. It has lived and thrived for almost three quarters of a century; and, to this day, thousands of people believe it—many of them people of unusual intelligence.

There are even some learned men of the colleges who profess to believe the myth. One of the most prominent churchmen in this country has gone up and down the land, declaring in his lectures to hundreds of audiences that Booth escaped. The author, while writing this chapter, was solemnly informed by a scientifically trained man that Booth had gone free.

Of course, Booth was killed. There can be no doubt of it. The man who was shot in Garrett's tobacco barn used every argument he could think of to save his life; and he had a splendid imagination; but, in his most desperate moments, it never occurred to him to deny that he was John Wilkes Booth. That was too absurd, too fantastic, to try even in the face of death.

And to make doubly sure that it was Booth who had been killed, Stanton sent ten men to identify the corpse after it reached Washington. One, as we have already recorded, was Dr. May. He had cut "a large fibroid tumor" from Booth's neck, and the wound in healing had left "a large and ugly scar." Dr. May, who identified him by that scar says:

> From the body which was produced by the captors, nearly every vestige of resemblance of the living man had disappeared. But the mark made by the scalpel during life remained indelible in death, and settled beyond all ques-

tion at the time, and all cavil in the future, the identity of the man who had assassinated the President.

Dr. Merrill, a dentist, identified the body by a filling he had recently put into one of Booth's teeth.

Charles Dawson, a clerk in the National Hotel, where Booth had stopped, identified the dead man by the initials "J. W. B." tattooed on Booth's right hand.

Gardner, the well-known Washington photographer, identified him; and so did Henry Clay Ford, one of Booth's most intimate friends.

When Booth's body was dug up by order of President Andrew Johnson, on February 15, 1869, it was identified again by Booth's close friends.

Then it was taken to Baltimore to be reburied in the Booth family plot in Greenmount Cemetery; but before it was reburied, it was identified again by Booth's brother and mother, and friends who had known him all his life.

It is doubtful whether any other man who ever lived has been as carefully identified in death as Booth was.

And yet the false legend lives on. During the eighties, many people believed that the Rev. J. G. Armstrong of Richmond, Virginia, was Booth in disguise, for Armstrong had coal-black eyes, a lame leg, dramatic ways, and wore his raven hair long to hide a scar on the back of his neck—so people said.

And other "Booths" arose, no less than twenty of them.

In 1872 a "John Wilkes Booth" gave dramatic readings and sleight-of-hand performances before the students of the University of Tennessee; married a widow; tired of her; whispered that he was the real assassin; and, stating that he was going to New Orleans to get a fortune that awaited him, he disappeared, and "Mrs. Booth" never heard of him again.

In the late seventies a drunken saloon-keeper with the asthma, at Granbury, Texas, confessed to a young lawyer named Bates that he was Booth, showed an ugly scar on the back of his neck, and related in detail how Vice-President Johnson had persuaded him to kill Lincoln and promised him a pardon if he should ever be caught.

A quarter of a century passed; and, on January 13, 1903, a drunken house-painter and dope-fiend, David E. George, killed himself with strychnine in the Grand Avenue Hotel in Enid, Oklahoma. But before he destroyed himself, he "confessed" that he was John Wilkes Booth. He declared that after he shot Lincoln, his friends had hidden him in a trunk and got him aboard a ship bound for Europe, where he lived for ten years.

Bates, the lawyer, read about this in the papers, rushed to Oklahoma, looked at the body, and declared that David E. George was none other than the asthmatic saloon-keeper of Granbury, Texas, who had confessed to him twenty-five years before.

Bates had the undertaker comb the corpse's hair just as Booth had worn his; wept over the remains; had the body embalmed; took it back to his home in Memphis, Tennessee, and kept it in his stable for twenty years, while trying to palm it off on the Government and claim the huge reward that had been offered—and paid—for the capture of Booth.

In 1908 Bates wrote a preposterous book entitled: "The Escape and Suicide of John Wilkes Booth, or the First True Account of Lincoln's Assassination, Containing a Complete Confession by Booth, Many Years after His Crime." He sold seventy thousand copies of his sensational paper-back volume; created a considerable stir; offered his mummified "Booth" to Henry Ford for one thousand dollars; and finally began exhibiting it in side-shows throughout the South, at ten cents a look.

Five different skulls are now being exhibited in carnivals and tents as the skull of Booth.

32

AFTER SHE LEFT the White House Mrs. Lincoln got into serious difficulties, and made an exhibition of herself that became national gossip.

In matters of household expense she was excessively penurious. It had long been customary for the Presidents to give a number of state dinners each season. But Mrs. Lincoln argued her husband into breaking the tradition, saying that these dinners were "very costly"; that these were war-times and public receptions would be more "economical."

Lincoln had to remind her once that "we must think of something besides economy."

When it came, however, to buying things that appealed to her vanity—such as dresses and jewelry—she not only forgot economy, but seemed bereft of all reason and indulged in a fantastic orgy of spending.

In 1861 she had come off the prairie, confidently expecting that as "Mrs. President" she would be the center of the glittering constellation of Washington society. But to her amazement and humiliation she found herself snubbed and ostracized by the haughty aristocrats of that Southern city. In their eyes, she, a Kentuckian, had been untrue to the South: she had married a crude, awkward "nigger-lover" who was making war upon them.

Besides, she had almost no likable personal qualities. She was, it must be admitted, a mean, common, envious, affected, mannerless virago.

Unable to attain social popularity herself, she was bitterly jealous of those who had achieved it. The then reigning queen of Washington society was the renowned beauty Adèle Cutts Douglas, the woman who had married Mrs. Lincoln's former sweetheart, Stephen A. Douglas. The glamorous popularity of Mrs. Douglas and Salmon P. Chase's daughter, inflamed Mrs. Lincoln with envy, and she resolved to win social victories with money—money spent on clothes and jewelry for herself.

"To keep up appearances," she told Elizabeth Keckley, "I must have money, more money than Mr. Lincoln can spare me. He is too honest to make a penny outside of his salary; consequently, I had, and still have, no alternative but to run in debt."

In debt she plunged, to the extent of seventy thousand dollars! A staggering sum when we remember that Lincoln's salary as President was only twenty-five thousand, and that it would have taken every penny of his income for over two years and nine months to pay for her finery alone.

I have quoted several times from Elizabeth Keckley. She was an unusually intelligent negro woman who had bought her freedom and come to Washington to set up a dress-making shop. Within a short time she had the patronage of some of the capital's leading social figures.

From 1861 to 1865 she was with Mrs. Lincoln almost daily in the White House, making dresses and serving her as a personal maid. She finally became not only Mrs. Lincoln's confidante and adviser, but her most intimate friend. The night that Lincoln lay dying, the only person Mrs. Lincoln kept calling for was Elizabeth Keckley.

Fortunately for history, Mrs. Keckley wrote a book about her experiences. It has been out of print for half a century, but dilapidated copies can be purchased now and then from rare-book dealers for ten or twenty dollars. The title is rather long: "Behind the Scenes, by Elizabeth Keckley, Formerly a Slave, but More Recently Modiste and Friend to Mrs. Abraham Lincoln: Or Thirty Years a Slave and Four Years in the White House."

Elizabeth Keckley records that in the summer of 1864, when Lincoln was running for a second term, "Mrs. Lincoln was almost crazy with fear and anxiety."

Why? One of her New York creditors had threatened to sue her; and the possibility that Lincoln's political enemies might get wind of her debts and use them as political thunder in the bitter campaign, drove her almost to distraction.

"If he is reëlected, I can keep him in ignorance of my affairs; but if he is defeated, then the bills will be sent in, and he will know all," she sobbed hysterically.

"I could go down on my knees," she cried to Lincoln "and plead for votes for you."

"Mary," he remonstrated, "I am afraid you will be punished for this overwhelming anxiety. If I am to be elected, it will be all right; if not, you must bear the disappointment."

"And does Mr. Lincoln suspect how much you owe?" inquired Mrs. Keckley.

And here was Mrs. Lincoln's answer, as reported on page 150 of "Behind the Scenes":

"God, no!—this was a favorite expression of hers [Mrs. Lincoln's]—and I would not have him suspect. If he knew that his wife was involved to the extent that she is, the knowledge would drive him mad."

"The only happy feature of Lincoln's assassination," says Mrs. Keckley, "was that he died in ignorance of these debts."

He hadn't been in his grave a week before Mrs. Lincoln was trying to sell his shirts with his initials marked on them, offering them at a shop on Pennsylvania Avenue.

Seward, hearing about it, went, with a heavy heart, and bought up the lot himself.

When Mrs. Lincoln left the White House, she took with her a score of trunks and half a hundred packing-boxes.

That created a good deal of nasty talk.

She had already been repeatedly and publicly accused of swindling the United States Treasury by falsifying an expense-account for the entertainment of Prince Napoleon, and her enemies pointed out that though she had come to the Executive Mansion with only a few trunks, she was now leaving it with a whole car-load of stuff. . . . Why? . . . Was she looting the place? Had she stripped it bare of everything she could?

Even as late as October 6, 1867—almost two and a half years after she left Washington—the "Cleveland Herald," speaking of Mrs. Lincoln, said:

"Let the country know that it required one hundred thousand dollars to make good the spoliation at the White House, and let it be proved who had the benefit of such plundering."

True, a great many things were stolen from the White House during the reign of the "rosy empress," but the fault was hardly hers. She made mistakes, of course: one of the first things she did was to discharge the steward and a number of the other employees, saying she was going to superintend the place herself, and put it on an economical basis.

She tried it, and the servants purloined almost everything except the door-knobs and the kitchen stove. The "Washington Star" for March 9, 1861, records that many of the guests who attended the first White House reception lost their overcoats and evening wraps. It wasn't long before even the White House furnishings were being carted away.

Fifty packing-boxes and a score of trunks! What was in them? Trash, for the most part: useless gifts, statuary, worthless pictures and books, wax wreaths, deer-heads, and a lot of old clothes and hats hopelessly outmoded—things she had worn back in Springfield years before.

"She had a passion," says Mrs. Keckley, "for hoarding old things."

While she was packing, her son Robert, recently graduated from Harvard, advised her to put a match to the old trumpery. When she scorned the idea, he said:

"I hope to heaven that the car that carries these boxes to Chicago catches fire and burns up all your old plunder."

The morning Mrs. Lincoln drove away from the White House, "there was scarcely a friend to tell her good-by," records Mrs. Keckley. "The silence was almost painful."

Even Andrew Johnson, the new President, failed to bid her farewell. In fact, he never even wrote her a line of sympathy after the assassination. He knew that she despised him, and he reciprocated her feelings.

Absurd as it seems now in the light of history, Mrs. Lincoln firmly believed then that Andrew Johnson had been back of the plot to assassinate Lincoln.

With her two sons, Tad and Robert, Lincoln's widow traveled to Chicago, stopped for a week at the Tremont House, found it too expensive, and moved to some "small, plainly-furnished" rooms at a summer resort called Hyde Park.

Sobbing because she couldn't afford better living quarters, she refused to see or even correspond with any of her former friends or relatives, and settled down to teaching Tad to spell.

Tad had been his father's favorite. His real name was Thomas, but Lincoln had nicknamed him "Tad" or "Tadpole" because as a baby he had had an abnormally large head.

Tad usually slept with his father. The child would lie around the office in the White House until he fell asleep, and then the President would shoulder him and carry him off to bed. Tad had always suffered from a slight impediment in his speech, and his father humored him; and, so with the ingenuity of a bright boy, he used his handicap as a foil to ward off attempts to educate him. He was now twelve years old, but he could neither read nor write.

Mrs. Keckley records that during his first spelling lesson, Tad spent ten minutes arguing that "a-p-e" spelled *monkey*. The word was illustrated with a small woodcut of what he believed to be a monkey, and it required the combined efforts of three people to convince him that he was wrong.

Mrs. Lincoln used every means in her power to persuade Congress to give her the hundred thousand dollars that Lincoln would have been paid had he lived out his second term. When Congress refused she was vitriolic in her denunciation of the "fiends" who had blocked her plans with "their infamous and villainous falsehoods."

"The father of wickedness and lies," she said, "will get these hoary-headed sinners when they pass away."

Congress did finally give her twenty-two thousand—approximately the amount that would have been due Lincoln had he served the rest of that year. With this she bought and furnished a marble-front house in Chicago.

Two years elapsed, however, before Lincoln's estate was settled; and, during that time, her expenses mounted and her creditors howled. Presently she had to take in roomers; then boarders; and at last she was obliged to give up her home and move into a boarding-house, herself.

Her exchequer became more and more depleted, until, in September, 1867, she was, as she phrased it, "pressed in a most startling manner for means of subsistence."

So she packed up a lot of her old clothes and laces and jewelry, and, with her face hidden under a heavy crêpe veil, she rushed to New York incognita, registered as a "Mrs. Clark," met Mrs. Keckley there, gathered up an armful of worn dresses, got into a carriage, drove over to the second-hand clothing dealers on Seventh Avenue, and tried to sell her wardrobe. But the prices offered were disappointingly low.

She next tried the firm of Brady & Keyes, diamond brokers, at 609 Broadway. Listening with amazement to her story, they said:

"Now listen, put your affairs in our hands, and we will raise a hundred thousand dollars for you in a few weeks."

That sounded rosy; so she wrote, at their request, two or three letters, telling of her dire poverty.

Keyes flaunted these letters in the face of the Republican leaders, threatening to publish them unless he got cash.

But the only thing he got from these men was their opinion of Mrs. Lincoln.

Then she urged Brady & Keyes to mail a hundred and fifty thousand circulars, appealing to the generosity of people everywhere for aid; but it was well-nigh impossible to get prominent men to sign the letter.

Boiling now with wrath at the Republicans, she turned for help to Lincoln's enemies. The New York "World" was a Democratic paper that had once been suspended by government order, and its editor arrested because of its violent attacks on Lincoln. Through its columns Mrs. Lincoln pleaded poverty, admitting that she was trying to sell not only her old clothes, but even such trifles as "a parasol cover" and "two dress patterns."

It was just before a state election; so the Democratic "World" printed a letter from her, fiercely denouncing such Republicans as Thurlow Weed, William H. Seward, and Henry J. Raymond of the "New York Times."

With its tongue in its cheek, "The World" solemnly invited its Democratic readers to send in cash contributions to care for the abandoned and suffering widow of the first Republican President. There were few contributions.

Next she tried to get the colored people to raise money for her, urging Mrs. Keckley to throw her heart and soul into the undertaking, and promising that if the Negroes raised twenty-five thousand dollars Mrs. Keckley would get a "cut" of three hundred dollars a year during Mrs. Lincoln's life, and all of the twenty-five thousand dollars at Mrs. Lincoln's death.

Then Brady & Keyes advertised a sale of her clothes and jewelry. Crowds thronged to their store, handling the dresses, criticizing them, declaring that they were out of style, that they were absurdly high-priced, that they were "worn" and "jagged under the arms and at the bottom of the skirts," and had "stains on the lining."

Brady & Keyes also opened a subscription-book at their store, hoping that if the sightseers would not buy they might donate money for Mrs. Lincoln.

Finally in despair, the merchants took her clothes and jewels to Providence, Rhode Island, intending to set up an exhibition and charge twenty-five cents admission. The city authorities wouldn't hear of it.

Brady & Keyes did finally sell eight hundred and twenty-four dollars' worth of her effects, but they charged eight hundred and twenty dollars for their services and expenses.

Mrs. Lincoln's campaign to raise money for herself not only failed, it also brought upon her a storm of public condemnation. Throughout the campaign she made a disgraceful exhibition of herself—and so did the public.

She "has dishonored herself, her country and the memory of her late lamented husband," cried the Albany "Journal."

She was a liar and a thief—such was the accusation brought against her by Thurlow Weed in a letter to the "Commercial Advertiser."

For years, back in Illinois, she had been "a terror to the village of Springfield," her "eccentricities were common talk," and "the patient Mr. Lincoln was a second Socrates within his own dwelling"—so thundered the "Hartford Evening Press." But the "Journal" of Springfield stated editorially that for years it had been known that she was deranged, and that she should be pitied for all her strange acts.

"That dreadful woman, Mrs. Lincoln," complained the Springfield, Massachusetts, "Republican," "insists on thrusting her repugnant personality before the world to the great mortification of the nation."

Mortified by these attacks, Mrs. Lincoln poured out her broken heart in a letter to Mrs. Keckley:

> Robert came up last evening like a maniac and almost threatening his life, looking like death because the letters of "The World" were published in yesterday's paper. . . . I weep whilst I am writing. I pray for death this morning. Only my darling Taddie prevents my taking my life.

Estranged now from her sisters and kindred, she finally broke even with Robert, defying and maligning him so bitterly that certain passages of her letters had to be deleted before publication.

When Mrs. Lincoln was forty-nine years old, she wrote the Negro dressmaker: "I feel as if I had not a friend in the world save yourself."

No other man in United States history has been so respected and loved as Abraham Lincoln; and possibly no other woman in United States history has been so fiercely denounced as his wife.

Less than a month after Mrs. Lincoln had tried to sell her old clothes, Lincoln's estate was settled. It amounted to $110,295, and was divided equally among Mrs. Lincoln and her two sons, each receiving $36,765.

Mrs. Lincoln now took Tad abroad and lived in solitude, reading French novels and avoiding all Americans.

Soon she was pleading poverty again. She petitioned the United States Senate to grant her a yearly pension of five thousand dollars. The bill was greeted in the Senate with hisses from the gallery and words of abuse from the floor.

"It is a sneaking fraud!" cried Senator Howell of Iowa.

"Mrs. Lincoln was not true to her husband!" shouted Senator Yates of Illinois. "She sympathized with the rebellion. She is not worthy of our charity."

After months of delay and torrents of condemnation she was finally given three thousand a year.

In the summer of 1871 Tad died of typhoid fever, passing away in violent agony. Robert, her only remaining son, was married.

Alone, friendless, and in despair, Mary Lincoln became the prey of obsessions. One day in Jacksonville, Florida, she bought a cup of coffee and then refused to drink it, swearing it was poisoned.

Boarding a train for Chicago, she wired the family physician, imploring him to save Robert's life. But Robert was not ill. He met her at the station and spent a week with her at the Grand Pacific Hotel, hoping to quiet her.

Often in the middle of the night she would rush to his room, declaring that fiends were attempting to murder her, that Indians "were pulling wires out of her brain," that "doctors were taking steel springs out of her head."

In the daytime she visited the stores, making absurd purchases, paying, for example, three hundred dollars for lace curtains when she had no home in which to hang them.

With a heavy heart Robert Lincoln applied to the County Court of Chicago, for a trial of his mother's sanity. A jury of twelve men decided that she was insane, and she was confined in a private asylum at Batavia, Illinois.

At the end of thirteen months she was, unfortunately, released—released, but not cured. Then the poor, ailing woman went abroad to live among strangers, refusing to write Robert or let him know her address.

One day while living alone in Pau, France, she mounted a step ladder to hang a picture above the fireplace; the ladder broke, and she fell, injuring her spinal cord. For a long time, she was unable even to walk.

Returning to her native land to die, she spent her last days at the home of her sister Mrs. Edwards, in Springfield, saying over and over: "You ought to pray now that I be taken to my husband and children."

Although she then had six thousand dollars in cash and seventy-five thousand in government bonds, nevertheless her mind was constantly racked by absurd fears of poverty, and she was haunted by the fear that Robert, then Secretary of War, would be assassinated like his father.

Longing to escape from the harsh realities that pressed upon her, she shunned every one, closed her doors and windows, pulled down the shades, darkened her room, and lighted a candle even when the sun was shining bright.

"No urging," says her physician, "would induce her to go out into the fresh air."

And there, amidst the solitude and soft quiet of the candlelight, her memory doubtless winged its way back across the cruel years, and, dwelling at last among the cherished thoughts of her young womanhood, she imagined herself waltzing once more with Stephen A. Douglas, charmed by his gracious manner and listening to the rich music of his melodious vowels and clear-cut consonants.

At times she imagined that her other sweetheart, a young man named Lincoln—Abraham Lincoln—was coming to court her that night. True, he was only a poor, homely, struggling lawyer who slept in an attic above Speed's store, but she believed he might be President if she could stimulate him to try hard, and, eager to win his love, she longed to make herself beautiful for him. Although she had worn nothing but the deepest black for fifteen years, she would, at such times, slip down to the stores in Springfield; and, according to her physician, she purchased and piled up "large quantities of silks and dress goods in trunks and by the cart load, which she never used and which accumulated until it was really feared that the floor of the store room would give way."

In 1882, on a peaceful summer evening, the poor, tired, tempestuous soul was given the release for which she had so often prayed. Following a paralytic stroke, she passed quietly away in her sister's house where, forty years before, Abraham Lincoln had put on her finger a ring bearing the words: "Love is eternal."

IN 1876, a gang of counterfeiters tried to steal Lincoln's body. It is an astonishing story, which few books on Lincoln say anything about.

"Big Jim" Kinealy's gang, one of the cleverest counterfeiting crews that ever vexed and perplexed the United States Secret Service, had its headquarters, during the seventies, in the guileless corn-and-hog town of Lincoln, Illinois.

For years Big Jim's suave and mild-mannered "shovers," as they were called, had been sneaking out across the country and shoving bogus five-dollar bills across the counters of credulous merchants. The profits had been fantastic. But by the spring of 1876, a deadly paralysis was creeping over the gang, for their supply of counterfeit currency was almost exhausted, and Ben Boyd, the master engraver who made their bogus greenbacks, was in prison.

For months Big Jim sniffed vainly about St. Louis and Chicago, trying to get another engraver to make counterfeit bills. Finally he resolved that somehow the invaluable Ben Boyd must be set free.

Big Jim conceived the unholy idea of stealing the body of Abraham Lincoln, and hiding it away. Then, while the whole North was in an uproar, Big Jim would calmly drive a hard and fabulous bargain: he would agree to return the sacred corpse in exchange for Ben Boyd's pardon and a huge pile of gold.

Dangerous? Not at all. For Illinois had upon her statute-book no law against the purloining of bodies.

So in June, 1876, Big Jim set about clearing the decks for action. He despatched five of his conspirators to Springfield, where they opened a saloon and dance-hall, masquerading as bartenders while making their preparations.

Unfortunately for him, one of his "bartenders" drank too much whisky one Saturday night in June, drifted into a red-light house in Springfield, and talked too much. He boasted that he was soon going to have a barrelful of gold.

He whispered the details: on the eve of the next fourth of July, while Springfield was shooting off rockets, he would be out in the Oak Ridge Cemetery, "stealing old Lincoln's bones," as he put it; and late that night he would bury them in a sand-bar under a bridge spanning the Sangamon.

An hour later the parlor-house madam was hurrying to the police, to tell her thrilling news. By morning she had blabbed it to a dozen other men. Soon the whole town had the story, and the masquerading bartenders dropped their towels and fled the city.

But Big Jim was not defeated. He was only delayed. He shifted his headquarters from Springfield to 294 West Madison Street, Chicago. He owned a saloon there. In the front room his man, Terrence Mullen, dispensed liquor to working-men; and in the back he had a sort of club-room, a secret rendezvous for counterfeiters. A bust of Abraham Lincoln stood over the bar.

For months a thief named Lewis G. Swegles had been patronizing this saloon and working himself into the good graces of Big Jim's gang. He admitted that he had served two terms in the penitentiary for stealing horses, and boasted that he was now "the boss body-snatcher of Chicago." He declared he supplied the medical schools of the town with most of their cadavers. That sounded plausible enough then, for grave-robbing was a national horror; medical colleges, in order to obtain bodies for dissection in their class rooms, were forced to buy them from ghouls who sneaked up to the rear door at two o'clock in the morning, with caps pulled low over their eyes and bulging sacks slung across their backs.

Swegles and Kinealy's gang perfected the details of their plan for rifling Lincoln's tomb. They would stuff the body into a long sack, pitch it into the bottom of a spring-wagon, and, with relays of fresh horses, would drive with all possible speed to northern Indiana; and there with only the water-fowl to see them, they would hide the body among the lonely dunes, where the wind from over the lake would soon wipe out all telltale tracks in the shifting sands.

Before leaving Chicago, Swegles bought a London newspaper; and, tearing out a piece, he stuffed the rest inside the bust of Lincoln that stood over the bar at 294 West Madison Street. That night, November 6, he and two of Big Jim's gang climbed aboard a Chicago & Alton train headed for Springfield, taking with them the fragment of torn newspaper, which they proposed to leave beside the empty sarcophagus as they dashed off with the body. The detectives finding the paper would naturally keep it as a clue. Then while the nation was rocking with excitement, one of the gang would approach the governor of the State and offer to return Lincoln's body for two hundred thousand dollars in gold and the freedom of Ben Boyd.

And how would the governor know that the self-styled spokesman was not an impostor? The gangster would carry with him the London newspaper; the detectives, fitting their fragment into the torn page, would accept him as the bona-fide representative of the ghouls.

The gang arrived in Springfield, according to schedule. They had chosen what Swegles called "a damned elegant time" for their adventure. November 7 was election day; for months the Democrats had been denouncing the Republicans for the graft and corruption that had besmirched Grant's second administration, while the Republicans had waved the "bloody shirt" of the Civil War in the face of the Democrats. It was one of the most bitter elections in United States history. That night, while excited crowds were milling about the newspaper offices and jamming the saloons, Big Jim's men hurried out to Oak Ridge Cemetery—dark now, and deserted—sawed the padlock off the iron door of Lincoln's tomb, stepped inside, pried the marble lid off the sarcophagus, and lifted the wooden casket half out.

One of the gang ordered Swegles to bring up the horses and spring-wagon which he had been delegated to have ready and waiting in a ravine two hundred yards northeast of the monument. Swegles hurried down the steep bluff until he was lost in the darkness.

Swegles was not a grave-robber. He was a reformed criminal

now employed as a stool-pigeon by the Secret Service. He had no team and wagon waiting in the ravine; but he did have eight detectives waiting for him in the memorial room of the tomb. So he raced around there and gave them the signal they had all agreed upon: he struck a match, lighted a cigar, and whispered the password *"Wash."*

The eight Secret Service men, in their stocking-feet, rushed out of their hiding-place, every man with a cocked revolver in each hand. They dashed around the monument with Swegles, stepped into the dark tomb, and ordered the ghouls to surrender.

There was no answer. Tyrrell, the district chief of the Secret Service, lighted a match. There lay the coffin, half out of the sarcophagus. But where were the thieves? The detectives searched the cemetery in all directions. The moon was coming up over the tree-tops. As Tyrrell rushed up onto the terrace of the monument, he could make out the forms of two men, staring at him from behind a group of statuary. In the excitement and confusion, he began firing at them with both pistols, and in an instant they were firing back. But they weren't the thieves. He was shooting at his own men.

In the meantime, the thieves, who had been waiting a hundred feet away in the darkness, for Swegles to return with the horses, dashed off through the woods.

Ten days later they were caught in Chicago, brought to Springfield, thrown into a jail, and surrounded by heavy guards day and night. For a time there was intense public excitement and indignation. Lincoln's son Robert, who had married into the wealthy Pullman family, employed the best lawyers in Chicago to prosecute the gang. They did what they could, but they had a hard time. There was no law in Illinois, then, against stealing a body. If the thieves had actually stolen the coffin, they might have been prosecuted for that, but they hadn't stolen it; they had not taken it out of the tomb. So the best the high-priced attorneys from Chicago could do was to prosecute the ghouls for having *conspired* to steal a coffin worth seventy-five dollars, the maximum penalty for which offense was five years. But the case did not come to trial for eight months; public indignation had died down by that time, and politics were at work; and, on the first ballot, four jurors actually voted for acquittal. After a few more ballots the twelve men compromised and sent the ghouls to the Joliet prison for one year.

Since Lincoln's friends were afraid that other thieves might steal the body, the Lincoln Monument Association hid it away for two years in an iron coffin under a heap of loose boards lying in a damp, dark passageway behind the catacombs—a sort of cellar. During that time thousands of pilgrims paid their respects to an empty sarcophagus.

For various reasons Lincoln's remains have been moved seventeen times. But they will be moved no more. The coffin is now imbedded in a great ball of steel and solid concrete, six feet beneath the floor of the tomb. It was placed there on September 26, 1901.

On that day the casket was opened, and human eyes gazed down for the last time upon his face. Those who saw him then remarked how natural he appeared. He had been dead thirty-six years; but the embalmers had done their work well, and he still looked very much as he had looked in life. His face was a trifle darker, and there was a touch of mold on one wing of his black tie.

BIBLIOGRAPHY

Badeau, Adam. *Grant in Peace*. Hartford, 1887.

Baker, Gen. La Fayette C. *History of the United States Secret Service*. L. C. Baker, Philadelphia, 1867.

Barton, William E. *The Life of Abraham Lincoln*. The Bobbs-Merrill Company, Indianapolis, 1925.

Barton, William E. *Lincoln at Gettysburg*. The Bobbs-Merrill Company, Indianapolis, 1930.

Barton, William E. *The Women Lincoln Loved*. The Bobbs-Merrill Company, Indianapolis, 1927.

Battles and Leaders of the Civil War. The Century Co., New York, 1887; 4 vols.

Beveridge, Albert J. *Abraham Lincoln*. Houghton Mifflin Company, Boston and New York, 1928.

Browne, Francis F. *The Every-day Life of Abraham Lincoln*. Brown & Howell Company, Chicago, 1913.

Carpenter, F. B. *Six Months at the White House with Abraham Lincoln*. Hurd & Houghton, New York, 1867.

Charnwood, Lord. *Abraham Lincoln*. Henry Holt & Company, New York, 1917.

Coggeshall, E. W. *The Assassination of Abraham Lincoln*. W. M. Hill, Chicago, 1920.

Columbia Historical Society Records.

Dewitt, D. M. *The Assassination of Abraham Lincoln and Its Expiation*. The Macmillan Company, New York, 1909.

Garland, Hamlin. *Ulysses S. Grant, His Life and Character*. The Macmillan Company, New York, 1898, 1920.

Grant, U. S. *Personal Memoirs*. The Century Co., New York, 1885, 1895; 2 vols.

Herndon, William H., and Weik, Jesse W. *The History and Personal Recollections of Abraham Lincoln*. The Herndon's Lincoln Publishing Company, Springfield, Illinois, 1888; 3 vols.

Keckley, Elizabeth. *Behind the Scenes, or Thirty Years a Slave and Four Years in the White House*. G. W. Carleton & Co., New York, 1868.

Lamon, Ward H. *Life of Abraham Lincoln*. Boston, 1872.

Lamon, Ward H. *Recollections of Abraham Lincoln, 1847–1865*. Edited by Dorothy Lamon Teillard. Teillard, Washington, D. C., 1911.

Lewis, Lloyd. *Myths after Lincoln.* Harcourt, Brace and Company, New York, 1929.

Macartney, Clarence E. *Lincoln and His Cabinet.* Charles Scribner's Sons, New York, 1931.

Macartney, Clarence E. *Lincoln and His Generals.* Dorrance and Company, Philadelphia, 1925.

Magazine of History.

Morrow, Honoré Willsie. *Mary Todd Lincoln, an Appreciation of the Wife of Abraham Lincoln.* William Morrow & Company, New York, 1928.

Nicolay, Helen. *Personal Traits of Abraham Lincoln.* The Century Co., New York, 1919.

Nicolay, John G., and Hay, John. *Abraham Lincoln: A History.* The Century Co., New York, 1890; 12 vols.

Oldroyd, Osborn H. *The Assassination of Abraham Lincoln.* Oldroyd, Washington, D. C., 1901.

Power, John C. *History of an Attempt to Steal the Body of Abraham Lincoln.* H. W. Rokker Printing and Publishing House, Springfield, Illinois, 1890.

Rhodes, James Ford. *History of the Civil War, 1861–1865.* The Macmillan Company, New York, 1917.

Rothschild, Alonzo. *Lincoln, Master of Men.* Houghton Mifflin Company, Boston and New York, 1912.

Sandburg, Carl. *Abraham Lincoln, the Prairie Years.* Harcourt, Brace and Company, New York, 1926.

Tarbell, Ida M. *The Life of Abraham Lincoln.* The Macmillan Company, New York, 1917.

Townsend, George A. *The Life, Crime and Capture of John Wilkes Booth.* Dick & Fitzgerald, New York, 1865.

Townsend, William H. *Lincoln and His Wife's Home Town.* The Bobbs-Merrill Company, Indianapolis, 1929.

Weik, Jesse W. *The Real Lincoln.* Houghton Mifflin Company, Boston and New York, 1922.

Wilson, Francis. *John Wilkes Booth; Fact and Fiction of Lincoln's Assassination.* Houghton Mifflin Company, Boston and New York.

Woodward, William E. *Meet General Grant.* Literary Guild of America, New York, 1928.